# CHRISTIAN BELIEFS AND ANTI-SEMITISM

# Christian Beliefs
## and Anti-Semitism

CHARLES Y. GLOCK and RODNEY STARK

HARPER & ROW, PUBLISHERS
NEW YORK AND LONDON

Volume One in a series based on
The University of California Five-Year Study of Anti-Semitism
in the United States,
being conducted by the Survey Research Center
under a grant from the Anti-Defamation League of B'nai B'rith

LIBRARY OF CONGRESS CATALOG CARD NUMBER: 65–21002

C-Q

# Contents

v

# Tables

# Preface

On Christmas Eve, 1959, a gang of German youths desecrated a Jewish synagogue in Cologne. Their crudely smeared swastikas forced humane men everywhere to face the rude fact that anti-Semitism had not perished with the Third Reich in the flames of Berlin, nor on the scaffold at Nuremberg.

Within days the Cologne incident was repeated in many other German cities. And this was only the beginning, for the wave spread beyond Germany, and then beyond Europe to the United States. By March 1960, barely two months after the first German incident, at least 643 similar incidents had occurred in the United States alone.[1] Synagogues across the nation suddenly bore the crude, splashed, epithets of bigotry and the ubiquitous swastika. Not synagogues alone, but Jewish cemeteries, stores, and homes were smeared and shattered in the epidemic of nightly anti-Semitic vandalism. On occasion Jews were personally tormented and beaten.

The mass media immediately reflected the outrage and alarm of millions of Americans who were profoundly shocked by the apparent durability of anti-Semitism. How could such feelings survive the grisly horrors of Nazism? Public shock increased as it became known that these acts were not a final effort by aged Fascists, but were done by youngsters reared and educated in supposedly enlightened, postwar America.

In a few weeks the storm of incidents began to subside. The mass media turned to new sensations, and public interest waned. Soon few Americans probably even remembered that such events had ever happened. But not everyone could forget. The victims could not, nor could the leaders

[1] David Caplovitz and Candace Rogers, *Swastika 1960: The Epidemic of Anti-Semitic Vandalism in America* (New York: Anti-Defamation League of B'nai B'rith, 1960), p. 9.

of the Anti-Defamation League of B'nai B'rith. The ADL was founded in 1912 to fight anti-Semitism in the United States. In the beginning its task was nearly overwhelming. But slowly times changed, and by 1960 the ADL leaders had begun to feel that violence against Jewish persons and property had become a thing of the past. They had turned their main attention instead to more subtle problems, such as discrimination against Jews by social clubs, schools, and industry. The incidents of 1960 came as a stunning and grievous contradiction of their hopes. And worse, if such things were still possible, what else? Could anything about anti-Semitism in contemporary America be taken for granted?

Thus, the officials of the ADL began to ask some old and stubborn questions once again. What accounts for the persistence of anti-Semitism in our democratic society? How is it that generation after generation of Americans come to regard their Jewish countrymen with suspicion and even contempt? Is it possible that such sentiments might be incorporated into the political doctrine of new extremist movements in the United States? The questions were urgent, but the ADL found that the answers were still by and large unknown.

Consequently, the ADL decided to commission a new social science investigation of the enduring phenomenon of anti-Semitism in the United States. They felt that such an effort would be extremely useful if it did no more than assess the extent, location, and character of contemporary anti-Semitism. But they also hoped to learn as much as possible about the causes of this social evil, in order to find more effective ways of combating it.

Once decided on this course, the ADL invited the Survey Research Center of the University of California at Berkeley to draw up a prospectus for a comprehensive study. The center's proposal was submitted to the Anti-Defamation League through the Regents of the University of California in the fall of 1960. The ADL responded promptly and committed itself to supplying the $500,000 which the program called for over a five-year period beginning July 1961. Thus was born what came to be called the University of California Five-Year Study of Anti-Semitism in the United States.

The plans for the study commit the associates of the Survey Research Center to conduct a series of interrelated projects during the period of the grant. Each of these projects focuses on a different aspect of American society which is considered crucial in determining the extent and course of anti-Semitism. All of these studies are underway and their findings will be reported in a series of books to be published by Harper & Row. This volume is the first.

Of the other projects, one is seeking to discover the process through which school children come to establish their images of, and relations with, persons of different religious, ethnic, and racial groups. In particular this study will be concerned with changes in beliefs and patterns of association that occur with the onset of dating. A second study is exploring the link between anti-Semitism and political extremism, with special interest in the ways in which political movements become anti-Semitic. This study will also attempt to estimate the potential for political anti-Semitism in contemporary America. A third study, already completed and to be published shortly, explored the impact of the Eichmann trial on American public opinion and the extent to which it influenced attitudes toward Jews. A fourth is a nationwide survey to determine the extent and location of present-day anti-Semitic beliefs and practices. A fifth study will explore Negro-Jewish relations within the context of the civil rights movement.

In attempting to study the role of religion in contemporary anti-Semitism we became indebted to many people. Our investigation forced us to "trespass" at times on a number of scholarly domains where we had no formal training. Fortunately, we were guided on our way by considerate specialists. Among these we particularly want to thank David Noel Freedman, Martin E. Marty, and Leo Trepp. We also received constant encouragement and counsel from our colleagues at the Survey Research Center, some of whom are working on other studies in this series: Gertrude Jaeger Selznick, M. Brewster Smith, Herbert McCloskey, Seymour Martin Lipset, Leo Lowenthal, Jane Hardyck, Stephen Steinberg, Earl Raab, and Joe L. Spaeth. We are particularly grateful to Ralph Lane for his tireless efforts in supervising the collection of data from the Roman Catholic sample. At various points along the way Polly Ham and Wendy Shuken kept the jungle of documents, records, correspondence, and data generated by the project from closing over us.

To the Anti-Defamation League of B'nai B'rith we owe much more than the generous financing which made the project possible. At all times they have stood ready to provide encouragement and aid. In particular we are indebted to the ADL's program director, Oscar Cohen. It was his vision which inspired the Five-Year Study and his indefatigable efforts which brought it into being and through to completion. We are also grateful for the support of the Charles Weinfeld Memorial Foundation toward this study.

Finally, we should like to thank all of the Protestant and Roman Catholic pastors of churches in the sample, and the 3,000 church members on whose beliefs, hopes, sentiments, and life histories our study is based.

*Berkeley, California*                                          C. Y. G.
*November 1, 1965*                                             R. S.

# Introduction: Religion and Anti-Semitism

> I believe that I am acting in accordance with the will of the Almighty Creator: by defending myself against the Jew, I am fighting for the work of the Lord.
>
> —ADOLF HITLER

For centuries, persecution of the Jews was justified in the name of God. The inspiration for the medieval ghettos and for the bloody pogroms of history was provided by the doctrine that the Jews had murdered Christ and thereby provoked God's eternal wrath and punishment.

But times have changed. Heretics no longer go to the stake; no respected churchmen speak of the "accursed Jews." Indeed, the official and sincerely meant policies of the major Christian bodies witness for the love of neighbor and the brotherhood of man.

In this era of growing religious harmony, it may seem fruitless or even unfortunate to raise the question of the role played by contemporary Christian teachings in shaping attitudes toward the Jews. Nevertheless, that is what this book is about. Here, we shall try to establish why we chose this topic and how we mean to pursue it.

Our general interest in anti-Semitism is not primarily historical, and we are only incidentally concerned with the forces producing bygone crimes against the Jews. The past can only be remembered, not changed. And it is the hope for change that is the basic motive of our inquiries; for if the church has had a change of heart toward Jewry, Western man has not. The flames of bigotry burn on.

But to call for change is a meaningless prescription unless we know

where we stand at present, and unless we understand the *means* for producing a different state of affairs. Thus, every element of our society which
influences anti-Semitism, whether for good or for evil, eventually must
be investigated.

On this basis, a study of what role (if any) religion plays today in
anti-Semitism, and *how* this comes about (if it does) seems an important
part of any broad effort to assess the current state of prejudice against
Jews. In fact, religion seems a particularly important object for study
because virtually nothing is known about what effect it presently has on
prejudice. The available clues are contradictory. On the one hand, both
Christian and Jewish religious leaders hail a major *rapprochement* between
the faiths: an era of good will, theological dialogues, mutual respect, and
cooperative undertakings. Yet, historically it is clear that the heart and
soul of anti-Semitism rested in Christianity. Can the legacy of these long
centuries of Christian agitation against the Jews have died out entirely?
We ought to know, because if it has not, a perhaps unnecessary source
of bigotry might be allowed to continue unopposed. On the other hand,
if modern Christianity is a positive force in allowing men to transcend
old prejudices, then this, too, ought to be understood so that it can be
made even more effective.

Our present ignorance in this matter must be blamed on social science.
Despite the fact that their centuries of suffering occurred primarily because
Jews were non-Christians living in militantly Christian lands, contemporary
social science studies have virtually ignored religion as a possible factor
in anti-Semitism.[1] Instead, recent studies seeking the causes of anti-
Semitism have pursued the effects of education, social class, ethnicity,
personality factors, politics, child-rearing practices, the link between circumcision and the "castration complex," and a host of similar "secular"
variables. Viewed in historical perspective this seems like an extraordinary
sin of omission.

Perhaps the main reason that religion has been ignored by contemporary
investigators of anti-Semitism lies in the impact of the Nazi holocaust.
It is hardly possible to comprehend the fact of six million murdered Jews;
such horror seems to transcend history, to mark a new and unique phenomenon which must be understood in new terms.

Furthermore, because Nazis were anti-Semites many investigators have

---

[1] In a recent inventory of all research done on anti-Semitism in America since
1930, of 183 studies digested, only 13 had to do with religion, and only one of
these could in any sense be called empirical research. Furthermore, this single study
was limited to description of intergroup perceptions of Protestants, Catholics, and
Jews. See Melvin M. Tumin, *An Inventory and Appraisal of Research on American
Anti-Semitism* (New York: Freedom Books, 1961).

assumed that the obverse, that all anti-Semites are Nazis, is also true. Consequently, to a great extent the study of anti-Semitism was transformed into the study of Nazism. The most famous and perhaps most significant research ever done on anti-Semitism, *The Authoritarian Personality*,[2] is an apt example. The famous "*f*-scale" is after all short for "fascist-scale."

This preoccupation with uncovering the roots of Nazism in order to understand anti-Semitism, or, indeed, regarding anti-Semitism *as* Nazism, was, we suspect, an important factor leading social science investigators to ignore religion as a possible cause. Because the Nazis were not religious (in fact many were explicitly antireligious), it seemed clear that religion could have played no significant role in the destruction of European Jewry.

Yet, most students of the Nazi era have concluded that one of its most central features was the acquiescence of the general population in the Nazi terror against Jews. The man in the street seemingly cared so little about what was being done to the Jews that he was willing to accept it without protest. This, of course, raises the question of the climate of mass opinion; to understand fully how the destruction of European Jewry occurred we must explain why popular sentiment was sufficiently antagonistic so that such horror met with at least acquiescence if not outright cooperation. It is in trying to understand this general sentiment, if not in trying to account for the anti-Semitism of the Nazi activists, that the omission of religion as a possible explanation seems especially serious.

However, not all scholars have in fact ignored religion in seeking to account for contemporary attitudes toward Jews. As a group, historians have been considerably more interested in the contribution of religion to these events than have sociologists and psychologists. Hilberg, for example, argues that traditional, religiously based anti-Semitism was a major factor in providing Hitler with the means for exploiting political anti-Semitism.[3] While Hitler was hardly given to invoking religion in his political speeches, he frequently did so when he discussed the Jewish question. Recently, Guenter Lewy has carefully reconstructed the extent to which the German Catholic hierarchy supported Hitler's anti-Semitism by promulgating historic religious doctrines on the Jews as "Christ-killers."[4]

If historians have remained sensitive to the role of religion in contemporary anti-Semitism, even that of the Third Reich, churchmen too have shown concern on this same issue. Beginning in the last decades,

---

[2] T. W. Adorno, *et al.* (New York: Harper & Row, 1950).

[3] Raul Hilberg, *The Destruction of the European Jews* (Chicago: Quadrangle Books, 1961).

[4] "Pius XII, the Jews, and the German Catholic Church," *Commentary*, February 1964.

liberal Christian leaders have been trying to expunge invidious depictions of the Jews from church teachings. Since then a number of major American Protestant bodies have adopted resolutions denouncing the age-old doctrine that the Jews are collectively guilty of the Crucifixion.

In addition, many Protestant bodies have been re-examining their Sunday school materials since recent studies by clergymen and Biblical scholars revealed the extent to which contemporary Sunday school texts teach harsh, anti-Jewish lessons.[5] It is worth quoting some of these Sunday school texts, for only their own prose does them justice.

One writer of a book for younger children widely used by a major denomination included the following warning note to the Sunday school teacher:

Do not use the expression "the wicked soldiers who were ill-treating Jesus," without taking care that the children do not identify "to be a soldier" with "to be wicked." . . . One should not speak of "wicked soldiers," but of "wicked Jews." In the Passion narrative the soldiers should be treated as simply doing what they are ordered to do.[6]

Another Sunday school text book offered this for the edification of young minds:

The Jews turned their backs on God, they refused His Son and they worshipped pagan gods. And they have been sorely punished for centuries as a result. . . . They are not really wanted anywhere.[7]

Other Sunday school texts reaffirmed the doctrine that Jewish suffering is divinely inspired. One author stated that the Jews continue to exist "to provide the world with tangible evidence of divine justice." Another explained: "God preserves them so that they may continue to expiate their national crime . . ."[8]

By bringing to national attention the hostile religious image of the Jews promulgated in many Sunday school lessons, these scholars stimulated renewed efforts by religious leaders to rectify church teachings. Today many of the major denominations have censored such blatant attacks upon Jews. Some have gone further and tried to incorporate not simply neutral, but positive, treatment of the Jews in Sunday school texts.

This developing theological reconsideration of doctrines on Jews has

---

[5] Among these are Bernhard E. Olson, *Faith and Prejudice* (New Haven: Yale University Press, 1962) and James Brown, "Christian Teaching and Anti-Semitism: Scrutinizing Religious Texts," *Commentary*, December 1957, pp. 494–501.

[6] Brown, *op. cit.*

[7] *Ibid.*

[8] *Ibid.*

recently received considerable attention in the press because of the delib-
erations of the Vatican Council. The move for reform was begun by Pope
John XXIII, who, in 1959, removed the phrase "perfidious Jews" (*"perfidi
Judaei"* and *"judaica perfidia"*) from the liturgy for Good Friday. Subsequently, during the first session of the Vatican Council called by Pope
John there were signs that the Catholic church was preparing to state
as its official position that the Jews were not and are not collectively guilty
of the Crucifixion. But it was not until late in the fall of 1965 that the
Council finally passed its schema on the Jews.

These reforms met strenuous opposition from the conservative Roman
curia who attempted to defeat the new schema and indeed, did succeed
between the third and fourth Council sessions in getting the preliminary
statement amended to delete its most forthright language. These efforts
on the part of the curia received considerable support from some conservative Protestants.

Despite opposition on the part of conservatives, a good deal of
progress has been made to rectify the centuries of religious teachings against the Jews. The motive of these clerical reformers has been
primarily one of moral concern, and their interest has been in doctrinal
inequities as such. There has been considerably less certainty that anything
besides specifically theological issues was at stake, for there has been
no indication from social science that these doctrines play any significant
role in generating anti-Semitism in the modern world. Still, many of these
clergymen have been worried that such teachings do indeed provide
Christians with a pious rhetoric for hating Jews. It is in part to assess
these fears that the present study was undertaken.

The basic questions prompting our inquiry are these: Does the Christian
faith currently have any effect on attitudes toward Jews, either positive or
negative? If such effects do occur (whether positive, negative, or even
both), through what process does this come to pass?

The book is organized around a theoretical model which postulates the
process through which religion may continue to foster anti-Semitism
among modern American Christians.[9] The analysis which is pursued

[9] This model was constructed on theoretical grounds *prior* to any collection
or analysis of empirical data. Thus, there are no *post hoc* hypotheses in succeeding
chapters that are not clearly identified as such, and *none* of these are of primary
importance to the theoretical model. *Post hoc* hypotheses are those offered as
explanations of empirical relationships already observed. Since they are necessarily
congruent with the data, they do not constitute predictions and face no possibility
of being refuted. Because our model was postulated in advance, the analysis in
subsequent chapters constitutes a legitimate test of our theories. Furthermore, without a priori hypotheses it would have been nearly impossible to provide any
intelligent basis for deciding what data to collect and what statistical tabulations
to examine.

constitutes a test of this theoretical model to determine whether or not it is true and if so, to what extent. Subsequent chapters are devoted to describing each element in the model, to postulating the links between elements through which Christian beliefs may produce anti-Semitism, and to confronting these postulates with empirical evidence to confirm or to refute them.

Having indicated the existence of this theoretical model, it would seem reasonable to provide the reader with a brief preliminary sketch of it here. However, it can be more effectively introduced and clarified piece by piece along the way. Consequently, we shall postpone discussing the workings of the model as a whole until all the pieces are assembled.

## Details of the Survey

So far this introduction has been concerned with a preliminary statement of the aims to be pursued in the rest of the book. In conclusion, something must be said about the means that will be employed.

Once the theoretical model of the religious sources of anti-Semitism had been constructed, the next step was to discover if it bore any resemblance to reality. Do any appreciable number of men possess all of the religious characteristics which we postulated? And, most important, if men are like this, are they much more likely than others to be anti-Semitic? Thus, to see the degree to which our theories are congruent with actuality an empirical study of individual behavior is required.

The data upon which our thesis will be tested in Chapters 1 through 11 were gathered through a survey of a random sample of the church-member population of four counties along the Western side of San Francisco Bay. In Chapter 12 the model developed and tested in the preceding chapters will be retested on data from a national sample of the adult population.

The sample of northern California church members was selected by first randomly sampling congregations from a list (weighted for size) of all Protestant and Roman Catholic congregations in the four counties of Marin, San Francisco, San Mateo, and Santa Clara. After thus selecting 97 Protestant congregations, and 21 Roman Catholic parishes, a random sample of members was obtained by sampling individual membership lists. Appendix A includes a detailed exposition of these procedures.

Each person who was selected in the sample through these means was sent a very lengthy questionnaire (See after Index) and asked to fill it out. Over a period of months, 72 per cent of the Protestants and 53 per cent of the Roman Catholics drawn in the sample responded, a total of 3,000 persons in all. Data collected from samples of Protestants and Catholics who did *not* respond, as shown in Appendix A, indicated that data from those who filled out questionnaires satisfactorily represented the entire sample.

Eighteen months after the questionnaires were mailed to the church-member sample the most important items were included in interviews conducted with a modified random sample of the national adult population. In all, 1,976 persons were interviewed. The sampling and interviewing were done by the National Opinion Research Center. Their techniques, developed through more than a decade of conducting nationwide surveys, are widely respected. A full account will be provided in another volume in this series which will be based entirely on these national data.[10]

To conclude this chapter a word must be said about our personal involvement in this subject. In formulating our theories and judging our data we have tried to be carefully objective and let the trail lead where it may. But obviously our decision to undertake such a study was not dispassionate. If the churches, no matter how inadvertently, lead men to hate Jews, we mean to raise the alarm. For all that, this book is not to be read as an indictment of religion. The good will and serious concern of most Christian leaders has already been demonstrated. It is not our intention to castigate them if the findings implicate religion in contemporary anti-Semitism. Rather we hope to provide them with the necessary understanding to transform the churches into a reliable force in man's struggle to free himself from bigotry.

[10] This study is being conducted by Dr. Gertrude Jaeger Selznick and Stephen Steinberg and will be published in 1967.

# PART I.      RELIGIOUS IDENTITY

*Religious identity comprises two basic features: the degree to which a man's world view contains a religious component, and the particular texture and quality of this component. In the two chapters which constitute Part I, each of these features will be examined in order to distinguish some general patterns of religious identity among present-day American Christians.*

CHAPTER 1

_____

# Orthodoxy

> Now faith is the substance of things hoped for, the evidence of
> things not seen.
>
> —Heb. 11:1 (A.V.)

Religion is many things. Among its aspects are symbols, practices, rituals, scriptures, but at the core of all religions is a set of beliefs about the nature, meaning, and purpose of reality. Other aspects of religion are only coherent within this context of a more or less systematic body of beliefs. For such beliefs, whether they postulate the nature of God, the nature of man, or the nature of matter, provide the rationale by which symbols and rituals are understood and justified. For example, prayer is at best solitary muttering unless it is warranted by some conception of a God who hears and cares. In this sense, theology is the bedrock of faith.

If religious roots for anti-Semitism are to be uncovered, the place to begin the search is in this bedrock of theology, in the doctrines and dogmas making up the Christian solutions to questions of ultimate meaning, or what Tillich has called "ultimate concern."[1]

This chapter will be devoted to developing satisfactory empirical means for measuring and evaluating the current state of religious belief among church members. To do so it will be necessary to put aside briefly the question of how religion affects anti-Semitism in order to establish a beginning for our investigation.

To examine the theological outlooks of contemporary Christians we

[1] Paul Tillich, _Systematic Theology_ (Chicago: University of Chicago Press, 1956), I, 12.

shall first examine a number of items on religious belief included in the questionnaire to see how well they distinguish various denominations and traditions from one another. From these beliefs, several will be selected to construct an index of religious orthodoxy in order to measure the commitment of persons to these theological outlooks. Then we shall demonstrate the validity of the index, that is, the degree to which it measures what it is intended to measure.

To provide a valid general measure of Christian orthodoxy we must concentrate on beliefs that are universal to the Christian tradition and avoid those that have been disputed among the various denominations. This is not to seek tenets on which all *persons* agree, for then it would not be possible to contrast the more and less orthodox, but rather to seek tenets broadly upheld by the various Christian *bodies*.

A universal and basic element in Christian theologies is an elaborate set of assertions about the nature and will of an all-powerful and sentient God. All Christian moral norms and religious practices are justified and understood as deriving from the intent of this Creator of human history. Without God, traditional Christian preachments become incoherent.

Commentators on the current American scene are unanimous in thinking all but a mere handful of Americans believe in God. Findings from national polls support this assumption; repeated Gallup surveys have found that 96 to 97 per cent of all American adults respond "yes" when asked, "Do you, personally, believe in God?"[2] Although a few observers have been somewhat uncomfortable about the seeming lack of sophistication of such an either-or probe, and wondered how many different images of God were subsumed within this gross summary, most have been content to accept these findings as a ratification of American piety, especially when contrasted with the much lower levels of belief in God disclosed by similar polling in European nations.

Given this virtual unanimity among the general public, it might seem pointless to examine belief in God among *members* of Christian churches. What could possibly be found but universal acceptance, which would prove useless for attempts to distinguish degrees of orthodoxy? Yet, it seems possible that there might be significant differences in the *images* of God held by different persons as well as in the *degree* they are certain about their belief. Looking at the data shown in Table 1, it is strikingly apparent that even in a sample of only church members, there are indeed important contrasts both in conceptions of God and in conviction. Furthermore, these variations sharply distinguish the denominations from one another.

[2] See American Institute of Public Opinion, survey of Dec. 18, 1954.

Table 1. BELIEF IN GOD

| "Which of the following statements comes closest to what you believe in God?" | Cong.[a] | Meth. | Epis. | D.of Christ | Pres.[e] | A.Luth.[b] | A.Bap. | M.Luth. | S.Bap. | Sects[c] | Total Prot. | Cath. |
|---|---|---|---|---|---|---|---|---|---|---|---|---|
| "I know God really exists and I have no doubts about it." | 41% | 60% | 63% | 76% | 75% | 73% | 78% | 81% | 99% | 96% | 71% | 81% |
| "While I have doubts, I feel that I do believe in God." | 34 | 22 | 19 | 20 | 16 | 19 | 18 | 17 | 1 | 2 | 17 | 13 |
| "I find myself believing in God some of the time, but not at other times." | 4 | 4 | 2 | 0 | 1 | 2 | 0 | 0 | 0 | 0 | 2 | 1 |
| "I don't believe in a personal God, but I do believe in a higher power of some kind." | 16 | 11 | 12 | 0 | 7 | 6 | 2 | 1 | 0 | 1 | 7 | 3 |
| "I don't know whether there is a God and I don't believe there is any way to find out." | 2 | 2 | 2 | 0 | 1 | d | 0 | 1 | 0 | 0 | 1 | 1 |
| "I don't believe in God." | 1 | d | d | 0 | 0 | 0 | 0 | 0 | 0 | 0 | d | 0 |
| No answer | 2 | 1 | 2 | 4 | d | d | 2 | 0 | 0 | 1 | 2 | 1 |
| Total | 100% | 100% | 100% | 100% | 100% | 100% | 100% | 100% | 100% | 100% | 100% | 100% |
| Number [of respondents] | (151) | (415) | (416) | (50) | (495) | (208) | (141) | (116) | (79) | (255) | (2,326) | (545) |

[a] The Congregationalists have recently merged with the Evangelical and Reformed Church to form a new denomination, the United Church of Christ. Because all of the respondents in our sample were formerly Congregationalists we have retained this more widely recognized name for the sake of clarity.

[b] Members of the Lutheran Church in America and the American Lutheran Church have been treated as a single group. Analysis showed there were no important differences between them.

[c] Included are Assemblies of God, Church of God, Church of Christ, Church of the Nazarene, Seventh Day Adventists, Four Square Gospel Church, and one independent tabernacle. The term "sects" is used to designate this group of churches in conformity with common sociological usage.

[d] Less than 0.5 per cent.

[e] Presbyterians in this sample were all members of the United Presbyterian Church.

In selecting the statement about God that came closest to their own views, only 41 per cent of the Congregationalists indicated unquestioning faith in a personal divinity. This proportion rises to 60 per cent of the Methodists, 63 per cent of the Episcopalians, reaches about the three-quarter mark among the denominations in the center of the table, and is virtually the unanimous response of Southern Baptists and members of the fundamentalist sects. Over-all, 71 per cent of the Protestants endorsed this traditionally orthodox position as compared with 81 per cent of the Roman Catholics.

Looking at the second line of the table, we may see that the greatest proportion of persons who rejected the first statement did not do so because they held a different image of God, but because they differed in their certainty. While they conceived of a personal divinity, they admitted having doubts about his existence. Denominational differences here too are marked; ranging from 34 per cent of the Congregationalists to 1 per cent of the Southern Baptists.

The third possible response (third line in the table) is simply a more "doubtful" version of the second and did not draw much support. However, the fourth response category is especially interesting, for it concerns a different conception of God, rather than differences in the certainty of faith. Again contrasts are striking: Sixteen per cent of the Congregationalists, 11 per cent of the Methodists, 12 per cent of the Episcopalians, down to none of the Southern Baptists, thought not of a personal God, but of some kind of "higher power." Over-all, 7 per cent of the Protestants held this impersonal conception of God, while 3 per cent of the Roman Catholics did so.

To complete the findings, it should be noted that 2 per cent of the Congregationalists, Episcopalians, and Methodists took an agnostic position and 1 per cent of the Congregationalists candidly said they did not believe in God.

Looking at the over-all figures, if responses to the first four categories are added together, the totals would indicate that 98 per cent of both Protestants and Roman Catholics believe to some extent in what they think of as God, which is a very close match with the usual Gallup results. What the data reveal, however, is how much variation in the strength of belief and the kind of God believed in is suppressed by a simplistic inquiry. And more important for our subsequent analysis, there is sufficient variation in the degree to which Christian church members are committed to this central tenet of religious ideology to warrant its use to measure their religiousness.

Gallup studies also report that Americans are virtually unanimous

Table 2. BELIEF IN THE DIVINITY OF JESUS

| "Which of the following statements comes closest to what you believe about Jesus?" | Cong. | Meth. | Epis. | D.of Christ | Pres. | A.Luth. | A.Bap. | M.Luth. | S.Bap. | Sects | Total Prot. | Cath. |
|---|---|---|---|---|---|---|---|---|---|---|---|---|
| "Jesus is the Divine Son of God and I have no doubts about it." | 40% | 54% | 59% | 74% | 72% | 74% | 76% | 93% | 99% | 97% | 69% | 86% |
| "While I have some doubts, I feel basically that Jesus is Divine." | 28 | 22 | 25 | 14 | 19 | 18 | 16 | 5 | 0 | 2 | 17 | 8 |
| "I feel that Jesus was a great man and very holy, but I don't feel Him to be the Son of God any more than all of us are children of God." | 19 | 14 | 8 | 6 | 5 | 5 | 4 | 0 | 0 | a | 7 | 3 |
| "I think Jesus was only a man, although an extraordinary one." | 9 | 6 | 5 | 2 | 2 | 3 | 2 | 1 | 1 | a | 4 | 1 |
| "Frankly, I'm not entirely sure there was such a person as Jesus." | 1 | 1 | 1 | 0 | 1 | a | 0 | 0 | 0 | 0 | 1 | 0 |
| Other and no answer | 3 | 3 | 2 | 4 | 1 | 0 | 2 | 1 | 0 | 1 | 2 | 2 |
| Total | 100% | 100% | 100% | 100% | 100% | 100% | 100% | 100% | 100% | 100% | 100% | 100% |
| Number | (151) | (415) | (416) | (50) | (495) | (208) | (141) | (116) | (79) | (255) | (2,326) | (545) |

a Less than 0.5 per cent.

in believing Jesus Christ was the Divine Son of God. But in light of our findings about God, we can expect this faith too needs to be qualified by degree of certainty as well as differences in the images of Christ.

Table 2 shows that indeed there are important contrasts in belief in the divinity of the central figure of Christianity. The pattern of denominational differences across the first line of the table is virtually identical to the pattern of belief in God. Differences range from 40 per cent of the Congregationalists who have no doubts that "Jesus is the Divine Son of God" to 99 per cent of the Southern Baptists. The total Protestant figure is 69 per cent in contrast to 86 per cent among Roman Catholics.

The second row of the table shows the proportion who see Christ as divine, but admit some doubts. Roughly a quarter each of the Congregationalists, Methodists, and Episcopalians gave this response, while only 5 per cent of the Missouri Synod Lutherans and none of the Southern Baptists did so.

The third statement acknowledges great respect for Jesus and his holiness, but denies his divinity. Again the denominations differ greatly. The next category is similar, but less reverent in tone, and drew fewer respondents. And, finally, 1 per cent of all Protestants, but none of the Roman Catholics, frankly doubted the historical existence of Jesus.

Variations in the degree to which Christian church members ratify faith in an orthodox conception of Christ come into even sharper focus when we examine some specific details of Christology. As shown in Table 3, only 57 per cent of all Protestants responded "completely true" when asked to evaluate the statement, "Jesus was born of a virgin," while 81 per cent of the Roman Catholics did so. But even more startling differences can be observed among the Protestant bodies: From 21 per cent of the Congregationalists the proportion rises to 99 per cent of the Southern Baptists.

The dispersion among Protestants is even slightly increased when we examine the second item in the table, which reports the proportions who thought it "completely true" that "Jesus walked on water." Firm believers in this miracle commonly credited to Christ form a small minority in the large, liberal denominations, constitute half of Protestants in general, make up 71 per cent of the Roman Catholics, and 99 per cent of the Southern Baptists. Like the existence of God, the Saviourhood of Christ produces mixed reactions among American Christians.

The extreme contrasts we have seen thus far among the various denominations are matched by widely different views on the authenticity of Biblical accounts of miracles. In Table 4 the proportions responding

Table 3.   ADDITIONAL BELIEFS ABOUT JESUS

|  | Cong. | Meth. | Epis. | D.of Christ | Pres. |
|---|---|---|---|---|---|
| Number | (151) | (415) | (416) | (50) | (495) |
| *"Jesus was born of a virgin."* "Completely true" | 21% | 34% | 39% | 62% | 57% |
| *"Jesus walked on water."* "Completely true" | 19 | 26 | 30 | 62 | 51 |

|  | A.Luth. | A.Bap. | M.Luth. | S.Bap. | Sects |
|---|---|---|---|---|---|
| Number | (208) | (141) | (116) | (79) | (255) |
| *"Jesus was born of a virgin."* "Completely true" | 68% | 69% | 92% | 99% | 96% |
| *"Jesus walked on water."* "Completely true" | 58 | 62 | 83 | 99 | 94 |

|  | Total Prot. | Cath. |
|---|---|---|
| Number | (2,326) | (545) |
| *"Jesus was born of a virgin."* "Completely true" | 57% | 81% |
| *"Jesus walked on water."* "Completely true" | 50 | 71 |

they believe the "miracles actually happened just as the Bible says they did," vary from 28 per cent of the Congregationalists and 37 per cent of the Methodists, 69 per cent of the American Luthern bodies, 89 per cent of the Missouri Lutherans, to 92 per cent of the Southern Baptists. Seventy-four per cent of the Roman Catholics ratified miracles in contrast to 57 per cent of all Protestants.

Members of the "liberal" denominations, on the left of the table, who did not accept the truth of Biblical miracles were about evenly divided between making a straightforward rejection of miracles (the bottom category) and a plausible-sounding, but confusing, "hedge." That is, 32 per cent of the Congregationalists, 31 per cent of the Methodists, and so on, with decreasing frequency across the table, responded that they believed the "miracles happened, but can be explained by natural causes."

If the word miracle has any coherent meaning, it refers to events in which natural laws are suspended and apparently violated, such as when a sea opens a dry path at a command or water is changed to wine. If an

Table 4. BELIEF IN MIRACLES

Reply to: "The Bible tells of many miracles, some credited to Christ and some to other prophets and apostles. Generally speaking, which of the following statements comes closest to what you believe about Biblical miracles?"

| | Cong. | Meth. | Epis. | D.of Christ | Pres. | A.Luth. | A.Bap. | M.Luth. | S.Bap. | Sects | Total Prot. | Cath. |
|---|---|---|---|---|---|---|---|---|---|---|---|---|
| "Miracles actually happened just as the Bible says they did." | 28% | 37% | 41% | 62% | 58% | 69% | 62% | 89% | 92% | 92% | 57% | 74% |
| "Miracles happened but can be explained by natural causes." | 32 | 31 | 22 | 16 | 20 | 14 | 16 | 4 | 0 | 3 | 19 | 9 |
| Doubt or do not accept miracles | 32 | 24 | 27 | 14 | 14 | 13 | 9 | 5 | 3 | 5 | 17 | 9 |
| Did not answer | 8 | 8 | 10 | 8 | 8 | 4 | 13 | 2 | 5 | 0 | 7 | 8 |
| Total | 100% | 100% | 100% | 100% | 100% | 100% | 100% | 100% | 100% | 100% | 100% | 100% |
| Number | (151) | (415) | (416) | (50) | (495) | (208) | (141) | (116) | (79) | (255) | (2,326) | (545) |

event can be explained by natural causes, it is, by definition, no miracle. This category was originally inserted in the questionnaire because when the item was pretested without such a response, a great many persons wrote in some approximation of this statement rather than to reply by either rejecting miracles outright or literally accepting them unequivocally. From discussions with some of the pretest respondents, we learned this position seemed to stem from a desire to avoid imputing fraud to Biblical writers. What these respondents wanted to say was that the events were natural, but inexplicable to people in Biblical times, and were thus given a miraculous interpretation in good faith. Be that as it may, the response seems most accurately classed as one variety of *rejection* of Biblical miracles, and will be interpreted as such in the present study.

Two more central Christian tenets will complete our exploration of beliefs which could be used to measure orthodoxy: belief in life after death and belief in the existence of the Devil. Again we see the marked differences in the proportions holding these beliefs across denominations (Table 5). But a much more interesting comparison is found by contrasting the proportions holding each belief *within* each denomination. Among the denominations on the left of the table, members are much more likely to accept an afterlife than to affirm belief in the Devil. Roman Catholics take a more unified position: 75 per cent over 66; and, similarly, the conservative Protestants take the "good" with the "bad." Thus, while many persons in the liberal bodies tend to question *both* an afterlife and the Devil, a substantial minority accept the comfort of belief in a hereafter, while rejecting the threat of a fiery alternative.

Our purpose in this section is to develop means for measuring the commitment of individuals to what can plausibly be considered orthodox Christian tenets. We now propose that from the seven items we have just examined, four can be selected from which to construct an index of orthodoxy. These are: the existence of a personal God, the divinity of Jesus Christ, the authenticity of Biblical miracles, and the existence of the Devil. In constructing the index, a respondent received a score of 1 for *each* of these belief questions on which he expressed his certainty of the truth of the orthodox Christian position. Respondents received a score of zero for each item on which they acknowledged doubt or disbelief about the orthodox response.[3] Thus, a person could score as high as 4, by being certain in his faith on all four items, or as low as zero by reporting doubt or disbelief on all four.

[3] The 216 persons who failed to answer one or more of the items were not scored. Subsequent analysis revealed them to be proportionately distributed across all categories of orthodoxy, and their deletion has no influence on findings. For a discussion of indexing procedures, see Appendix B.

Table 5.  BELIEF IN LIFE BEYOND DEATH AND THE DEVIL

| | Cong. | Meth. | Epis. | D.of Christ | Pres. | A.Luth. | A.Bap. | M.Luth. | S.Bap. | Sects | Total Prot. | Cath. |
|---|---|---|---|---|---|---|---|---|---|---|---|---|
| Number | (151) | (415) | (416) | (50) | (495) | (208) | (141) | (116) | (79) | (255) | (2,326) | (545) |
| *"There is a life beyond death."* | | | | | | | | | | | | |
| "Completely true." | 36% | 49% | 53% | 64% | 69% | 70% | 72% | 84% | 97% | 94% | 65% | 75% |
| "Probably true." | 40 | 35 | 31 | 32 | 21 | 23 | 19 | 10 | 3 | 4 | 24 | 16 |
| "Probably or definitely not true." | 21 | 13 | 13 | 0 | 7 | 5 | 7 | 4 | 0 | 2 | 9 | 5 |
| Did not answer | 3 | 3 | 3 | 4 | 3 | 2 | 2 | 2 | 0 | 0 | 2 | 4 |
| Total | 100% | 100% | 100% | 100% | 100% | 100% | 100% | 100% | 100% | 100% | 100% | 100% |
| *"The Devil actually exists."* | | | | | | | | | | | | |
| "Completely true." | 6% | 13% | 17% | 18% | 31% | 49% | 49% | 77% | 92% | 90% | 38% | 66% |
| "Probably true." | 13 | 15 | 16 | 34 | 17 | 20 | 17 | 9 | 5 | 5 | 15 | 14 |
| "Probably or definitely not true." | 78 | 66 | 60 | 38 | 48 | 26 | 29 | 10 | 1 | 5 | 43 | 14 |
| Did not answer | 3 | 6 | 7 | 10 | 4 | 5 | 5 | 4 | 2 | 0 | 4 | 6 |
| Total | 100% | 100% | 100% | 100% | 100% | 100% | 100% | 100% | 100% | 100% | 100% | 100% |

Orthodoxy Index

Table 6. ORTHODOXY AND DENOMINATION

| Orthodoxy Index | Cong. | Meth. | Epis. | D.of Christ | Pres. | A.Luth. | A.Bap. | M.Luth. | S.Bap. | Sects | Total Prot. | Cath. |
|---|---|---|---|---|---|---|---|---|---|---|---|---|
| High 4 | 4% | 10% | 14% | 18% | 27% | 43% | 43% | 66% | 88% | 86% | 33% | 62% |
| 3 | 18 | 20 | 23 | 36 | 29 | 20 | 20 | 21 | 9 | 10 | 21 | 19 |
| 2 | 18 | 23 | 21 | 23 | 16 | 12 | 18 | 7 | 3 | 3 | 16 | 6 |
| 1 | 12 | 17 | 18 | 7 | 12 | 12 | 7 | 6 | 0 | 0 | 12 | 4 |
| Low 0 | 48 | 30 | 24 | 16 | 16 | 13 | 12 | 2 | 0 | 1 | 18 | 9 |
| Total | 100% | 100% | 100% | 100% | 100% | 100% | 100% | 100% | 100% | 100% | 100% | 100% |
| Number | (141) | (381) | (373) | (44) | (457) | (195) | (130) | (111) | (76) | (247) | (2,155) | (500) |

As can be seen in Table 6, the Orthodoxy Index shows the same relationship to various denominations that was observed in our examination of the items included in it. Moving across the table from left to right, the proportion scoring high on orthodoxy rises from 4 per cent of the Congregationalists to 88 per cent of the Southern Baptists. Furthermore, among both Protestants and Catholics, although less so among the latter, the Orthodoxy Index distributes respondents widely, revealing many degrees of ideological commitment.

Having constructed the index, it remains to be demonstrated whether it sensitively measures what we mean it to. Looking at the first three items in Table 7, we see that among both Protestants and Catholics the

Table 7.   VALIDATION OF THE ORTHODOXY INDEX

(Per cent in each category of Orthodoxy Index who answered "completely true.")

| | Orthodoxy Index | | | | |
| | Low | | | | High |
| | 0 | 1 | 2 | 3 | 4 |
|---|---|---|---|---|---|
| | *"There is a life beyond death."* | | | | |
| Protestants | 12% | 35% | 65% | 79% | 97% |
| Catholics | 15 | 24 | 47 | 71 | 96 |
| | *"Jesus was born of a virgin."* | | | | |
| Protestants | 6% | 20% | 38% | 74% | 96% |
| Catholics | 11 | 10 | 59 | 91 | 98 |
| | *"Jesus walked on water."* | | | | |
| Protestants | 3% | 11% | 24% | 63% | 95% |
| Catholics | 9 | 10 | 41 | 66 | 92 |
| | *"A child is born into the world already guilty of sin."* | | | | |
| Protestants | 3% | 8% | 12% | 22% | 55% |
| Catholics | 9 | 19 | 47 | 61 | 89 |
| | *"The Pope is infallible in matters of faith and morals."* | | | | |
| Protestants | 2% | 2% | 2% | 2% | 1% |
| Catholics | 11 | 19 | 44 | 63 | 85 |
| | *Number* | | | | |
| Protestants | (394) | (248) | (339) | (454) | (720) |
| Catholics | (46) | (21) | (32) | (97) | (304) |

index powerfully and consistently predicts acceptance of other central Christian tenets: life beyond death, the virgin birth, and Christ's walking on water.

But the bottom two statements in the table give even more impressive demonstrations of the sensitivity and validity of the index. Here it is used to predict tenets which are central to *some* traditions in Christianity, *but not to others*. The concept of original sin is emphasized by some Protestant theologies but not by others, and the table shows that while the proportions feeling this concept is absolutely true rise across categories of the index, even among the most orthodox Protestants only half take this position. However, for Roman Catholics, original s an important doctrine, and acceptance of it is predicted powerfully by the Orthodoxy Index. Thus, the index does not predict just *any* Christian teaching, but is sensitive to disagreements among Christian denominations. This is further demonstrated by belief in papal infallibility, a specifically Roman Catholic teaching. A handful of Protestants in each category of orthodoxy—most of whom probably erred in marking their response—accept this statement as "completely true." However, among Catholics, acceptance is accurately predicted by the Orthodoxy Index. These findings clearly indicate that our index, made up of general belief items, is also a valid register of orthodoxy specific to particular groups. As a result, we can use one index to classify all our respondents rather than having to make separate indexes for classifying members of the various denominations.

With orthodoxy defined and operationalized, we may now turn our attention to a second feature of religious commitment: ritual participation.

## Ritual Participation

Although theology is the bedrock of faith, it seems worthwhile to give some attention to the degree to which persons act on their faith to fulfill the ritual expectations of Christianity. Beyond knowing the degree of a man's orthodoxy it will prove valuable to know the degree to which he participates in the worship that a traditional conception of God demands. Subsequently, we shall be able to explore the interplay between these two aspects of religious commitment.

While various world religions differ in placing emphasis on public or private ritual requirements, Christianity has historically valued both subtypes of ritual involvement. Hence, while Christians have been enjoined to attend church regularly and participate in various sacraments, they have also been expected to perform frequently such personal ritual acts as prayer.

On this basis we can perhaps expect to find so high a correlation between meeting public and private ritual expectations that measures of each can be legitimately combined to form a single measure of ritual commitment. However, as with orthodoxy, we need to select ritual acts which are encouraged by all denominations rather than rituals specific to a few bodies.

While some Christian bodies lay emphasis on private reading of the Bible, or saying table grace, others do not stress these activities. However, all bodies put a premium on personal prayer. Similarly, while only some denominations expect frequent participation in institutional sacraments such as Holy Communion, all attempt to secure regular attendance at Sunday worship services. The generality of prayer and church attendance recommends them as measures of public and private ritual involvement.

As can be seen in Table 8, Christians are slightly more likely to

Table 8.   RITUAL PARTICIPATION

|  | Cong. | Meth. | Epis. | D.of Christ | Pres. |
|---|---|---|---|---|---|
| Number | (151) | (415) | (416) | (50) | (495) |
| Attend church weekly or nearly so | 45% | 51% | 56% | 68% | 68% |
| Pray at least several times weekly | 61 | 62 | 71 | 80 | 77 |

|  | A.Luth. | A.Bap. | M.Luth. | S.Bap. | Sects |
|---|---|---|---|---|---|
| Number | (208) | (141) | (116) | (79) | (255) |
| Attend church weekly or nearly so | 65% | 75% | 73% | 84% | 94% |
| Pray at least several times weekly | 75 | 75 | 81 | 92 | 91 |

|  | Total Prot. | Cath. |
|---|---|---|
| Number | (2,326) | (545) |
| Attend church weekly or nearly so | 63% | 80% |
| Pray at least several times weekly | 74 | 82 |

pray at least several times a week than to attend church every, or nearly every, week. This tendency is more pronounced among members of the denominations at the top of the table than in the more conservative bodies. In the main, however, praying and attending church are similarly distributed among the denominations, which suggests that most persons are likely to do both or neither. And in fact the correlation coefficient between these two ritual activities was .67 among Catholics and .50 among Protestants.[4]

This high correlation supported our expectation that private and public ritual involvement could be treated unidimensionally.[5] Hence, the

[4] Yule's $Q$ was used.
[5] This unidimensionality may be a consequence of having a sample made up entirely of church members. By belonging to a specific church, these respondents are probably predisposed to high attendance. Prayerful, but nonattending, persons may tend not to belong to any church congregation, and hence to be excluded from our sample.

two items were combined to construct an index of ritual involvement. Persons who both attended church every, or nearly, every week and prayed at least several times a week were classified as high on the index. Those who reported performing either of these ritual activities as frequently as this were scored as medium. Persons who fell below this level of performance on both items were classified as low.

The validity of the index was established by its powerful prediction of other public and private ritual acts, such as saying table grace, reading the Bible, participating in other church activities, and placing great value on one's church membership.

## The Connection Between Orthodoxy and Ritual Involvement

Having found means for measuring both orthodoxy and ritual involvement, we shall bring this chapter to a close by briefly exploring the interrelations between these two aspects of religious commitment.

While one can easily imagine persons who hold orthodox beliefs, but are ritually inactive, and persons who are ritually active, but little concerned with belief, the fact seems to be that people tend to be either active believers or inactive nonbelievers. Table 9 reveals the strong relationship between the orthodoxy and ritual involvement indexes.

Among Protestants only 17 per cent of those in the lowest category

Table 9.   ORTHODOXY AND RITUAL INVOLVEMENT

| Rank on Ritual Index | Orthodoxy Index | | | | |
|---|---|---|---|---|---|
| | Low 0 | 1 | 2 | 3 | High 4 |
| Protestants: | | | | | |
| High | 17% | 34% | 48% | 54% | 68% |
| Medium | 38 | 43 | 40 | 38 | 28 |
| Low | 45 | 23 | 12 | 8 | 4 |
| Total | 100% | 100% | 100% | 100% | 100% |
| Number | (393) | (234) | (339) | (448) | (706) |
| Catholics: | | | | | |
| High | 31% | 30% | 52% | 70% | 83% |
| Medium | 26 | 40 | 45 | 24 | 15 |
| Low | 43 | 30 | 3 | 6 | 2 |
| Total | 100% | 100% | 100% | 100% | 100% |
| Number | (42) | (20) | (31) | (97) | (301) |

of orthodoxy score high on ritual involvement, while 68 per cent of those highest on orthodoxy are also high on ritual. Among Roman Catholics the Orthodoxy Index similarly predicts ritual involvement. While these data indicate that ideological and ritual commitment are highly correlated, they also illustrate the relevance of our earlier concern to distinguish between these aspects of religiousness. For the fact is that they are not entirely measures of the same thing, but to some degree they can be regarded as independent expressions of religious involvement: Persons do not *always* exhibit the same degree of religiousness on both dimensions. For example, 31 per cent of those Catholics who did not express certainty in any of the four basic beliefs in the Orthodoxy Index, nevertheless prayed at least several times a week and attended Mass every, or nearly every week. Thirty-two per cent of the Protestants who were certain of all four belief items fell short of this frequency of performance on one or both ritual acts.

Given the moderate independence of these two dimensions of religious commitment, we shall be able to contrast the effects of both kinds of involvement in our subsequent analysis as well as explore their joint impact on attitudes and behavior.

## Conclusion and Preview

As we briefly outlined in our opening chapter, this book will be fashioned like a chain; each chapter will introduce a new concept, or variable, which will be added to a sequential model of the way in which Christianity may influence attitudes toward Jews.

The present chapter has been devoted to the first link in this chain. In it we have attempted to outline the general concept of religious orthodoxy and to construct adequate means for measuring certain aspects of this phenomenon. To accomplish this necessary task we have turned aside, briefly, from our central concern with discovering what potential for hostility and prejudice may lurk within religious orientations, and in turn with learning how religion may enable people to transcend such propensities. Having now established a beginning for our story we may return to this quest. In the next chapter we shall seek to isolate and explain a particular aspect of religious imagery which may turn faith into a holy cause.

# CHAPTER 2

# Particularism

> For thou are an holy people unto the LORD thy God: the LORD thy God hath chosen thee to be a special people unto himself, above all people that are upon the face of the earth.
>
> —Deut. 7:6 (A.V.)

> Do not unite yourselves with unbelievers; they are no fit mates for you. What has righteousness to do with wickedness? Can light join darkness? Can Christ agree with Belial, or a believer join hands with an unbeliever? Can there be a compact between the temple of God and the idols of the heathen?
>
> —II Cor. 6:14–16 (N.E.V.)

In this chapter we shall try to show that certain kinds of theologies necessarily imply a narrow and precisely defined sphere of persons who qualify as properly religious. In subsequent chapters, we shall suggest that one consequence of such clear specification of religious legitimacy is the identification of a number of persons and groups as religiously illegitimate.

The particular component of religious perspectives which we mean to isolate and clarify asserts an exclusive patent on religious "truth." The fanatic intolerance of contrary creeds generated by this kind of religious self-righteousness has been proved in blood throughout history. In this spirit Moslems slew, and were slain by, the hated infidel. It inspired the racks and stakes of the Inquisition, the St. Bartholomew's Day Massacre, the burning of convents, the decimation of the Albigenses and Taborites— the record is so long, so brutal, and so well known that it need not be recounted. Our interests, for the moment, are better served by a dispassionate effort to clarify and specify than by tales of inhumanity committed in the name of faith.

Our central concern in this chapter will be with what we shall call religious particularism—a precise and narrow conception of proper religious status, tantamount to religious chauvinism. Webster's *New World Dictionary* defines particularism as: "1. the theological doctrine that redemption is possible only for certain individuals. 2. Undivided adherence or devotion to one particular party, system, interest, etc." The discussion of this concept will comprise three parts. In the first we shall attempt to clarify what we mean by religious particularism and select ways adequately to measure it. The second part will examine the conditions under which a religious perspective includes or develops a particularistic component. In the last section these theoretical notions will be empirically tested.

## Defining and Measuring Religious Particularism

Most simply put, religious particularism is the belief that only one's own religion is legitimate. In contrast with the bland sentiments of former President Eisenhower, who stressed the importance of "a deeply felt religious faith—and I don't care what it is,"[1] men with a particularistic outlook most emphatically do care *what* it is. To the particularistic mind there are not faiths, but one true faith.

Eric Hoffer has provided a perceptive portrait in miniature of the particularistic vision: "The true believer is apt to see himself as one of the chosen, the salt of the earth, the light of the world, a prince disguised in meekness, who is destined to inherit this earth and the kingdom of heaven too."[2]

In our pluralistic, modern society particularism can take broader or narrower forms.[3] Some may feel that any faith is acceptable so long as it acknowledges a supreme being. Others may specifically limit religious legitimacy to Christians, and still others may reject all but their own specific denomination. A few persons even call down a pox upon all but themselves and their immediate families.[4] In the words of Coleridge, "He

---

[1] Quoted in Will Herberg, *Protestant, Catholic, Jew* (Garden City, N.Y.: Anchor Books, 1959), p. 84.

[2] Eric Hoffer, *The True Believer* (New York: Mentor Books, 1951), p. 93.

[3] Particularism, as used here, can be applied as aptly to political as to religious outlooks, indeed to any ideology that serves as a system of ultimate values. In this sense of an exclusive destiny, the Birchite and the Communist are indistinguishable from the Jehovah's Witness.

[4] Max Weber viewed conceptions of "chosen people" as a natural outgrowth of ethnic conflict, a horizontal form of status differentiation. Granted that most groups

who begins by loving Christianity better than truth, will proceed by loving his own sect or church better than Christianity, and end in loving himself . . . better than all."

Whether broad or narrow, a particularistic outlook discredits all persons whose religious status lies beyond the boundaries of what is seen as the "true" faith. Obviously, the wider these boundaries, the fewer *actual* persons and groups who will be excluded. Thus, the breadth of particularism has great practical importance for those concerned about conflict among men. However, the quality of seeing one's own group as singularly legitimate is the same in broader and narrower instances.

It is clear in what we have said so far that a particularistic view of one's own religious status implies invidious judgments of the religious legitimacy of persons of another faith. However, we wish for analytic purposes to separate these two questions. Thus, we shall concentrate first on the question of seeing one's own group as singularly possessed of the true faith, and only later examine the connection of such views with hostility toward religious outsiders. For, as we shall argue later in this chapter and throughout this volume, although particularism is very likely to result in religious hostility, it need not, and indeed does not, always do so. Some persons seem able both to regard their religion as having a patent on truth and to refrain from drawing any conclusions about the state of religious outsiders from this conviction. Such a capacity, even if it is far from typical, is of great importance to efforts to find ways in which men can accommodate one another's differences.

Thus, in what follows we shall develop the concept of religious particularism independent of religious hostility. In discussing certain historical examples this separation may not be kept entirely clear because the particularism and hostility present were so intermingled. But for our empirical measure of particularism, and in subsequent analysis, this distinction will be imposed.

A supreme test of proper faith in Christian tradition rests on the

---

tend to prefer their own customs and regard them as superior to those of others, such ethnocentricism lacks the cutting edge of religious particularism, although the two often coincide. We must distinguish between a sense of being "chosen people" and being "God's chosen people." A man with funny clothes and poor manners is not nearly so far beyond the pale as a man encumbered with a false religion. Weber does make the interesting point, however, that "the idea of a chosen people derives its popularity from the fact that it can be claimed to an equal degree by any and every member of the mutually despising groups . . ." Thus, the poorest medieval serf could regard himself as infinitely superior to the most learned and wealthy Jewish physician. This is a comfort which people are likely to be reluctant to give up. See Max Weber, "Ethnic Groups," in Talcott Parsons *et al., Theories of Society* (New York: The Free Press of Glencoe, 1961), I, 308.

question of salvation, of what is required of men in order that they may be saved. This suggests that if one wants to discover particularistic conceptions of religious legitimacy the place to look is at the criteria imposed on salvation—who are viewed as eligible and who as ineligible for entrance into God's kingdom?

Our respondents were asked a number of questions about the requirements for salvation, but, for the moment, we shall give attention to three items which seem most specifically to plot the boundaries of those who may aspire to be saved.

The first of these determines whether or not respondents see salvation as limited to Christians. Table 10 shows the proportion of persons in each denomination who thought "belief in Jesus Christ as Saviour," was "absolutely necessary for salvation," or "probably would help." (The remainder felt it would make no difference, and a few did not answer.) While only a minority of Congregationalists felt belief in Christ was absolutely necessary,[5] the proportion rises to virtual consensus among the conservative bodies, reaching 97 per cent among Missouri Lutherans and Southern Baptists. However, a sizable minority of members in the liberal bodies moderately favored this view, feeling that belief in Christ "probably would help in gaining salvation." Clearly the implication of these data is that a majority of Christian church members feel that only Christians qualify for salvation.

However, as is evident from the second item in Table 10, they are somewhat reluctant to translate this positive requirement into a negative sanction. Far fewer persons in all denominations were willing to say that "being completely ignorant of Jesus as might be the case for people living in other countries," would "definitely" prevent salvation. A sizable proportion, however, felt this could "possibly" be the case. Again, differences in the proportions holding this view increase systematically among the denominations, reading from left to right across the table.

The third question in the table drastically narrows the scope of salvation from Christians in general to the person's own denomination in particular. Here again fewer persons took an adamant position. Only 3 per cent of the Congregationalists, rising to 16 per cent of the Missouri Lutherans and Southern Baptists felt "being a member of your particular religious faith" was necessary for salvation. These findings suggest that

---

[5] This is no surprise since many members of the liberal groups rejected the existence of life after death, questioned the divinity of Christ, and of course rejected the very notion of salvation. When questioned about the requirements for salvation, such people chose either not to answer or to say that a particular requirement made no difference. The tables in this chapter include those who did not believe in salvation.

Table 10.   THE REQUIREMENTS FOR SALVATION

| | Cong. | Meth. | Epis. | D.of Christ | Pres. | A.Luth. | A.Bap. | M.Luth. | S.Bap. | Sects | Total Prot. | Cath. |
|---|---|---|---|---|---|---|---|---|---|---|---|---|
| Number | (151) | (415) | (416) | (50) | (495) | (208) | (141) | (116) | (79) | (255) | (2,326) | (545) |
| *"Belief in Jesus Christ as Saviour."* | | | | | | | | | | | | |
| "Absolutely necessary for salvation." | 38% | 45% | 47% | 78% | 66% | 77% | 78% | 97% | 97% | 81% | 65% | 51% |
| "Probably would help in gaining salvation." | 36 | 37 | 36 | 18 | 23 | 16 | 17 | 1 | 1 | 2 | 23 | 37 |
| *"Being completely ignorant of Jesus as might be the case for people living in other countries."* | | | | | | | | | | | | |
| "Definitely prevent salvation." | 3% | 7% | 3% | 8% | 11% | 15% | 17% | 36% | 41% | 23% | 14% | 4% |
| "May possibly prevent salvation." | 13 | 23 | 16 | 38 | 24 | 29 | 31 | 28 | 39 | 40 | 25 | 24 |
| *"Being a member of your particular religious faith."* | | | | | | | | | | | | |
| "Absolutely necessary for salvation." | 3% | 6% | 7% | 8% | 8% | 14% | 12% | 16% | 16% | 16% | 11% | 28% |
| "Probably would help in gaining salvation." | 30 | 32 | 29 | 28 | 27 | 27 | 34 | 29 | 20 | 36 | 30 | 45 |

the days when bitter Christian factions saw themselves as having a monopoly on religious authenticity have largely passed. And while Roman Catholics are commonly accused of believing theirs to be the "One True Faith," only 28 per cent thought only Catholics could be saved. While it is true that Roman Catholics seem more prone to such a view than Protestants, still the overwhelming majority did not take such a position. On the other hand, sizable proportions from all denominations displayed a muted chauvinism in replying that membership in their particular faith "probably would help" one to gain salvation.

While these three items do not exhaust available measures of religious particularism, as we shall see shortly, they seem well suited jointly to distinguish the degree to which Christians limit the sphere of persons whom they will acknowledge as being properly religious.

Following the indexing procedures described in the last chapter, these three items were scored to make a summary measure of religious parochialism.[6] The Particularism Index assigns persons scores from zero to 6; the higher the score, the greater the adherence to a particularistic perspective. As with the Orthodoxy Index, the question of whether or not the Particularism Index actually measures what it is intended to measure must be answered.

The question of validity is a knotty one which is often given short shrift in social science. In general, the various scales and indexes used by researchers rely on face validity, that is, on the face of them they seem to bear on the concept they are assigned to measure. The items in the Particularism Index clearly meet this criterion, for their manifest content concerns the religious boundaries of salvation: Who are the properly faithful?

While this face validity lends confidence to our operationalization, the quest for validity need not rest here. Several further strategies are available. One of these is to see whether the measure sensitively predicts other narrow conceptions of who may be saved.

Table 11 demonstrates this predictive power of the Particularism Index. Among both Roman Catholics and Protestants, the proportions who hold "prayer" and "holy baptism" as "absolutely necessary for salvation" increase dramatically with the degree of particularism (from left to right across the table). Further confirmation is given by the pattern of response to the third item in the table. While some Protestant groups, particularly those in a "high church" or liturgical tradition, place great

[6] The scoring on each question was: Absolutely necessary = 2; probably would help = 1; probably has no influence = 0. Thus the index ranges from 6 (highest particularism) to 0 (lowest).

Table 11. VALIDATION OF THE PARTICULARISM INDEX

| | Particularism Index | | | | | | |
| | Low 0 | 1 | 2 | 3 | 4 | 5 | High 6 |
|---|---|---|---|---|---|---|---|
| *Per cent who said prayer "absolutely necessary for salvation."* | | | | | | | |
| Protestants | 16 | 36 | 49 | 59 | 69 | 87 | 98 |
| Catholics | 25 | 17 | 37 | 59 | 75 | 92 | 100 |
| *Per cent who said holy baptism "absolutely necessary for salvation."* | | | | | | | |
| Protestants | 2 | 9 | 27 | 34 | 50 | 67 | 84 |
| Catholics | 13 | 27 | 41 | 79 | 90 | 98 | 93 |
| *Per cent who said "regular participation in Christian sacraments" is "absolutely necessary for salvation."* | | | | | | | |
| Protestants | 1 | 4 | 14 | 17 | 35 | 46 | 72 |
| Catholics | 0 | 10 | 7 | 33 | 70 | 92 | 100 |
| *Per cent who said "practicing artificial birth control" would "definitely prevent salvation."* | | | | | | | |
| Protestants | 0 | 0 | a | a | 2 | 5 | 16 |
| Catholics | 8 | 8 | 14 | 19 | 34 | 47 | 57 |
| *Number of respondents* | | | | | | | |
| Protestants | (167) | (286) | (483) | (436) | (396) | (166) | (61) |
| Catholics | (24) | (48) | (125) | (109) | (93) | (49) | (14) |

a Less than 0.5 per cent.

emphasis on regular participation in Christian sacraments, others do not. Catholicism makes such participation an essential article of faith. Thus, particularism ought massively to predict making salvation conditional on participation in the sacraments among Roman Catholics, but less strongly elicit such a judgment among Protestants. This is precisely what the data show. Among Catholics *none* of the respondents with a zero score on the Particularism Index thought participation in the sacraments was absolutely necessary for salvation, while *100 per cent* of those highest in particularism thought so. Among Protestants, the proportions responding "absolutely necessary" increase markedly with parochialism, but only about three-fourths (72 per cent) of the most particularistic group took this position. Hence, the index, though built from broad notions of who may be saved, also reflects criteria peculiar to some denominations.

This is further demonstrated by the last item in the table. Artificial birth control is widely approved by Protestant leaders but condemned as mortal sin by the Catholic hierarchy. There has been speculation, however, that many devout Catholic laymen reject this stipulation of the church. The data show that virtually no Protestants feel artificial birth control will prevent salvation (although the most particularistic are slightly more inclined to this view) and also show how widely this tenet is rejected by Catholics. High rank on the Particularism Index strongly predicts belief that birth control perils salvation, but even among the most particularistic Catholics only 57 per cent accept this view. Over-all, only 23 per cent of Roman Catholics and 2 per cent of Protestants see artificial birth control as insuring damnation.

Aside from its intrinsic interest, this finding also demonstrates that the Particularism Index is not merely a measure of unreflective affirmation of all traditional criteria for salvation. Rather, it implies a discriminating judgment of who may qualify as properly religious persons from the standpoint of a Christian perspective.

It can be seen in Table 11 that in spreading respondents across seven points of the index, from zero through 6, some of the categories turned out to contain relatively few cases. For this reason it was necessary to collapse the index, observing the natural cutting points in the data.[7] Looking at Table 11, two such breaks consistently occur on all items: between scores 1 and 2 and between 3 and 4.

By cutting the index along these two breaks, a three-point measure of particularism was constructed. The first category (Low) contains all persons scoring zero or 1 on the original index. The Medium group comprises those who scored 2 or 3. High includes all who scored 4, 5, or 6. With the index thus collapsed, many more cases are available in each category, thereby permitting further analysis. For example, the least numerous type, low particularism, contains 453 Protestants and 72 Roman Catholics.

The validation pursued thus far has shown that the Particularism Index effectively measures the degree to which church members impose limits on eligibility for salvation. To a certain extent the criteria of eligibility imply human responsibility, and hence, freedom to qualify. They concern what men must do to satisfy divine will. But particularism also includes a self-image of having been selected, favored, set apart by the divine which, to a degree, implies a worthiness attached to some men by God in the manner of a status *imposed* rather than one to be attained. While it is true that traditional Christianity emphasizes that all men are free,

---

[7] This is especially true among Roman Catholics, who make up only about a fifth of the sample to begin with. Only 24 Catholics were classified in the least particularistic (zero) category, and only 14 in the pure particularistic class (6), and among Protestants there were only 61 pure particularists, and 167 nonparticularists. This shortage of cases at some points in the index would have seriously hampered further analysis. Such small numbers of cases would not have permitted the introduction of further variables; when fewer than 15 cases occur in a cell of a table the stability of any percentage based on that cell becomes questionable.

indeed exhorted, to come into the faith, there seems to also be a certain self-righteousness attached to having been born a Christian.

It remains to be seen whether or not the Particularism Index also taps this capacity for seeing one's own religious group as God's Elect, as the Chosen People "above all people that are on the face of the earth."[8] All respondents were asked who, if anyone, they thought were God's "Chosen People" today? Table 12 shows the relationship between the

Table 12.    PARTICULARISM AND BELIEF THAT CHRISTIANS ARE GOD'S
CHOSEN PEOPLE TODAY

Reply to: "Who do you think are God's 'Chosen People' today?"

| | Low | Particularism Index Medium | High | Total |
|---|---|---|---|---|
| *Per cent who said "Christians":*[a] | | | | |
| Protestants | 11 | 32 | 62 | **41** |
| Catholics | 31 | 43 | 56 | **46** |
| Per cent of Protestants who said "Protestants" | b | b | 2 | **1** |
| Per cent of Catholics who said "Roman Catholic" | 11 | 25 | 28 | **24** |
| *Number responding:* | | | | |
| Protestants | (453) | (919) | (623) | **(1,995)** |
| Catholics | (72) | (234) | (156) | **(462)** |

[a] Persons who said "Protestants," "Roman Catholics," or "Christians."
[b] Less than 0.5 per cent.

Particularism Index and identification of Christians as the chosen people. Among both Protestants and Roman Catholics, though more so among the former, particularism as measured by the index is strongly related to seeing Christians as God's own.

The data in the third and fourth lines of the table are also worth noting. Here we may observe that virtually no Protestants (1 per cent) restricted their definition of the chosen people to Protestants alone, although many thought Christians were elect. But slightly more than half of the Catholics, who were classified in the upper table as designating Christians as God's chosen people actually restricted their response to Roman Catholics. In light of the popular image that Catholics think their church is the One True Faith, the percentage who made this choice (24 per cent) may seem rather small. Yet it is clear that a sizable minority of Catholics do reject the religious legitimacy of Protestants, while Protestants consider Catholics among the faithful. This is not to say that

[8] Deut. 7:6 (A.V.).

Protestants do not vigorously denounce aspects of Catholic doctrine and worship. Our data indicate they do, but in the final analysis they grant Catholics a place among the properly religious. The propensity of Catholics either to count all Christians or only fellow Catholics among God's Chosen People increases systematically as they score higher on the Particularism Index. Thus, the index seems a valid and sensitive measure of the extent to which the respondent holds a narrow and chauvinistic conception of religious legitimacy.

## Particularism in Historical Perspective

We have now developed what we mean by the concept of particularism and have settled on an empirical measure of it. Furthermore, it has been shown that particularism is a relatively common aspect of contemporary Christianity. For the immediate needs of this study it would be possible to let the matter rest here and move on to examine the role played by Christian particularism in the process leading to anti-Semitism. However, in our judgment it is important to inquire about the forces which give rise to particularism. In the last section of this chapter we shall demonstrate the degree to which particularism is a product of commitment to Christian orthodoxy. But why is this the case? Must such a connection exist?

The answers, we suggest, cannot be found in a study of Christianity alone. Rather it seems likely that the rise of particularism in Christianity must be attributed to the working of more general social phenomena—when certain conditions exist *any* religious ideology (and perhaps any ideology) evolves a particularistic outlook.

In what follows we shall briefly suggest what some of these conditions are. It must be emphasized that this is a mere sketch toward a theory; to provide a more complete theoretical statement would require an extended historical analysis which is presently beyond our means and which would carry us far afield from the central question of this study. Nevertheless, it seems important to give some consideration to these general issues because they have received so little scholarly attention and because it places our line of argument in a broader and more useful perspective.

There are two classes of factors which affect the generation and maintenance of particularism. The first are ideological or theological attributes; the second comprise aspects of the society in which the ideology flourishes. The first govern the development of what can be called the particularistic *idea*; the second limit or facilitate the degree to which this idea can be acted upon.

The first aspect of theologies, necessary to produce the particularistic idea, is *a generality of ideological claims.* Whatever the content of beliefs, a theological system cannot become particularistic unless or until these beliefs are credited to be universally applicable and true, the only truth, and mutually exclusive with other contradictory beliefs.

At first glance, this thesis may seem tautological, as though we are only saying that religions which regard themselves as the true faith will regard themselves as the true faith. But this is not the case, for this characteristic of theological systems is not by itself sufficient to produce particularism. Such an assumption of universal applicability may be associated with theologies which are nevertheless so vaguely specified that little or nothing fails to meet these requirements. Consider, for example, theologies which posit that all religions are manifestations of the same generalized revelation, idiosyncratically developed in different cultural circumstances. From this view all religions are true, and their differences trivial. The universal assertion here is limited to the notion that there has been a general revelation by divinity to all men. Such a view is insufficient for particularism. An example of such an outlook can be found in the Bahai faith, and modern Unitarianism approaches this view. However, many theologies are not so limited in their tenets, which leads us to a second necessary element for the development of particularism.

Given universality of ideological claims, the degree to which a theology is likely to lead to particularism is a function of the *specificity of that theology.* Simply put, this refers to the elaborateness of a theological system—the degree to which it details a view of divine nature, intent, and demands. In a general way, specificity is simply a function of the number of discrete tenets in the theology. The greater the number of tenets, or the more detailed the belief system, the greater the specificity of "proper" doctrine and the narrower the way of "truth."

Even given both these conditions, *there must exist some conception of persons or groups who do not meet the criteria of proper religiousness posited by the theology* in order for a religion to become particularistic. It seems implausible to suppose that any religious group which contained all men would come to think of itself as special or chosen, for whom would they be chosen in contrast to, from whom would they be distinguished? However, the greater the specificity of any theology the greater the likelihood that more persons and groups will in fact be excluded from religious legitimacy, and the greater the *degree* of violation of proper religiousness which becomes possible. If "outsiders" are considered as relatively stable in their own religious behavior, then it follows that if some group increases the number of requirements for proper faith, the likelihood of

excluding any given person or group is increased. The number of standards which may be violated simultaneously also increases, thus raising
the degree of violation.

If historical religions which had elaborate belief systems are examined
it is clear that specificity alone is insufficient to produce particularism.
The Roman and Greek cults, for example, had detailed notions of the
will and intent of divinity, as well as what was required properly to
worship and seek the gods. But they claimed no universal, exclusive truth,
and flourished side by side without much conflict. However, we are not
suggesting that particularism is possible only in monotheistic religions.
Polytheistic systems may consider a specific *set* of gods as the complete
and only divinity, and thus generate the grounds for a particularistic outlook. Hence, polytheism *may* lead to claims of universality, but monotheism
seems particularly likely to do so.

Given that a theology or an ideology has generated a particularistic
idea of its own status, there still remains the matter of if, and how, this
idea will be socially enacted. Here, we suggest, the primary considerations
are matters of power. The concept of power—the ability to impose one's
wishes upon a group or a society—is one of the more complicated and
ambiguous notions in social science. However, we mean to use it in a
relatively conventional sense. Furthermore, our concern is not with power
per se, but with certain aspects of social arrangements which affect *access*
to power. Specifically, we shall be concerned with the degree to which
the bearers of a particularistic ideology *have* power in their society, and
the degree to which power *exists* in their society.

The question of a particularistic group holding extensive power in a
given society is largely governed by whether they constitute a majority or
a minority. Although we recognize that in some peculiar circumstances a
religious minority may rule over a majority, for the purposes of this
discussion we shall treat such groups as if they were in fact a majority.
That is, we are primarily concerned with who is at the mercy of whom.

If the particularistic idea is the property of a minority (or less powerful) group, they face different options for enacting their idea than when
it is the majority who are particularistic. A minority can either risk their
survival by acting out their particularism in the face of majority opposition,
or they may adopt some strategy of isolation. It is typical of recent particularistic American cults that they have turned inward and sought means
to insulate themselves from the dissenting majority. Sometimes this is
accomplished within the heart of the dissenting majority through careful
control of members, as was the case for followers of the late Father
Divine, for example. Others have sought actual geographic isolation by
trekking into the wilderness.

For a minority that chooses to act out their particularism openly, the risks are considerably greater. Their typical strategy is to seek to rise above their powerlessness through conversion of the powerful. But this entails confrontation and collision between the minority's conviction of superiority and the majority's objection to this as unwarranted pride, and a threat to prevailing institutions besides. When the majority too is particularistic the confrontation is typically hostile and even violent, for example, the friction between the various American cults and their Christian environment. But friction can occur even when the majority is not particularistic. The confrontation between ancient Judaism and the classical world is instructive here. The ancient Jews, having spread colonies throughout the Mediterranean world, and armed with their particularistic view of a true and *only* god, embarked upon a campaign of active proselytization although in a minority status.[9] The antagonistic response of classical society followed. For even Rome, with its permissive, eclectic, and somewhat instrumental approach to religion,[10] the Rome which boasted of raising temples to the gods of every conquered nation, found itself unable easily to accommodate a religion that claimed not merely to be true, but to be singularly true.[11]

The social conflict stemming from particularism is even more pronounced when particularism is the property of the majority (or the powerful), and when a dissenting minority exists or arises. For if the minority has the problem of a lack of power, the majority has the positive burden of power. In order for humane and liberal conditions to prevail, a particularistic majority must resist the temptations of power. This, of course, constitutes the historical burden of Christianity, imposed after the conversion of Constantine, when the church rose triumphant over the Roman Empire. The burden proved unbearable. What followed was the

[9] Because Judaism was not allowed to seek converts during the centuries of its suppression by Christianity, and because it does not do so today, it is incorrectly assumed often that Judaism was never a conversionist faith. But in immediately pre-Christian times Judaism was a potent religious force that enjoyed considerable success in gaining converts. An excellent account is provided in several of the remarkable historical volumes of James Parkes, especially his *The Conflict of the Church and the Synagogue* (Cleveland and New York: Meridian Books, 1961).

[10] This eclectic spirit of Roman religion has been captured best by Gibbon's famous passage: "The various modes of worship which prevailed in the Roman world were all considered by the people as equally true; by the philosopher as equally false; and by the magistrate as equally useful."

[11] It is often said in defense of particularistic religions—such as ancient Judaism, Christianity, and Islam—that they were universalistic because they placed no restrictions upon who might come into the faith. This is all well and good, but the conflict produced by particularism occurs when it is confronted by persons who do not choose to come into the "true faith." It is this aspect which is of concern to this study. We are not concerned with attitudes toward Jewish converts to Christianity, but with attitudes toward Jews who remain Jews.

brutal and bloody imposition of "the truth"; for the truth, like fortune, is always on the side of the largest battalions.

Islam too provides an instance of a particularistic majority faced with the burden of power. Like Christians, the Moslems failed to restrict its use in the enactment of their particularistic idea. The infidels were an abomination in the eyes of Allah and must be brought into the faith. During the wars through which Islam exploded across Africa and into Southern Europe, infidel prisoners were readily accepted into the "true faith" upon their conversion, and typically slain if they rejected this opportunity to embrace the truth. For a brief period the ancient Jews too faced the burdens of power and turned it upon the pagan Canaanites.

Despite these similarities, in important ways Christianity produced a unique blend of the particularistic idea with social reality. If the ancient Jews and Islam approximated the Christian tendency to impose "the truth" upon those outside the faith, the practical limits of their definition of who was religiously legitimate were much broader, and comparatively vague. For there remained in both Islam and ancient Judaism considerable freedom for internal dissent. Even at the height of their power, Judaism and Islam were riddled with sects and factions disputing the exact nature of the true faith. Thus their particularism encompassed a good deal of latitude; "the truth" never became monolithic, and the notion of heresy remained rudimentary at best.

Christianity, on the other hand, though in early centuries it too accommodated considerable factionalism and schism, soon evolved into a monolith. The suppression of all internal dissent is peculiarly Christian— the barbaric campaigns against groups who, although they claimed to be Christians, rejected some tenet of the Church Universal;[12] the rise of the inquisitions, the very embodiment of monolithic particularism, which, through the centuries, committed hundreds of thousands to a variety of grotesque deaths. Such are not to be found in either ancient Judaism or Islam.

The primary factor in the monolithic development of Christian particularism was the extent to which internal power existed in Christian society. Such power varies according to the degree of effective social

[12] During the campaign against the Albigenses, the papal legate reported to Pope Innocent III, ". . . our men, sparing neither rank nor sex nor age, slew about 20,000 souls with the edge of the sword; and, making a huge slaughter, pillaged and burned the whole city, by reason of God's wrath wondrously kindled against it." When later asked about the danger that some Christians might also be slain in these wholesale annihilations of cities, the legate is reported to have advised, "Slay all, the Lord will know his own." [Quotations from H. C. Lea, *A History of the Inquisition in Spain* (New York: Macmillan, 1906–1967), I, 215 and 135.]

organization. By social organization we mean those attributes of societies such as communications, responsive lines of authority, the organization of force, and the like, which allow governmental consolidation of power. In most earlier societies (and in most of today's underdeveloped countries), the authority of the central government was weak, the enforcement of its policies was problematic at best.

Historically, it is clear that Islam never accomplished a social organization sufficient to produce much centralized power. Rather it remained a loose-knit conglomoration of tribes, minor rulers, and competing domains. Similarly, ancient Judaism did not develop a truly powerful monarchy, rather, authority remained fragmented and decentralized.

Christianity, on the other hand, inherited at least the remains of one of the most effectively organized and centralized societies prior to modern times—the Roman Empire. In such a setting, the *means* by which monolithic particularism could be imposed lay at hand. With the emergence of the Bishop of Rome as predominant in the church, there developed a structure of centralized religious authority built upon the existing centralized power of the Empire. It was the development of a Supreme Pontif which permitted Christian suppression of internal dissent. Similarly, it was the failure of a strong caliphate to develop in Islam or of a supreme high priest in Judaism that made the suppression of internal dissent impossible.

Thus, Christianity represented a unique combination of social factors. To its particularistic theology were added majority status and the means for effective centralization of authority. As a result Christianity was posed with unique access to power, the power to define its particularism to include only the single interpretation advocated by the Papacy, and the power to suppress all who disagreed. The bloody pages of church history show that this power was not managed with humility or restraint.

Eventually, however, Christianity did begin to accommodate factionalism; denominations emerged to shatter the monolith. It is instructive that this diversity did not come about because a more tolerant attitude grew up in Rome. It was not a gradual restraint from using power, but the corrosion of power that permitted the rise of Protestantism. Dissent won its existence only through force of arms, and the church only began to learn to live with dissent when dissent could live in spite of the church.

It must not go unacknowledged that these new dissenters in their turn were equally intolerant and dealt death and torture to orthodox Christians and other dissenters as well. During the years 1542–1546 alone, Calvin had 58 persons executed. The sixty-year total for the Geneva theocracy was 150 heretics burned at the stake, including, on October 27, 1553, the famous physician-scholar, Servetus. By virtue of usually being in a minority position, however, Christians who broke with Rome were typically victims rather than tormentors.

It is important to recognize that the monolithic enactment of ideological particularism did not remain uniquely Christian, but has been matched by particularistic political movements in the twentieth century. The Nazis found the notion of heresy quite agreeable, and it remains a major preoccupation of Communism. The cries of deviationism, revisionism, bourgeois mentality, and left sectarianism, sound depressingly like the earlier cries of manichaeism, gnosticism, and pelagianism.

Upon examination it is clear that these political ideologies have the necessary ideological aspects to develop a particularistic idea. Communism is regarded as the final unfolding of history, a universal truth for all men in all future times. Furthermore, this truth is greatly detailed; the economic and political organization of proper Marxist societies is elaborately specified by the doctrine. In addition, there is a clear conception of others who fail to adhere to these principles.

Given such a particularistic notion, the monolithic quality of Communism, with its internal heresy hunting, follows from the efficient centralization of authority inherent in the modern state. Communists need only to control these vast resources of power to make it possible for the leaders to enact a narrow definition of proper Marxist doctrine. Like early Christianity, the early days of Bolshevism were marked by freewheeling internal argument of proper doctrine, but as power was consolidated this soon ceased.

Thus Communism, where it rules (and Nazism when it did), repeats the circumstances of the church with relatively similar consequences. The opportunities inherent in power seem irresistible for men who know all the answers. It is obviously untrue that all tyranny stems from particularism, but the taste for tyranny seems a ubiquitous feature of particularism wherever it arises.

This summary of factors affecting particularism is admittedly sketchy, meant only to provide a very general setting for our subsequent use of the concept. It is in no sense offered as proof of our speculations. Indeed, even with exhaustive scholarship it would be exceedingly difficult to test such sociological hypotheses on historical materials. It would be impossible to locate all relevant historical cases, and often difficult to obtain any agreement on whether or not various characteristics were present or absent in specific instances. Thus, all our historical references were intended only as illustrations of certain points.

However, some test of our speculations can be provide
notions concerning the ideological requirements for a particula
look are correct, they need not apply only to religious groups, t
equally apply to individuals. That is, persons whose theology n
conditions previously specified ought to be prone to a particularis
ception of themselves and their own group, while those who lack such a
theology ought not to hold a particularistic view.

This makes possible a rigorous, empirical test of our hypothesis.
Means for classifying respondents in our survey according to their degree
of religious particularism have already been developed. We have also
constructed measures of religious commitment, including an index of
commitment to orthodox Christian theology. At this point it seems
appropriate to bring these two concepts together.

Before doing so, one extremely important caveat must be introduced:
We are arguing that religious doctrines of a certain kind, under certain
circumstances, will come to be interpreted in a way which justifies and
generates hostility toward religious dissenters. We are *not* arguing that
such interpretations of doctrine are the *only* logical conclusions that can
be drawn from a given theology. It is simply never true that theologies,
or ideologies in general, are so logically integrated that there exist no
alternative ways of interpreting them. The old saw that "religion is a violin
on which any tune can be played" is much closer to the truth. Thus, it is
entirely beside the point that many Bible texts can be collected to show
the tolerant and universalistic character of Christian doctrine. While the
presence of such texts enables modern theologians to find a new Christian
perspective in keeping with enlightened views of the brotherhood of man,
*these texts were not made the basis of such a tolerant theology in earlier
days.* We are concerned here, not with all the potential interpretations of
a religious doctrine, but with the commonly understood and predominant
interpretations made from such doctrines in particular eras. It is on this
basis that we characterize the mainstream of Christian thought down to
relatively modern times as particularistic.

### Religious Commitment and Particularism

As amply illustrated in the last section, historic Christianity meets
the conditions specified for developing a particularistic outlook. The
faith claims universal application, is highly specified, in fact may be the
most theologically detailed religion ever to appear in human society,
and relevant deviants from its tenets have always existed both within
Christendom and surrounding it.

Similarly, these conditions seem to be met by some Christians and some Christian groups in contemporary America. That is, persons who embrace traditionally orthodox Christian theology claim universality for an elaborate doctrine amidst persons and groups who reject these teachings. Thus, we are led to predict on the basis of our theoretical notions that those who are ideologically committed to orthodox Christianity will be highly prone to a particularistic vision, while those relatively uncommitted to this ideology will likely reject particularism.

Empirically, this prediction requires that the Orthodoxy Index display a powerful relationship with the Particularism Index. This is well confirmed by the data shown in Table 13. Among both Protestants and

Table 13.   ORTHODOXY AND RELIGIOUS PARTICULARISM

| Rank on Particularism Index | Orthodoxy Index | | | | |
|---|---|---|---|---|---|
| | Low 0 | 1 | 2 | 3 | High 4 |
| *Protestants:* | | | | | |
| Low | 58% | 38% | 25% | 13% | 4% |
| Medium | 36 | 48 | 57 | 56 | 36 |
| High | 6 | 14 | 18 | 31 | 60 |
| Total | 100% | 100% | 100% | 100% | 100% |
| Number | (344) | (219) | (299) | (420) | (602) |
| *Catholics:* | | | | | |
| Low | 55% | 35% | 18% | 14% | 8% |
| Medium | 40 | 40 | 68 | 55 | 51 |
| High | 9 | 25 | 14 | 31 | 41 |
| Total | 100% | 100% | 100% | 100% | 100% |
| Number | (43) | (20) | (28) | (85) | (260) |

Roman Catholics, ideological commitment strongly predicts particularism. Sixty per cent of the Protestants with a maximum score on the Orthodoxy Index qualify as highly particularistic, while only 6 per cent of those least orthodox are high on particularism. Conversely, 58 per cent of the least committed are low on particularism as compared with 4 per cent of the most committed. Particularism systematically increases with the degree of orthodoxy. A similar pattern can be observed among Roman Catholics, although there is a tendency for Roman Catholics to be less likely than Protestants to be either high or low on particularism and to fall into the medium category.

Looking at the relationship from another direction, while many of the most orthodox among both Protestants and Catholics are not classed as high on particularism (though very few are low), of those who are

high on particularism 83 per cent of the Protestants and 91 per cent of
the Catholics fall into the two highest categories of orthodoxy. Clearly,
the data show there is an impressive correlation between orthodoxy and
particularism as predicted.

To seek further confirmation of these findings we may see in Table 14

Table 14.   ORTHODOXY AND BELIEF THAT CHRISTIANS ARE GOD'S
CHOSEN PEOPLE TODAY

(Per cent who think Christians are God's Chosen People today)

|  | Orthodoxy Index | | | | |
|  | Low 0 | 1 | 2 | 3 | High 4 |
|---|---|---|---|---|---|
| Protestants |  |  |  |  |  |
| Per cent | 14 | 23 | 29 | 49 | 65 |
| Number | (344) | (219) | (299) | (420) | (602) |
| Catholics |  |  |  |  |  |
| Per cent | 20 | 28 | 35 | 45 | 54 |
| Number | (43) | (20) | (28) | (85) | (260) |

the power of orthodoxy to predict perceptions of Christians as God's
Chosen People today. Among Protestants the proportion holding this
belief rises from 14 per cent of those lowest in orthodoxy to 65 per cent
of those in the highest category. The same comparison among Roman
Catholics is 20 per cent versus 54 per cent.

These findings lend great plausibility to our hypothesis that a particularistic definition of religious legitimacy is to a great extent a function
of being ideologically involved in orthodox Christianity. If this is so,
then we would expect that our second dimension of religious commitment,
ritual involvement, *would not* be independently related to particularism.
That is, we ought to expect that religious activity by itself has no effect
on particularism, but only when connected with a theological orientation
which meets the conditions of our theory. Particularism is not a consequence of what *one does* in connection with his religion, but of what
*one believes.* This expectation can easily be tested by examining the
particularism of persons who differ in their ritual involvement, but who
are equally orthodox.

Table 15 precisely bears out this expectation. Looking at Protestants
we can see that *within* each category of ideological involvement (reading
down), the degree of ritual involvement does not produce differences in
the proportions who scored low on particularism. Among the least orthodox, for example, 57 per cent of those high on ritual involvement were
low on particularism, 55 per cent of those medium on ritual, and 59 per

Table 15.   RELIGIOUS PARTICULARISM IS A FUNCTION OF ORTHODOXY,
NOT OF RITUAL INVOLVEMENT

(Per cent who scored Low on Particularism Index)

| Rank of Protestants on Ritual Index | Orthodoxy Index | | | | |
|---|---|---|---|---|---|
| | Low 0 | 1 | 2 | 3 | High 4 |
| High | | | | | |
| Per cent | 57 | 30 | 21 | 8 | 4 |
| Number | (59) | (77) | (145) | (233) | (464) |
| Medium | | | | | |
| Per cent | 55 | 45 | 31 | 18 | 5 |
| Number | (132) | (97) | (116) | (147) | (103) |
| Low | | | | | |
| Per cent | 59 | 30 | 23 | 19 | 4 |
| Number | (151) | (46) | (37) | (33) | (26) |

| Rank of Catholics on Ritual Index | Orthodoxy Index | | |
|---|---|---|---|
| | Low (0, 1) | Middle (2, 3) | High (4) |
| High | | | |
| Per cent | 32 | 14 | 7 |
| Number | (19) | (74) | (211) |
| Medium | | | |
| Per cent | 56 | 19 | 5 |
| Number | (18) | (32) | (39) |
| Low | | | |
| Per cent | 45 | 17 | 14 |
| Number | (22) | (17) | (7) |

cent of those low. Among the most orthodox, 4 per cent of those high on ritual, 5 per cent of those medium, and 4 per cent of those low, were low on particularism. These patterns suggest no consistent or meaningful independent relationship between ritual involvement and particularism. On the other hand, no matter what degree of ritual involvement, differences in particularism across the Orthodoxy Index are consistent and large (reading the table from left to right).

A similar lack of an independent ritual effect applies to Roman Catholics. Here, because of insufficient cases, it was necessary to collapse the Orthodoxy Index.

As ritual involvement produced no effect on particularism independent of ideology, the same is true of religious denomination. Earlier in this chapter we showed that denomination was highly related to particularism, the more traditionally orthodox groups being more given to particularism than the more modernist church bodies. This relationship was entirely an artifact of differences in ideological involvement. That is to say, orthodox believers in the more liberal groups were as likely to be particularistic as were the orthodox in conservative bodies. Similarly the nonorthodox, regardless of their denominational affiliation, were equally unlikely to be particularistic.[13] Hence, in subsequent development of our inquiry we shall not introduce denomination into the analysis, although items being presented prior to construction of indexes will be shown by denomination in order to preserve the intrinsic interest of denominational comparisons.

Having touched on these matters it seems proper also to raise the question of spuriousness and "controls" here in order to make clear our reasons for ignoring it thus far. Briefly, spuriousness refers to assigning a casual interpretation to the relationship between two variables, when in fact they are related only because of their joint association with some additional variable or variables which are not controlled in the analysis. A common illustration of this error is to cite the high positive correlation between the number of fire engines at the scene of a fire and the amount of damage done by the blaze. Knowledge of such a correlation might lead a person with limited experience to assert that fire engines cause damage; hence, the more trucks the worse for the property owner. Obviously, these two phenomena are highly related because *each* is caused by the same variable, so far unmentioned, i.e., the size of the fire. To prove by statistical means that they are not independently related, but are produced by a mutual cause, one would examine fires that are very large but where few fire trucks arrive and also small fires to which many fire engines come. In the first case damage is found to be very great; in the second damage is slight. Statistically, the original positive correlation between the number of trucks and the amount of the damage "vanishes" when one controls for the size of the fire.[14] This procedure, a part of what is often called multivariate analysis, has been developed to attempt to approximate the rigor of laboratory experiments for studies of events which cannot be taken into a laboratory, including most interesting social events.

In this tradition, the typical report of casual analysis of survey data would begin to introduce test factors or controls immediately upon presenting the first data which attempted to test a casual statement. Having reached that point in this book, normally we would now begin to suggest other factors which might actually be producing the apparent correlation between orthodoxy and particularism. Foremost among these would likely

---

[13] Slight remnants of a denominational effect which remained when ideology was controlled were accounted for by social class.

[14] Actually the correlation should become negative, showing that firetrucks prevent damage.

be social class, the argument being that perhaps lower-status persons are both more likely to hold orthodox Christian beliefs and to be particularistic than are persons of higher status. If the relationship between orthodoxy and particularism disappeared when social class was controlled,[15] that is, when examined separately among the higher- and lower-status groups, then we would have to admit that our theory was rejected by the data and that the original relationship was spurious.

However, we do not intend to begin controls until later. Because we feel that introducing a variety of such test factors at each stage in the analysis adds confusion and redundancy, we shall defer this matter until our entire theoretical chain has been developed and each link shown to hold initially. Then we shall test the entire sequence at one time, seeking confidence that no uncontrolled factors have produced spurious findings. This is quite as proper statistically as doing the job piecemeal and, it seems to us, vastly more efficient and readable.[16]

### Summary

So far we have outlined and linked two concepts: religious orthodoxy and particularism. We have seen that commitment to an orthodox Christian theology strongly implies a particularistic image of being God's Chosen People, singularly qualified for eternal salvation. A frequent consequence of such a view of one's own group is an invidious contrast with all religious "outsiders."

In Part II we shall explore the implications of particularism for hostile definitions of non-Christians. We shall be primarily interested in the connection between Christian particularism and historic and contemporary religious images of the Jew, but attention will also be paid to images of non-Christians in general.

[15] It did not.

[16] We must hasten to point out that such a deferment is only possible for analyses which take the form of examining a single, causal link, the effect of X on Y, or, as in the present case, the effect of A on B on C on D on E. When one is investigating the influence of a number of different factors on a single variable, or the effect of a single variable on a number of "consequences," such a format is probably unworkable.

# PART II.    RELIGIOUS OUTSIDERS

*To speak of "outsiders" requires some frame of reference that provides a conception of an "inside." The previous chapters were devoted to specifying some religious frames of reference, or "insides." The following section will survey the view from these various vantage points. Specifically, we shall ask who is seen as an outsider from where, and what feelings arise toward persons who are viewed as religious outsiders.*

# CHAPTER 3

# Prophets and Crucifiers: The Historic Jew

Therefore when they were gathered together, Pilate said unto them, Whom will ye that I release unto you? Barabbas, or Jesus which is called Christ?

For he knew that for envy they had delivered him.

When he was set down on the judgement seat, his wife sent unto him, saying, Have thou nothing to do with that just man: for I have suffered many things this day in a dream because of him.

But the chief priests and elders persuaded the multitude that they should ask Barabbas, and destroy Jesus.

The governor answered and said unto them, Whether of the twain will ye that I release unto you? They said, Barabbas.

Pilate saith unto them, What shall I do then with Jesus which is called Christ? They all say unto him, Let him be crucified.

And the governor said, Why, what evil hath he done? But they cried out the more, saying, Let him be crucified.

When Pilate saw that he could prevail nothing, but that rather a tumult was made, he took water, and washed his hands before the multitude, saying, I am innocent of the blood of this just person: see ye to it.

Then answered all the people, and said, His blood be on us, and on our children.

—Matt. 27:17–25 (A.V.)

Two contrasting and mutually reinforcing themes dominate traditional Christian religious imagery of the historic Jew. The first of these concerns the mutual Old Testament heritage of Christians and Jews. In staking the origins of their faith in the Old Testament, Christians have had to claim direct descent from the faith of Moses and to acknowledge the special religious virtue of ancient Jewry. From this view, prior to the coming of Jesus, Jews had an exclusive claim on religious legitimacy, and, in a sense, Christianity and Judaism were one.

The second theme proclaims the Jewish fall from grace and, hence, the consequent Christian monopoly on legitimate succession to God's favor. The primary elements in this theme are interpretations of those acts and events through which Jews are seen to have forfeited their religious destiny. Combined with common religious origins, this second view of history provides an image of Jews, not as unenlightened pagans, but as renegades from true faith, and cruel persecutors of the faithful, indeed, the very crucifiers and revilers of the Son of God.

In this chapter we shall attempt to examine both of these themes. First we shall see to what extent modern Christians perceive and acknowledge mutual roots with Judaism. Then we will take up Christian conceptions of the events surrounding the separation of the two faiths, particularly the traditions of deicide and racial guilt.

### The Mutual Heritage of the Old Testament

A crucial issue in the theological disputes between Jews and Christians during the first three centuries A.D. concerned legitimate succession from the Old Testament faith. Having emerged from its initial status as a Jewish sect, when Paul won Peter and his followers to the doctrine that gentiles could come into the faith without adopting Mosaic law, Christianity, nevertheless, was irrevocably committed to the Old Testament as a prophetic basis for New Testament fulfillment. The proclamation of the divinity of Jesus was not to be taken as raising up a new god; rather Christ was claimed to be the son of the old and eternal Yahweh, and Christianity the final resolution of an established religious tradition. The majority of Jews vigorously rejected these claims.

Given the crucial importance of the Hebrew texts to Christianity, succession was the pressing doctrinal question. The whole texture of the Old Testament is ethnocentric, steeped in the conviction that Jews are the Chosen People of God. This tradition threatened to leave Christianity severed from its origins, an apostate movement. Thus, the Christian condition as non-Jews had to be reconciled with the doctrine of the Chosen People. But how was it that God had changed his allegiance? Was he inconsistent? Were Christians outside the true faith? Neither of these alternatives was a possible interpretation for the early Christian elders. Hence some mechanism was necessary to demonstrate that Christians were legitimate heirs to God's favor.

The theology developed was essentially as follows. Christ fulfilled the prophesies of the Old Testament and was God's ultimate revelation to men, marking the start of a new set of conditions for man's relation to God. Because Christ's death was an atonement for human sins, now only through Christ could men qualify for God's kingdom. Since the Jews refused to accept the authenticity of Christ, they were unredeemed and excluded from the community of saints. Until such time as the Jews repented their rejection of the Saviour, they were fallen from grace and disqualified from God's favor. Thus, legitimate succession as the men of God passes from the Jews to Christians, and continuity between Old and New Testaments is preserved.[1]

The relevance of these historic problems of legitimacy for a study of contemporary religion lies in the viability of the issues. Matters of common origins with Judaism and the subsequent claim of legitimate succession from the Old Testament remain central doctrinal matters to be taught each new generation of Christians. As Bernhard Olson put it:

. . . Present day [Sunday School] texts abound in reminders that the Church's founders, its earliest followers, and its scriptures were Jewish. Christianity's basic beliefs and practices were rooted in one or another tradition of Jewish thought, and the earliest ideological conflicts took place within the matrix of first-century Judaism.

It it as impossible, therefore, for a Christian teacher to communicate the Christian message without reference to Judaism as it would be to teach American history without referring to England and the founding fathers.[2]

Modern Christian children who receive religious instruction learn Old Testament stories that are largely concerned with the heroes and heroics of God's Chosen People. The child comes to identify himself with these figures, the marvelous Samson, the heroic David, and Moses, the liberator and stern father; these stories teach him about the heroes of *his* faith. It is usually reasonably clear that these Chosen People were Jews; yet the child is not a Jew. Thus, the lessons must show how ancient Jewish heroes can now be the property of Christians. This, of course, leads to teachings about how the Jews lost their religious heritage. This will provide the focus for the next section. For the moment we shall concentrate on Christians' perception of common origins with Jews.

[1] See the Epistle to the Hebrews.
[2] Bernhard E. Olson, "The Victims and the Oppressors" (Doctoral Dissertation, Yale University Divinity School, 1959), p. 84.

Primarily we shall be concerned to understand in what ways and to what degree Christians perceive the "Jewishness" of the Old Testament. Are Jews acknowledged to be the "Israelites" and the central characters of the Old Testament, or have some portions of the Old Testament been Christianized and the Jews reduced to minor background players? We shall begin our exploration of the data with the broad image of the Jews as the Chosen People in the Old Testament, and then take up more specific questions.

As can be seen in Table 16, about three-quarters of Christian church

Table 16.    THE CHOSEN PEOPLE

Reply to "The Old Testament tells that God picked a certain group to be His 'Chosen People.' Can you tell us whom God picked as His 'Chosen People'?"

|  | Cong. | Meth. | Epis. | D.of Christ | Pres. |
|---|---|---|---|---|---|
| Number | (151) | (415) | (416) | (50) | (495) |
| Per cent replying: | | | | | |
| "The Jews" | 83% | 75% | 71% | 80% | 78% |
| "The Christians" | 8 | 10 | 8 | 4 | 9 |

|  | A.Luth. | A.Bap. | M.Luth. | S.Bap. | Sects |
|---|---|---|---|---|---|
| Number | (208) | (141) | (116) | (79) | (255) |
| Per cent replying: | | | | | |
| "The Jews" | 70% | 82% | 80% | 84% | 85% |
| "The Christians" | 14 | 9 | 14 | 6 | 6 |

|  | Total Prot. | Cath. |
|---|---|---|
| Number | (2,326) | (545) |
| Per cent replying: | | |
| "The Jews" | 79% | 75% |
| "The Christians" | 9 | 11 |

members identify the Jews as the group spoken of in the Old Testament as chosen by God. Since there is little fluctuation among denominations, it seems plausible to assume that Christians do recognize in a general way that the origins of their faith lie in ancient Judaism. However, approximately 10 per cent seem to have expunged the Jew from the Old Testament, designating the "Christians" as the *original* Chosen People, and a similar number either rejected both Christians and Jews as the Old Testament Chosen People, or said they did not know who they might have been. Hence, even on this broadest view of the Jewish role in the Old Testament, there is some propensity on the part of a small minority to Christianize the whole Biblical tradition.

When we turn to major figures in the Old Testament, this Christianizing tendency increases. As shown in Table 17, an appreciable number

Table 17.  THE RELIGION OF BIBLICAL CHARACTERS

| | Cong. | Meth. | Epis. | D.of Christ | Pres. |
|---|---|---|---|---|---|
| Number | (151) | (415) | (416) | (50) | (495) |
| *"Do you think of Moses, David, and Solomon as:"* | | | | | |
| "Jews" | 72% | 67% | 79% | 74% | 69% |
| "Christians" | 15 | 20 | 11 | 16 | 18 |
| *"When you think of Peter and Paul and the other Apostles, do you think of them as:"* | | | | | |
| "Christians" | 70% | 73% | 70% | 76% | 72% |
| "Jews" | 15 | 13 | 15 | 10 | 14 |

| | A.Luth. | A.Bap. | M.Luth. | S.Bap. | Sects |
|---|---|---|---|---|---|
| Number | (208) | (141) | (116) | (79) | (255) |
| *"Do you think of Moses, David, and Solomon as:"* | | | | | |
| "Jews" | 57% | 64% | 58% | 43% | 62% |
| "Christians" | 28 | 26 | 33 | 46 | 17 |
| *"When you think of Peter and Paul and the other Apostles, do you think of them as:"* | | | | | |
| "Christians" | 76% | 74% | 73% | 84% | 73% |
| "Jews" | 9 | 11 | 13 | 9 | 12 |

| | Total Prot. | Cath. |
|---|---|---|
| Number | (2,326) | (545) |
| *"Do you think of Moses, David, and Solomon as:"* | | |
| "Jews" | 66% | 72% |
| "Christians" | 20 | 15 |
| *"When you think of Peter and Paul and the other Apostles, do you think of them as:"* | | |
| "Christians" | 73% | 61% |
| "Jews" | 13 | 19 |

of Christians "think of Moses, David, and Solomon as: Christians." Again, an over-all majority identified these Biblical figures as Jews; yet 20 per cent of the Protestants and 15 per cent of the Roman Catholics thought of them as Christians.[3] Furthermore, this Christianizing tendency

[3] We must not think, however, that all who acknowledged Moses, David, and Solomon as Jews did so without ambivalence, for an examination of comments written in the margins of questionnaires reveals that many bothered to note their

is markedly related to denomination. While 11 per cent of the Episcopalians and 15 per cent of the Congregationalists identified Moses, David, and Solomon as Christians, 33 per cent of the Missouri Lutherans and 46 per cent of the Southern Baptists did so. Indeed, among the Southern Baptists, more persons thought these Old Testament figures were Christians than thought they were Jews!

To find this Christianizing tendency so common, especially among the more conservative denominations, suggests that one possible way to resolve any ambivalence which might stem from seeing the ancient Jews both as "founding fathers" of the faith and as crucifiers and rejecters of Jesus is to deny their claim as founders.

When we consider New Testament figures, the question of religious identity becomes historically more ambiguous. Clearly, the apostles and the earliest converts were Jews, and it is also clear that they continued to regard themselves as Jews; for early Christianity was for some time a Jewish sect movement. Yet because they did accept the divinity of Jesus and founded the Christian church, they could as well be considered Christians. Given this option, Christian church members overwhelmingly regard Peter, Paul, and the other apostles as Christians. As can be seen in Table 17, slightly more than two-thirds of the Protestant respondents and more than three-fifths of the Catholics held this image. A small minority, however, comprising 13 per cent of the Protestants and 19 per cent of the Roman Catholics, identified them as Jews. These tables suggest there are three basic stances among Christians on the matter of the identity of early religious figures. The largest group sees the Old Testament figures as Jews and those of the New Testament as Christians. A second group Christianizes both Old and New Testament figures, while a small third group seems to identify both with Judaism.

Perhaps even more revealing, while a sizable minority of Christians think of Moses, David, and Solomon as Christians, and also think of the apostles as Christians, their Christianizing of religious figures stops short when presented with the infamous Judas Iscariot.

---

reluctance to surrender a Christian claim on these Old Testament figures. As a middle-aged housewife member of the Assemblies of God, who marked "Jews" in response to the question, replied: "I actually think of them as Kings and prophets of God, and not necessarily as what we know as Jews today."

As we remarked earlier about responses to the question of who were the Chosen People of the Old Testament, some respondents who answered "Jews" were still loath to identify the Israelites or the Old Testament Jews with "what are called Jews today." Thus, if anything, the estimates based on our structured items are under- rather than over-estimates of the extent of the Christianizing of the Old Testament, or at least of denying its Jewishness. Viewed in this light these findings seem to deserve serious attention.

Christians generally refuse to call Judas a Christian; on the contrary, they are quite likely to remember him as a Jew. Or, having so Christianized the Old Testament as to have little basis for making him a Jew, they refuse to assign Judas any religious identity. As shown in Table 18, 44 per cent

Table 18. JUDAS

Reply to: When you think of Judas, who betrayed Christ, do you think of him as:"

|  | Cong. | Meth. | Epis. | D.of Christ | Pres. |
|---|---|---|---|---|---|
| Number | (151) | (415) | (416) | (50) | (495) |
| "A Jew" | 46% | 36% | 44% | 34% | 46% |
| "A Christian" | 25 | 27 | 30 | 30 | 22 |
| "None of these" | 19 | 24 | 15 | 18 | 20 |

|  | A.Luth. | A.Bap. | M.Luth. | S.Bap. | Sects |
|---|---|---|---|---|---|
| Number | (208) | (141) | (116) | (79) | (255) |
| "A Jew" | 45% | 48% | 43% | 43% | 54% |
| "A Christian" | 25 | 19 | 21 | 11 | 8 |
| "None of these" | 21 | 22 | 20 | 38 | 26 |

|  | Total Prot. | Cath. |
|---|---|---|
| Number | (2,326) | (545) |
| "A Jew" | 44% | 47% |
| "A Christian" | 23 | 28 |
| "None of these" | 22 | 13 |

of the Protestants and 47 per cent of the Roman Catholics thought Judas was a Jew (only 13 and 19 per cent of these groups thought the apostles were Jews). Seeing Judas as a Jew is not meaningfully related to denomination.

It is extremely important to recognize that no particular answer on any of these items we have been examining necessarily implies any hostility toward Jews. For example, one surely ought to be able to believe that Judas was a Jew without holding the Jews responsible for him. Furthermore, while we have given relatively great attention to these tendencies, the majority of Christians do acknowledge the Jewishness of the Old Testament and perceive the two faiths as rooted in a common religious tradition.

These findings provide a basis for turning now to exploring perceptions and beliefs about events surrounding the separation of Judaism and Christianity from these mutual beginnings.

### Historic Conflict: The Jew as Crucifier and Apostate

The crucial questions that have haunted Jewish-Christian relations for nearly two millennia are: What collective role did the Jews play in the Crucifixion, and what were their motives for rejecting the Messianic claims made about Jesus? Despite a conciliatory voice raised now and again by Christian churchmen, Christians have been taught through the centuries that the Jews, as a people, bore the responsibility for deicide, and forfeited their mandate from God because they had become sinful, mercenary, and proud.

In the pages that follow we shall attempt to determine the degree to which these age-old Christian images of the Jews find support among the rank-and-file members of contemporary churches. First we shall explore the Crucifixion story, and then examine the motives imputed to the ancient Jews for rejecting Jesus.

*The Crucifixion*

The primary source for the threadbare epithet, "Christ-killer," is the Book of Matthew, Chapter 27, which was quoted at the beginning of this chapter. Here we are told that Jesus was seized on complaints by the chief priests and elders and taken before Pontius Pilate, the Roman Procurator of Judea, for judgment. The chief priests and elders informed Pilate that Jesus claimed to be King of the Jews, a charge tantamount to treason under both Roman and Jewish law. But, Matthew goes on to tell us, Pilate felt sympathetic toward Jesus and realized that the priests were persecuting Jesus out of envy. Pilate's wife, because she had dreamed he ought have nothing to do with the whole affair, further encouraged him to release Jesus.

Pilate attempted such a release by taking advantage of a custom by which a condemned prisoner was pardoned at feast time. He gave the multitude a choice between Jesus and one Barabbas, accused of murder and sedition.

This attempt was frustrated, Matthew charges, because the priests and elders persuaded the people to ask for the release of Barabbas. Thus forestalled, Pilate is reported to have protested that Jesus had done nothing. But he was drowned out by the multitude who shouted, "Let him be crucified." Fearing tumult, Pilate is portrayed as backing down, and, calling for water, washing his hands before the mob to make clear his refusal to take responsibility for the blood of Jesus.

At this, Matthew reports, the people cried out, "His blood upon us, and on our children." Thus the Jewish throng is shown to call down a blood curse of eternal guilt upon themselves and their future generations.

The major themes in this account are these:

1.   Pilate, although perhaps weak and ineffectual, tried to prevent the Crucifixion.

2.   The Jewish multitude, stirred up by their priests and elders, forced the Crucifixion to be carried out.

3.   By virtue of their demands, and by calling down a curse upon themselves, the Jews assumed collective responsibility for the death of Jesus.

Items to assess the current status of these major themes were included in the questionnaire. We shall consider them in the order presented above.

The overwhelming majority of the respondents believed the Biblical accounts that Pontius Pilate, the Roman Procurator of Judea, opposed the Crucifixion of Jesus. As can be seen in Table 19, 79 per cent of both

Table 19.   THE ROLE OF PONTIUS PILATE

Reply to: "Do you think Pontius Pilate wanted to spare Jesus from the Cross?"

|  | Cong. | Meth. | Epis. | D.of Christ | Pres. |
|---|---|---|---|---|---|
| Number | (151) | (415) | (416) | (50) | (495) |
| "Yes" | 68% | 71% | 77% | 86% | 80% |
| "No" | 5 | 7 | 7 | 4 | 7 |
| "Don't know" | 25 | 18 | 13 | 6 | 9 |

|  | A.Luth. | A.Bap. | M.Luth. | S.Bap. | Sects |
|---|---|---|---|---|---|
| Number | (208) | (141) | (116) | (79) | (255) |
| "Yes" | 80% | 82% | 91% | 82% | 92% |
| "No" | 7 | 4 | 4 | 14 | 2 |
| "Don't know" | 9 | 9 | 3 | 1 | 2 |

|  | Total Prot. | Cath. |
|---|---|---|
| Number | (2,326) | (545) |
| "Yes" | 79% | 79% |
| "No" | 6 | 7 |
| "Don't know" | 11 | 10 |

the Protestants and the Roman Catholics responded "yes" when asked, "Do you think Pontius Pilate wanted to spare Jesus from the Cross?" Among the Protestants, the proportion taking this position increases moderately from the more liberal to the more conservative bodies. Yet even among the most liberal groups, from two-thirds to three-quarters of the respondents believed Pilate opposed the Crucifixion. In addition, a mere handful of these Christian respondents felt Pilate did *not* want to spare Jesus. Six per cent of the Protestants and 7 per cent of the Roman Catholics gave this answer. Of the remainder, most reported they did not know whether or not Pilate was sympathetic to Jesus.

Turning to Table 20, we may see that approximately half of the Protestants and Catholics not only believed Pilate wanted to spare Jesus, but that he failed to do so because "a group of powerful Jews wanted Jesus dead." Among Protestants, the proportions taking this view rise from 36 per cent of the Congregationalists to 62 per cent of the Missouri Synod Lutherans. Conversely, the proportions who felt Pilate failed to stop the Crucifixion because "a group of powerful Romans wanted Jesus dead," decreases from 24 per cent of the Congregationalists to 13 per cent of the Southern Baptists. Over-all, 19 per cent of the Protestants and 16 per cent of the Roman Catholics held this view. An additional small group gave a mixture of reasons why Pilate went along with the Crucifixion, ranging from "It was God's Will," to "fiends" were responsible. The remaining persons in the various denominations did not think Pilate wanted to spare Jesus, except for a few who did not answer the item. Among those persons who believed Pilate *did* want to spare Jesus, the proportions blaming the Jews were of course higher; 62 per cent among the Protestants, and 48 per cent of the Roman Catholics took this position.

These data indicate widespread acceptance of the belief that the Jews overwhelmed Pilate to bring about the death of Jesus. This is further confirmed by Table 21, which shows that 58 per cent of the Protestants and 61 per cent of the Roman Catholics picked the Jews as the group "most responsible for crucifying Christ." The denominational pattern among Protestants is the same liberal-to-conservative increase observed in the two previous tables. Approximately a quarter of both Protestants and Catholics fixed primary responsibility for the death of Christ upon the Romans.

Thus, the three elements in the traditional Christian interpretation of the Crucifixion remain the predominant view among members of present-day American churches: The majority believe that Pilate wished to spare Jesus, but yielded to powerful Jewish pressure, and thus that the ancient Jews bear the primary responsibility for the Crucifixion. We must emphasize that to hold any or all of these beliefs does not *necessarily* imply hostility toward the ancient Jews. One could obviously give these responses in a neutral way, as mere recollections of historical events long past, without intending any particular evaluation of motives. We shall consider this point more fully later.

## Table 20.  PILATE'S ACQUIESCENCE

Reply to: "If you think Pilate really wanted to spare Jesus, why didn't he?"

| Reasons Given | Cong. | Meth. | Epis. | D.of Christ | Pres. | A.Luth. | A.Bap. | M.Luth. | S.Bap. | Sects | Total Prot. | Cath. |
|---|---|---|---|---|---|---|---|---|---|---|---|---|
| "A group of powerful Jews wanted Jesus dead." | 36% | 38% | 47% | 50% | 49% | 43% | 50% | 62% | 53% | 62% | 47% | 46% |
| "A group of powerful Romans wanted Jesus dead." | 24 | 21 | 18 | 18 | 19 | 23 | 18 | 21 | 13 | 15 | 19 | 16 |
| Other[a] | 7 | 10 | 9 | 14 | 9 | 12 | 11 | 6 | 11 | 11 | 11 | 13 |
| Didn't think Pilate wanted to spare, or didn't know. | 33 | 31 | 26 | 18 | 23 | 22 | 21 | 11 | 23 | 12 | 23 | 25 |
| Total | 100% | 100% | 100% | 100% | 100% | 100% | 100% | 100% | 100% | 100% | 100% | 100% |
| Number | (151) | (415) | (416) | (50) | (495) | (208) | (141) | (116) | (79) | (255) | (2,326) | (545) |

[a] Such responses as "It was God's Will," "Both Romans and Jews," "a mob," "fiends," etc.

Table 21. RESPONSIBILITY FOR THE CRUCIFIXION

Reply to: "What group do you think was most responsible for crucifying Christ?"

| | Cong. | Meth. | Epis. | D.of Christ | Pres. |
|---|---|---|---|---|---|
| Number | (151) | (415) | (416) | (50) | (495) |
| "The Jews" | 48% | 47% | 55% | 68% | 58% |
| "The Romans" | 36 | 33 | 27 | 20 | 28 |

| | A.Luth. | A.Bap. | M.Luth. | S.Bap. | Sects |
|---|---|---|---|---|---|
| Number | (208) | (141) | (116) | (79) | (255) |
| "The Jews" | 54% | 64% | 72% | 66% | 73% |
| "The Romans" | 24 | 23 | 20 | 18 | 13 |

| | Total Prot. | Cath. |
|---|---|---|
| Number | (2,326) | (545) |
| "The Jews" | 58% | 61% |
| "The Romans" | 26 | 22 |

## Jewish Motives for Rejecting Jesus as the Messiah

Since Jesus was himself a Jew, and brought his message to the Jews, Christians have long been preoccupied with explaining how it came to pass that God's Chosen People rejected their promised Messiah. Two basic explanations have been offered: that the evilness, selfishness, and conceit of the Jews led them to contempt for Jesus; or that they simply erred or were misled by wicked priests. The first of these, which in its most elaborate version included a belief that the Jews were in league with the Devil, has provided a reservoir of hatred for Jews and has served as a major theme for pogroms from early medieval times down to the present.[4]

To investigate Christian beliefs about these motives, respondents were offered a series of reasons why the Jews might have rejected Jesus and were asked to mark each with which they agreed. The form of the question perhaps led to a slight *under*estimation of the proportion who acknowledged belief in a given statement. Persons were asked to check only those choices with which they agreed rather than to indicate whether they agreed or disagreed with each. Respondents were probably very inclined to check only several of the choices listed and as a result many may have passed up choices with which they also agreed. These "weaker" choices would likely have been registered too had each been asked about separately.

[4] Joshua Trachtenberg, *The Devil and the Jews* (Cleveland and New York: Meridian Books, 1961).

Yet, even with what are probably conservative estimates, the data indicate that belief that the Jews rejected Jesus out of "bad" motives is rather common among church-member Christians.

Furthermore, looking at Table 22, we may also see that imputing "bad" motives to the Jews for their rejection of Jesus is markedly related to denomination. The first item in the table shows that 44 per cent of the Protestants and 39 per cent of the Catholics agreed with the statement, "They couldn't accept a Messiah who came from humble beginnings." This conjures up an image of the ancient Jews as undemocratic, preoccupied with worldly status and position, and too haughty to recognize their Lord in the ascetic and unworldly person of Jesus. Among Protestants, the proportion attaching this interpretation to the behavior of the ancient Jews increases from 26 per cent of the Congregationalists to 66 per cent of the Southern Baptists.

The second item in the table attributes strongly "evil" motivation for the "apostasy" of the ancient Jews, and the support given this answer is somewhat less than that of the first. Over-all, 21 per cent of the Protestants and 16 per cent of the Roman Catholics agreed that "because the Jews hated Gentiles they could not accept Christ's message of brotherhood." Again among Protestants the support given this interpretation markedly increases from left to right across the table, from 13 per cent of the Congregationalists to 44 per cent of the Southern Baptists.

On the last answer in the table, 18 per cent of the Protestants and 16 per cent of the Catholics agreed that the Jews rejected Jesus because they "were sinful and had turned against God." Among Protestants only 8 per cent of the Congregationalists, as compared with 39 per cent of the Southern Baptists, accepted this view.

Looking at the data over-all, it seems legitimate to suggest that the belief that the Jews rejected Jesus for some "evil" motive is relatively common among contemporary Christians, and especially so among conservative Protestant groups.

Historically, Christians have often explained Jewish rejection of Jesus as not a matter of evil motives but of mere ignorance and error. As can be seen in Table 23, nearly half of the Protestants and the Catholics think the Jews rejected Jesus because "they were deceived by wicked priests who feared Christ." Although such a statement imputes questionable judgment to Jews, it can hardly be called hostile. Still, interestingly enough, the conservative Protestant groups, towards the right side of the table, who were the highest supporters of "bad" motives, do not give appreciably greater support to this item than do the more liberal bodies.

Indeed, the pattern of support among Protestants seen on the items which imputed hostile motives to the ancient Jews is reversed when we

Table 22. THE REJECTION OF CHRIST: HOSTILE MOTIVES

Reply to: "Why did the Jews reject Jesus?"

| Per Cent Who Agreed That:[a] | Cong. | Meth. | Epis. | D.of Christ | Pres. | A.Luth. | A.Bap. | M.Luth. | S.Bap. | Sects | Total Prot. | Cath. |
|---|---|---|---|---|---|---|---|---|---|---|---|---|
| Number | (151) | (415) | (416) | (50) | (495) | (208) | (141) | (116) | (79) | (255) | (2,326) | (545) |
| "They couldn't accept a Messiah who came from humble beginnings." | 26% | 37% | 35% | 54% | 44% | 42% | 49% | 53% | 66% | 67% | 44% | 39% |
| "Because the Jews hated Gentiles they could not accept Christ's message of brotherhood." | 13 | 15 | 15 | 34 | 21 | 21 | 25 | 26 | 44 | 29 | 21 | 16 |
| "The Jews were sinful and had turned against God." | 8 | 9 | 11 | 8 | 15 | 19 | 17 | 29 | 39 | 40 | 18 | 16 |

[a] Respondents could check as many or few of these explanations as they agreed with; hence total responses on this and the succeeding table exceed 100 per cent.

Table 23. THE REJECTION OF CHRIST: BENIGN MOTIVES

Reply to: "Why did the Jews reject Jesus?"

| Per Cent Who Agreed That: | Cong. | Meth. | Epis. | D. of Christ | Pres. | A.Luth. | A.Bap. | M.Luth. | S.Bap. | Sects | Total Prot. | Cath. |
|---|---|---|---|---|---|---|---|---|---|---|---|---|
| Number | (151) | (415) | (416) | (50) | (495) | (208) | (141) | (116) | (79) | (255) | (2,326) | (545) |
| "They were deceived by wicked priests who feared Christ." | 46% | 41% | 49% | 38% | 43% | 49% | 43% | 54% | 52% | 47% | 45% | 42% |
| "They made an unfortunate but honest mistake." | 19 | 21 | 21 | 20 | 15 | 13 | 12 | 12 | 8 | 11 | 16 | 21 |
| "Jesus did not actually fulfill the Old Testament prophesies concerning the Messiah, so the Jews saw no reason to accept Him." | 35 | 27 | 31 | 16 | 20 | 18 | 15 | 10 | 6 | 5 | 21 | 14 |

look at the second item in this table, which suggests that the ancient Jews were relatively blameless for their action. While approximately 20 per cent of the members of the more liberal groups on the left of the table replied that the Jews "made an unfortunate but honest mistake," only 8 per cent of the Southern Baptists did so. In general, Christians were not markedly inclined to accept this interpretation, only 16 per cent of the Protestants and 21 per cent of the Roman Catholics doing so.

The last item in the table may be something of a surprise. It was included as an afterthought, to provide a response for persons who felt the Jews were somewhat justified in rejecting the Messianic claims made about Jesus, perhaps because they themselves doubted or rejected the divinity of Christ. Over-all, 21 per cent of the Protestants and 14 per cent of the Catholics agreed that "Jesus did not actually fulfill the Old Testament prophesies concerning the Messiah, so the Jews saw no reason to accept Him." It can be said with some accuracy that Christian theologians have been forced to devote a good deal of apologetic writing reconciling the otherworldly salvation of the Christ story with the Old Testament prophesies of a temporal Lord who would lead God's Chosen People to pre-eminence in this world. Obviously, many modern Christians reject these reconciliations and ratify the skepticism of ancient Jewry concerning the claim of Jesus to be the Christ. It is no surprise that these proportions, which change markedly from 35 per cent of the Congregationalists to 6 per cent of the Southern Baptists, closely coincide with the proportions who doubted or rejected the divinity of Christ (see Table 2). Indeed, of persons who rejected Jesus as the divine Son of God, 42 per cent said he failed to fulfill the Old Testament prophesies, while only 14 per cent of those who were confident Jesus was divine agreed with this statement. Thus, willingness of Christians to accept the traditional Jewish justification for rejecting Jesus is largely a function of having rejected the divinity of Christ themselves.

Earlier in this chapter we noted that to believe the Jews were primarily responsible for the Crucifixion does not necessarily imply any hostility. This same caveat applies to many of the reasons we have just examined for Jewish rejection of Jesus. However, several of these responses do seem to imply a hostile image of the historic Jew. In particular, to say the Jews rejected Jesus because they "were sinful and had turned against God" would seem to indicate that a respondent bore ill will toward ancient Jewry.

## Summary and Preview

In this chapter three main findings have emerged. First of all we saw that most Christians acknowledged their mutual roots with Judaism, although a minority Christianized such major Old Testament figures as Moses, David, and Solomon. Secondly, these church members overwhelmingly supported Christian traditions concerning the Crucifixion: Pilate opposed the Crucifixion, but was overruled by the Jewish multitude; hence the Jews were the group "most responsible for crucifying Christ."

Lastly, Christians seem inclined to assign questionable or even evil motives to the Jewish rejection of Jesus. More than 40 per cent of the respondents supported such assertions as "They couldn't accept a Messiah who came from humble beginnings," and "They were deceived by wicked priests who feared Christ."

In sum, the traditional images of the historic Jew remain viable features of the contemporary Christian outlook.

But even though Christians assign negative motives and wicked acts to ancient Jewry, we cannot directly infer from this that they harbor ill will toward modern Jews and regard them as heirs to this ancient "guilt." However, it does seem clear that implicating the historic Jew in these events will predispose some to extend this indictment to modern Jewry, and we may anticipate that orthodoxy and particularism will play a crucial role in producing this propensity to link the contemporary Jew with the "sins" of his ancestors. It is this linkage which provides the major focus of the next chapter.

CHAPTER 4

# Religious Images of the Contemporary Jew

Give proof that the curse which the Jews called down upon their
nation still rests on them and their children to this very day.
—Discussion question in a Sunday school text of the Lutheran Church—Missouri Synod, United States, 1955

In a 1939 pastoral letter, Konrad Gröber, the Roman Catholic Archbishop
of Freising, Germany, advised his flock that the Jews were entirely
responsible for the Crucifixion of Christ and that "their murderous hatred
[of Him] has continued in later centuries."[1] Indeed, echoed Bishop Hilfrich
of Limburg, for their murder of God the Jews have been under a curse
since the original Good Friday.[2] Such religious attitudes toward contemporary Jews were fairly typical of the Roman Catholic hierarchy in Nazi
Germany.[3] At about the same time in America, Father Charles E. Coughlin
and revivalist preachers such as Gerald B. Winrod and Gerald L. K. Smith
thundered similar notions.[4] The similarities were neither coincidental nor
particularly surprising, for these same threadbare notions have furnished
a rhetoric for justifying pogroms and the repression of Jewry since the

[1] Pastoral letter of January 30, 1939, *Amtsblatt für die Erzdiözese Freiburg*,
February 8, 1939, p. 15, quoted in Guenter Lewy, "Pius XII, the Jews, and the
German Catholic Church," *Commentary*, February 1964, pp. 23–35.
[2] Quoted in Lewy, *op. cit.*
[3] See *Ibid.*
[4] See Gustavus Myers, *History of Bigotry in the United States* (New York:
Capricorn Books, 1960).

rise of Christendom. Today these same shibboleths feed the hate mills of anti-Semitic extremists in the United States. Thus, the charges first leveled at the ancient Jews by early Christian writers are used to indict modern-day Jews as cursed for deicide: "Jesus in very strong terms denounced the Jews, and pronounced judgment upon them. . . . This explains why these judgments are falling upon the Jews, from Jesus' time until today; they are receiving just what they measured out to Christians."[5]

Such a sinister linking of modern Jews with the "crimes" attributed to their far-distant ancestors depends, in the first instance, upon believing that the ancient Jews actually were responsible for the death of Jesus. In the last chapter we have seen that typically modern American Christians *do* attribute such guilt to the ancient Jews. However, although we know the connection between contemporary and ancient Jewish "guilt" was commonly made in times past, and even recently by such extremists as the Nazis and various members of the present-day "lunatic fringe," few have seriously suggested that such views are still common in respectable circles.

In this chapter we shall see to what extent these traditional views of Jewry do remain among contemporary Christians. Furthermore, we shall move beyond these connections of the modern Jew with his ancient fore-bears and try to assess general Christian conceptions of the religious status of their Jewish countrymen. Are Jews regarded as wicked, sinful, and damned, or as legitimate participants in the religious life of the nation? As answers to these questions emerge from the data we shall see how they connect with the concepts and findings developed in earlier chapters.

### The Modern Jew as an Accursed Christ-killer

To see how commonly Christian church members do, in fact, perceive contemporary Jews as guilty of the Crucifixion and consequently cursed by God, we shall draw on two items included in the questionnaire to measure just such sentiments.

The first of these suggests that Jews are still to be blamed for the Crucifixion: "The Jews can never be forgiven for what they did to Jesus until they accept Him as the True Saviour." It is true that this statement presupposes that modern Jews are perceived as not accepting Jesus as Christ; but this was justified, since only 6 per cent of the Protestants and 10 per cent of the Catholics thought that Jews did "believe in Christ."

Turning to the data in Table 24, we may read the frequency with

[5] *Women's Voice,* March 26, 1953, p. 9.

## Table 24.  DEICIDE

Reply to: "The Jews can never be forgiven for what they did to Jesus until they accept Him as the True Saviour."

| | Cong. | Meth. | Epis. | D.of Christ | Pres. | A.Luth. | A.Bap. | M.Luth. | S.Bap. | Sects | Total Prot. | Cath. |
|---|---|---|---|---|---|---|---|---|---|---|---|---|
| "Agree" | 10% | 12% | 11% | 20% | 31% | 37% | 40% | 70% | 80% | 79% | 33% | 14% |
| "Uncertain" | 23 | 35 | 31 | 42 | 32 | 32 | 26 | 16 | 6 | 4 | 27 | 32 |
| "Agree" plus "uncertain" | (33) | (47) | (42) | (62) | (63) | (69) | (66) | (86) | (86) | (83) | (60) | (46) |
| "Disagree" | 58 | 44 | 49 | 34 | 28 | 27 | 22 | 8 | 8 | 8 | 33 | 44 |
| No response | 9 | 9 | 9 | 4 | 9 | 4 | 12 | 6 | 6 | 9 | 7 | 10 |
| Total | 100% | 100% | 100% | 100% | 100% | 100% | 100% | 100% | 100% | 100% | 100% | 100% |
| Number | (141) | (415) | (416) | (50) | (495) | (208) | (141) | (116) | (79) | (255) | (2,326) | (545) |

which Christians ratified the suggestion that the Jews are still unforgiven for the death of Jesus. Among Protestants, one-third of the respondents agreed with this statement, and 14 per cent of the Roman Catholics did so. Furthermore, 27 per cent of the Protestants and 32 per cent of the Catholics replied they were uncertain whether or not they agreed with this statement. *Thus, 60 per cent of the Protestants and 46 per cent of the Roman Catholics at least acknowledged the possibility that this was a true statement about the modern Jew.* Looking at differences within Protestantism, striking contrasts obtain: While only 10 per cent of the Congregationalists and 12 per cent of the Methodists agreed with the statement, 70 per cent of the Missouri Lutherans and 80 per cent of the Southern Baptists agreed. Thus, among conservative Protestants there is virtual consensus that modern Jews remain unforgiven "for what they did to Jesus."

Before pursuing these findings further, let us consider an even more extreme religious image of the contemporary Jew: as cursed by God. Respondents were asked whether or not they agreed that "The reason the Jews have so much trouble is because God is punishing them for rejecting Jesus."

To agree with this statement is to place the responsibility for their centuries of persecution and tribulation upon the Jews themselves, indeed to justify mistreatment of the Jew as divinely ordained. Looking at the data in Table 25, we may immediately see that this extreme view is much less often agreed to by contemporary Christians than was the previous item. Still, only 53 per cent of the Protestants and 52 per cent of the Roman Catholics would reject the statement outright. Over-all, 13 per cent of the Protestants agreed, and another 26 per cent indicated they were uncertain whether or not the Jews are being punished by God. Eleven per cent of the Roman Catholics agreed with the statement, and 30 per cent were uncertain.

Looking at differences among Protestants a pattern similar to that found in the previous table is apparent. One per cent of the Congregationalists agreed, while 35 per cent of the Southern Baptists did so. The third line of the table, in bold face, shows the total percentage who at least considered the statement as possibly true; here the proportions increase from 20 per cent of the Congregationalists to 66 per cent of the Missouri Lutherans.

A national study of the Protestant clergy, presently being conducted by Jeffrey K. Hadden,[6] included this same item attributing Jewish trouble

[6] These data were collected under the auspices of the Danforth Foundation. We are indebted to Professor Hadden for making them available to us. A report of findings of this study is in preparation.

**Table 25.** DIVINE PUNISHMENT

Reply to: "The reason the Jews have so much trouble is because God is punishing them for rejecting Jesus."

| | Cong. | Meth. | Epis. | D.of Christ | Pres. | A.Luth. | A.Bap. | M.Luth. | S.Bap. | Sects | Total Prot. | Cath. |
|---|---|---|---|---|---|---|---|---|---|---|---|---|
| "Agree" | 1% | 4% | 5% | 14% | 11% | 13% | 9% | 32% | 35% | 34% | 13% | 11% |
| "Uncertain" | 19 | 25 | 23 | 26 | 28 | 35 | 35 | 34 | 24 | 22 | 26 | 30 |
| "Agree" plus "uncertain" | (20) | (29) | (28) | (40) | (39) | (48) | (44) | (66) | (59) | (56) | (39) | (41) |
| "Disagree" | 72 | 63 | 65 | 54 | 54 | 48 | 44 | 28 | 37 | 32 | 53 | 52 |
| No response | 8 | 8 | 7 | 6 | 7 | 4 | 12 | 6 | 4 | 12 | 8 | 7 |
| Total | 100% | 100% | 100% | 100% | 100% | 100% | 100% | 100% | 100% | 100% | 100% | 100% |
| Number | (151) | (415) | (416) | (50) | (495) | (208) | (141) | (116) | (79) | (255) | (2,326) | (545) |

to divine punishment. Distressingly, Hadden's tabulations show that this image of the modern Jew is about as widely held by ministers as by their parishioners. While 3 per cent of the Episcopalian clergymen agreed, as did 6 per cent of the Methodists and 7 per cent of the Presbyterians, 21 per cent of the American Lutheran, 22 per cent of the American Baptist, and 38 per cent of the Missouri Lutheran ministers did so.

Surely few students of contemporary America would have predicted that these virulent images of the Jew are so commonly held. How does such an outlook continue to linger after the horrors of the Nazi era, and amid the apparent contemporary climate of interfaith cooperation and brotherhood?

The theoretical notions developed in earlier chapters suggest that certain kinds of complex religious ideologies contribute to a particularistic outlook which in turn produces negative sentiments toward religious outsiders. If this is so, then we would expect that this lingering of hostile religious images of the Jew is highly related to the degree to which orthodoxy and particularism characterize modern Christianity.

The logic of this expectation is as follows. Religious particularism, a function of an encompassing and elaborate theology, specifies that one's own religious group has a monopoly on legitimate religious status. Implicit in such a view is the judgment that all persons and groups beyond the boundaries of this legitimacy are violating crucial values and norms; hence, an invidious, hostility-laden comparison will be drawn between the "faithful" and the "pagans." Historical circumstances make the Jew an especially salient and visible religious outsider relative to the Christian majority. First of all, the Jews are the only sizable and readily identifiable group of religious "deviants" in Christendom.[6] Though Buddhists, Moslems, and all the other non-Christian faiths may be equally beyond the pale of the true faith, their adherents live in distant lands, while Jews are close at hand. Furthermore, the mutual origins of Judaism and Christianity make the Jew consistently relevant and visible in Christian teachings. Thus, Christian particularism can be expected markedly to influence invidious judgments of the religious legitimacy of the Jew today, as well as in the past. The fact that Christianity has undergone massive alterations in recent centuries, especially the past one, leading away from orthodoxy and particularism, seems related to a diminished religious fervor against the Jews. But, to the degree that particularism remains it can be expected to retain its power to engender hostile definitions of Judaism.

Since we have previously developed measures of these concepts, the

---

[6] Atheists have no ethnic or organizational identity.

foregoing theoretical expectations can be readily put to empirical tests. In the remainder of this section we shall see the degree to which orthodoxy and particularism account for the retention of traditional images of Jews as unforgiven crucifiers whose troubles stem from Divine wrath.

In Table 26 we may see the joint effect of orthodoxy and particularism

Table 26.   ORTHODOXY, PARTICULARISM, AND JEWISH GUILT

(Per cent who agreed: "The Jews can never be forgiven for what they did to Jesus until they accept Him as the True Saviour.")

| Rank on Particularism Index | Orthodoxy Index | | |
|---|---|---|---|
| | High | Medium | Low |
| *Protestants:* | | | |
| High | | | |
| Per cent | 77 | 42 | 29 |
| Number | (360) | (183) | (52) |
| Medium | | | |
| Per cent | 63 | 20 | 8 |
| Number | (219) | (403) | (235) |
| Low | | | |
| Per cent | 13 | 5 | 1 |
| Number | (24) | (131) | (280) |
| *Catholics:* | | | |
| High | | | |
| Per cent | 33 | 10 | a |
| Number | (105) | (30) | (9) |
| Medium | | | |
| Per cent | 13 | 6 | 0 |
| Number | (135) | (66) | (25) |
| Low | | | |
| Per cent | 5 | 0 | 0 |
| Number | (19) | (17) | (29) |

a Too few cases for stable percentage.

on the belief that "The Jews can never be forgiven for what they did to Jesus until they accept Him as the True Saviour." The percentages represent the proportion of persons who agreed with this statement. Looking at Protestants it is clear that our theoretical expectations are borne out. Of those persons who are high both on orthodoxy and particularism, 77 per cent agreed. Of those low on both measures only 1 per cent agreed. The proportion taking this hostile religious view of the contemporary Jew falls with the degree of orthodoxy, regardless of particularism, and falls with the degree of particularism regardless of orthodoxy. Thus, each factor has a marked independent effect on taking this view of Jews, and their joint effect is very powerful indeed.

Among Catholics the findings are consistent with our theoretical expectations, but the effects do not appear to be so dramatic. Mostly, this smaller effect comes about because Catholics in general were much less likely to accept this statement about Jews than were Protestants. Thus, the statistical limit placed on the percentage-point differences which would be obtained was much lower. Nevertheless, taking such a position on modern Jews is pretty much restricted to those high on both measures, and is virtually absent among other Catholics.

This lower propensity of Catholics to impose hostile definitions on religious outgroups is a phenomenon we shall have occasion to consider in some detail as our analysis proceeds. However, a few general remarks seem appropriate here. Minority status is a condition peculiar to American Catholicism and has led the church in America to respond in an exceedingly atypical way. While the church in Europe and South America has a record of suppressing religious freedom, the American church has, from the early days of the Republic, consistently opposed religious restrictions and especially church-state bonds. For example, the Roman Catholic church played an important role in the fight to remove religion from the public schools during the nineteenth century. Similarly, American Catholics have vociferously opposed all religious tests for public office. While there is no reason to question the sincerity of the vigorous leadership Catholics have given to the struggle for religious tolerance, it must be pointed out that in a Protestant nation, religious intolerance is likely to be mainly anti-Catholic. Thus, Catholics have had an enormous stake in strengthening the climate of religious liberty. Given this long preoccupation with religious liberty, one might well expect that American Catholics would have developed a great reluctance to impose hostile evaluations on any religious group. Thus, although Catholics are as inclined toward particularism as Protestants are, there is perhaps a tendency among them to suspend translating positive judgments of their own group into negative judgments of non-Catholics.

Such a tendency, while much less pronounced, can perhaps also be seen among Protestants. *Not all* of the Protestants who rank high on both ideological commitment and parochialism agreed with this negative statement about Jews. We shall have occasion later to try to understand how some orthodox and particularistic persons resist making invidious judgments of religious outsiders.

Turning now to Christian perceptions of the Jews as cursed, a pattern similar to that revealed in Table 26 can be observed. In Table 27 percentages indicate the proportions who agreed that "The reason the Jews have so much trouble is because God is punishing them for rejecting

Table 27.    ORTHODOXY, PARTICULARISM, AND JEWISH PUNISHMENT

(Per cent who agreed "The reason the Jews have so much trouble is because God is punishing them for rejecting Jesus.")

| Rank on Particularism Index | Orthodoxy Index | | |
|---|---|---|---|
| | High | Middle | Low |
| *Protestants:* | | | |
| High | | | |
| Per cent | 35 | 12 | 6 |
| Number | (360) | (183) | (52) |
| Medium | | | |
| Per cent | 29 | 7 | 2 |
| Number | (219) | (403) | (235) |
| Low | | | |
| Per cent | 4 | 3 | 1 |
| Number | (24) | (131) | (280) |
| *Catholics:* | | | |
| High | | | |
| Per cent | 25 | 13 | ᵃ |
| Number | (105) | (30) | (9) |
| Medium | | | |
| Per cent | 13 | 2 | 0 |
| Number | (135) | (66) | (25) |
| Low | | | |
| Per cent | 11 | 0 | 0 |
| Number | (19) | (17) | (29) |

ᵃ Too few cases for stable percentage.

Jesus." Both orthodoxy and particularism independently, and strongly, influence crediting the notion that the Jews are cursed. And as in the previous table, their mutual effect on taking this hostile view of Jews is extensive. Among Protestants the differences range from 35 per cent of those high on both measures to 1 per cent of those low on both.

Because this image of the Jew as cursed is much less commonly held than the belief that the Jews are still unforgiven for the Crucifixion, the size of the differences which could be obtained in this table was less. For this reason we should report that if we add the "uncertain" to the "agree" response, then 20 per cent of those Protestants low on both measures supported the statement as compared with 70 per cent of those high on both. This provides a relationship approaching the magnitude of that found in Table 26.

Among Roman Catholics the findings are virtually the same as for Protestants: Twenty-five per cent of those high on both indexes agreed with the statement, while no Catholic low on both did so.

Thus, our theoretical explanation for the incidence of these images of the modern Jew as still condemned in the eyes of God is very consistent with the statistical relationships found in the data. The prevalence of such beliefs coincides with the prevalence of commitment to an orthodox Christian ideology and to particularistic conceptions of Christian supremacy.

We have earlier suggested that religious hostility toward the modern Jew is partly a function of historic traditions, especially those concerning the Crucifixion, which maintain the Jew as a salient and highly visible religious outsider. We shall now introduce the belief that the historic Jews were guilty of crucifying Jesus into the preceding analysis in order to determine the impact of this belief on contemporary religious images of Jewish religious guilt, and also to investigate the interplay between these historic teachings and orthodoxy and particularism. This combination of factors is shown in Table 28, which contains the same data as Table 26 except that a fifth variable, belief or disbelief that the Jews were the group "most responsible for crucifying Christ," has been added. A five-variable table is somewhat complex, and there are a number of different generalizations which can be drawn from these data. To clarify the discussion we shall number these generalizations and explicate each separately.

Among Protestants, these were the patterns of belief:

1.   Persons who believe the ancient Jews were responsible for the Crucifixion were more likely to agree that the modern Jew is still to blame than those who did not implicate the Jews in the Crucifixion. This generalization is true regardless of the degree of orthodoxy or particularism.

2.   Orthodoxy markedly affected the propensity to blame the modern Jew regardless of whether or not the person thought the ancient Jews were most responsible for the Crucifixion.

3.   Particularism greatly influenced the image of the contemporary Jew no matter what one believed about the historic Jew, except among those persons low on orthodoxy who thought the ancient Jews were not the group most responsible for the Crucifixion.

4.   Perhaps the most dramatic finding in the table is that *persons with a particularistic outlook were primarily the ones who linked the contemporary and historical Jew*. Among the most orthodox believers who thought the ancient Jews were implicated in the Crucifixion, 86 per cent of those high on particularism thought the modern Jews were still unforgiven for "what they did to Jesus," as did 69 per cent of those medium on particularism, and *only* 19 per cent of those low on particularism. Thus, with orthodoxy and historic image held constant, we can see the enormous impact of particularism on drawing a hostile link between the

Table 28.  INFLUENCE OF ORTHODOXY AND PARTICULARISM ON LINKING OF MODERN JEWS WITH THE CRUCIFIXION

(Per cent who agreed "The Jews can never be forgiven for what they did to Jesus until they accept Him as the True Saviour.")

ORTHODOXY INDEX

| RANK ON PARTICULARISM INDEX | High | | Medium | | Low | |
|---|---|---|---|---|---|---|
| | Group Most Responsible for Crucifixion | | Group Most Responsible for Crucifixion | | Group Most Responsible for Crucifixion | |
| | Jews | Not Jews[a] | Jews | Not Jews[a] | Jews | Not Jews[a] |
| *Protestants:* | | | | | | |
| High | 86% (242) | 70% (78) | 52% (103) | 28% (54) | 40% (21) | 0% (22) |
| Medium | 69 (152) | 59 (49) | 25 (221) | 13 (123) | 10 (114) | 7 (85) |
| Low | 19 (16) | [b] (5) | 9 (67) | 2 (46) | 1 (135) | 1 (101) |
| *Catholics:* | | | | | | |
| High | 33 (80) | 33 (15) | 12 (17) | [b] (9) | [c] (4) | • (2) |
| Medium | 15 (92) | 3 (34) | 6 (35) | 4 (27) | [c] (9) | • (11) |
| Low | [b] (12) | [b] (5) | [c] (10) | 0 (15) | [c] (13) | [c] (9) |

NOTE: Figures in parentheses show total number of respondents.
[a] Includes persons who answered "the Romans," "the Christians," "none of these."
[b] Too few cases to compute meaningful percentage.
[c] Although too few cases to compute meaningful percentage, none of the respondents agreed with the statement.

ancient and the modern Jews. But the power of particularism to predict hostility toward the modern Jew is not limited to only those who explicitly saw the ancient Jews as Christ-killers. Among the most orthodox believers who did not specifically indict the ancient Jews, 70 per cent of those high on particularism still agreed that the modern Jew is unforgiven.

5.   The combined impact of particularism, orthodoxy, and belief that the Jews were the group most responsible for the Crucifixion provided a massive prediction of how Protestants would regard the contemporary Jew. *Eighty-six per cent of those high on particularism and orthodoxy, and who implicated the ancient Jews, held a negative religious image of the modern Jew. On the other hand, only 1 per cent of those low on both and who did not blame the ancient Jews held such an image.*

Among Roman Catholics similar patterns obtain. However, Catholics were considerably less likely than Protestants to agree in the first place that "the Jews can never be forgiven"; thus the actual percentage-point differences are considerably smaller. *However, a majority of Catholics who did agree with the statement scored high on particularism and orthodoxy and also blamed the ancient Jews for the Crucifixion.*

Table 29 takes precisely the same form as Table 28, except that here the negative religious image of the contemporary Jew is the belief that "The reason the Jews have so much trouble is because God is punishing them for rejecting Jesus."

Again the same pattern of relationship can be seen. While agreement to this statement was considerably less common among Christian church members than it was for the previous item, thus limiting the absolute size of the percentage-point differences, still the same effects obtain. Particularism plays the major role in determining one's response to this question, but orthodoxy and perceptions of the historic guilt of the Jews also play a part.

An additional question allows further insight into Christian images of the connection of modern Jews with the "sins" of their forebears. All respondents were asked whether or not they thought it true that "among themselves, Jews think Christians are ignorant for believing Christ was the Son of God." This statement depicts Jews as active apostates from the "true faith," privately disdainful of those who accept Jesus as the promised Messiah. As can be seen in Table 30, Christians frequently agreed with this statement. Twenty-one per cent of the Protestants and 13 per cent of the Roman Catholics were entirely sure this statement about Jews was true, and an additional 20 per cent of the Protestants and 25 per cent of the Catholics felt Jews were "somewhat like this." Thus, 41 per cent of the Protestants and 38 per cent of the Catholics were at least inclined

Table 29. INFLUENCE OF ORTHODOXY AND PARTICULARISM ON BELIEF THAT MODERN JEWS ARE CURSED BY GOD

(Per cent who agreed "the reason the Jews have so much trouble is because God is punishing them for rejecting Jesus.")

ORTHODOXY INDEX

| RANK ON PARTICULARISM INDEX | High Group Most Responsible for Crucifixion | | Medium Group Most Responsible for Crucifixion | | Low Group Most Responsible for Crucifixion | |
|---|---|---|---|---|---|---|
| | Jews | Not Jews[a] | Jews | Not Jews[a] | Jews | Not Jews[a] |
| *Protestants:* | | | | | | |
| High | 44% (242) | 20% (76) | 17% (101) | 6% (53) | 14% (21) | 0% (22) |
| Medium | 32 (151) | 22 (50) | 9 (222) | 4 (126) | 4 (115) | 1 (85) |
| Low | 6 (16) | [b] (5) | 5 (65) | 2 (46) | 1 (136) | 5 (101) |
| *Catholics:* | | | | | | |
| High | 28 (80) | 20 (15) | 24 (17) | [b] (9) | [c] (4) | [c] (2) |
| Medium | 14 (92) | 6 (34) | 3 (35) | 0 (27) | [c] (9) | [c] (11) |
| Low | [b] (12) | [b] (5) | [c] (10) | [c] (5) | [c] (13) | [c] (9) |

NOTE: Figures in parentheses show total number of respondents.

[a] Includes persons who answered "the Romans," "the Christians," "none of these."
[b] Too few cases to compute meaningful percentage.
[c] Although too few cases to compute meaningful percentage, none of the respondents agreed with the statement.

Table 30.   THE IGNORANCE OF CHRISTIANS

Agreement with: "Among themselves, Jews think Christians are ignorant for believing Christ was the Son of God."

| | Cong. | Meth. | Epis. | D.of Christ | Pres. |
|---|---|---|---|---|---|
| Number | (151) | (415) | (416) | (50) | (495) |
| "Jews are like this." | 15% | 13% | 18% | 24% | 18% |
| "Jews are somewhat like this." | 17 | 21 | 19 | 20 | 20 |
| Total | 32% | 34% | 37% | 44% | 38% |

| | A.Luth. | A.Bap. | M.Luth. | S.Bap. | Sects |
|---|---|---|---|---|---|
| Number | (208) | (141) | (116) | (79) | (255) |
| "Jews are like this." | 24% | 18% | 33% | 44% | 33% |
| "Jews are somewhat like this." | 18 | 21 | 24 | 16 | 24 |
| Total | 42% | 39% | 57% | 60% | 57% |

| | Total Prot. | Cath. |
|---|---|---|
| Number | (2,326) | (545) |
| "Jews are like this." "Jews are somewhat like this." | 21% | 13% |
| Total | 41% | 38% |

to accept this image of the modern Jew. Among Protestants, complete agreement ranged from 13 per cent of the Methodists to 44 per cent of the Southern Baptists. Thus, for many Christians, modern Jews are not only seen as still guilty for the Crucifixion of Christ, but as actively hostile to followers of Jesus. Response to this statement about the Jews, like the images we have examined previously in this chapter, was strongly related to orthodoxy, particularism, and to belief that the historic Jews were implicated in the Crucifixion.

To summarize what we have learned so far in this chapter, it is apparent that images of the contemporary Jew as unrepentant and still guilty of the Crucifixion are not to be shrugged off as the mad notions of insignificant hate merchants. On the contrary, sizable minorities in Christian congregations embrace such beliefs about Jews, and indeed, about half at least consider it possible that such statements about Jews are accurate. If there is some truth in the notions of church members that they constitute the moral backbone of their communities, the upstanding and outstanding citizenry, then we can only conclude that far from being bizarre, images of Jews as deicides and the objects of divine wrath are "respectable" in modern America.

The data also indicate that it is not Christian orthodoxy directly, nor the teaching that the Jews were implicated in the Crucifixion, which led to these negative beliefs about modern Jewry. Both do have some impact, but *primarily* they function to engender bigotry when *combined* with a particularistic conception of one's own religion.

## The Religious Legitimacy of the Modern Jew

We have seen that modern Christians frequently regard Jews as still responsible for the Crucifixion and as subject to divine punishment. In this section we shall explore broader aspects of the images Christians hold of the religious condition of modern Jewry.

The overwhelming majority of Christian church members were aware of both the major similarities and differences in religious beliefs and practices between Jews and Christians. For example, 84 per cent of the Protestants and 78 per cent of the Catholics acknowledged that Jews worshiped God. Only 5 per cent of the Protestants and 8 per cent of the Roman Catholics erred in thinking Jews regard the New Testament as "God's word." And 77 per cent of the Protestants and 66 per cent of the Catholics replied that Jews believe in the Ten Commandments. The proportions who recognized the common elements in Christianity and Judaism, as might be expected, decreased from the more liberal to the more conservative Protestant bodies.

In general, Christians were also willing to agree that Jews are sincere in their faith. Seventy-seven per cent of the Protestants and 79 per cent of the Catholics judged Jews to be "truly religious." But on the basis of our earlier findings we might suppose that many who accept the Jews as truly religious do so with the reservation that Jews are also truly wrong in their religion, and hence in an inferior religious condition. To pursue our understanding of how Christians view Jews, we shall examine some concrete evaluations of the religious efficacy of Judaism.

From a traditional Christian point of view, a primary test of all religion and religious acts is based on the question of salvation—how will a man's chances to be saved be affected? In the Middle Ages, of course, there was no doubt among Christians that Jews were doomed to eternal perdition. Since belief in literal salvation has diminished among Christians, such a view of the Jew has correspondingly diminished. Furthermore, in recent years, many Christian groups have been moving toward a more universalistic view of salvation—the Roman Catholic Church acknowledges that non-Catholics can indeed be saved, and some Protestant groups suggest that men of good will in all religions will be received by God. However, we might expect that many Christians still believe in a literal salvation exclusively available to Christians and beyond the reach of Jews.

Looking at the data in Table 31, we see that this is indeed the case.

Table 31.    DENOMINATION AND JEWISH SALVATION

(Per cent who said "being of the Jewish religion" would "definitely" or "possibly" prevent salvation.)

| Cong. | Meth. | Epis. | D.of Christ | Pres. | A.Luth. | A.Bap. | M.Luth. | S.Bap. | Sects |
|---|---|---|---|---|---|---|---|---|---|
| 7% | 12% | 13% | 26% | 19% | 32% | 32% | 54% | 53% | 55% |
| (151) | (415) | (416) | (50) | (495) | (208) | (141) | (116) | (79) | (255) |

| Total Prot. | Cath. |
|---|---|
| 25% | 12% |
| (2,326) | (545) |

NOTE: Figures in parentheses show total number of respondents.

Twenty-five per cent of the Protestants and 12 per cent of the Roman Catholics believed that "being of the Jewish religion" would definitely or possibly prevent salvation. Of even greater interest, the proportions holding this view increase among Protestants from 7 per cent of the Congregationalists to 54 per cent of the Missouri Lutherans and 53 per cent of the Southern Baptists. For the majority of conservative Protestants, Jews are seen as beyond the boundaries of God's grace. Among the liberal bodies, however, only a handful exclude Jews from salvation. It must be remembered, however, that many persons in the liberal bodies also reject the orthodox view of salvation. For such persons, the question of the consequence of Jewishness for salvation is irrelevant.

But Christian orthodoxy is not the only factor which ought to influence Christians to judge the Jew as beyond the bounds of salvation. Particularism ought also to play a role. Table 32 supports these expectations. Among Protestants, 62 per cent of those ranking high on both orthodoxy and particularism doubt that Jews can be saved, while only 1 per cent of those low on both measures did so. And both factors display an independent effect on thinking Jews can be saved.

Among Catholics a similar pattern obtains, although the much lower propensity of Catholics to reject salvation for the Jews limits the size of the relationship.

Table 32.   ORTHODOXY, PARTICULARISM, AND JEWISH SALVATION

(Per cent who thought that "being of the Jewish religion"
would definitely or possibly prevent salvation.)

| Rank on Particularism Index | Orthodoxy Index | | |
|---|---|---|---|
| | High | Middle | Low |
| *Protestants:* | | | |
| High | | | |
| Per cent | 62 | 36 | 23 |
| Number | (360) | (183) | (52) |
| Medium | | | |
| Per cent | 40 | 23 | 12 |
| Number | (219) | (403) | (235) |
| Low | | | |
| Per cent | 4 | 4 | 1 |
| Number | (24) | (131) | (280) |
| *Catholics:* | | | |
| High | | | |
| Per cent | 27 | 13 | a |
| Number | (105) | (30) | (9) |
| Medium | | | |
| Per cent | 11 | 16 | 12 |
| Number | (135) | (66) | (25) |
| Low | | | |
| Per cent | 0 | 6 | 3 |
| Number | (19) | (17) | (29) |

a Too few cases for stable percentage.

Although our discussion of particularism has explicitly concerned religious outsiders in general, so far we have only tested these hypotheses on Christian images of Jews. To lend confidence to our assertion that orthodoxy and particularism combine to disqualify all religious outsiders, and that our findings are not idiosyncratic of perceptions of Jews alone, let us turn for a moment to another non-Christian religious group. In doing so we will also get some relative idea of the degree to which Jews, viewed from a Christian perspective, are seen as religious aliens. Table 33 shows the effect of orthodoxy and particularism on doubting that members of the Hindu religion can be saved. The relationship is even stronger than that seen in Table 32. Among Protestants 73 per cent of those high on both indexes doubt that a Hindu can be saved, while 3 per cent of those low on both measures had similar doubts. The same comparison among Catholics is 30 per cent versus 3 per cent.

Over-all, Christians are slightly more likely to reject salvation for

Table 33.   ORTHODOXY, PARTICULARISM, AND HINDU SALVATION

(Per cent who thought "being of the Hindu religion" would
definitely or possibly prevent salvation.)

| Rank on Particularism Index | Orthodoxy Index | | |
|---|---|---|---|
| | High | Middle | Low |
| *Protestants:* | | | |
| High | | | |
| Per cent | 73 | 51 | 42 |
| Number | (360) | (183) | (52) |
| Medium | | | |
| Per cent | 50 | 28 | 15 |
| Number | (219) | (403) | (235) |
| Low | | | |
| Per cent | 12 | 10 | 3 |
| Number | (24) | (131) | (280) |
| *Catholics:* | | | |
| High | | | |
| Per cent | 30 | 23 | ▪ |
| Number | (105) | (30) | (9) |
| Medium | | | |
| Per cent | 16 | 15 | 8 |
| Number | (135) | (66) | (25) |
| Low | | | |
| Per cent | 5 | 0 | 3 |
| Number | (19) | (17) | (29) |

▪ Too few cases for stable percentage.

Hindus than for Jews. While 25 per cent of all the Protestants rejected salvation for the Jews, 32 per cent barred Hindus. Among Catholics, 12 per cent rejected Jews and 15 per cent doubted Hindus could be saved. These differences are not very great. Considering that Jews share many beliefs and practices with Christians, while Hinduism and Christianity are widely different, it becomes apparent that for most of those Christians who do restrict the boundaries of salvation, close does not count. Christians can be saved, and no one else.

Sizable groups of Christian church members seem to believe that Jews, along with Hindus, fail the ultimate test of proper faith—admission to divine salvation. We have remarked, however, that because many Christians no longer accept the notion of salvation in an orthodox sense, such a test is irrelevant to many of our respondents. Furthermore, while still having a generally invidious view of the propriety of Judaism as a faith, one could admit that under exceptional circumstances an individual Jew might gain salvation. For this reason, we shall now give attention to a somewhat more general test of the religious legitimacy of Judaism—the rather sensitive matter of conversion.

If one adheres to a conversionist faith which he regards as superior to the faith of others, he will likely propose to convert persons from inferior faiths to his own. Christianity is only challenged by Islam for claim to being the most conversionist faith in history. Thus to expect Christians to favor converting non-Christians is somewhat obvious. But the question is, who do they see as *requiring* conversion? There was a time when most Christian denominations regarded all other denominations as in need of conversion. These days have virtually passed except for the most parochial sects on the Christian perimeter. Methodists do not typically worry that their Baptist neighbors are lost in unredeemable error. One might suppose that in the ecumenical, "religious community" spirit of contemporary America, many will have come to see the Jews as also beyond need of conversion.

To hold, on the other hand, that the Jews ought to be converted to Christianity is implicitly a judgment that their current religious condition is inferior—that Judaism is not seen as a proper faith in the same way that one Protestant denomination regards another as a legitimate religious involvement. While such missionary efforts may stem from the most benign motives, they nevertheless constitute an unambiguous denial that Judaism is an appropriate accommodation of divine will.

Thus, the willingness of Christians to convert Jews to Christianity, while it implies that Jews are not totally wicked and beyond hope, seems another legitimate basis for determining whether or not Judaism is regarded as a proper religion. Table 34 shows the proportion of persons in the

Table 34.   CONVERTING THE JEWS

(Per cent who said they personally approved of "converting Jews to Christianity.")

| Cong. | Meth. | Epis. | D.of Christ | Pres. | A.Luth. | A.Bap. | M.Luth. | S.Bap. | Sects |
|---|---|---|---|---|---|---|---|---|---|
| 21% | 29% | 33% | 46% | 46% | 61% | 59% | 73% | 90% | 84% |
| (151) | (415) | (416) | (50) | (495) | (208) | (141) | (116) | (79) | (255) |

| Total Prot. | Cath. |
|---|---|
| 48% | 48% |
| (2,326) | (545) |

NOTE: Figures in parentheses show total number of respondents.

various denominations who said they personally approved of "converting Jews to Christianity." Over-all, nearly half of both Roman Catholics and Protestants (48 per cent) approved. Judged on this basis, virtually half of these Christians reject Judaism as a legitimate faith. Among Protestants, the proportions who agreed increase from 21 per cent of the Congregationalists to 90 per cent of the Southern Baptists. Thus, the more conservative groups overwhelmingly suggest Jews ought to change their faith. Virtually identical proportions in each denomination also perceived their pastor as favoring the conversion of Jews.

As with previous negative images of the religious condition of Jewry, regarding the Jews as needing conversion ought to be highly related to particularism and orthodoxy. The data in Table 35 show that this is indeed

Table 35.   ORTHODOXY, PARTICULARISM, AND PERCENTAGE WHO APPROVED
OF CONVERTING JEWS TO CHRISTIANITY

| Rank on Particularism Index | Orthodoxy Index | | |
|---|---|---|---|
| | High | Medium | Low |
| *Protestants:* | | | |
| High | | | |
| Per cent | 83 | 60 | 29 |
| Number | (360) | (183) | (52) |
| Medium | | | |
| Per cent | 74 | 44 | 32 |
| Number | (219) | (403) | (235) |
| Low | | | |
| Per cent | 67 | 34 | 16 |
| Number | (24) | (131) | (280) |
| *Catholics:* | | | |
| High | | | |
| Per cent | 63 | 37 | ᵃ |
| Number | (105) | (30) | (9) |
| Medium | | | |
| Per cent | 58 | 45 | 40 |
| Number | (135) | (66) | (25) |
| Low | | | |
| Per cent | 63 | 29 | 17 |
| Number | (19) | (17) | (29) |

ᵃ Too few cases for stable percentage.

the case. Among Protestants, 83 per cent of those high on both indexes personally approve of converting Jews to Christianity, while only 16 per cent of those low on both indexes approve. Among Roman Catholics the same comparison is 63 per cent among the highs versus 17 per cent among the lows, a very similar finding. Thus, particularism and orthodoxy can be seen to have independent effects on attitudes toward converting the Jews, and their joint influence on this judgment is very great.

## Summary

Hostile religious images of the modern Jew as Christ-killer, beyond salvation, and in need of conversion to Christianity are far from dead in the Christian churches. Such notions were advocated by from a quarter to more than half of our respondents. However, such a description does not equally characterize the various denominations. Among the more liberal Protestant groups, such as the Congregationalists and Methodists, these views are rather uncommon. Among conservatives such as the Missouri Lutherans and Southern Baptists, such attitudes toward Jews are almost unanimous. The conservatives are, of course, also the most particularistic and orthodox respondents. And the data clearly show that these factors crucially affect the religious image held of the contemporary Jew.

On the other hand, as we have remarked before, some persons who are highly involved in orthodox Christian ideology and hold a very particularistic conception of Christian supremacy do not translate these factors into a negative evaluation of the Jews. This is especially true of Roman Catholics. The particular concern of American Catholicism with religious liberty has been suggested as a likely inhibiting force which prevents such translations from taking place. Such an explanation may also apply, to a lesser extent, to Protestants. In the next chapter we shall explore this hypothesis. Can norms of religious libertarianism disconnect the link between the particularistic vision and religious hostility?

# CHAPTER 5

# Religious Libertarianism

> From the polluted fountain of indifferentism flows that absurd and erroneous doctrine or rather raving which claims and defends liberty of conscience for everyone. From this comes, in a word, the worst plague of all, namely, unrestrained liberty of opinions and freedom of speech.
>
> —Pope Gregory VI (1765–1846), *Encyclical Mirari Vos*

The ideal of religious liberty is a relatively recent development in Western society and has been realized in practice only intermittently. The traditional Christian doctrine, promulgated by the Church Universal and subsequently reaffirmed by the various Protestant reformers, defined religious differences as intolerable; since there could be but one truth, to suffer the preaching of false doctrine was unthinkable. Could God's vicars permit men to be led into error and eternal perdition? The answer to this question was regarded as self-evident for centuries. Only grudgingly have Christians come to tolerate one another's "heresies." Indeed, as recently as 1885 Pope Leo XII could write, "The equal toleration of all religions . . . is the same thing as atheism. . . . The Church deems it unlawful to place all the religions on the same footing as the true religion."[1] A medieval Pope would hardly have considered it necessary to argue the point.

As the first stirrings of the Renaissance jarred Europe from the Long Night, notions of religious toleration found occasional expression, particularly among the early scientific intellectuals. Perhaps the most important medieval precursor of the scientific movement, William of Occam, was also one of the earliest critics of religious authoritarianism. Indeed, Lewis

---

[1] *Immortale Dei,* Nov. 1, 1885.

Feuer persuasively credits the scientific intellectuals, whose emergence and eventual ascendancy revolutionized Western culture, as the primary developers and proponents of doctrines of religious freedom.[2]

While such philosophical views probably stemmed from many sources, it seems reasonable to suppose that they came to command wide attention primarily where religious conflicts lent them relevance. For the early men of science, the parochial tyranny of the churches posed a profound and dangerous impediment.[3] A doctrine of freedom of thought on religious matters was an obvious solution to their problem of finding a way to make their lives and study less precarious in a hostile religious environment.

By the time of the American Revolution, however, religious conflict was not simply the problem of an intellectual class or of a dissenting minority, but had become a "social problem" that constituted a threat to political order. Given the fact of internal religious cleavages which could not be rectified by suppression or amalgamation, nation-states faced a need for some mechanism by which the endemic disruptive tension of religious conflict could be suppressed or otherwise managed.[4] Institutionalizing ideals of religious liberty provided a solution to this problem; religion was made a private and personal affair not subject to social approval and men were freed to follow the dictates of their own conscience.

European nations enacted ideals of religious freedom into law and practice somewhat later than the United States, probably simply because repression of dissent remained possible somewhat longer. The organizing American colonies, many of which were founded by dissenting sects fleeing European repression, found that no particular religious body was sufficiently predominant to claim sovereignty. The one denomination which might have made a bid for legal establishment, the Church of England, was in bad odor for Tory sympathy during the Revolution. Thus, religious liberty was virtually a prerequisite for organizing the colonies into a federal system.[5]

[2] The Scientific Intellectual (New York: Basic Books, 1963).
[3] See A. D. White, A History of the Warfare of Science with Theology in Christendom (New York: Dover, 1960).
[4] The religious schisms the Reformation left among the German princes were a major factor in frustrating the creation of a German state until late in the nineteenth century.
[5] The prominence of deists and freethinkers among the "Founding Fathers" should not be overlooked in accounting for the embodiment of religious liberty in the American Constitution. However, this probably only lent speed to the enterprise, for there seems no other solution by which the diverse religious groups could have been welded into a common political unit. Of course, with leaders committed to sectarianism, the problem might not have been solved. It is interesting to recall, too, that disestablishment of denominations in various states came a good deal later, and typically, as disadvantaged sects gained adherents and political power.

But if norms and values of religious liberty are sufficient to mute religious conflict, they are insufficient to provide any ultimate values to integrate and legitimate the social system. Nor can the religious ideology of any group within the system do so since, by definition, there are several conflicting religions all of which must be denied primacy. For this reason, the integrating values of social systems in which there is religious pluralism tend to emphasize the common elements of the political, economic, and geographic domains. Religious ideas may enter into this value system too, but these will be limited to religious elements common to all of the disputing religions. Such common elements are likely to be vague and platitudinous, as is the case with the "deactivated" public religion of the United States.[6]

The recent Congressional hearings on the 147 different proposals to amend the Constitution to restore prayer to the public schools provided an excellent occasion for seeing this public, national religion on display. Representative Frank Becker (Republican, N.Y.), a leading proponent of the amendment, told the committee: "Invocations, duties, oaths taken on the Bible are as American and as universal as a taste for apple pie, or ice cream or watermelon." Representative Louis Wyman (Republican, N.H.) said he would approve of requiring a person to swear his belief in a Supreme Being in order to obtain a driver's license, but was quick to add: "It does not make the slightest difference so long as the Supreme Being is acknowledged in some form, whether it is Buddha, Allah, or God."[7]

This public religion, while susceptible to attacks on its authenticity or even good taste, could hardly be called particularistic in any narrow sense. Clearly it tries to embrace all of the major American religious bodies. One of the sternest serious critics of this national religion, William Lee Miller, recognizes that our religious diversity may have inevitably led to a sterilized religious rhetoric. In his view, ". . . the presence and growing importance of . . . other major faiths may be one of the causes which—inadvertently, as it were—produce the effect of a kind of generalizing and secularizing of the old amalgam of evangelical Protestantism and Americanism into a contemporary public, patriotic religiosity."[8] Indeed, it seems likely that the more one embraces firm ideals of religious liberty the more one is constrained to give up adherence to a narrow par-

[6] See Charles Y. Glock and Rodney Stark, *Religion and Society in Tension* (Chicago: Rand McNally, 1965), Chapter 9.

[7] Quoted in Murray Kempton, "Vessels of Christ," *New Republic*, May 16, 1964, p. 14.

[8] William Lee Miller, "American Religion and American Political Attitudes," *Religious Perspectives in American Culture*, ed. James Ward Smith and A. Leland Jamison (Princeton: Princeton University Press, 1961), pp. 81–118.

ticularism and instead take up an "interdenominational" theology. But while this may be a tendency, even a strong one, it is not a necessity. It may well be easier to stop thinking of a man as different than to remark his difference and refrain from hostility, but the latter can be done.

Our concern with religious libertarianism is, of course, its potential role in disconnecting the predispositions of persons holding orthodox and particularistic conceptions of Christianity to impute religious illegitimacy to persons of other faiths, particularly Jews. While religious liberty is an official policy of the United States, and hence there are strong traditions of sticking to one's own religious business, it is not universally accepted by Americans. Various sects continually challenge libertarian norms by seeking to impose restrictions upon those who reject their doctrines. The continuing recurrence of antievolution campaigns is a case in point. Furthermore, although a good deal of variation in religious outlook is permitted in contemporary America, neither the courts nor public opinion will countenance just *any* theological position. American "pluralism" has plain boundaries. To clarify some of the issues which will be of concern in our subsequent introduction of religious libertarianism into the empirical analysis, we briefly sketch the limits of religious freedom in America.

One of the most constant examples of the persecution of religious violators, thus indicating that American pluralism has patrolled boundaries, is provided by what are commonly called "cults," the name itself connoting an invidious public view of certain religious outlooks. Briefly, cults are all of those religious groups which are publicly regarded as being too far removed from the religious mainstream to qualify as members of the legitimate American religious genus, but are instead seen as mutants who constitute a new breed.

Such movements are frequently exposed to public hatred, contempt, and ridicule, are sometimes harassed by public officials, the police, and the courts, and are occasionally the objects of mob violence. The majority of leaders of American cults during the past century have gone to jail, fled the threat of imminent imprisonment, or been lynched.[9] Many of these leaders clearly seem to have been bounders and charlatans of the

[9] For example: The Mormon founder Joseph Smith and his brother Hyrum were killed by a vigilante mob in Carthage, Illinois; James J. Strang, one of Smith's successors, led a fragment of the Mormons to Mackinac Island in upper Michigan where he was also shot by vigilantes; the main body of Mormons in Utah were forced to give up polygamy and conform to American values when Western settlement caught up with them; and orthodox rurals continue to be swept up in posse raids. James Humprey Noyes, leader of the Oneida Colony, had constant legal troubles and finally fled to Canada to escape the jurisdiction of New York courts; and Ben Purnell of the House of David was under indictment when he died. In more recent times, Edna Ballard and her son Donald, of the Mighty I AM, were

worst sort, but this is irrelevant to the issue at hand, namely, that they were especially tempting targets for surveillance and prosecution because they were publicly defined as "kooks" and "heretics" and thus as fair game. Police do not commonly infiltrate or "bug" the meetings of the major denominations, searching for actionable evidence. But this often does happen to cults, and as a result their sins invariably find them out. And though cult leaders are primarily jailed for fraud, the case typically rests in part on a judgment that the *doctrine of the cult is fraudulent*. A Christian pastor could hardly be tried for obtaining money under false pretenses because he led members to tithe in order to gain salvation. A cult leader can be tried for doing so.

The boundaries of American pluralism are also violated by atheists, freethinkers, and agnostics. This fact tends to be overlooked by intellectuals and scholars, who occupy the one structural situation in America where irreligiousness is common and goes generally unopposed.[10] However, to the degree that the greater society is, or comes to be, aware of this fact, hostility toward the academic and scholarly community is forthcoming. In the larger American society the agnostic is *persona non grata*. No candidate for major political office, regardless of his actual religious outlook, may be elected without demonstrating his commitment to a legitimate religious institution.[11]

Our primary concern with the boundaries of American pluralism is, of course, with the degree to which Judaism is accommodated within it. Officially there is little question that Judaism is indeed legitimate. The compulsiveness with which clergymen of all "three" major faiths are included at public occasions such as political conventions suggests that public leaders are making a strenuous effort to impose legitimacy upon

---

sentenced to jail in 1942; Arthur L. "The Voice" Bell of Mankind United, and twelve of his assistants, were sentenced to jail for "sedition" at about the same time, and Bell has been in and out of California courts ever since. Krishna Venta, the self-styled Los Angeles Christ, was blown to kingdom come by a dynamite blast touched off by the husbands of several of his converts. And Reinhold Schmidt, interplanetary sage of the Flying Saucer cult, was sentenced to prison in 1961. The list could be extended indefinitely.

[10] Among graduate students in the arts and sciences at the best American universities, a larger proportion report they have no religion than acknowledge themselves as belonging to any one of the three main faiths: Protestant, Catholic, or Jew (See Glock and Stark, *op. cit.*, Chapter 14).

[11] It is interesting to note, however, that candidates are also probably constrained from being too strongly attached to their religion; they must make it clear that their basic commitment is to the public religion. Had Richard Nixon been a "strong" Quaker, he probably could not have been nominated. Nor could John F. Kennedy have been elected as a "strong" Catholic. Significantly, both were criticized by spokesmen of their respective faiths for being heterodox.

Jewry despite contrary public opinion. This is to be applauded. But the fact of anti-Semitism remains as a clear proof that Jews are seen as quite beyond the boundaries of American pluralism by a significant portion of the public.

Thus, religious libertarianism in America remains problematic at best, limited both by the degree to which any value of religious toleration is accepted and by the sphere of religions judged as warranting the benefits of freedom.

To what extent can variations in religious libertarianism inform our study of the religious roots of anti-Semitism? Clearly, this should be a crucial factor. We have suggested earlier that the comparative reluctance of Roman Catholics to link their particularistic vision with negative judgments of the religious status of Jews may stem from the particular salience of religious libertarianism for American Catholicism. And we might expect that the relatively smaller proportion of Protestants whose particularism does not seem to be translated into religious hostility toward the Jew may also be influenced by values of religious libertarianism. In order to determine whether or not this is the explanation, it will be necessary to construct a measure of religious libertarianism that can be introduced into our analysis.

## Defining and Measuring Religious Libertarianism

By religious libertarianism we do not mean approval of religious differences, but rather an unwillingness to take punitive action toward persons who are perceived to violate one's own religious standards. In this sense, religious libertarianism is nonaction rather than a positive basis for action; to be a religious libertarian is to refrain from punishing or otherwise discriminating against persons on the basis of perceived religious "shortcomings."

The various religious standards which may be violated, and thus raise the question of religious libertarianism, differ greatly from denomination to denomination. However, it will be most useful for purposes of analysis if we can select some religious standards upheld by all of the Christian bodies so as to have a basis for determining relative unwillingness to punish religious violations. Since belief in God is a tenet common to all of these groups, despite some differences in the conceptions of God and the certainty of belief, this seems a proper general test of religious libertarianism: Will Christians grant ordinary civil liberties to atheists? And if not, how far will they go in punishing persons who do not believe in God?

The questionnaire contained a battery of proposed actions against "a man [who] publicly admitted he did not believe in God." Respondents were asked to indicate whether they agreed or disagreed with each of these proposed actions.

The responses can be seen in Table 36. The actions proposed have been arranged in the table according to the support they were given. The most agreed-to action against an atheist was to bar him from teaching in a public high school. Thirty-nine per cent of the Protestants and 36 per cent of the Catholics agreed with this statement. As can be seen, the proportions agreeing that freedom ought to be denied an atheist increase from the more liberal Protestant groups on the left to the more conservative on the right. A similar pattern obtains on the other items.

Both Protestants and Catholics were slightly less likely to recommend preventing an atheist from teaching in a private university than they were to object to such a person in a public high school. Twenty-nine per cent of the Protestants took this view, as compared with 31 per cent of the Roman Catholics. Roughly a quarter of both Protestants and Catholics agreed that an atheist "should not be allowed to preach his beliefs to others." About the same proportions also felt an atheist "should not be allowed to hold public office."

When it came to removing an atheist's book from the public library, however, support was about half that given the two previous items. Only 12 per cent of the Protestants and 14 per cent of the Roman Catholics advocated such a step. Significantly, this seems to represent a definite stance on the part of many Christians to extend tolerance to the books of atheists rather than any general rejection of book censorship as such. Fifty-four per cent of Protestants and 60 per cent of Catholics elsewhere in the questionnaire indicated that they personally approved of the "censorship of movies and books." The last two items, firing an atheist from a defense plant and from a job in a supermarket, went virtually unsupported.

For the sake of comparison it ought to be reported that in 1954, during the McCarthy era, Americans in general were much more likely to support similar actions against an admitted Communist.[12] Thus, the violation of political standards of propriety seems somewhat more likely to beget illiberal sanctions from Americans than is religious deviation.

Nevertheless, the data indicate that a sizable minority of these Christian

[12] See Samuel A. Stouffer, *Communism, Conformity, and Civil Liberties* (Garden City, N.Y.: Doubleday, 1955). Lest these differences be attributed to social class, the church members in our sample were also much less willing to discriminate against atheists than were persons selected in Stouffer's sample of community leaders to approve of punishing Communists.

Table 36. TOLERANCE OF ATHEISTS

Reply to: "Suppose a man publicly admitted he did not believe in God. Would you agree or disagree that the following actions should be taken against him?"

| Per cent Who Agreed | Cong. | Meth. | Epis. | D.of Christ | Pres. | A.Luth. | A.Bap. | M.Luth. | S.Bap. | Sects | Total Prot. | Cath. |
|---|---|---|---|---|---|---|---|---|---|---|---|---|
| Number | (151) | (415) | (416) | (50) | (495) | (208) | (141) | (116) | (79) | (255) | (2,326) | (545) |
| "He should not be allowed to teach in a public high school." | 33% | 33% | 34% | 44% | 40% | 40% | 45% | 39% | 57% | 54% | 39% | 36% |
| "He should not be allowed to teach in a private university." | 17 | 23 | 22 | 26 | 30 | 34 | 29 | 31 | 46 | 48 | 29 | 31 |
| "He should not be allowed to preach his beliefs to others." | 11 | 19 | 24 | 18 | 23 | 30 | 21 | 32 | 32 | 36 | 24 | 28 |
| "He should not be allowed to hold public office." | 20 | 23 | 26 | 16 | 29 | 28 | 27 | 40 | 41 | 34 | 28 | 23 |
| "A book he wrote should be removed from the library." | 4 | 8 | 6 | 8 | 10 | 13 | 14 | 13 | 27 | 34 | 12 | 14 |
| "He should be fired from a defense plant." | 3 | 6 | 7 | 6 | 8 | 8 | 9 | 9 | 13 | 11 | 8 | 5 |
| "He should be fired from a job in a supermarket." | 1 | 1 | 1 | 2 | 1 | 1 | 2 | 1 | 3 | 7 | 1 | 1 |

church members declared themselves willing to take some rather extensive punitive actions against a confessed atheist. Nearly four in ten would not permit such an individual to teach in a public high school, and nearly a third would keep him from a private university. Religious liberty for an atheist, then, is far from unanimously extended by American Christians.

Following the same procedures used in previous chapters, four of these items were used to construct an index of religious libertarianism.[13] The completed measure ranged from a score of zero, given persons who agreed that all four sanctions should be imposed on an admitted atheist, to 4, which indicates that a libertarian response was made to all four items.

Turning to the question of validity, the index was found strongly to predict agreement to the other items reported in Table 36 that were not included in the measure. Furthermore, the index was strongly related to other items which suggest restrictions on the civil liberties of religious deviants. Two such items are shown in Table 37.

The index of religious libertarianism is strongly related to willingness to deny freedom of speech and assembly to missionaries from non-Chris-

Table 37.    VALIDATION AND INTERPRETATION OF THE INDEX OF
RELIGIOUS LIBERTARIANISM

Index of Religious Libertarianism

| Per Cent Who Agreed | Low 0 | 1 | 2 | 3 | High 4 | Total |
|---|---|---|---|---|---|---|
| *"We should not allow missionaries from non-Christian religions to spread their teachings in a Christian community."* | | | | | | |
| Protestants | 69% | 42% | 27% | 20% | 11% | 23% |
| Catholics | 62 | 37 | 23 | 17 | 13 | 21 |
| *"Would you agree that a person who says there is no God is likely to hold dangerous political ideas?"* | | | | | | |
| Protestants | 81% | 62% | 48% | 35% | 16% | 34% |
| Catholics | 79 | 70 | 42 | 40 | 18 | 35 |
| *Total number* | | | | | | |
| Protestants | (170) | (273) | (273) | (262) | (1,109) | (2,086) |
| Catholics | (34) | (60) | (64) | (70) | (253) | (481) |

[13] The items included were: "He should not be allowed to teach in a public high school." "He should not be allowed to teach in a private university." "A book he wrote should be removed from the library." "He should not be allowed to hold public office." Scoring was zero for each "agree" answer, and 1 for each "disagree." The 304 persons who failed to answer one or more of the four items were not scored on the index. However, an analysis of the unscored group showed they took a middle position on items used to validate the index, indicating that nonresponse was randomly distributed among the various degrees of religious libertarianism.

tian religions. Of those with zero libertarianism scores, 69 per cent of the Protestants and 62 per cent of the Roman Catholics agreed that "We should not allow missionaries from non-Christian religions to spread their teachings in a Christian community." Only 11 per cent of the Protestants and 13 per cent of the Roman Catholics with maximum scores (4) on the libertarianism index agreed with the statement.

The index was also strongly related to suspecting atheists of political unreliability. Among Protestants, 81 per cent of those with zero scores agreed that "A person who says there is no God is likely to hold dangerous political ideas," while only 16 per cent of those with maximum scores agreed. Among Roman Catholics these groups showed 79 and 18 per cent agreement respectively.

Looking at the total column, however, and recalling the total Protestant and Roman Catholic comparisons in Table 36, an important finding comes to light: *Protestants and Roman Catholics are about equally libertarian as measured by these items.* This fact forces a reconsideration of our earlier expectations that religious libertarianism will account for the greater reluctance of Catholics to translate particularism into negative sentiments toward Jews and Hindus. Statistically, this cannot be the case, since it would be necessary for Roman Catholics to be considerably more predisposed toward religious libertarianism than Protestants if this interpretation were to be supported.

Thus, we are faced with a seeming perplexity: Roman Catholics are no more likely to uphold civil liberties for atheists than are Protestants, yet Catholics are considerably less likely than Protestants to impose negative religious evaluations upon Jews and Hindus. Seemingly Catholics can accommodate *religious* deviation better than Protestants can, but this greater tolerance does not extend to deviation based on *irreligiousness*. Historically, this makes a good deal of sense. Roman Catholic concern has been with the extension of norms of toleration to persons who worship differently from the majority—that is, with escaping the penalties of the anti-Catholic prejudice of a Protestant majority. But Catholics have little stake in liberty for nonbelievers; indeed opposition to skepticism may well serve to emphasize their common religiousness with potentially hostile religious groups.

A further explanation of Catholics' relative reluctance to impose hostile definitions on deviant religious groups, such as Jews and Hindus, may lie in their evaluation of Protestantism. We have commented in chapters 2 and 3 that although Protestants have profound reservations about many Catholic beliefs and practices, they do not doubt the ultimate legitimacy of Catholicism as a Christian faith. That is, Protestants did not think Protestants, rather than Christians in general, are God's Chosen People, and were considerably less likely than Catholics to think that being a member of their particular faith was necessary for salvation. While the majority of Catholics did not restrict the designation of God's Chosen People today to themselves, they were much more likely to do so than were Protestants.

This suggests that from the view of the Roman Catholic, especially in past decades, Protestants represented a severe strain on proper religious status, indeed were regarded as beyond the True Faith. In facing the need to accommodate these severe strictures to the facts of living in a predominantly Protestant society, Catholics may have been forced to a very broad view of religious legitimacy. That is, from the original Catholic view there may have seemed little difference among Protestants, Jews, and the various other non-Christian faiths—all were heretical.[14] In re-defining their outlook to accord religious legitimacy to Protestants, Roman Catholics may well have been forced to make a considerably greater extension of tolerance than was required of Protestants who sought to see Catholics as legitimate. One reason why this may be the case lies in the *asymmetry between Protestants and Catholics in the matter of shared and discrepant beliefs.*

The traditional religious beliefs of most Protestant denominations are also, for the most part, believed by Catholics. The fact that Catholics *also* hold a number of "additional" beliefs can be somewhat overlooked from a Protestant perspective, the important thing being that *no major Protestant tenets are disbelieved by Catholics.* For Roman Catholics the situation is quite the opposite; Catholics are faced with a Protestantism *that does indeed deny many important Catholic tenets.* For example, both Protestants and Catholics accept the doctrine of the Trinity, but Protestants generally do not share with Catholics special reverence for Mary and the saints. While Protestants and Catholics share belief in the authority of Scriptures, Catholics also accept the authority of tradition. While most Protestant bodies retain the ritual of communion, they reject the "additional" Catholic doctrines concerning transubstantiation—that the bread and wine are literally transmuted into the blood and flesh of Christ. Thus, Protestantism likely poses a greater strain on accommodation for Catholics than Catholicism does for Protestants. In order to define Protestants as legitimate, Catholics may in fact have been led to grant a general dispensation of religious hostility toward all groups sincere in some form of worship.

Unfortunately, none of these speculations can be put to a direct

[14] Indeed, Renan was impressed by the similarity of the accusations made against Jews and Protestants by French Catholics. See Ernest Renan, *Discours et Conferences* (7th ed.; Paris: Calmann-Levy, 1922).

empirical test with our data, although they do seem to account for a number of our findings. Although religious libertarianism as we have measured it does not account for the less powerful influence of particularism on Roman Catholic images of the religious status of the modern Jew, our interest in this concept continues. While Protestant-Catholic differences can be expected to remain, religious libertarianism may still play an important role in both groups by intervening at various points in the process we have developed and examined so far. Norms of religious libertarianism could well prevent some men with orthodox Christian ideologies from adopting a particularistic view of religious legitimacy, and further may prevent particularism from being translated into religious hostility toward outsiders.

To see whether or not religious libertarianism has this "suspending" influence is particularly relevant for all concerned with combating religious prejudice. It is surely beyond the proper scope of any social action to request men to surrender their commitment to an orthodox Christianity, and there seem grounds also to wonder whether or not particularism can be legitimately opposed. But such barriers do not apply to a doctrine of religious libertarianism—this is a message which men may honorably promote. The question then is: Are such messages of any use? Can persons with a particularistic religious vision nevertheless manage to adopt a libertarian view of religious outsiders, or is religious libertarianism restricted to persons who have little basis for religious prejudice anyway? We shall now consider these questions.

## Religious Libertarianism and Religious Hostility

Earlier in this chapter we suggested that religious libertarianism was apt to be highly associated with having relinquished commitment to traditional Christian theology; that apparent tolerance was often little more than a reflection of a lack of concern for the standards from which nonconformity is permitted. But we also indicated that this *need* not be the case, that devout Christians could nevertheless permit others religious freedom.

Table 38 indicates that both these suggestions are confirmed by the data.[15] Religious libertarianism is highly associated with a lack of commitment to traditional Christian orthodoxy. Of Protestants classified as

[15] The Religious Libertarianism Index was collapsed from the form in which it appears in Table 37; and in all subsequent tables High includes those with scores of 4 on the original index, Medium includes those with scores of 2 and 3, while Low includes those with scores of zero and 1.

Table 38.   ORTHODOXY AND RELIGIOUS LIBERTARIANISM

|  | Orthodoxy Index | | |
| --- | --- | --- | --- |
|  | High | Medium | Low |
| Protestants high on religious libertarianism | 39% | 52% | 71% |
| Number | (627) | (735) | (608) |
| Catholics high on religious libertarianism | 43% | 54% | 73% |
| Number | (270) | (120) | (59) |

High on the Index of Orthodoxy, 39 per cent scored High on the Index of Religious Libertarianism, while 71 per cent of those Low on orthodoxy scored High on libertarianism. Among Catholics the same comparison is 43 per cent versus 73 per cent. Thus, in general, we must conclude that religious libertarianism finds the bulk of its support among those least committed to Christian orthodoxy. This suggests that societies can perhaps only sustain libertarian norms when sufficient numbers of persons no longer firmly embrace a precise religious ideology. Nevertheless, a great many persons who are highly involved in traditional Christian ideology do support norms of religious libertarianism; thus our second expectation is also supported. This will allow us to inquire what effect religious libertarianism may have in reducing religious hostility; to what degree can it disconnect that process we have previously examined whereby Christians come to regard the modern Jew as tainted with the guilt of the Crucifixion and suffering God's punishment.

To pursue such questions we must introduce the Index of Religious Libertarianism into the relationships shown in Chapter 4 (tables 28 and 29). This proved difficult technically, but not altogether impossible. The problem lay in the fact that the tables were already so complex that the number of cases in each cell was somewhat small. Introducing an additional variable resulted in having so few cases in many cells of the tables that they could not provide a stable basis for computing percentages. Indeed, the loss of cases among Roman Catholics was so great that conclusions could hardly be drawn. Fortunately there are ways around these difficulties. However, before we turn to different methods, we examine several crucial cells in this complex table for which sufficient cases remained to warrant percentaging.

Table 39 includes *only* persons who were classified as High on both ideological involvement and particularism and who thought the Jews were the group most responsible for the Crucifixion. The data clearly show the important role religious libertarianism can play in disconnecting the potential of these factors for hostility towards modern Jews. Among

Table 39.   INFLUENCE OF RELIGIOUS LIBERTARIANISM[a]

Reply to "The Jews can never be forgiven for what they did to Jesus until they accept him as the true Saviour."

| | Index of Religious Libertarianism | | |
|---|---|---|---|
| Per Cent Who Agreed: | Low | Medium | High |
| Protestants | | | |
| Per cent | 93 | 84 | 73 |
| Number | (78) | (58) | (90) |
| Catholics | | | |
| Per cent | 39 | 32 | 26 |
| Number | (18) | (25) | (27) |

[a] Among only those who were High on the indexes of Orthodoxy and of Particularism and who thought the Jews were the group most responsible for the Crucifixion.

Protestants, 93 per cent of those low on libertarianism agreed that "The Jews can never be forgiven for what they did to Jesus until they accept Him as the True Saviour," but the proportion agreeing falls to 73 per cent of those high on libertarianism. Among Catholics, who are much less likely to agree with this statement in any event, a similar decline in agreement occurs as religious libertarianism increases. Thus, even among those most likely to take an invidious view of the modern Jew, religious libertarianism mutes hostility. We must grant that this muting is far from complete—73 per cent of the most libertarian Protestants who have all of the other predisposing characteristics still translate them into a negative religious image of the modern Jew. Still the effect is of sufficient strength to warrant serious attention by those committed to combating religious intolerance.

### Religious Hostility Toward Jews Recapitulated

In Parts I and II of this volume we conducted a search for the sources of religious hostility toward the modern Jew. In Part III we shall attempt to assess the implications of this hostility for anti-Semitic sentiments and actions in nonreligious aspects of modern life. Before turning to these new questions it may be useful to recapitulate our basic conceptual scheme of religious hostility and to consolidate our empirical evidence.

Figure 1 summarizes the theoretical discussions contained in chapters 1–5. Orthodox faith that claims universal truth and specifies in detail what that truth is leads persons to take a particularistic conception of their religious status. They think of themselves as having a patent on religious virtue and hence discredit all persons who do not share in their faith. Particularism leads Christians to be especially negative in their historic image of ancient Jewry, to see the Jews as implicated in the Crucifixion of Jesus. The combination of these factors markedly predisposes Christians to hold a negative religious image of the modern Jew as unforgiven for the "sins" of his ancient forebears, and suffering God's punishment. Norms of religious libertarianism (as indicated by the broken lines) may intervene at each connection in this process and to some extent prevent subsequent factors from developing.

In order to demonstrate empirically the full power of this process it

**FIGURE 1**

**THE PROCESS OF RELIGIOUS HOSTILITY TOWARD MODERN JEWS**

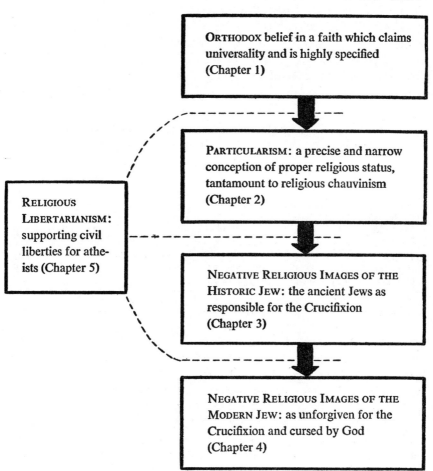

ORTHODOX belief in a faith which claims universality and is highly specified (Chapter 1)

PARTICULARISM: a precise and narrow conception of proper religious status, tantamount to religious chauvinism (Chapter 2)

RELIGIOUS LIBERTARIANISM: supporting civil liberties for atheists (Chapter 5)

NEGATIVE RELIGIOUS IMAGES OF THE HISTORIC JEW: the ancient Jews as responsible for the Crucifixion (Chapter 3)

NEGATIVE RELIGIOUS IMAGES OF THE MODERN JEW: as unforgiven for the Crucifixion and cursed by God (Chapter 4)

is necessary to combine four of these factors into a single index—we have already seen that lack of cases makes it impossible fully to examine these relationships simultaneously in a multiple cross-tabulation. An examination of the factors influencing hostile religious images of the modern Jews revealed that each has an effect independent of all of the others. Thus, their effects ought to be additive and, in combination, massively predict invidious beliefs about the religious status of Jews. To test this hypothesis, an Index of Religious Dogmatism was constructed.[16] The word "dogmatism" was used to denote the intransigence, militancy, and doctrinal literalism that characterize a religious perspective built on an orthodox theology, a particularist conception of one's religious status, a rejection of religious liberty, and belief in the tradition that the ancient Jews killed Christ. Thus, the Religious Dogmatism Index summarizes those elements of traditional Christianity which, we have postulated, make up the process through which the modern Jew comes to be the object of religious hostility.

The powerful findings in Table 40 fulfilled our expectations. Among Protestants, *93 per cent* of those highest on the Dogmatism Index (8)

Table 40.   RELIGIOUS DOGMATISM AND JEWISH GUILT

(Per cent who agreed "The Jews can never be forgiven for what they did to Jesus until they accept Him as the True Saviour.")

| | Religious Dogmatism Index | | | | | | | |
|---|---|---|---|---|---|---|---|---|
| | Low 0 | 1 | 2 | 3 | 4 | 5 | 6 | 7 | High 8 |
| Protestants | | | | | | | | |
| Per cent | 1 | 3 | 5 | 11 | 30 | 43 | 66 | 80 | 93 |
| Number | (74) | (97) | (205) | (234) | (269) | (233) | (225) | (117) | (78) |
| Catholics | | | | | | | | |
| Per cent | 0[a] | 0 | 0 | 4 | 0 | 8 | 27 | 30 | 39 |
| Number | (4) | (14) | (31) | (44) | (52) | (71) | (71) | (43) | (18) |

[a] Percentage would not normally be computed; appears here only because of its descriptive interest.

agreed "the Jews can never be forgiven for what they did to Jesus until they accept Him as the True Saviour," while only *1 per cent* of those lowest on the index agreed with this statement. The proportions agreeing systematically increase with the degree of dogmatism. Among Roman

[16] The scoring was as follows: Orthodoxy Index: High = 2, medium = 1, low = 0. Particularism Index: High = 2, medium = 1, low = 0. Religious Libertarianism Index: Low = 2, medium = 1, high = 0. The Jews responsible = 2; the Jews not responsible = 0. Thus the index ranged from 8 (highest dogmatism) through 0 (lowest dogmatism).

Catholics the effects are equally systematic, but of course agreement is considerably lower in all cases than among Protestants. Thus, while no Catholic in the lowest three points of the index agreed with the statement, 39 per cent of those in the highest category agreed. Given the reluctance of Catholics to accept this statement a percentage-point difference between high and low categories equal to that found among Protestants was statistically impossible.

However, the association among the variables is roughly equivalent in both instances. Indeed, looking at these findings in another way it is possible to say that our theoretical model works somewhat *better* among Catholics than among Protestants. While 58 per cent of the Protestants who agreed with this statement fall into the upper three points on the scale, 83 per cent of the Catholics who agreed are found here. If one thinks of our theoretical scheme as an attempt to specify what kind of person will agree with this negative image of the modern Jew, then it appears that among Catholics virtually everyone who agreed closely approximates our description. Thus, our model seems to come somewhat closer to specifying completely the *necessary* conditions among Catholics, while it comes closer to specifying fully the *sufficient* conditions among Protestants: Virtually every Protestant who met the maximum conditions specified by our theory agreed with the statement. In addition, virtually no one completely lacking these characteristics, whether Protestant or Catholic, agreed.

A similar pattern appears in Table 41, where the effect of the Dog-

Table 41.   RELIGIOUS DOGMATISM AND JEWISH PUNISHMENT

Reply to: "The reason the Jews have so much trouble is because God is punishing them for rejecting Jesus."

| | Religious Dogmatism Index | | | | | | | | |
|---|---|---|---|---|---|---|---|---|---|
| | Low 0 | 1 | 2 | 3 | 4 | 5 | 6 | 7 | High 8 |
| *Per cent who agreed:* | | | | | | | | | |
| Protestants | | | | | | | | | |
| Per cent | 1 | 1 | 2 | 3 | 8 | 17 | 28 | 35 | 56 |
| Number | (74) | (97) | (206) | (236) | (273) | (233) | (227) | (118) | (75) |
| Catholics | | | | | | | | | |
| Per cent | ᵃ | 0 | 0 | 0 | 6 | 11 | 23 | 23 | 26 |
| Number | (4) | (15) | (32) | (44) | (52) | (75) | (72) | (43) | (19) |
| *Per cent who agreed or were uncertain:* | | | | | | | | | |
| Protestants | 12 | 21 | 23 | 32 | 40 | 53 | 63 | 70 | 80 |
| Catholics | ᵃ | 13 | 22 | 27 | 48 | 40 | 53 | 58 | 53 |

ᵃ Too few cases to compute stable percentage.

matism Index in seeing Jews as still being punished by God can be observed. Both Protestants and Catholics were less likely to agree with this statement than they were to support the image of the Jews as still unforgiven for the Crucifixion. However, agreement to this statement too is in large part a function of particularism, orthodoxy, seeing the ancient Jews as crucifiers, and a lack of religious libertarianism, all of which are measured jointly by the index. While agreement was lower on this item, uncertainty was a good deal higher. Sizable proportions of church members were unwilling either fully to accept or deny that the Jews' troubles came from divine wrath. When agreement and uncertainty are combined (bottom half of the table) the magnitude of the findings closely approximates that reported in Table 40.

Thus, the data strongly confirm that the process we have postulated by which Christians come to have religiously based hostility toward Jews operates dramatically in contemporary America. It must be pointed out that only a minority of modern Christians fully meet all of the characteristics specified by the theory, but to the degree they do have these characteristics Christians seem constrained to view Jews with suspicion and contempt.

# PART III.  PREJUDICE

*So far in this volume it has been established that certain attributes of Christian theology and teachings strongly predispose church members to hold hostile religious images of the modern Jew. In this section we shall see if, and to what extent, these religious images provide a basis for anti-Semitism of a secular kind.*

# CHAPTER 6

# The Concept of Anti-Semitism*

I determine who is a Jew.

—HERMANN GOERING

Anyone who approaches the topic of anti-Semitism does so with the oppressive, almost incomprehensible, knowledge of six million Jewish corpses strewn across Europe by the Nazi madness. In the face of these terrible and too contemporary facts, one risks seeming insensitive and pedantic by raising objections about what is commonly meant by anti-Semitism. Yet a phenomenon that has left such brutal scars on the human conscience deserves much more than dirges, polemics, and penitence. It demands clear explanation. But such explanation has been left generally unaccomplished despite the enormous amount of research that has been done on the topic in recent years.[1]

A major reason for this failure seems to be the virtually impregnable barriers to separating an understanding of anti-Semitism from the moral and emotional qualities of the phenomenon itself. As shall be seen in

* This chapter draws heavily on the work done by Gertrude Jaeger Selznick and John Larkins in early 1962 to provide a conceptual basis for all of the projects on anti-Semitism then planned by the Survey Research Center of the University of California at Berkeley, of which the present study is one. Further insights into how best to conceptualize anti-Semitism were forthcoming in working seminars lead by Dr. Selznick and participated in by all investigators associated with the various studies. In particular, we would like to acknowledge the contributions made by M. Brewster Smith, Joe L. Spaeth, Earl Raab, and Seymour Martin Lipset.

[1] Indeed, an entire volume has been written to summarize this vast literature; see Melvin M. Tumin, *An Inventory and Appraisal of Research on American Anti-Semitism* (New York: Freedom Books, 1961).

detail in this and the next chapter, it is clear enough that many fundamental and even obvious questions concerning anti-Semitism have been ignored by most investigators. But these questions must be raised if the study of anti-Semitism is to rise above the level of mere polemics to something that may prove useful in understanding and counteracting this age-old evil.

In order even to raise coherent questions about the causes of anti-Semitism, it is first necessary to make some decisions about what we mean by this term and to develop adequate conceptual and empirical tools for investigating it. Consequently, in this chapter we shall be concerned with establishing some very broad distinctions in the way anti-Semitism can best be conceived. Subsequent chapters will develop these distinctions further and, in addition, assess the implications of religiously based hostility toward Jews for anti-Semitism in general.

Let it be clear at the start that the decision about what will be called anti-Semitism is, in the first instance, a matter of ethics and morality. There is no reason intrinsic to social science, as such, that Jews should not be hated and persecuted. The techniques of scholarship could as well be brought to bear on questions of how to stir up bigotry as how to extinguish such acts and sentiments. Indeed, the medical and organizational skills of German professional men were enlisted to shape and implement the incredible "final solution."

These limits to social science per se are no basis for condemnation. As men, social scientists must take moral responsibility for their work, and are also entirely free to search for ethical solutions to man's countless dilemmas. Simply because, in the end, the weighing of evidence must not be biased by an investigator's moral commitments is no reason to suggest that social scientists are, or should be, morally uncommitted. To think otherwise seems absurd. Yet, such an image of the social scientist as a moral eunuch has been widely circulated for polemical effect by those whose ideological sensibilities have been offended by the facts unearthed by social science.

Consequently, it is on moral grounds that we define and condemn anti-Semitism as the hatred and persecution of Jews as a group; not the hatred of persons who happen to be Jews, but rather the hatred of persons *because* they are Jews. But to translate this moral definition into a suitable social science concept it is necessary to state more precisely what we mean by such terms as hatred and persecution.

Antagonism toward Jews, or any racial, ethnic, or cultural group, can take many forms. There can be secret and silent hatred that is never expressed in overt action. There can be insults and discrimination, rumors and vilification. Anti-Semitism may take the form of a series of inaccurate, but invidious, beliefs about Jews; it may constitute anger, fear, revulsion, disdain, or any number of unpleasant feelings. And as the history of the Jews sadly proclaims, anti-Semitism can mean physical violence, pogroms, and even death camps.

In general usage, the term anti-Semitism includes any and all of these myriad forms that antagonism toward Jews may take. While this is suitable for the requirements of everyday conversation, the lack of precision raises some difficulties when carried over into research. Yet in virtually all of the studies that have been made of the phenomenon, anti-Semitism has been used in its vague, everyday meaning, leaving its many facets unspecified and, hence, unexplored. This constitutes a major and abiding flaw in research, and as a result we have learned much less about anti-Semitism than we ought. Clearly there are crucial differences in the variety of things called anti-Semitism. From a sheerly pragmatic standpoint it obviously matters a great deal whether a man merely holds some unfavorable attitudes toward Jews or whether he is also willing to harm them physically. Furthermore, by treating anti-Semitism in such an undifferentiated way we have been prevented from observing processes and interrelations among its various facets. For example, through what stages does a man pass to reach the point where he will take part in smearing swastikas on a synagogue? In this volume we shall certainly do little more than begin to grope for answers to such basic questions, but we shall at least try to pose the rudiments of a scheme for systematically asking such questions.

To begin we shall distinguish three very general components which can be treated as a very simplified dynamic scheme making up the phenomenon of anti-Semitism: *beliefs→feelings→actions*. All of the many things usually meant by anti-Semitism can be classified as one of these three components. Furthermore, we suggest this order represents a developmental sequence of anti-Semitism. Negative beliefs about Jews may ultimately produce negative feelings toward Jews which in turn may reach sufficient intensity so that, provided an appropriate opportunity, persons may engage in hostile acts against Jews. This hypothesized sequence assumes that not only does the manifestation of anti-Semitism proceed from beliefs to feelings to actions, but that the extent of the process provides a basis for making statements about the intensity of anti-Semitism.

A classification into three components has been suggested several times before;[2] yet it has not, to our knowledge, been utilized in research. This

[2] Bernard Kramer, "Dimensions of Prejudice," *Journal of Psychology*, 1949, pp. 389–451; and Isador Chein, "Notes on a Framework for the Measurement of Discrimination and Prejudice," Appendix C in Marie Jahoda, Morton Deutsch, and Stuart Cook, *Research Methods in Social Relations*, Part One (New York: Dryden Press, 1951).

is *not* to say that previous researchers have only dealt with one component of anti-Semitism, for example, only studied anti-Semitic beliefs. On the contrary, many measures of anti-Semitism have tapped each of these components. They have done so, unfortunately, in a haphazard way. No distinctions among these various classes of items have been made and the measures have simply lumped all of these manifestations of anti-Semitism together. Differences in the mix of items in various measures tapping a particular component of anti-Semitism probably account for the great differences in estimates of the degree of anti-Semitism prevalent in modern society. For example, if willingness to engage in hostile actions toward Jews is, as we suspect, much less common than negative beliefs about Jews (which seem a necessary basis for such actions) then a measure in which half the items explore anti-Semitic acts ought to show much less general anti-Semitism than one in which action makes up only 10 per cent of the items. Thus, even for purposes of description, let alone explanation, it seems useful and necessary to distinguish among anti-Semitic beliefs, feelings, and actions.

Of course, things are not quite as simple as this three-fold scheme suggests. Undoubtedly there is a certain amount of "feedback" that operates among these components of anti-Semitism. For example, if one's anti-Semitic feelings increase, as a result of increased anti-Semitic beliefs, these feelings may subsequently operate to encourage acceptance of new anti-Semitic beliefs. Or, similarly, further to justify an anti-Semitic act, one's negative feelings and beliefs about Jews may increase after the fact. Still, the simpler statement of the process seems a sufficient starting place for an exploration of the religious roots of anti-Semitism, and makes it possible to ask to just what extent negative beliefs are in fact accompanied by negative feelings and to what degree beliefs and feelings produce a predisposition to behave in hostile ways. It also enables us to ask whether there are significant subdimensions within each of these components or whether, for example, anti-Semitic beliefs are all elements of a single negative portrait of the Jews.

In the chapters that follow we shall seek answers to these questions as we also attempt to assess the impact of religious teachings and traditions on contemporary beliefs, feelings, and actions toward Jews. Since a separate chapter will be devoted to each of these components of anti-Semitism, we shall defer more detailed discussion of each.

One final consideration is the matter of the validity of using responses to a questionnaire about beliefs, feelings, and hypothetical action as a basis for estimating anti-Semitism. The whole matter of whether attitudes "really" mean anything or whether surveys are themselves meaningful is a concern we shall leave for a more specialized forum; needless to say, we feel surveys of this kind do really mean something. However, a more germane issue of validity concerns the honesty and candor one might expect persons to display in answering such a questionnaire. Will they say how they really feel about Jews, or will they gloss over their hostilities and give "acceptable" answers? Our major reason for thinking that they will be honest by and large, aside from the obvious point that answers were entirely anonymous, arises out of the logic by which we have decided to trichotomize the phenomenon of anti-Semitism itself into belief, feeling, and action.

It may come as something of a surprise to readers long immersed in the literature on prejudice, but nobody, not even the most rampant anti-Semite, thinks of himself as a bigot. A corollary of this is that, in the main, prejudice is a *rational* pattern of behavior.

A great deal of the writing on prejudice of various kinds, drawing on Freud's contribution to our understanding of the irrational in human behavior, has been marred by what could best be described as misplaced irrationality. While it might be argued that it is irrational for persons to *hold* particular beliefs about Jews, although this too is subject to debate,[3] it seems unwarranted to think of the hostility and aggression following *from* such beliefs as essentially irrational. Considering many of the beliefs which have a long tradition as anti-Semitic stereotypes, it would be an irrational man indeed who thought such things were true of Jews without disliking or even hating Jews for being this way. The point then is, given negative beliefs about the character and intentions of Jews, persons do not see themselves as odd or demented for hating them. They do not think of themselves as bigots, because a bigot is, of course, a person who unreasonably hates, and very few persons see their own feelings as unreasonable. Perhaps a few examples selected from the many similar comments that appeared as afterthoughts penned in the last pages of the questionnaire booklet will make this point entirely clear.

A middle-aged Protestant housewife wrote:

This questionnaire is apparently for the use of finding out if I am prejudiced against Negroes or Jews *which I can say I am not*. I feel they should have a place in the community if they earn the right. So far the Negroes are uneducated and unclean and haven't earned their place in the average community. The Jews are neither and they fit in most any place, *but they are underhanded and sneaky.* [her italics]

---

[3] Given their particular location in society and the culture in which they are nourished, it seems reasonable enough to expect many persons to believe what they do about Jews. Not humane or accurate on their part, but nonetheless reasonable.

A retired Protestant executive wrote:

Some of my replies in connection with races and faiths, other than my own, might seem prejudiced to some. But during my forty years of business life I have had a very good opportunity to observe the characteristics of the Negro and the Jew. Granted that some are much better men and women than I am. However, in my opinion, by far more than the majority of them retain the distinctive traits attributed to their race and/or faith . . . Jews, as a rule, try almost every devious trick in the book to alleviate themselves from the fulfill-ment of their just obligations.

Both of these respondents were well-educated and were obviously aware of the "enlightened" public norms concerning prejudice. But al-though they knew they did not agree with these tolerant views, neither felt himself unreasonable or intemperate. If anything, they seem extremely sincere and even reflective in their antagonism toward Negroes and Jews. One may well challenge their judgments, but once made, these judgments logically generate sufficient grounds for ill will. It is for this reason that our study, and others making up the Survey Research Center's general project on anti-Semitism, will give initial attention to the ways in which persons come to hold these negative beliefs about Jews. For this seems the basic issue from which the feeling and action components of anti-Semitism follow.

This at least subjectively rational character of prejudice strongly militates against the possibility that people covered up and denied their actual sentiments. A person who feels his position is legitimate is not easily embarrassed about it, especially within the privacy of an anonymous questionnaire. But there is even further reason for putting some stock in the honesty of these responses: A rather large number of people proved their lack of self-consciousness in a most direct way, by selecting anti-Semitic responses.[4]

---

[4] This is not to say that no one disguised his anti-Semitism in answering the questionnaire, but as will be seen from the consistency of responses, this was not common.

CHAPTER 7

# Anti-Semitic Beliefs

> A wave of anti-Semitism is sweeping the world as a reaction against (1) Jewish control of news channels, (2) international Jewish banking, and (3) atheistic Communism, which was originally spawned in Jewish capitalism and Jewish intellectualism.
>
> —REV. GERALD B. WINROD (1940)

If, as was pointed out in the last chapter, the term anti-Semitism has usually been treated as an undifferentiated mixture of beliefs, feelings, and actions concerning Jews, notions of what constitutes an anti-Semitic belief have also confused polemical, emotional, and analytic elements. A good many studies have been willing to consider *any* acknowledgment that Jews are in *any way* different from non-Jews as being fundamentally anti-Semitic. Throughout his recent study, based on data from several national surveys, Stember used the two following items, among others of course, as measures of anti-Semitism: "Do you think there are any differences between Jews and other people?" "Do you think Jews are different from other people in any way?"[1]

In short, it could be said honestly that anyone who acknowledged the existence of a group of people identifiable as Jews would have been called an anti-Semite in such investigations. This is ridiculous. In order to argue

[1] Charles Herbert Stember, *Education and Attitude Change* (New York: Institute of Human Relations Press, 1961). Stember recognizes some ambiguities are involved in using these items and acknowledges that the question might be answered in a factual, rather than only an unfavorable, way. Yet his use and discussion of the items assumes persons will primarily respond "yes" in an unfavorable way. As will be pointed out, even if this were true, we would still not want to call the response anti-Semitism per se.

107

seriously that such a wide definition of anti-Semitism is reasonable, one would also have to argue that there is no such thing as a Jew. For clearly, if there are no criteria by which a Jew may be identified, no way a Jew can be distinguished from a non-Jew, then there are, in effect, no Jews.

Such groups as Jewish charities, Jewish defense organizations, and the like, by their very existence, make such definitions of anti-Semitism absurd, yet these same groups have shown a propensity to accept and employ such definitions. While there are indeed polemical advantages in such dual conceptions, clearly such premises betray all efforts to conduct a sober assessment of the status, origins, and effects of anti-Semitism.

Furthermore, these militant definitions, which seemingly rest on the notion that Jews do not really exist, have greatly confused the issues. A major difficulty concerns the fact that Jews often ratify many of the beliefs which have been classified as anti-Semitic under these loose definitions. This should be no surprise, for clearly Jews do exist and can be differentiated from non-Jews by certain cultural characteristics; if this were not the case, anti-Semitism would be meaningless and irrelevant. However, having decided to class as anti-Semitic *any* statements concerning Jewish "differences," regardless of content, researchers have been gravely threatened to find Jews accepting some of these statements too. For if Jews hold such beliefs, how then can we call gentiles anti-Semitic for doing likewise? The usual solution adopted in this dilemma has been most unfortunate. Instead of re-examining their premises, investigators have conjured up the notion of Jewish self-hatred or Jewish anti-Semitism to resolve the problem. Jews too can be infected with the virus of anti-Semitic bigotry, we are told.

This is not to say that there have not been occasional Jews who made a career of anti-Semitism and others who in a more private way have felt hatred toward their ethnic brethren. Such renegades are common to all social groups. But surely the existence, for example, of former priests who earn their living through anti-Catholic writings and speeches has not led us to serious discussions of Catholic self-hatred. The point is that, as it has been generally employed, the term Jewish self-hatred has been a convenient polemic to cover the extreme chauvinism employed in defining anti-Semitism. The real problem is to sort out beliefs that merely indicate differences between Jews and gentiles and those that imply invidious differences—to separate mere description or honest criticism from contempt.

But if just any belief about Jews is not to be called anti-Semitic, what kinds of beliefs can be so labeled? This, of course, raises moral and ethical questions which may lie on the border of the purely sociological.

Yet the problem seems answerable only on some objective, rather than emotional, grounds. In this study we shall be concerned with *beliefs about Jews which, on the face of them, provide a reasonable basis for negative sentiments and perhaps hostile actions toward Jews.* That is, we shall select beliefs which, if true, would seem grounds for feeling at least uneasy, and perhaps even violent hatred, toward Jews.

This does not necessarily mean that such beliefs invariably do lead men to be hostile toward Jews. This is a question we shall take up later in connection with negative feelings toward Jews. However, although such beliefs may be held without producing any negative reaction toward Jews, due to extreme tolerance, saintliness, or even stupidity, they ought strongly to predispose men toward negative sentiments and rarely produce admiration. We should not classify beliefs as anti-Semitic which may be ambiguous in their implications—beliefs which may both form part of an anti-Semitic belief system or as easily be held by persons who bear no ill will toward Jews. These issues will be developed further as we examine specific items.

## A Measure of Anti-Semitic Beliefs

A long battery of items was included in the questionnaire to assess the portrait of the contemporary Jew held by members of Christian churches. Some of these items made strongly negative statements about Jews, some were relatively neutral, and some could well be considered favorable beliefs about Jews. All respondents were asked for each statement, "Do you feel Jews tend to be like this?" The answers supplied were "yes," "somewhat," and "no." In what follows we shall report how members of the various denominations answered these questions, both to get a general understanding of how church people perceive the modern Jew and to seek some suitable items to construct an index of anti-Semitic beliefs. A number of standard themes recur in the secular negative stereotype of the Jew. In examining responses to these questions about Jews, it seems useful to group items within some of these general themes.

### The Avaricious Jew

Perhaps the most constant theme in anti-Semitism from medieval times down to the present is of the Jew as a cheap, miserly manipulator of money, forever preoccupied with materialism, and consequently possessing virtually unlimited economic power. From Shakespeare's creation of the grasping Shylock to Hitler's ravings about Jewish international bankers,

this particular belief about Jewish character and wealth has been one
of the most significant tenets in the faith of anti-Semitism. Its penetration
of our culture is demonstrated by the widespread use of the verbs "to
Jew," meaning to cheat, and "to Jew down," meaning to drive down the
price unfairly by bickering. A good deal of careful scholarship has connected the origins of these beliefs with money-lending arrangements in
the Dark Ages. Christian doctrine once held that lending money at interest
was usury and proscribed such activity for all Christians. The Jewish
interpretation of this same Old Testament prohibition was that it only
applied to lending to one another, and that lending at interest to gentiles
was permissible. Because of the economic difficulties created by the
Church's ban on lending at interest, it was inevitable that Christians, particularly rulers, would borrow from the Jews (for only lending, not bor-
rowing, was sinful). Often the role of money lender was forced on the
Jews, and frequently the loans were not repaid. But for several centuries
the Jews provided the only credit resources of Europe. From this comes
the legend of Jewish economic power and usury. Despite the number of
times that this stereotype has been exposed as unfounded,[2] the notion that
"the Jews have all the money" has continued. We may now see how
commonly these images are held by contemporary Christian church
members. A number of items in the questionnaire dealt with various
aspects of Jewish avariciousness. These appear in Table 42.

The first three items in the table attempt to assess beliefs about the
extent of Jewish economic success. Looking at these items it is clear that
the majority of our respondents believe Jews occupy a powerful economic
position. In response to the statement, "On the average, Jews are wealthier
than Christians," 33 per cent of the Protestants and 30 per cent of the
Roman Catholics said "yes." An additional 23 and 28 per cent respectively responded "somewhat." Thus, more than half of all the church
members in the sample were inclined to believe this statement about
Jewish wealth.

Responses to the second question in the table reveal that virtually
the same proportions in each denomination as believed Jews are wealthier
also believed that "international banking tends to be dominated by Jews."
This belief has played a major role in political anti-Semitism and has been
used to conjure up images of the Jews funding munitions industries and
profiting from both sides in time of war. The tremendous banking power
of the House of Rothschild has lent further support to such beliefs, which
also nicely coincide with medieval traditions of money-lending and the

---

[2] A careful study by *Fortune* (February 1936), showed that Jews had virtually
no role in banking or heavy industry.

## Table 42. IMAGES OF THE AVARICIOUS JEW

| | Cong. | Meth. | Epis. | D.of Christ | Pres. | A.Luth. | A.Bap. | M.Luth. | S.Bap. | Sects | Total Prot. | Cath. |
|---|---|---|---|---|---|---|---|---|---|---|---|---|
| Number | (151) | (415) | (416) | (50) | (495) | (208) | (141) | (116) | (79) | (255) | (2,326) | (545) |
| *"On the average, Jews are wealthier than Christians."* | | | | | | | | | | | | |
| "Yes" | 23% | 28% | 31% | 36% | 34% | 34% | 30% | 36% | 37% | 48% | 33% | 30% |
| "Somewhat" | 26 | 24 | 21 | 20 | 22 | 25 | 30 | 22 | 24 | 23 | 23 | 28 |
| *"International banking tends to be dominated by Jews."* | | | | | | | | | | | | |
| "Yes" | 26% | 24% | 28% | 30% | 27% | 25% | 23% | 22% | 27% | 28% | 26% | 23% |
| "Somewhat" | 23 | 24 | 24 | 20 | 21 | 21 | 22 | 22 | 25 | 23 | 22 | 22 |
| *"The movie and television industries are pretty much run by Jews."* | | | | | | | | | | | | |
| "Yes" | 51% | 46% | 59% | 46% | 52% | 48% | 35% | 54% | 25% | 28% | 47% | 46% |
| "Somewhat" | 26 | 30 | 22 | 38 | 23 | 25 | 30 | 18 | 27 | 19 | 25 | 28 |
| *"Jews are more likely than Christians to cheat in business."* | | | | | | | | | | | | |
| "Yes" | 9% | 10% | 14% | 22% | 17% | 20% | 16% | 21% | 28% | 26% | 17% | 14% |
| "Somewhat" | 12 | 16 | 12 | 22 | 18 | 16 | 16 | 20 | 15 | 22 | 16 | 15 |
| *"Because Jews are not bound by Christian ethics, they do things to get ahead that Christians generally will not do."* | | | | | | | | | | | | |
| "Yes" | 11% | 12% | 17% | 18% | 17% | 17% | 15% | 22% | 22% | 27% | 17% | 14% |
| "Somewhat" | 20 | 17 | 15 | 32 | 20 | 20 | 26 | 22 | 27 | 21 | 19 | 21 |
| *"Jews tend to wear flashy clothes and jewelry."* | | | | | | | | | | | | |
| "Yes" | 16% | 15% | 23% | 8% | 20% | 17% | 16% | 20% | 15% | 22% | 18% | 15% |
| "Somewhat" | 23 | 22 | 28 | 34 | 27 | 31 | 20 | 20 | 22 | 21 | 25 | 28 |

international dispersion of the Jewish people. As worded in the present form, however, the belief does not necessarily imply hostility; and many persons, as will be seen shortly, were making what they felt to be a factual response devoid of ill will.

Christian perceptions of Jewish economic power increase sharply on the third item on the table. Here virtually three-fourths were inclined to believe, "The movie and television industries are pretty much run by Jews." Indeed, about half answered this question with an unqualified "yes."

Denominational differences among Protestants on each of these three items are rather modest and show no consistent trends. Since none of these items is necessarily hostile, this is about what we would expect. However, denominational patterns do begin to come into focus on subsequent items where neutrality has been replaced by unfriendly implications.

The first of these more hostile beliefs, the fourth in the table, states, "Jews are more likely than Christians to cheat in business." Over-all, 17 per cent of the Protestants and 14 per cent of the Roman Catholics answered "yes." An additional 16 per cent of Protestants and 15 per cent of the Catholics responded "somewhat." Hence, about a third of our respondents found some truth in this statement. Among Protestants, the proportions answering "yes" rose from 9 per cent of the Congregationalists to 26 per cent among the sects and 28 per cent of the Southern Baptists, and 43 and 48 per cent of those in these two conservative groups thought the Jews at least "somewhat" inclined to cheat in business.

Rather similar distributions can be seen in responses to the fifth question: "Because Jews are not bound by Christian ethics, they will do things to get ahead that Christians generally will not do." Among Protestants, 17 per cent agreed and 19 per cent answered "somewhat"; among Roman Catholics 14 per cent and 21 per cent gave these responses. Again, within the Protestant group, differences increased from left to right, from 11 per cent of the Congregationalists who said "yes," to 27 per cent of those in sects who did so.

Thus, a majority of Christians are convinced Jews hold powerful economic positions in society, and a substantial minority see Jews as behaving unethically in pursuit of material gain. Not only are Jews wealthy, they cheat and connive. Open-end responses to a series of sentence completions provided an occasion for many respondents to put these images of the avaricious Jew in their own words.[3] For example:

"I can't understand why Jews . . ." or "It's a shame that Jews . . .
    "are so prosperous in business and live so high here."

[3] See Questionnaire following Index.

"are such money-grabbers."

"have no ethics and will take every chance to squeeze some profits."

"seek world domination. It is very serious."

"like to take advantage in business deals by double dealing and unfair practices."

The last question in the table concerns Jewish materialism from a slightly different perspective, a preoccupation with tasteless displays of wealth: "Jews tend to wear flashy clothes and jewelry." Altogether, 18 per cent of the Protestants responded "yes," and 25 per cent said "somewhat." Among Roman Catholics 15 per cent and 28 per cent gave these responses. Differences between the various Protestant groups are slight and inconsistent.

Thus we have seen that beliefs about Jews as materialistic, dishonest, and vulgar are relatively common among contemporary Christian church members.

## The Egocentric and Exclusive Jew

A second general theme in anti-Semitic beliefs depicts Jews as conceited, insolent, overbearing, and, as a result of convictions of superiority, clannish and exclusive. As can be seen in Table 43, such beliefs are commonly held by Christians in our sample.

The first item asserts, "Jews believe they are better than other people." Among Protestants 16 per cent agreed and 24 per cent thought this was somewhat true; and Roman Catholics agreed in rather similar proportions —13 and 23 per cent. The proportions holding this image of the Jew increase moderately from the more liberal to the more conservative Protestant bodies with more than half of the Southern Baptists and sect members ratifying it.

Agreement rises sharply on the second item: "Jews want to remain different from other people, and yet they are touchy if people notice these differences." Here an image of Jews as inclined to exclusiveness is combined with feelings that Jews demand special treatment for themselves. Fifty-seven per cent of the Protestants and 49 per cent of the Roman Catholics at least felt that Jews are "somewhat" like this. Differences among Protestant groups who answered either "yes" or "somewhat" range from 49 per cent of the Congregationalists to 67 per cent of the Southern Baptists.

Perceptions of Jewish exclusiveness increase markedly on items that have a more clearly neutral tone. Hence, 34 per cent of the Protestants agreed that "Jews like to be with other Jews and tend to avoid non-Jews," while an additional 38 per cent felt this was somewhat true. Thirty-three

Table 43. DENOMINATION AND THE EGOCENTRIC, EXCLUSIVE JEW

| | Cong. | Meth. | Epis. | D.of Christ | Pres. | A.Luth. | A.Bap. | M.Luth. | S.Bap. | Sects | Total Prot. | Cath. |
|---|---|---|---|---|---|---|---|---|---|---|---|---|
| Number | (151) | (415) | (416) | (50) | (495) | (208) | (141) | (116) | (79) | (255) | (2,326) | (545) |
| *"Jews believe they are better than other people."* | | | | | | | | | | | | |
| "Yes" | 10% | 12% | 17% | 18% | 16% | 14% | 12% | 22% | 25% | 24% | 16% | 13% |
| "Somewhat" | 23 | 22 | 23 | 22 | 24 | 25 | 28 | 18 | 28 | 27 | 24 | 23 |
| *"Jews want to remain different from other people, and yet they are touchy if people notice these differences."* | | | | | | | | | | | | |
| "Yes" | 20% | 23% | 32% | 30% | 28% | 27% | 26% | 28% | 41% | 32% | 28% | 23% |
| "Somewhat" | 29 | 30 | 26 | 32 | 27 | 29 | 35 | 35 | 25 | 21 | 29 | 26 |
| *"Jews like to be with other Jews and tend to avoid non-Jews."* | | | | | | | | | | | | |
| "Yes" | 29% | 29% | 34% | 22% | 35% | 33% | 25% | 25% | 46% | 45% | 34% | 33% |
| "Somewhat" | 38 | 42 | 38 | 56 | 39 | 38 | 39 | 39 | 35 | 32 | 38 | 35 |
| *"Jewish parents tend to be very concerned about making sure that their children marry Jews."* | | | | | | | | | | | | |
| "Yes" | 66% | 66% | 68% | 68% | 69% | 69% | 69% | 75% | 89% | 76% | 69% | 72% |
| "Somewhat" | 25 | 25 | 23 | 24 | 22 | 21 | 18 | 18 | 6 | 12 | 21 | 18 |

per cent of the Catholics answered "yes" on this question and 35 per cent chose "somewhat."

An overwhelming consensus obtains among church members in thinking, "Jewish parents tend to be very concerned about making sure their children marry Jews." Ninety per cent of both Protestant and Roman Catholics thought this at least somewhat true, and seven out of ten were in full agreement with the statement. As we shall discuss later, while an anti-Semite may infuse hostility into a belief such as this, a great many of the persons who agreed with this statement did so simply to acknowledge a rather obvious fact about the Jewish community and felt no particular objections to such a state of affairs.

In summary, however, clearly many Christians do see the Jew in a negative light as egocentric, touchy, and exclusive. As respondents wrote in:

"I can't understand why Jews . . ." or "It's a shame that Jews . . .
 "feel compelled to be so clannish."
 "are sometimes so overbearing and pushy."
 "believe they are being picked on all the time."
 "brag so much."
 "are always screaming persecution, when they hate everyone else."
 "think they're too damn good to associate with others. Who needs them?"

## The Unpatriotic and Subversive Jew[4]

Having barred Jews from citizenship or otherwise meaningful participation in civic affairs for centuries, Europeans suspected Jews lacked any great patriotic fervor and cared little about the destiny of "the Fatherland." In addition, the internationalism of Jews, dispersed in ghettos all across Europe, cast doubt on their loyalty to *any* particular nation. But while these beliefs about Jews were common, they lacked great relevance so long as Jews were shut out from national life. All this changed with emancipation.

Following the suspension of medieval restrictions on Jews, which occurred in most European states during the nineteenth century, Jews began to take up active roles in national life: to seek political office, to enlist in the army, and otherwise to become full citizens. This entry of Jews into the general society was opposed intransigently by parties of the

[4] This section has been broadly informed by Hannah Arendt's, *The Origins of Totalitarianism* (New York: Meridian Books, 1958); and Werner Cohn's "The Politics of American Jews," in Marshall Sklare (ed.), *The Jews: Social Patterns of an American Group* (Glencoe, Ill.: The Free Press, 1958), pp. 614–626.

right, especially in Germany, Austria, and France. Indeed, the famous Dreyfus case was merely the focal point for a general struggle between the old aristocracy and the Republican left over the admission of Jews to citizenship, and represented an effort to portray Jews as potential sub-versives unfitted for the officer corps.[5] This image of Jews reached venomous heights during the Nazi reign of terror. The Jews, as Hitler's all-purpose scapegoats, were endlessly identified as saboteurs and defeatists who stabbed Germany in the back during World War I.

A second theme in beliefs about Jewish subversiveness is related to the political bonds between Jews and left-wing parties following the nine-teenth century emancipation. Jewish emancipation was achieved by the left, which proposed a secular or national concept of citizenship—that national residence alone, rather than religious affiliation, should determine citizenship. Opposition from the right, determined that the state should remain Christian and citizenship require proper religious status, explicitly rejected Jewish political rights.

Consequently, as Jews moved into participation in civic life, their only political option lay with the left. Only leftist parties would acknowl-edge their rights and permit their membership. Soon democratic parties of the left had leading Jewish members. As Cohn noted:

In parties of the moderate and constitutional left, Jews were often able to play prominent roles as intellectuals, journalists, and parliamentarians; one recalls names like Lasker and Rathenau in Germany and Cremieux and Blum in France. Undoubtedly, moderate democratic movements have claimed the allegiance of the overwhelming majority of Europe's Jews. When a strictly Orthodox rabbi, Dob Berush B. Isaac Meisels, was elected, with Catholic help, to represent Cracow in the provisional Austrian Reichsrat of 1848, he took his seat to the left of the aisle. Observing the surprise of the presiding officer at seeing an Orthodox rabbi among the liberals of the left, Meisels remarked, "*Juden haben keine Recht,*" (Jews have no right.) This describes—*mutatis mutandis*—the situation to this day.

It was the most normal thing for a Jew to support one of the moderate left parties.[6]

For many Jews, however, liberal parties did not provide an entirely adequate solution to their problems and aspirations for full membership in society. These parties remained, for the most part, within the religious and cultural traditions of their societies. Within their ranks Christians were still Christians, and Jews tended to remain Jews. The sense of separa-

[5] See Arendt, *op. cit.*, and Paul-Marie de la Gorce, *The French Army* (New York: George Braziller, 1963).
[6] Cohn, *op. cit.*, p. 616.

tion, though greatly muted, still remained. Furthermore, Jews who became prominent in liberal parties experienced violent and vitriolic attacks from the anti-Semitic right. The sacrifices required of liberal Jewish politicians often seemed excessive. Consequently, Jews perhaps had strong motives for their prominence in radical and revolutionary parties which typically rejected the very cultural traditions that separated Jews and Christians. This was perhaps especially true in Czarist Russia where legal emancipation had not even been granted and where there was no opportunity for Jewish political participation within the legal framework of the state. Subsequently, Jewish intellectuals played major roles in the Bolshevik revolution.

While it is undoubtedly true, as Cohn noted, that the majority of Jews who participated in politics at all were associated with moderate democratic movements, the prominence of a few in the extreme left coincided with the anti-Semitic line of rightist parties. The right was thus provided an opportunity to combine the "revolutionary menace" and the "Jewish menace," which ultimately culminated in Hitler's constant ravings against "Jew-Communists."

Beginning in medieval suspicions, then, and amplified by Jewish association with the political left following the emancipation, the image of the Jew as unpatriotic and subversive took on major emphasis in European versions of anti-Semitism.

The waves of immigrants during the late nineteenth century brought this European image of the Jew to America. However, it failed to become a salient part of American politics and, indeed, seems not to have become so important a theme in American anti-Semitism as the stereotype of the avaricious Jew.[7]

However, events in the 1930s and 1940s etched the beliefs about Jewish "Bolshevism" and "subversion" somewhat deeper into American public consciousness. For a number of reasons, American Jews were prominent in the Communist party and the Trotskyite and other radical left movements during the depression and following World War II. While only a tiny proportion of Jews were active in left radicalism during this period, they were highly visible and made up a significant proportion of the membership of the various parties and groups. A traditional associa-

[7] The very surprising finding that anti-Semitism seems to have played no important role in generating support for even so explicitly anti-Semitic a political movement as that led by Rev. Charles Coughlin was made by Seymour Martin Lipset [see "Three Decades of the Radical Right: Coughlinites, McCarthyites, and Birchers," in Daniel Bell (ed.), *The Radical Right* (Garden City, N.Y.: Doubleday, 1963), pp. 313–377]. Lipset's paper was written as part of the same research project that produced the present volume.

tion with the left brought from Europe, the lack of vigorous opposition by Western democracies to the menace and the anti-Semitic madness of the Nazis, the anti-Semitism of American *bunds* and other Fascist groups which appeared here during this same depression period, and the high representation of Jews among American intellectuals, who, as a group, seemed prone to radical leftism at this time, probably all played an important role in accounting for this overrepresentation of American Jews in Marxist and Stalinist groups. Because many Communists were Jews, many Americans readily accepted the fallacy that many Jews were Communists.[8]

Following the war, when the rise of the cold war again lent new impetus to Communist-hunting, this association between Jews and Communism was further reinforced by the Jewishness of principal figures in the famous spy trials. The basic commitment of national leaders and parties to democratic principles prevented these facts from being exploited in mainstream politics. But they were of course seized upon avidly by extremists already committed to political anti-Semitism and probably too had some diffuse effect upon public opinion where grass-roots anti-Semitism provided a receptive predisposition to impute evil to Jews.

In any event, while political anti-Semitism has never become a significant force in American national politics, the stereotype of the Jew as a political unreliable has had a long career and received considerable reinforcement from the visibility of Jews in radical left movements.

The question remains, with the demise of a viable radical left, how widely held is this image of the Jew among American church members today? Turning to Table 44, we may find some answers to this question.

The first item in the table indicates that a Jewish-Communism link is not believed by the majority of Christian church members. In response to the statement, "Jews are less likely than Christians to oppose Communism," 8 per cent of all Protestants said "yes," and another 7 per cent said "somewhat." Roman Catholics gave somewhat greater support to these statements, with 10 per cent saying "yes" and 11 per cent "somewhat." Within Protestantism the proportions who saw at least some truth in the statement vary from 8 per cent of the Disciples of Christ to 23 per cent of the Southern Baptists. While these percentages are not as high as those we have seen in relation to the avaricious and egocentric-exclusive images, still they must not be dismissed as minor. When 15 per cent of the Protestants and 21 per cent of the Roman Catholics do to some degree hold the belief that Jews are soft on Communism, this seems serious. Prejudice, after all, is not a matter of majority vote.

[8] Irving Howe and Louis Coser, *The American Communist Party: A Critical History* (New York: Praeger, 1962).

Table 44.  DENOMINATION AND THE UNPATRIOTIC, SUBVERSIVE JEW

| | Cong. | Meth. | Epis. | D.of Christ | Pres. | A.Luth. | A.Bap. | M.Luth. | S.Bap. | Sects | Total Prot. | Cath. |
|---|---|---|---|---|---|---|---|---|---|---|---|---|
| Number | (151) | (415) | (416) | (50) | (495) | (208) | (141) | (116) | (79) | (255) | (2,326) | (545) |
| *"Jews are less likely than Christians to oppose Communism."* | | | | | | | | | | | | |
| "Yes" | 4% | 5% | 8% | 2% | 7% | 13% | 5% | 10% | 13% | 11% | 8% | 10% |
| "Somewhat" | 8 | 6 | 8 | 6 | 8 | 7 | 5 | 5 | 10 | 7 | 7 | 11 |
| *"Jews, in general, are inclined to be more loyal to Israel than to America."* | | | | | | | | | | | | |
| "Yes" | 5% | 9% | 10% | 12% | 11% | 14% | 13% | 20% | 20% | 24% | 13% | 10% |
| "Somewhat" | 20 | 15 | 15 | 18 | 20 | 16 | 13 | 22 | 24 | 22 | 18 | 16 |
| *"Jewish boys were less likely than Christian boys to volunteer for service in the armed forces during the last war."* | | | | | | | | | | | | |
| "Yes" | 7% | 8% | 11% | 4% | 10% | 10% | 9% | 15% | 13% | 12% | 10% | 10% |
| "Somewhat" | 7 | 8 | 11 | 14 | 12 | 11 | 11 | 13 | 18 | 11 | 11 | 12 |

The creation of the state of Israel following World War II and the major role American Jews played in funding and supporting the new Jewish state gives special relevance to the second item in the table. Here respondents were asked whether they had perceived in American Zionism and the ubiquitous Israel bond activities some signs of disloyalty toward the United States by American Jews. Thirty-one per cent of the Protestants and 26 per cent of the Catholics felt it at least somewhat true that "Jews, in general, are inclined to be more loyal to Israel than to America." Many respondents penned in further comments on this issue. One wrote: "I don't know why they don't all move over there. I guess the money is too good here and they're more loyal to money than even to Israel."

Among Protestant denominations the proportions believing that Jews are more loyal to Israel increase sharply from left to right across the table. Twenty-four per cent of the Methodists thought it at least somewhat true (only 9 per cent were certain) while 44 per cent of the sect members accepted it (24 per cent said "yes").

The third line in the table looks at what might be called an alleged symptom of Jewish lack of patriotism, the old "draft-dodger" stereotype. Respondents were asked to assess the truth of the statement, "Jewish boys were less likely than Christian boys to volunteer for service in the armed forces during the last war." As can be seen in the table, this image of the Jew was less commonly held than that of greater Jewish loyalty to Israel, but believed slightly more frequently than was the notion that Jews are soft on Communism. Twenty-one per cent of the Protestants and 22 per cent of the Roman Catholics felt this statement was at least somewhat true. As with previous items, within Protestantism an increasing proportion support the statement as one reads from left to right across the denominations.

In summary, perceptions of the Jew as soft on Communism, more loyal to Israel than to America, and as a draft dodger are relatively widely held: From 20 to 30 per cent of these Christian church members indicated their support for these images of the subversive and unpatriotic Jew.

## Jewish Intellectualism and Success

The ambivalence of beliefs about Jews is evidenced by the fact that Jews are frequently thought to be especially intelligent and talented by persons who nonetheless dislike them. Indeed, one theme in anti-Semitism is that the Jew constitutes a grave threat because he is such a worthy opponent. Inadvertently, in constructing the questionnaire, all the items on Jewish intellectualism and talent were favorably or neutrally worded.

As we shall discuss in some detail shortly, items that contain no explicit hostility can be agreed to by both anti-Semitic and non-anti-Semitic persons and thus are of little use for measuring anti-Semitism. Nevertheless, the data seem worth reporting simply to give some estimate of how commonly this image of the Jew is held even if we can only infer whether or not the belief is part of a negative or positive portrait, and is likely both.

Turning to Table 45, we see that approximately half of the persons in the sample were inclined to agree that "An unusual number of the world's greatest men have been Jews." Furthermore, there is little variation among Protestant groups; roughly the same proportions agreed in each denomination.

Roughly a third of the persons in all denominations thought it likely true that "Jewish children tend to get better grades in school than Christian children do." Of perhaps even greater interest is the last item in the table, which shows that more than 90 per cent of both Protestants and Catholics are inclined to see Jews as highly motivated—"Jews are ambitious and work hard to succeed." This last item is an excellent illustration of how a belief about Jews may be negative, neutral, or positive depending on the belief context in which it is set. Given the virtual unanimity this item provoked, it is clear that many persons felt it was true who also rejected all negative items about Jews, while many who held explicitly hostile images of Jews believe this statement too. Obviously, then, the meaning of the belief differs greatly depending on what else one thinks of Jews.

Having examined these available items on beliefs about Jews we may now select some to serve as a measure of anti-Semitic beliefs. As stated at the beginning of this chapter, we shall consider as anti-Semitic *only* beliefs which manifestly make a negative assertion about Jews and exclude items, like the one concerning Jewish ambition and hard work, where the meaning of the belief is problematic. That is, such neutral beliefs *may* be encompassed in an anti-Semitic portrait, but they need not imply anti-Semitism.

As it turns out, this decision to exclude apparently neutral items from an anti-Semitism index need not rest purely on moral and conceptual considerations. For our assertions that such neutral items can be held by both anti-Semites and persons favorable or neutral toward Jews were supported by the data. A factor analysis of the items we have just presented revealed there were two interpretable independent (orthogonal) factors underlying these data. The first of these contained negative statements about Jews; the second was made up of items which could be accepted without implying anything unfavorable about Jews. Thus, both

Table 45. DENOMINATION AND JEWISH INTELLECTUALISM AND SUCCESS

| | Cong. | Meth. | Epis. | D.of Christ | Pres. | A.Luth. | A.Bap. | M.Luth. | S.Bap. | Sects | Total Prot. | Cath. |
|---|---|---|---|---|---|---|---|---|---|---|---|---|
| Number | (151) | (415) | (416) | (50) | (495) | (208) | (141) | (116) | (79) | (255) | (2,326) | (545) |
| *"An unusual number of the world's greatest men have been Jews."* | | | | | | | | | | | | |
| "Yes" | 38% | 34% | 40% | 38% | 36% | 31% | 28% | 31% | 32% | 36% | 35% | 30% |
| "Somewhat" | 23 | 20 | 19 | 20 | 17 | 13 | 19 | 23 | 19 | 18 | 18 | 20 |
| *"Jewish children tend to get better grades in school than Christian children do."* | | | | | | | | | | | | |
| "Yes" | 20% | 14% | 22% | 16% | 19% | 14% | 16% | 16% | 6% | 16% | 17% | 14% |
| "Somewhat" | 21 | 17 | 23 | 16 | 17 | 16 | 15 | 20 | 15 | 11 | 18 | 16 |
| *"Jews are ambitious and work hard to succeed."* | | | | | | | | | | | | |
| "Yes" | 76% | 75% | 79% | 74% | 76% | 73% | 75% | 80% | 71% | 77% | 76% | 77% |
| "Somewhat" | 17 | 18 | 15 | 20 | 16 | 19 | 18 | 14 | 14 | 13 | 16 | 15 |

persons who accepted and persons who rejected unfavorable items about Jews were inclined to accept neutral items. For example, many agreed that "Jews like to be with other Jews and tend to avoid non-Jews," or that "Jewish parents tend to be very concerned about making sure their children marry Jews," as mere statements of fact implying nothing unfavorable about Jews. For others, these statements represented an image of the exclusive and "clannish" Jew.

Thus, while the correlations between negative and neutral images of Jews were reasonably high (each of the two items above was correlated with "Jews cheat in business"; the correlation coefficients were +.385 and +.352 respectively) it seems clear that such neutral beliefs are best regarded as *correlates of* anti-Semitism, rather than as anti-Semitism per se.

The second important finding of the factor analysis is that the negative items fell in a single factor. Thus, there is no need to distinguish several types of anti-Semitic beliefs and construct separate measures of each. Instead, these data suggest that anti-Semitic beliefs tend to form a single coherent negative picture of the Jew rather than a variety of pictures held independently of one another. Since the underlying logic of factor analyses, and their proper interpretation and use in the social sciences, are still a matter of considerable doubt and some confusion, we have employed this technique in a very incidental way, as one of several tests of these notions. Further attention to the validity and internal consistency of the measure finally arrived at will be given shortly.

Thus far we have specified that only beliefs which on the face of them clearly imply a negative image can be used to measure anti-Semitism. In presenting items included in the questionnaire a number of negative statements about Jews have been reported under three major historic themes in anti-Semitism: the avaricious Jew, the egocentric and exclusive Jew, and the subversive and unpatriotic Jew. To construct a measure of anti-Semitic beliefs it seemed appropriate to select two items from each of these three general categories. Table 46 lists these six items and presents an intercorrelation matrix of these items separately for Protestants and Roman Catholics. As is apparent in the table, these items are very highly intercorrelated. Indeed, the average product moment correlation among them is .547 among Protestants and .591 among Roman Catholics. By normal standards correlation coefficients as large as those in the table are very high. This gives further confidence to our decision to treat anti-Semitic beliefs as unidimensional, as primarily forming a single hostile portrait of the Jew.

On the basis of these findings, the six items were combined to form an index of anti-Semitic beliefs. Persons received a score of 2 for each

Table 46.    PRODUCT-MOMENT CORRELATIONS AMONG ITEMS
IN INDEX OF ANTI-SEMITIC BELIEFS

Items Included in the Index of Anti-Semitic Beliefs
1. Jews believe they are better than other people.
2. Jewish boys were less likely than Christian boys to volunteer for service in the armed forces during the last war.
3. Jews are more likely than Christians to cheat in business.
4. Jews, in general, are inclined to be more loyal to Israel than America.
5. Jews want to remain different from other people, and yet they are touchy if people notice these differences.
6. Because Jews are not bound by Christian ethics they do things to get ahead that Christians generally will not do.

| Item | Item | | | | | |
|------|------|------|------|------|------|------|
|      | 1    | 2    | 3    | 4    | 5    | 6    |
| | | | PROTESTANTS | | | |
| 1 | X | .570 | .445 | .567 | .713 | .603 |
| 2 |   | X    | .407 | .580 | .539 | .558 |
| 3 |   |      | X    | .467 | .428 | .592 |
| 4 |   |      |      | X    | .525 | .635 |
| 5 |   |      |      |      | X    | .577 |
| 6 |   |      |      |      |      | X    |

Average product-moment correlation = .547

| | | | CATHOLICS | | | |
|------|------|------|------|------|------|------|
| 1 | X | .662 | .520 | .615 | .766 | .634 |
| 2 |   | X    | .508 | .601 | .589 | .643 |
| 3 |   |      | X    | .474 | .473 | .639 |
| 4 |   |      |      | X    | .537 | .645 |
| 5 |   |      |      |      | X    | .563 |
| 6 |   |      |      |      |      | X    |

Average product-moment correlation = .591

item to which they responded "yes," a score of 1 for each they answered "somewhat," and a score of zero for each they answered "no." Thus, the index has a possible range of 12 ("yes" on all six statements) to zero ("no" on all six).

However, an index ranging from zero to 12 is somewhat unwieldy and produces tables that are rather difficult to read. For this reason the index was collapsed into four categories that coincided with the empirical breaking points in the data. The first category, High, contains all persons who scored 8 or more in the index. In order to achieve such a score, a person must have answered "yes" on at least four of the six questions or answered "yes" on two and "somewhat" on the remaining four. Since these items were all selected for their manifest hostility, scores of 8 or higher are very high indeed. Such persons clearly acknowledge their belief in an extensive portrait of Jews as evil men. The Medium High category contains those who earned scores of 5 through 7; and again, to gain this classification a respondent had to express considerable anti-Semitism. The third category we decided to call Medium, despite the fact that it contains persons with scores as low as 1 (and as high as 4). We did this because the overtly hostile tone of the items in the index would tend to be forgotten if we had called this category Low. It is true that relative to this index those in the Medium category earned low scores. However, were we to refer to this as a low anti-Semitism score it would suggest these are persons who hold only mildly negative beliefs about Jews. But this was not the case; instead the Medium category contains persons who hold some strongly negative beliefs about Jews, but who do not hold as many of them as persons who scored higher. The last category, None, is a pure group—only persons who answered "no" to all six items are classified here. Only these persons can properly be judged as not anti-Semitic—all others supported some overtly anti-Semitic beliefs.

## Validation of the Index of Anti-Semitic Beliefs

In previous chapters a good deal of attention has been given to the question of the validity of the indexes constructed to measure various concepts. Our concern has been to establish some reasonable empirical grounds for believing that an index measured what we intended it to measure. Because of our criticism of the conceptual confusion of much of the previous work done on anti-Semitism it seems especially important to show that our index means what we intend.

The initial selection of items to include in a measure of anti-Semitic beliefs was based on the requirement that they be manifestly hostile statements about Jews—that such assertions should provide a reasonable basis for negative sentiments. While the question of anti-Semitic feelings or sentiments will provide the central issue of the next chapter, it can be reported here that respondents concurred in our judgments that each of these items was in fact a hostile statement about Jews. For each statement in the battery of belief items about Jews, respondents were asked: "Whether or not you think Jews are like this, we would ask you to suppose that the statement actually were true. If the statement were true, how would it tend to make you feel toward Jews? Would you tend to feel friendly or unfriendly toward them because of this?"

In judging their feelings about each statement, supposing it were true, respondents overwhelmingly selected the items included in the index as those that would make them feel unfriendly. As we shall discuss in

Chapter 8, there was a tendency for respondents to say these beliefs would not make them feel either friendly or unfriendly; nevertheless, enormous differences in the proportions responding "unfriendly" were found from item to item. Thus, for example, while only 4 per cent of both Protestant and Roman Catholics said it would make them feel unfriendly toward Jews if Jews actually were wealthier than Christians, 61 per cent of the Protestants and 54 per cent of the Roman Catholics admitted they would feel unfriendly if Jews really were more likely than Christians to cheat in business. Similarly, items asserting that Jews want their children to marry Jews, control television and the movies, and are ambitious and work hard to succeed elicited unfriendliness in from 1 to 7 per cent of the respondents, while items included in the Anti-Semitic Belief Index made from 40 to 60 per cent admit potential hostility. Thus, it seems beyond doubt that the index contains items that are markedly distinguishable for their manifest hostility—such beliefs imply a negative portrait of the Jew.

A second means of establishing the validity of the index is to use it to predict statements about Jews other than those included in the index. As can be seen in Table 47, the index strongly predicts belief that Jews

Table 47.    VALIDATION OF THE INDEX OF ANTI-SEMITIC BELIEFS

Anti-Semitic Belief Index[a]

| | None | Medium | Medium High | High |
|---|---|---|---|---|
| *Number* | | | | |
| Protestants | (327) | (770) | (296) | (252) |
| Catholics | (107) | (183) | (75) | (44) |
| PER CENT REPLYING "YES" AND "SOMEWHAT" | | | | |
| *"Jews are less likely than Christians to oppose Communism."* | | | | |
| Protestants | 6 | 10 | 22 | 43 |
| Catholics | 7 | 16 | 44 | 55 |
| *"International banking tends to be dominated by Jews."* | | | | |
| Protestants | 31 | 53 | 67 | 80 |
| Catholics | 34 | 49 | 71 | 80 |
| *"Jews tend to wear flashy clothes and jewelry."* | | | | |
| Protestants | 18 | 29 | 65 | 74 |
| Catholics | 18 | 44 | 55 | 80 |
| PER CENT GIVING CLEARLY NEGATIVE RESPONSE ON OPEN-END BATTERY | | | | |
| Protestants | 28 | 41 | 61 | 75 |
| Catholics | 22 | 46 | 64 | 65 |

[a] Index includes only persons who responded to all six items.

are soft on Communism. Among Protestants, only 6 per cent of those who were scored None on the Anti-Semitic Belief Index held this belief about Jews, while 43 per cent of those scored High did so. Among Roman Catholics, the differences increase similarly—from 7 per cent of those who were scored None up to 55 per cent of those scored High. Since belief that Jews are less likely than Christians to oppose Communism was not widespread (see Table 44) compared with certain other beliefs included in the index, it could not be expected that all those scored High would hold this belief. However, the powerful relationship between the index and this belief demonstrates the consistency of the index.

The two other items in the table are not clearly negative in their content, and we have pointed out that many persons could hold such beliefs without ill will. On the other hand, they are potentially objectionable beliefs and if held by persons who have a negative image of Jews, could well be infused with negative meaning. The data suggest that both points are true. More than 30 per cent of the persons who did not even respond "somewhat true" to any of the six beliefs in the index did think Jews dominate international banking. On the other hand, 80 per cent of those high on the index held this belief. The powerful relationship between the index and this item suggests that the image of the Jew as an international banker is likely infused with anti-Semitic meaning, but shows too that such a belief ought not be taken as anti-Semitic per se.[9] The statement that "Jews tend to wear flashy clothes and jewelry" borders close to negative meaning, the word "flashy" connoting impropriety to many people when applied to dress. But the alleged flaw, if one feels it is a flaw, is surely not grievous and is a slight basis for ill will. The suggestion of negative meaning is indicated by the fact that a far smaller proportion of persons classified as None on the index (18 per cent) believed this statement than thought Jews dominated international banking. Correspondingly, 74 per cent of the Protestants who scored high and 80 per cent of the Roman Catholics accepted this belief. These findings lend further confidence to interpreting the index as a sensitive measure of anti-Semitic beliefs.

Earlier in this chapter we reported that several sentence completion items were included in the questionnaire. Persons were asked to finish the following two sentences about Jews: "It's a shame that Jews . . ." and

---

[9] For example, in order for a belief that Jews dominate international banking to operate as a basis for ill will against Jews, it is probably necessary further to believe that because these bankers are Jews their power will be abused. Thus, some conspiracy theory beyond mere control of banks is required to turn this belief into anti-Semitism.

"I can't understand why Jews. . . ." Similar statements about Catholics, Protestants, and Negroes were also included in this battery. Some of the answers written in by our respondents have been included in the discussion of various negative beliefs about Jews. However, these responses are of more than descriptive use. Coders were asked to consider what each respondent had written in to complete both statements and evaluate these as indicating negative, neutral, or positive images of Jews.[10] Thus, we have an independent measure of how respondents regarded Jews that is not based on any content supplied by the questionnaire. That is, persons were not simply asked to agree or disagree with a characteristic imputed to Jews by the authors, but were forced to fashion an answer of their own. These open-end responses, then, provide a further test of the validity of the Index of Anti-Semitic Beliefs.

As can be seen on the last two rows in Table 47, the expected relationship between the index and negative response on the open-end questions about Jews is strong and clear. Among those scored None, 28 per cent of the Protestants and 22 per cent of the Roman Catholics wrote in answers classified as negative, while among those scored High on the index, 75 per cent of the Protestants and 65 per cent of the Roman Catholics did so. In summary, then, there seems to be a firm empirical basis for considering the index an accurate measure of anti-Semitic beliefs.

Having established some grounds for putting confidence in the index, we may now finally attempt to answer the question: How anti-Semitic are Christian church members? The answer provided by the data in Table 48 is: Only 20 per cent of the Protestants and 26 per cent of the Roman Catholics rejected all six anti-Semitic beliefs and hence can be exonerated from the charge of being anti-Semites. Looking at the various Protestant bodies, the proportion classified as None is as large as 26 per cent among the Congregationalists and Episcopalians, and as small as 5 per cent among the Southern Baptists and 8 per cent in the sects. Thus, the overwhelming majority of all church members hold some clearly invidious beliefs about Jews, and virtually everyone in the most conservative Protestant bodies does so. Similarly, the proportions who could be called extreme anti-Semites, those classified as High on the index, vary among the denominations from 7 per cent of the Congregationalists up to 26 per cent of those in the sects. Over-all, 33 per cent of the Protestants and 29 per cent of the Roman Catholics are High or Medium High on the anti-Semitism index (boldface line on Table 48). Clearly, an unprejudiced image of Jews is not characteristic of present-day Christians.

[10] An intercoder reliability of 95 per cent agreement was obtained before actual coding of these data was carried out.

Table 48. CHRISTIAN ANTI-SEMITISM

| Index of Anti-Semitic Beliefs[a] | Cong. | Meth. | Epis. | D.of Christ | Pres. | A.Luth. | A.Bap. | M.Luth. | S.Bap. | Sects | Total Prot. | Cath. |
|---|---|---|---|---|---|---|---|---|---|---|---|---|
| High | 7% | 9% | 12% | 21% | 18% | 19% | 12% | 23% | 24% | 26% | 15% | 11% |
| Medium high | 14 | 14 | 19 | 15 | 18 | 17 | 19 | 16 | 22 | 27 | 18 | 18 |
| High and medium high | (21) | (23) | (31) | (36) | (36) | (36) | (31) | (39) | (46) | (53) | (33) | (29) |
| Medium | 53 | 51 | 45 | 46 | 46 | 40 | 56 | 45 | 49 | 39 | 47 | 45 |
| None | 26 | 26 | 24 | 18 | 18 | 24 | 13 | 16 | 5 | 8 | 20 | 26 |
| Total | 100% | 100% | 100% | 100% | 100% | 100% | 100% | 100% | 100% | 100% | 100% | 100% |
| Number | (115) | (297) | (305) | (33) | (353) | (140) | (104) | (81) | (55) | (159) | (1,645) | (409) |

[a] Index includes only persons who responded to all six items.

### Religion and Secular Anti-Semitic Beliefs

In Parts I and II, we have searched for a religious basis for anti-Semitism. It was suggested that commitment to traditional Christian ideology predisposed persons to adopt a particularistic conception of religious legitimacy, narrowly to consider their own religious status as the only acceptable faith. These features of Christianity were then linked with historical images of the Jews as apostates from true faith and as the crucifiers of Jesus. Subsequently it was shown that orthodoxy, particularism, and a negative religious image of the historic Jew, combined with a rejection of values of religious libertarianism, overwhelmingly predicted a hostile *religious* image of the contemporary Jew.

As suggested in the Introduction, there seems clear evidence that historically anti-Semitism stemmed mainly from religiously inspired hatred of Jews. The question that concerns us, however, is whether such a tendency continues in the modern world; whether and to what extent the configuration of religious influences we have delineated so far make men vulnerable to accepting secular anti-Semitic imagery.

In Chapter 5, a Religious Dogmatism Index was constructed to summarize four concepts: orthodoxy, particularism, lack of religious libertarianism, and an historic image of the Jews as crucifiers. We may begin an assessment of the religious roots of secular anti-Semitic beliefs by using this Dogmatism Index once again.

We saw, in tables 40 and 41, that the Dogmatism Index powerfully predicted negative religious images of the contemporary Jew. In Table 49 we see that dogmatism is also strongly related to holding secular anti-Semitic beliefs.[11]

Among Protestants, 29 per cent of those High on the Dogmatism Index scored high on the Index of Anti-Semitic Beliefs, while only 9 per cent scored None. In contrast, only 7 per cent of those who were least dogmatic scored High on anti-Semitic beliefs, while 27 per cent scored as having None. Furthermore, 52 per cent of those High on dogmatism were High or Medium High on anti-Semitic beliefs, while only 34 per cent of those Medium on dogmatism, and 20 per cent of those Low, earned similar scores.

Among Roman Catholics a similar relationship can be seen. The proportions High or Medium High on anti-Semitic beliefs decrease from 37 per cent among those high on dogmatism to 26 per cent of those

[11] The Dogmatism Index was collapsed in the following way: High includes persons who scored 6, 7, and 8; Medium, those with scores of 4 and 5; and Low, those who scored 0, 1, 2, and 3.

Table 49.    DOGMATISM AND ANTI-SEMITIC BELIEFS

| Rank on Index of Anti-Semitic Beliefs | Religious Dogmatism Index | | |
|---|---|---|---|
| | High | Middle | Low |
| *Protestants:* | | | |
| High | 29% | 13% | 7% |
| Medium high | 23 | 21 | 13 |
| **Subtotal** | **(52)** | **(34)** | **(20)** |
| Medium | 39 | 48 | 53 |
| None | 9 | 18 | 27 |
| Total | 100% | 100% | 100% |
| Number | (522) | (421) | (310) |
| *Catholics:* | | | |
| High | 12 | 8 | 9 |
| Medium high | 25 | 18 | 11 |
| **Subtotal** | **(37)** | **(26)** | **(20)** |
| Medium | 47 | 49 | 43 |
| None | 16 | 25 | 37 |
| Total | 100% | 100% | 100% |
| Number | (78) | (111) | (117) |

Medium and 20 per cent of those Low. While the percentage-point differences across the Dogmatism Index are smaller among Roman Catholics than among Protestants when the proportions High and Medium are examined, the differences are somewhat greater for Catholics when the proportions scored as None on anti-Semitism are examined. Over-all, then, among both Protestants and Roman Catholics, it can be seen that the Dogmatism Index does indeed markedly influence the acceptance of secular beliefs about Jews as avaricious, exclusive, and subversive.

However, this is far from the whole story. We have shown in Part II that the Dogmatism Index was massively associated with holding negative *religious* images of the modern Jew as an unforgiven crucifier being punished by God. The logic of the model we have been developing of the religious roots of anti-Semitism ultimately assigns primary importance to these specifically religious hostile beliefs about Jews. That is, the elements of the modern Christian perspective summarized by the Dogmatism Index ought to affect secular anti-Semitism *primarily* because these elements lead men to discredit and dislike Jews on religious grounds. Put another way, the elements measured by the Dogmatism Index produce a kind of religious anti-Semitism, which in turn makes men inclined to credit invidious traits attributed to Jews by secular traditions. It is easy to believe new tales of wrongdoing about those one already believes to be knaves.

This process is summarized in Figure 2. We have just seen that there

FIGURE 2

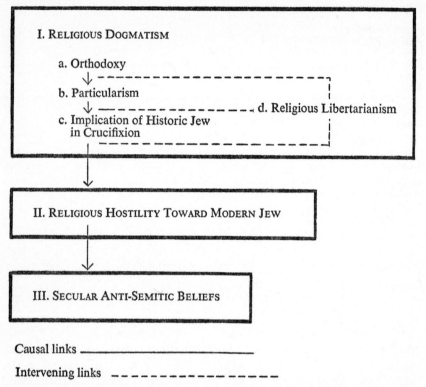

Causal links _____

Intervening links  _ _ _ _ _ _ _ _ _ _ _ _ _ _ _ _ _

is a strong relationship between Box I (the Dogmatism Index) and Box III (secular anti-Semitic beliefs). We have suggested that there is no particular reason for dogmatism to influence anti-Semitic beliefs *directly*, but that this relationship holds *only* through the intervening link of Box II (religious hostility).

If this is the case, if dogmatism only produces anti-Semitism through the mechanism of religious hostility, then the relationship between dogmatism and anti-Semitism seen in Table 49 should *disappear* when religious hostility is controlled. Statistically this must be the case; such a finding is sometimes called "complete interpretation."[12] This is a complex argument, crucial to the main thesis of this book, and requires careful explication to clarify its meaning.

If some variable $(A)$ *only* influences another variable $(C)$, through its influence on some third variable $(B)$, then there should be no rela-

[12] Herbert Hyman, *Survey Design and Analysis* (Glencoe, Ill.: The Free Press, 1955).

tionship between *A* and *C* when *B* does not vary. A classic example of this logic is the relationship between whether or not a mother works (*A*) and the likelihood that her children will be juvenile offenders (*C*). A reasonably strong correlation has been found to exist—with the children of working mothers more likely to get in trouble with the law. However, in trying to determine *why* such a relationship should exist, investigators took up the question of child supervision (*B*). In so doing they discovered that there were no differences in the delinquency rates of working and nonworking mothers when their children were equally subject to supervision. Thus, they established that the reason for the original findings was that working mothers find it more difficult to have their children well supervised and thus their working leads to poor supervision which in turn leads to a greater chance that their children will get in trouble.

This is the kind of investigation we shall now take up. Having found that dogmatism strongly influences the likelihood that church members will hold *secular* anti-Semitic beliefs, we shall now test the underlying logic on which this entire volume has been based: that religious hostility toward the modern Jew, generated by the factors in the Dogmatism Index, accounts for this link between dogmatism and anti-Semitic beliefs.

In order to test this hypothesis it was necessary to construct a simple measure of religious hostility toward the modern Jew. This Religious Hostility Index was made up of two items which will be familiar from previous chapters: "The Jews can never be forgiven for what they did to Jesus until they accept Him as the True Saviour," and "Among themselves, Jews think Christians are ignorant for believing Christ was the Son of God." Answers to these two questions were scored in the way previous indexes in this volume have been constructed, and the resulting index ranges from 4 (persons who firmly accepted both statements) down to zero (persons who absolutely rejected both).[13]

In order to determine statistically whether or not religious hostility is in fact the *mechanism* by which religious dogmatism influences anti-Semitic beliefs, it is necessary to introduce the Index of Religious Hostility into the relationship shown in Table 49. Turning to Table 50 we may see the overwhelming confirmation of our hypothesis. Looking at the Protestants, *within* each category of the Religious Hostility Index the relationship between dogmatism and anti-Semitic beliefs has vanished into meaningless patterns. Reading across the table it is clear that *there is no meaningful independent relationship between being religiously dogmatic*

---

[13] Scoring on "The Jews can never be forgiven . . .": Agree = 2; uncertain = 1; disagree = 0. On "Among themselves Jews think . . .": Jews are like this = 2; somewhat like this = 1; not like this = 0.

Table 50.  DOGMATISM, RELIGIOUS HOSTILITY, AND ANTI-SEMITISM

(Per cent of respondents who ranked High or Medium High
on Index of Anti-Semitic Beliefs)

| Rank on Index of Religious Hostility Toward Modern Jews | Religious Dogmatism Index | | |
|---|---|---|---|
| | High | Middle | Low |
| *Protestants:* | | | |
| High (4) | | | |
| Per cent | 77 | 62 | ᵃ |
| Number | (97) | (50) | (7) |
| Score of 3 | | | |
| Per cent | 53 | 54 | 56 |
| Number | (75) | (73) | (32) |
| Score of 2 | | | |
| Per cent | 35 | 34 | 38 |
| Number | (79) | (93) | (92) |
| Score of 1 | | | |
| Per cent | 19 | 21 | 15 |
| Number | (21) | (96) | (151) |
| Low (zero) | | | |
| Per cent | 5 | 16 | 10 |
| Number | (19) | (82) | (217) |
| *Catholics:* | | | |
| High (4) | | | |
| Per cent | ᵃ | ᵃ | ᵃ |
| Number | (6) | (1) | (1) |
| Score of 3 | | | |
| Per cent | 55 | ᵃ | ᵃ |
| Number | (20) | (5) | (3) |
| Score of 2 | | | |
| Per cent | 37 | 39 | 33 |
| Number | (27) | (28) | (15) |
| Score of 1 | | | |
| Per cent | 32 | 19 | 23 |
| Number | (28) | (37) | (22) |
| Low (zero) | | | |
| Per cent | 12 | 12 | 6 |
| Number | (26) | (32) | (31) |

ᵃ Too few cases to compute stable percentages.

*and anti-Semitic.* On the other hand, *within* each degree of dogmatism the effect of religious hostility is powerful indeed (reading down the table). For example, among those who were scored High on religious dogmatism, 78 per cent of those who scored 4 on religious hostility were anti-Semitic, while among those who scored zero only 5 per cent were anti-Semitic. The same effect prevails among those scoring Medium and Low on dogmatism. A virtually identical pattern can be seen among Catholics. This strongly confirms our thesis. We have previously seen that Catholics were much less likely than Protestants to translate their religious dogmatism into religious hostility. But what this table shows is that if Catholics do make this translation they are just as likely as Protestants to be anti-Semitic.

In Chapter 5 (Tables 40 and 41) it was demonstrated that religious hostility is overwhelmingly the product of religious dogmatism. What we have established now, in Table 50, is *not* that dogmatism has no impact on secular anti-Semitism, but that this connection operates *only* through the generation of the intervening condition: religious hostility. Dogmatism makes it very likely that persons will become religiously hostile toward the modern Jew. If they do they are very likely to accept secular anti-Semitic beliefs about Jews as well. But when religious dogmatism fails to develop into religious hostility it seems to have no further consequences for anti-Semitism.

This finding seems extremely important for church leaders who would seek to suspend the process by which the church serves, albeit inadvertently, to foster hatred of Jews. By massively assaulting the current belief among Christians that their Jewish neighbors continue to bear the stigmas of deicide and divine punishment, the churches might well be able to interrupt the invidious process through which religious dogmatism is transmuted into anti-Semitism.

## Religious Bigotry

The basic pieces making up our model of the religious sources of anti-Semitism have now all been assembled. We have seen that they interrelate in the manner postulated and together they powerfully predict holding secular anti-Semitic beliefs. To simplify subsequent use of this religious model, we may now finally join all of the parts into a single variable, or summary measure. We shall call this the Index of Religious Bigotry. By this name we mean to indicate the entire chain of religious factors by which men come to think ill of persons who do not meet certain standards of religious propriety. Religious bigotry is more than a propensity for religious hostility; it includes the fulfillment of these propensities. To construct this summary measure of our model of the religious roots of anti-Semitism, the Index of Religious Hostility toward the modern Jew and the Dogmatism Index were combined into a single measure.[14]

By merging these indexes, it will be possible to examine more complex relationships between religion and anti-Semitism with simpler statistical tables. For example, in examining the relationship in Table 50 among

[14] The scores in each index were added, thus the Religious Bigotry Index ranges from 0 through 6.

dogmatism, hostility, and anti-Semitic beliefs, it would have been unduly complex to show the complete range of the Index of Anti-Semitic Beliefs. Consequently, only the percentage scored High or Medium High on the index were shown in the table. After the two independent variables are combined into a single index, however, the complete findings may be easily shown in Table 51. The findings in boldface show in a linear fashion

Table 51.   RELIGIOUS BIGOTRY AND ANTI-SEMITIC BELIEFS

| Rank on Index of Anti-Semitic Beliefs | Index of Religious Bigotry | | | | | | |
|---|---|---|---|---|---|---|---|
| | 0 | 1 | 2 | 3 | 4 | 5 | 6 |
| *Protestants:* | | | | | | | |
| High | 2% | 3% | 9% | 20% | 16% | 28% | 54% |
| Medium high | 8 | 12 | 19 | 17 | 30 | 29 | 24 |
| **High and medium high** | **(10)** | **(15)** | **(28)** | **(37)** | **(46)** | **(57)** | **(78)** |
| Medium | 57 | 54 | 52 | 49 | 45 | 40 | 22 |
| None | 33 | 31 | 20 | 14 | 9 | 3 | 0 |
| Total | 100% | 100% | 100% | 100% | 100% | 100% | 100% |
| Number | (216) | (233) | (206) | (146) | (159) | (124) | (97) |
| *Catholics:* | | | | | | | |
| High | 6% | 4% | 6% | 7% | 18% | 29% | 50% |
| Medium high | 0 | 13 | 13 | 32 | 22 | 29 | 33 |
| **High and medium high** | **(6)** | **(17)** | **(19)** | **(39)** | **(40)** | **(58)** | **(83)** |
| Medium | 42 | 48 | 50 | 46 | 51 | 42 | 17 |
| None | 52 | 35 | 31 | 15 | 9 | 0 | 0 |
| Total | 100% | 100% | 100% | 100% | 100% | 100% | 100% |
| Number | (31) | (54) | (78) | (59) | (33) | (21) | (6)[a] |

[a] The stability of a percentage based on so few cases is questionable, and this finding is presented only for its descriptive interest.

those reported earlier in Table 50. The proportions scored High and Medium High on the Index of Anti-Semitic Beliefs rise enormously from left to right across the Index of Religious Bigotry—from 10 to 78 per cent among Protestants and from 6 to 83 per cent among Roman Catholics. Yet, by being able to examine the full range of the Anti-Semitism Index, further interesting findings come to light. For example, among both Protestants and Catholics *every* person who earned a maximum score of 6 on the Religious Bigotry Index accepted some of the anti-Semitic belief items. Not a single person in this category, indeed virtually no one in any of the top three categories, was able to reject all six of the invidious statements about Jews. Furthermore, half of those scored 6 on Religious Bigotry were in the *top* category of anti-Semitic beliefs, and thus exhibit that they hold an extensive negative portrait of the Jews.

Thus, it would appear that religion not only played a crucial historical role in the rise of anti-Semitism, but that even today it continues to reinforce and foster hatred of the Jews. But do all aspects of religious involvement have this consequence? Given the conditions specified by our model, do other manners in which people may exhibit greater concern about religion increase or decrease their tendency to discredit Jews?

It will be recalled that in Chapter 1 an Index of Ritual Involvement in religion was developed. In Chapter 2 it was shown that ritual involvement in no way influenced particularism, independent of orthodoxy. That is, particularism was entirely a function of what people *believed* about their faith and had nothing to do with what they *did* to observe their faith. However, it seems time to resume our interest in ritual involvement. What effect does ritual involvement—church attendance and private prayer— have upon anti-Semitism?

Table 52 provides the answer. First of all, no matter whether one is ritually involved or uninvolved, religious bigotry remains an equally powerful predictor of anti-Semitism. However, among Protestants, ritual

Table 52.  BIGOTRY, RITUAL, AND ANTI-SEMITISM

(Per cent distribution of respondents who ranked High or Medium High
on Index of Anti-Semitic Beliefs

| Rank on Index of Ritual Involvement | Index of Religious Bigotry | | | | | | |
|---|---|---|---|---|---|---|---|
| | 0 | 1 | 2 | 3 | 4 | 5 | 6 |
| *Protestants:* | | | | | | | |
| Low | | | | | | | |
| Per cent | 10 | 23 | 41 | 40 | 79 | a | a |
| Number | (63) | (49) | (35) | (30) | (14) | (4) | (4) |
| Medium | | | | | | | |
| Per cent | 11 | 14 | 44 | 48 | 68 | 54 | 67 |
| Number | (95) | (88) | (64) | (42) | (39) | (26) | (18) |
| High | | | | | | | |
| Per cent | 11 | 12 | 13 | 29 | 33 | 62 | 82 |
| Number | (57) | (94) | (102) | (72) | (104) | (89) | (74) |
| *Catholics:* | | | | | | | |
| Low | | | | | | | |
| Per cent | a | 0 | a | a | a | a | a |
| Number | (3) | (9) | (5) | (2) | (4) | (0) | (0) |
| Medium | | | | | | | |
| Per cent | 11 | 15 | 26 | 30 | a | a | a |
| Number | (9) | (13) | (19) | (10) | (4) | (1) | (2) |
| High | | | | | | | |
| Per cent | 5 | 22 | 13 | 43 | 60 | 65 | a |
| Number | (9) | (32) | (53) | (48) | (25) | (20) | (4) |

a Too few cases to compute stable percentages.

involvement does seem independently to affect anti-Semitism in a rather complex way. For Catholics there seems to be no consistent relationship. Among Protestants, at the lowest level of religious bigotry, ritual involvement has no effect upon anti-Semitism. In the intermediate levels of religious bigotry (scores 1–4), ritual involvement seems to make persons much less likely to be anti-Semitic, but this reverses in the highest categories of religious bigotry, where ritual involvement seems to make men more anti-Semitic. Upon reflection, this makes a good deal of sense. Persons with intermediate scores on the model can be thought of as religiously cross-pressured. They have some of those attributes that provide a religious rationale for anti-Semitism, but they also lack some of these attributes. For them, concern for religion as evidenced by church attendance and private prayer seems to decrease the invidious potential of those elements of religious bigotry which they possess. Lacking a complete set of those religious elements which foster anti-Semitism perhaps leads men to a greater openness to the doctrines of brotherhood to which they may be more exposed through increased ritual involvement. On the other hand, when persons approximate our conception of the religious bigot, increased activity in the life of the church makes them more likely to be anti-Semites.

CHAPTER **8**

---

# Anti-Semitic Feelings

> Gradually I began to hate them . . . For me this was the time of the greatest spiritual upheaval I have ever gone through. I had ceased to be a weak-kneed cosmopolitan and become an anti-Semite.
> —ADOLF HITLER

To read the pages on Jews in *Mein Kampf,* or any of the countless tracts and periodicals devoted to anti-Semitism, is to be exposed to raw, virtually uncensored, emotions. The fear and loathing, the almost helpless rage that permeates these documents is seldom matched in print. But to come to grips specifically with this wrathful aspect of anti-Semitism is extremely difficult, for such feelings do not occur independently of some kind of belief structure.

No matter how wildly untrue, some version of "the truth" about Jews seems a necessary correlate of these emotions. Even Hitler never just vented pure rage against the Jews, but invariably connected his outrage to some hideous fantasy about the nature of Jews, for example, "the nightmare vision of the seduction of hundreds of thousands of girls by repulsive, crooked-legged Jew bastards."[1] His violent feelings were based on what he considered to be true of Jewish actions and intentions. He *believed*[2] that young Jews *did* lie in wait "satanically glaring and spying on the

---

[1] Quoted in Alan Bullock, *Hitler: A Study in Tyranny* (New York: Bantam Books, 1958), p. 12.

[2] Because Hitler often admitted that he used anti-Semitism opportunistically, some people suggest he was not a sincere anti-Semite, that he did not really believe what he said about Jews. This is absurd, at best. It seems much more reasonable that he felt no qualms about exploiting anti-Semitism to suit his purposes because he hated Jews uncontrollably anyway. Surely there was no way in which it was

unsuspicious girl whom he plans to seduce, adulterating her blood and removing her from the bosom of her own people."[3]

The problem this linkage poses for the study of anti-Semitism is in how to separate feelings from the beliefs which make them coherent. This seems to be possible only in a partial way. It would be possible, of course, to employ one of several psychological devices, such as the semantic differential,[4] that are intended to measure "pure affect," or only emotional responses, toward some stimulus object. However, our conviction that sentiments do not generally occur in the absence of some rationale or belief structure, although such a structure may be extremely crude or simplistic, gives us pause as to what such "pure affect" measures really mean. This is not to suggest that such measures do not have real meaning, only that it is extremely difficult to determine just what it is. In what kind of an image of the Jew, for example, are certain feelings anchored?

For this reason we decided to attempt to uncover what may be less purely emotional responses, but for which it is possible to specify meaning. Thus, having determined that a man does believe that some particular negative characteristic is true of Jews in general, we want to know how he feels about it. Does it make him angry or not? Our reasons for taking this approach are more than methodological, for in the practical events of the real world this is a major consideration. It matters greatly whether or not a particular belief about Jews makes men angry, and especially under what conditions anti-Semitism can be limited to mere belief. How is it possible to suspend the translation of beliefs into feelings? For we can more easily live in a world in which these feelings have diminished, even if we must endure the beliefs for some time to come.

In this rather brief chapter we shall attempt to assess the extent to which the anti-Semitic beliefs we have just examined produce admissions of hostility toward Jews. For each anti-Semitic belief item included in the questionnaire, respondents were first asked whether or not they thought it was true. Then each respondent was asked to *suppose* that the statement actually were true, and asked how this would make him feel toward Jews: friendly, unfriendly, or neither way.

---

opportunistic and to Hitler's advantage to tie up large amounts of his desperately scarce rail transport to the collapsing Eastern Front in order to transport Jews to the death camps, and yet this is precisely what he did. The irrationality of such an act is a major reason why Western leaders were reluctant to believe the reports about the death camps during the war. Such a use of transport was strategically incomprehensible. It can only be explained in a system of priorities where the destruction of Jews was at least on a par with military victory.

[3] Quoted in Bullock, *op. cit.*, p. 12.

[4] Charles E. Osgood, George J. Suci, and Percy H. Tannenbaum, *The Measurement of Meaning* (Urbana: University of Illinois Press, 1957).

By asking *all* respondents to evaluate their feelings about each alleged characteristic of the Jews, regardless of whether or not they thought it true, it was possible to get some general estimate of the potential hostility contained in each stereotype. In the preceding chapter we have drawn on these general evaluations of the relative invidiousness of each item to lend confidence to our selection of belief items that were unambiguously negative. In this chapter, however, we are not interested in how persons *would* feel about things they believe are actually not true of Jews, but how people say they feel toward Jews on the basis of negative qualities they do in fact impute to Jews. Thus, the responses of persons who rejected the truth of an anti-Semitic statement must be disregarded in measuring the feeling component of anti-Semitism.

On the other hand, it will be evident that a number of respondents, having admitted an anti-Semitic belief, claimed it had no effect on their feelings toward Jews. It seems likely that some of these respondents lied, if not to us, at least to themselves. For others, however, it may be true that they can resist hard feelings toward persons despite believing them to be of bad character. In any event, it seems reasonable that our estimate of anti-Semitic feelings will be somewhat lower than is the actual state of affairs. This may weaken the strength of the relationships we report, but gives assurance that the relationships are minimal rather than inflated.

Two main questions must be asked of these empirical data: (1) What are the relative capacities of these anti-Semitic beliefs for generating ill will, and (2) What proportion of American church members have such negative feelings toward Jews?

In order to answer these questions, Table 53 has been set up to show two things about each feeling question. First, the proportions who felt unfriendly because of some trait imputed to the Jews are shown for both those who thought the item entirely true and those who thought it somewhat true. The figures in boldface show how those who rejected the truth of the statement would feel had the statement been true. Beneath these data, for each item, are shown the total percentage of Protestants and of Catholics who *both* believed the item and *also* acknowledge hard feelings because of this belief.

Looking, then, at the first item in the table, we may see that 80 per cent of the Protestants who believe Jews cheat in business admitted that this made them feel unfriendly toward Jews, while 73 per cent of those who thought the item only somewhat true admitted unfriendliness. Among Roman Catholics these same percentages are 74 and 56, respectively. It is apparent on this, and the other five items on the table, that persons who were certain of the truth of a given negative belief about the Jews were more likely to admit feeling unfriendly because of it than were persons who thought the statement only "somewhat" true. This seems to reflect a certain ambivalence on the part of persons who chose the "somewhat" response. This is further suggested by the fact that persons who felt these statements were *not* true typically were more likely to say that they would

Table 53.   ANTI-SEMITIC BELIEFS AND FEELINGS

Jews are more likely than Christians to cheat in business.

*Per Cent Who Feel* (**or Would Feel**) *"Unfriendly"*
*Among Those Who Answered:*

|  | "Yes" | "Somewhat" | No |
|---|---|---|---|
| Protestants | 80% | 73% | 66% |
| Number | (364) | (357) | (1,310) |
| Catholics | 74% | 56% | 58% |
| Number | (74) | (79) | (322) |

Per cent who *both* think the statement is at least "somewhat" true *and* who say it makes them feel "unfriendly."

| Protestants | 26% |
|---|---|
| Catholics | 21% |

Because Jews are not bound by Christian ethics, they do things to get ahead that Christians generally will not do.

*Per Cent Who Feel* (**or Would Feel**) *"Unfriendly"*
*Among Those Who Answered:*

|  | "Yes" | "Somewhat" | No |
|---|---|---|---|
| Protestants | 67% | 60% | 63% |
| Number | (364) | (416) | (1,095) |
| Catholics | 65% | 39% | 53% |
| Number | (71) | (109) | (260) |

Per cent who *both* think the item is at least somewhat true *and* who feel unfriendly about it.

| Protestants | 22% |
|---|---|
| Catholics | 20% |

Jewish boys were less likely than Christian boys to volunteer for service in the armed forces during the last world war.

*Per Cent Who Feel* (**or Would Feel**) *"Unfriendly"*
*Among Those Who Answered:*

|  | "Yes" | "Somewhat" | No |
|---|---|---|---|
| Protestants | 61% | 53% | 54% |
| Number | (204) | (239) | (1,256) |
| Catholics | 67% | 49% | 49% |
| Number | (51) | (65) | (304) |

Per cent who *both* think the statement is at least "somewhat" true *and* who say it makes them feel "unfriendly."

| Protestants | 15% |
|---|---|
| Catholics | 16% |

(Table continued)

Table 53.  (Continued)

Jews believe they are better than other people.

| | *Per Cent Who Feel* **(or Would Feel)** *"Unfriendly"* *Among Those Who Answered:* | | |
|---|---|---|---|
| | "Yes" | "Somewhat" | **No** |
| Protestants | 52% | 38% | **48%** |
| Number | (338) | (520) | **(954)** |
| Catholics | 56% | 45% | **53%** |
| Number | (64) | (120) | **(242)** |

Per cent who *both* think the item is at least somewhat true *and* who feel unfriendly about it.

| | |
|---|---|
| Protestants | 23% |
| Catholics | 18% |

Jews want to remain different from other people, and yet they are touchy if people notice these differences.

| | *Per Cent Who Feel* **(or Would Feel)** *"Unfriendly"* *Among Those Who Answered:* | | |
|---|---|---|---|
| | "Yes" | "Somewhat" | **No** |
| Protestants | 37% | 24% | **26%** |
| Number | (592) | (626) | **(594)** |
| Catholics | 34% | 17% | **22%** |
| Number | (114) | (132) | **(183)** |

Per cent who *both* think the item is at least somewhat true *and* who feel unfriendly about it.

| | |
|---|---|
| Protestants | 20% |
| Catholics | 14% |

Jews, in general, are inclined to be more loyal to Israel than to America.

| | *Per Cent Who Feel* **(or Would Feel)** *"Unfriendly"* *Among Those Who Answered:* | | |
|---|---|---|---|
| | "Yes" | "Somewhat" | **No** |
| Protestants | 41% | 41% | **56%** |
| Number | (264) | (382) | **(1,184)** |
| Catholics | 37% | 30% | **50%** |
| Number | (51) | (83) | **(303)** |

Per cent who *both* think the item is at least somewhat true *and* who feel unfriendly about it.

| | |
|---|---|
| Protestants | 14% |
| Catholics | 11% |

feel unfriendly, if such a thing were true, than were those who judged the item somewhat true.[5] Thus, persons who were certain one way or the other were more likely to acknowledge the hostile character of these items than were persons who qualified their agreement.

[5] In 10 of 12 possible comparisons, a higher proportion of persons who answered "no" on the item indicated unfriendliness than did persons who thought the item somewhat true, with one tie and one reversal of this tendency.

Looking further in the table we see that 26 per cent of the Protestants and 21 per cent of the Roman Catholics in the sample[6] *both* believed that Jews are more likely than Christians to cheat in business and *also* admitted feeling unfriendly toward Jews because of it.

On the second item in the table, approximately two-thirds of both Protestants and Roman Catholics who believed Jews will do unethical things to get ahead admitted this made them feel unfriendly. Furthermore, 22 per cent of all Protestants and 20 per cent of the Roman Catholics both believed this statement and felt hostile about it.

Similarly, the draft-dodger stereotype elicited unfriendliness from about two-thirds of those who thought it completely true, and from about half of those who thought it somewhat true. Fifteen per cent of the Protestants and 16 per cent of all Catholics both believed and were unfriendly about it.

The potential for hostility of the fourth item is somewhat less than for the previous three, with only a little more than half of those who answered "yes" indicating it made them feel unfriendly. Apparently Christians are more hostile about being cheated than about alleged Jewish egocentrism. Over-all, 23 per cent of the Protestants and 18 per cent of the Catholics agreed "Jews believe they are better than other people" and said it made them unfriendly.

Only about a third of those who said "yes" to the statement that "Jews want to remain different from other people, and yet they are touchy if people notice these differences," said it would make them unfriendly; however, 20 per cent of the Protestants and 14 per cent of the Catholics did both believe and object.

Finally, about 40 per cent of those who fully believed that Jews are more loyal to Israel than America said it made them unfriendly toward Jews.

Thus we may conclude that hostility is more readily admitted, and likely more deeply felt, when a trait imputed to the Jews represents a direct threat. Thus Jewish cheating and unethical behavior can be seen as personally victimizing the Christian and Jewish draft-dodging as unfairly imposing an added military burden upon Christians. But other alleged Jewish traits, such as conceit and touchiness, are less significant impositions, and accordingly the admitted hostility is less widespread.

We have seen that as many as a quarter of the total sample acknowledged both belief and concomitant unfriendliness toward Jews on certain traits. However, it seems useful to get some more general estimate of the prevalence of admitted anti-Semitic feelings among Christian church members. Consequently, the six items on feelings toward Jews were scored

---

[6] Only persons who answered both the belief and friendliness items are included in these computations.

into an index. If a person answered that a particular statement about Jews was not true, he automatically received a score of zero on the Feelings Index. But if a respondent indicated the statement was at least somewhat true, then he received a score of 1 for saying this made him feel unfriendly and a score of zero for indicating he would feel neither friendly nor unfriendly toward Jews because of this.[7] The Feelings Index produced through this scoring technique was divided into three categories: None—persons who rejected the truth of all beliefs, or accepted some but denied that any would make them feel unfriendly; Medium—persons who admitted that one, two, or three of the items they believed true made them feel unfriendly toward Jews; and High—persons who said that four, five, or six of these items were true and made them feel unfriendly.

Table 54 shows how the members of each denomination were distributed on this index. The most significant finding is that a large minority of church members (44 per cent of the Protestants and 37 per cent of the Catholics) indicate that they have anti-Semitic beliefs which are

Table 54.   ANTI-SEMITIC FEELINGS

| Index of Anti-Semitic Feelings | Cong. | Meth. | Epis. | D.of Christ | Pres. |
|---|---|---|---|---|---|
| High (4, 5, 6) | 5% | 7% | 9% | 13% | 12% |
| Medium (1, 2, 3) | 37 | 37 | 36 | 28 | 37 |
| None (zero) | 58 | 56 | 55 | 59 | 51 |
| Total | 100% | 100% | 100% | 100% | 100% |
| Number | (119) | (304) | (309) | (38) | (362) |

| Index | A.Luth. | A.Bap. | M.Luth. | S.Bap. | Sects |
|---|---|---|---|---|---|
| High | 12% | 12% | 17% | 16% | 5% |
| Medium | 25 | 38 | 33 | 35 | 42 |
| None | 63 | 50 | 50 | 49 | 53 |
| Total | 100% | 100% | 100% | 100% | 100% |
| Number | (147) | (103) | (85) | (55) | (173) |

| Index | Total Prot. | Cath. |
|---|---|---|
| High | 10% | 8% |
| Medium | 34 | 29 |
| None | 56 | 63 |
| Total | 100% | 100% |
| Number | (2,103) | (405) |

[7] Virtually no respondents said such characteristic of Jews would make them feel friendly; the few who did were also given zero scores on anti-Semitic feeling.

accompanied by hard feelings toward Jews. Among the Protestant bodies the proportion who both hold anti-Semitic beliefs and have anti-Semitic feelings is as high as 50 per cent among the more conservative bodies.

These findings allow only one conclusion: *Not only do the vast majority of Christian church members exhibit an affinity for anti-Semitic beliefs, but nearly half frankly admit to anti-Semitic feelings.*

But now we pose a slightly different question: To what extent does the Religious Bigotry Index predict *both* holding anti-Semitic beliefs *and* having hard feelings toward Jews because of them. It will be recalled that the scores on the Index of Anti-Semitic Feelings were partly determined by anti-Semitic beliefs. Persons who held no anti-Semitic beliefs were by definition scored zero on feelings. The rest of the respondents received a score only if they acknowledged unfriendly feelings toward Jews on the basis of those beliefs they held. Thus, on the Feelings Index persons are, in effect, "excused" for holding an anti-Semitic belief if they could do so without rancor. That is, for the purposes of Table 55, we have adopted a more complex definition of anti-Semitism which requires both beliefs and feelings.

Looking at Table 55, we see the powerful impact of religious bigotry upon this more complex form of anti-Semitism. Among Protestants, while 32 per cent of those without a religious basis for anti-Semitism nevertheless held both anti-Semitic beliefs and feelings, approximately two-thirds (65 per cent) of those scored high on the bigotry index did so. Similarly, among Catholics 19 per cent of those low on bigotry held anti-Semitic beliefs and feelings, 83 per cent of those in the highest category did so. The impact of religious bigotry remains powerful even when anti-Semitism is treated in a more complex way.

Table 55. RELIGIOUS BIGOTRY AND ANTI-SEMITIC BELIEFS AND FEELINGS
(Per cent Holding Anti-Semitic Beliefs and Feelings)

| | Index of Religious Bigotry | | | | | | |
|---|---|---|---|---|---|---|---|
| | Low 0 | 1 | 2 | 3 | 4 | 5 | High 6 |
| *Protestants:* | | | | | | | |
| Per cent | 32 | 39 | 48 | 56 | 58 | 63 | 65 |
| Number | (209) | (231) | (207) | (154) | (156) | (126) | (98) |
| *Catholics:* | | | | | | | |
| Per cent | 19 | 28 | 32 | 46 | 53 | 64 | 83[a] |
| Number | (31) | (54) | (73) | (56) | (34) | (22) | (6) |

[a] Too few cases for a stable percentage; presented for descriptive interest only.

Having seen that certain features of Christian fervor and theology greatly predispose church members toward anti-Semitic beliefs and feelings, we shall turn our attention in the next chapter to anti-Semitic actions.

# CHAPTER 9

# Anti-Semitic Actions

> We decree and order that from now on, and for all time, Christians shall not eat or drink with Jews, nor admit them to feasts, nor cohabit with them, nor bathe with them. Christians shall not allow Jews to hold civil honors over Christians, or to exercise public offices in the state.
>
> —POPE EUGENIUS IV, Decree, 1442

> 1. Marriages between Jews and citizens of German or kindred stock shall be prohibited. Marriages concluded despite the law shall be considered void even when they are concluded abroad.
>
> 2. Nonmarital sexual intercourse between Jews and citizens of German or kindred stock shall be prohibited.
>
> 3. Jews shall not employ in their households female citizens of German or kindred stock under 45 years of age.
>
> —German law enacted September 15, 1935

We come now to the sticks and stones of prejudice: What are people who believe evil of the Jews and who dislike them because of it willing to *do* about it?

With his characteristic zeal for "works," Western man has tragically been willing again and again to "do something about the Jews." Sometimes this has meant violence and bloodshed. Almost always this has meant a cruel structure of laws and customs which imprison the Jews in physical and spiritual bondage. The origin of these cultural traditions of discrimination against the Jews was in early and medieval Christianity. Beginning in the fourth century, armed with its newly gained power over the collapsing Roman Empire, the Church began to institute "defensive" measures against the Jews. For if the conversion of the Jews must be sought with patience, the Church leaders deemed it prudent that in the interim Jews be prevented from contaminating the life and faith of true believers. The first of these measures precluded social contact between Jews and Christians. Intermarriage, sexual intercourse, and eating together were among acts proscribed between Christians and Jews. Progressively, the Church increased its pressure on the Jews. In the sixth century, the Third Synod of Orléans forbade Jews from employing Christian servants and from showing themselves in the streets during Passion Week. In the seventh century, the Talmud was ordered burned, and at about the same time the Synod of Clermont disqualified Jews from holding public office. In the thirteenth century the Church, speaking through the Synod of Vienna, outlawed Jews from even discussing religion with Christians, for as Pope Innocent III wrote to the Count de Nevers in about 1200: "The Jews, like Cain, are doomed to wander the earth as fugitives and vagabonds, and their faces are covered with shame."[1] Slowly the Church inspired and erected the walls of the ghetto, walls that were to shut the Jews away from humanity for centuries—indeed, the Papacy maintained a ghetto under its direct dominion in Rome until 1870!

If the Roman Catholic Church was responsible for forging these legal instruments of repression, the early Protestant reforms did not include repeal of these canon laws against the Jews. Instead, the Protestants fervently carried on this legacy of bigotry.[2]

---

[1] It must be emphasized that while the popes and the higher clergy were responsible for imposing these cruel restrictions upon the Jews, *no pope ever lent support to acts of violence against Jews.* Frequently, papal pronouncements condemned such acts. Thus, to blame the Church for Jewish massacres is not wholly justified. Yet, the local clergy, monks, and even saints were often in the forefront of the mobs, leading them on to riot and murder, and the people too were often among the most devout and faithful Christians. Thus, to either exonerate or implicate "the Church" in the bloody pogroms depends upon how broadly or narrowly one defines "the Church." Still, it must be recognized that many popes exerted their power to protect the Jews even while they imposed terrible restrictions upon them.

[2] For all his genius and humanity, Martin Luther became a violent and brooding anti-Semite. Initially he was optimistic about converting the Jews, but as his efforts failed, he became increasingly angry. His later writings are filled with a horror of the Jews, and he called for their deportation from Germany. In one thundering pronouncement he demanded that "all their cash and jewels and silver and gold" be taken from them and that "their synagogues or schools be set on fire, that their houses be broken up and destroyed . . . and they be put under a roof or stable like gypsies . . . in misery and captivity as they incessantly lament and complain to God about us" [quoted in William L. Shirer, *The Rise and Fall of the Third Reich* (New York: Simon and Schuster, 1960), p. 236]. To the older Luther, even the conversion of the Jews he had once hoped for seemed fraught with danger, for could they be trusted even then? "If a Jew, not converted at heart, were to ask for baptism at my hands, I would take him on to the bridge, tie a stone round his neck, and hurl him into the river; for these wretches are wont to make jest of our religion" (*Table Talk,* CCLXXV).

Thus was the pattern of anti-Semitic law and action in times past fashioned by Christian doctrine. In our own day, these traditions have served as a basis in custom for the continued persecution of the Jews. A revealing chart constructed by Hilberg shows that *every* restriction imposed upon the Jews by the Nazis, short of the monstrous "final solution," had an earlier counterpart in canon law.[3]

The common acts of anti-Semitism in contemporary America are a far cry from those imposed by canon law. Yet they are rooted in this same centuries-old tradition of isolating the Jews from contact with the larger community and occasionally include violence. These customs were *established* by religion. But we must now see to what extent they are still carried on out of religious motives.

### Measuring Anti-Semitic Action

Given the kind of data on which this study is based, it is only possible for us to discuss anti-Semitic action in a somewhat hypothetical way. We simply do not know what varieties of acts against Jews these respondents may have taken in the past or will take at some future time. We can, however, examine how they say they would act should they be faced with certain situations. It must be admitted immediately that there is undoubtedly a great discrepancy between what people say they would do, and what they really end up doing when the occasion arises. A great many aspects of real situations undoubtedly act to deflect many persons from carrying out their anticipated response. Thus, both persons who state they would act in an anti-Semitic way and those who say they would not might do the opposite thing in real life. To a certain degree, then, intentions stated about hypothetical situations are merely attitudes and do not represent actions. Nevertheless, despite all these inadequacies in our data when compared with the stuff of real life, there is obviously a considerable correlation between what people say they will do and what they actually do. People who say they will act in a certain way are more likely to act that way than people who say they will not. It is because of such a correlation, although it is obviously far from perfect, that it seems useful to consider the ways people say they would behave in certain circumstances.

A second qualification that must be made of this chapter involves the worth of the items included in the questionnaire to assess how people think they might act toward or concerning Jews in certain circumstances. Very few such items were included in the study, and these in retrospect turned out not to be very well designed. It is perhaps true that all survey studies

[3] Raul Hilberg, *The Destruction of the European Jews* (Chicago: Quadrangle Books, 1961), pp. 5–6.

Table 56. VACATION RESORTS

Hypothetical situation: "Suppose you heard an argument between three of your friends over the practice of many vacation resorts of not permitting Jews as guests. One friend said Jews have a right to be admitted to any vacation resort. The second said Christians have a right to their own private resorts if they want them. The third said regardless of what Christians or Jews might expect, any resort owner has the right to run his business and pick his customers any way he wants to. With whom would you tend to agree?"

| | Cong. | Meth. | Epis. | D.of Christ | Pres. | A.Luth. | A.Bap. | M.Luth. | S.Bap. | Sects | Total Prot. | Cath. |
|---|---|---|---|---|---|---|---|---|---|---|---|---|
| *Per cent who would say:* | | | | | | | | | | | | |
| Jews have a right to be admitted anywhere. | 36% | 43% | 44% | 54% | 45% | 40% | 40% | 38% | 24% | 39% | 42% | 48% |
| Christians have a right to their own resorts if they want them. | 5 | 6 | 4 | 0 | 4 | 3 | 6 | 6 | 6 | 4 | 4 | 2 |
| Resort owners have a right to pick their own customers. | 51 | 42 | 44 | 34 | 41 | 42 | 38 | 40 | 51 | 39 | 42 | 40 |
| Other | 5 | 6 | 5 | 8 | 7 | 9 | 10 | 14 | 12 | 11 | 8 | 5 |
| No answer | 3 | 3 | 3 | 4 | 3 | 6 | 6 | 2 | 7 | 7 | 4 | 5 |
| Total | 100% | 100% | 100% | 100% | 100% | 100% | 100% | 100% | 100% | 100% | 100% | 100% |
| Number | (151) | (415) | (416) | (50) | (495) | (208) | (141) | (116) | (79) | (255) | (2,326) | (545) |

would be changed in a number of ways if the investigators were ever to repeat them. Hindsight is very edifying. Despite certain flaws in our items, we shall try to exploit fully the potential of what data we have, but any extensive investigation of anti-Semitic behavior is beyond our means. Fortunately, subsequent studies in this series profited from our errors and will take up anti-Semitic acts in great detail.

The first item on anti-Semitic acts concerns an argument over the practice of discriminating against Jews at vacation resorts. Respondents were asked with which of three friends, each taking a different position on this practice, they would agree. Respondents could take the position that Jews have a right to be admitted anywhere, that Christians have a right to their own resorts, or that the resort owners have the right to pick their customers as they choose. As can be seen in Table 56, respondents were about equally inclined to assert human rights and property rights. Forty-two per cent of the Protestants and 48 per cent of the Catholics felt Jews have a right to be admitted anywhere—among Protestants the proportion taking this position varied from 54 per cent of the Disciples of Christ down to 24 per cent of the Southern Baptists. Thus, somewhat less than half advocated human rights, and 42 per cent of the Protestants and 40 per cent of the Catholics instead advocated the right of resort owners to pick their own customers. Few in any body, however, felt Christians had a right to their own resorts; only 4 per cent of the Protestants and 2 per cent of the Catholics took this position. The great value church members put on property rights will be seen in Chapter 10, where their attitudes on racial relations are examined. As shown here, however, this propensity, which is extensive in all denominations, is confounded with feelings of anti-Semitism per se. Consequently, the full meaning of these results is difficult to establish.

The rather elaborate item reported in Table 57 faces Christians with a more unambiguously anti-Semitic situation. Respondents were asked to suppose they were in a store operated by a Jew when a customer came in to complain about a purchase and, during an argument with the storekeeper, called him "a crook like all the Jews." Respondents were then asked a series of questions about how they might feel and act in such a situation.

1. What if you were in a store operated by a Jew, and a customer came in to complain about a purchase and during the argument with the storekeeper called him "a crook like all the Jews." How would you feel and act in this circumstance?
   a. Would you be inclined to understand the customer's feelings?
      ☐ Yes ☐ No ☐ Uncertain

2. With whom would you be inclined to feel sympathetic?
   ☐ the customer    ☐ the owner
   ☐ both            ☐ neither
3. What would you most likely do?
   ☐ Leave the store quietly
   ☐ Stay and say nothing
   ☐ Speak up on the side of the customer
   ☐ Speak up on the side of the owner
4. What if you knew the owner had actually cheated the customer?
   Would it change your feelings about the customer's remark or not?
   ☐ It would likely change my feelings in that case
   ☐ It would not change my feelings
   ☐ I don't know what effect it would have

The first line in the table shows the proportion who responded they would *not* be inclined to understand this customer's feelings. A majority, but far from an overwhelming one, said they would *not* understand. Fifty-nine per cent of both Protestants and Roman Catholics took this position, while proportions among Protestant denominations varied from about two-thirds of those in the liberal bodies on the left of the table down to barely half of those in the more conservative groups. Of the remainder, 13 per cent over-all indicated support for the customer while the rest said they were "uncertain" whether or not they would "understand."

While the majority registered their disapproval of such behavior by this disgruntled customer, many fewer in all bodies, and less than half over-all, said they would sympathize with the shop owner in this situation. Forty-six per cent of Protestants and Catholics said they would sympathize with the Jewish storekeeper, while among Protestants 53 per cent of the Congregationalists, Methodists, and Episcopalians would do so, and only 30 per cent of the Southern Baptists would.

Christians are, however, virtually unanimous in what they think they would do in such a situation: keep silent. Eighty-six per cent of the entire sample indicated they would say nothing. Of these about a third would leave the store, while the other two-thirds would stay. Only 9 per cent of the total sample said they would speak out on behalf of the owner; 1 per cent would speak out on behalf of the customer; and 5 per cent failed to answer the question. Thus, while the majority said they would disapprove of such an anti-Semitic outburst, virtually all would condone it by their silence.

The last line in the table is particularly revealing. While only a small minority unambiguously took the side of the customer in this incident, information that he had in fact been cheated would cause the overwhelming

## Table 57.  SENSITIVITY TO AN ANTI-SEMITIC INCIDENT

Hypothetical situation: "What if you were in a store operated by a Jew, and a customer came in to complain about a purchase, and during the argument with the storekeeper called him "a crook like all the Jews." How would you feel and act in this circumstance?"

| | Cong. | Meth. | Epis. | D.of Christ | Pres. | A.Luth. | A.Bap. | M.Luth. | S.Bap. | Sects | Total Prot. | Cath. |
|---|---|---|---|---|---|---|---|---|---|---|---|---|
| Number | (141) | (415) | (416) | (50) | (495) | (208) | (141) | (116) | (208) | (255) | (2,326) | (545) |
| *"Would you be inclined to understand the customer's feelings?"* | | | | | | | | | | | | |
| Per cent who would *not* be inclined to understand the customer's feelings. | 65% | 64% | 66% | 66% | 60% | 54% | 56% | 53% | 51% | 52% | 59% | 59% |
| *"With whom would you be inclined to feel sympathetic?"* | | | | | | | | | | | | |
| Per cent who responded: "the owner" | 53 | 53 | 53 | 42 | 47 | 39 | 52 | 41 | 30 | 36 | 46 | 46 |
| *"What would you most likely do?"* | | | | | | | | | | | | |
| Per cent who would either leave quietly or stay and say nothing. | 85 | 83 | 85 | 88 | 87 | 84 | 83 | 80 | 90 | 87 | 86 | 86 |
| *"What if you knew the owner had actually cheated the customer? Would it change your feelings about the customer's remark or not?* | | | | | | | | | | | | |
| Per cent for whom such knowledge would *not* change their feelings. | 22 | 28 | 27 | 28 | 22 | 20 | 20 | 24 | 24 | 18 | 24 | 25 |

majority to change, or at least question, their previous position. Only a quarter of the sample said such information would not cause them to change their feelings. Now it is clear, in retrospect, that many of these respondents failed to grasp the implications of this last question and were simply saying that they would feel differently toward the shopkeeper if he were guilty instead of innocent. Morally, of course, the shopkeeper's individual culpability in no way justifies the anti-Semitic charge that *all* Jews are crooks and that he is just like them. This failure by many respondents to see the moral implications of the last question partially invalidates it as a measure of their willingness to condone anti-Semitic incidents, but it does dramatically demonstrate their inability to *perceive* moral issues as they often arise in real life. And herein lies a major difficulty in overcoming the social injustices that discredit aspirations to a free, humane, and enlightened way of life. It does little good for men to hold high principles if they are unable to recognize when and how these principles relate to their affairs.

In summary, not only do a large proportion of these Christians fail to take an explicit private stand against anti-Semitic behavior, nearly all would do nothing to indicate disapproval, and the vast majority would consider condoning such a remark about Jews if the shopkeeper had actually cheated. It will be recalled from Chapter 7 that about 30 per cent of these respondents personally agreed with the customer's belief that Jewish businessmen are cheats, which provides them with a substantial basis for sympathy in such matters.

Reservations over the degree to which these items actually tap a propensity for anti-Semitic behavior are greatly reduced when we examine the extent to which these responses are related to anti-Semitic beliefs. As shown in Table 58, the Index of Anti-Semitic Beliefs strongly predicts responses on these hypothetical action situations. Looking at the first item in the table, among Protestants only 39 per cent of those classified as High on anti-Semitic beliefs said they would not be inclined to understand the customer's anti-Semitism in the store incident, while 83 per cent of those who scored None on anti-Semitic beliefs said they would *not* understand. A similar pattern obtains among Roman Catholics.

The same relationship can be seen in the second item, where among Protestants only 29 per cent of those High on anti-Semitic beliefs said they would be inclined to feel sympathetic toward the Jewish store owner, while 68 per cent of those scored None would feel sympathetic.

Furthermore, changing one's mind about the incident if it turned out the Jewish store owner had actually cheated is powerfully related to anti-Semitic beliefs. Seventy-one per cent of the Protestants and 80 per

Table 58. ANTI-SEMITIC BELIEFS AND ANTI-SEMITIC ACTIONS

Index of Anti-Semitic Beliefs

| | High | Medium High | Medium | None |
|---|---|---|---|---|
| *Per cent who would not be inclined to understand the customer's anti-Semitism.* | | | | |
| Protestants | 39 | 54 | 69 | 83 |
| Number | (251) | (289) | (753) | (322) |
| Catholics | 46 | 46 | 63 | 76 |
| Number | (43) | (74) | (182) | (107) |
| *Per cent who would be inclined to feel sympathetic toward the Jewish store owner.* | | | | |
| Protestants | 29 | 44 | 55 | 68 |
| Number | (250) | (291) | (754) | (321) |
| Catholics | 38 | 37 | 47 | 59 |
| Number | (44) | (74) | (181) | (106) |
| *Per cent who would likely change their feelings if they knew the owner had actually cheated (only for those who originally opposed the customer).* | | | | |
| Protestants | 71 | 59 | 52 | 34 |
| Number | (98) | (155) | (520) | (203) |
| Catholics | 80 | 77 | 44 | 39 |
| Number | (20) | (34) | (115) | (81) |

cent of the Catholics who were High on anti-Semitic beliefs said they would likely change their feelings in this case, while only 34 per cent of the Protestants and 39 per cent of the Catholics who rejected all of the anti-Semitic beliefs said they would change their minds.

Consequently, there are persuasive empirical grounds for having some confidence that these questions about hypothetical life situations do imply a propensity for anti-Semitic actions. The actions these respondents anticipate taking are strongly related to their beliefs about the character of Jews.

A second group of items in the questionnaire also bore upon the matter of anti-Semitic action—maintaining social relations with Jews. These items have the strength of asking about actual rather than hypothetical behavior, but the degree to which they constitute an aspect of anti-Semitism is not entirely clear. Obviously, the impassioned anti-Semite curtails his social relations with Jews. The heart of discrimination against Jews in contemporary American lies in the systematic way in which gentiles exclude Jews from their clubs, resorts, social activities, and homes. Thus, knowing how much or how little one has to do with Jews socially ought to measure directly this anti-Semitic pattern of exclusion. Unfortunately things are not quite that simple. Not everyone has an equal chance for social relations with Jews, regardless of how he might feel about them. This is partly overcome in our sample since all respondents lived in the same major metropolitan area; consequently, differences in their access to Jews are considerably less than would exist among respondents in a national sample. Still, there are some differences within this metropolitan area in the number of Jews living in a given neighborhood. Furthermore, it could be argued that in many instances a lack of social contact with Jews is less an instance of anti-Semitism than a state of affairs that *facilitates* the maintenance of anti-Semitism. It can be argued that because persons do not have Jewish friends, they continue to be anti-Semitic rather than that they do not have Jewish friends because they are anti-Semitic. There is probably considerable truth in both interpretations of the meaning of a lack of social contact with Jews—it both represents, and facilitates the maintenance of, anti-Semitic attitudes. Recognizing that there is likely a two-way effect between social contact and anti-Semitism, still it seems worthwhile to give attention to the extent to which these Christians do have social contact with Jews and the extent to which this is correlated with their anti-Semitic beliefs and feelings.

The data in Table 59 show that the vast majority of Christian church members are acquainted with at least one Jew. Only 13 per cent of the Protestants and 12 per cent of the Roman Catholics indicated they were not presently acquainted with a single Jew. Among the Protestants the proportion who have no Jewish acquaintances varies from 7 per cent of the Congregationalists and Episcopalians up to 38 per cent of the Southern Baptists.

Fewer persons in all denominations claimed to know at least one Jew well; 25 per cent of the Protestants and 19 per cent of the Roman Catholics indicated they did not. Again these proportions vary greatly among the Protestant bodies, ranging from less than 20 per cent for the more liberal bodies to more than half of the Southern Baptists.

Roughly similar proportions say they have *never* entertained a Jew in their homes; 13 per cent of the Episcopalians and 15 per cent of the Congregationalists have not done so, while 35 per cent of the American Baptists and 58 per cent of the Southern Baptists have not.

Upon reflection, it seems likely that these estimates of the extent of social contact with Jews are somewhat inflated. Jews are estimated to make up only 1 per cent of the total population of the sample area. If 75 per cent of our sample have had Jews in their home, one suspects that Jews in the area would have few opportunities for a quiet evening at home. But if people are inclined to exaggerate how well they know Jews and how

Table 59.   SOCIAL CONTACT WITH JEWS

|  | Cong. | Meth. | Epis. | D.of Christ | Pres. |
|---|---|---|---|---|---|
| Number | (151) | (415) | (416) | (50) | (495) |
| Not presently acquainted with a single Jew | 7% | 8% | 7% | 16% | 8% |
| Do not know a single Jew well | 18 | 19 | 16 | 28 | 23 |
| Have *never* entertained a Jew in own home | 15 | 20 | 13 | 20 | 21 |

|  | A.Luth. | A.Bap. | M.Luth. | S.Bap. | Sects |
|---|---|---|---|---|---|
| Number | (208) | (141) | (116) | (79) | (255) |
| Not presently acquainted with a single Jew | 17% | 21% | 16% | 38% | 25% |
| Do not know a single Jew well | 31 | 38 | 33 | 52 | 36 |
| Have *never* entertained a Jew in own home | 30 | 35 | 32 | 58 | 45 |

|  | Total Prot. | Cath. |
|---|---|---|
| Number | (2,326) | (545) |
| Not presently acquainted with a single Jew | 13% | 12% |
| Do not know a single Jew well | 25 | 19 |
| Have *never* entertained a Jew in own home | 26 | 24 |

many they know, this tendency is probably general enough so that the relative differences among groups of respondents are accurate. That is, Southern Baptists may have contact with Jews much less often than they report doing so, as do the Congregationalists, but the differences in reported contact between the two bodies is probably of about the same magnitude as the actual differences.

Consequently, even if these reports of social contact are descriptively inaccurate, they ought to serve satisfactorily to identify persons who have greater or lesser contact with Jews.

## Religious Bigotry and Anti-Semitic Actions

We have seen that anti-Semitic beliefs and feelings among contemporary Christians seem to a great extent rooted in their religious outlook and traditions. The degree to which these religious factors also foster a propensity for anti-Semitic actions must now be determined. The relative muddiness of the data on anti-Semitic acts makes it likely that these relationships will not be as powerful and clear-cut as those in previous chapters; nevertheless, the model ought to produce convincing results.

As can be seen in Table 60, the model of religious roots of anti-Semitism, summarized in the Index of Religious Bigotry, is indeed strongly related to items on anti-Semitic action. The first three items in the table refer to the hypothetical incident in the store when the irate customer called the store owner "a crook like all the Jews." The first item reports

Table 60.   RELIGIOUS BIGOTRY AND ANTI-SEMITIC ACTIONS[a]

Index of Religious Bigotry

|  | 0 | 1 | 2 | 3 | 4 | 5 | 6 |
|---|---|---|---|---|---|---|---|
| | *Per cent who would NOT understand the customer's anti-Semitic remark.* | | | | | | |
| Protestants | 74 | 71 | 69 | 58 | 57 | 60 | 58 |
| Number | (224) | (249) | (222) | (159) | (183) | (143) | (110) |
| Catholics | 78 | 60 | 65 | 59 | 58 | 46 | 42 |
| Number | (33) | (56) | (81) | (64) | (33) | (24) | (7)[b] |
| | *Per cent who would sympathize with the Jewish store owner.* | | | | | | |
| Protestants | 64 | 62 | 57 | 53 | 46 | 42 | 35 |
| Number | (224) | (249) | (222) | (160) | (183) | (144) | (121) |
| Catholics | 58 | 56 | 48 | 43 | 58 | 44 | 14 |
| Number | (33) | (56) | (81) | (64) | (36) | (24) | (7)[b] |
| | *Per cent who would NOT change their minds if owner had actually cheated (only for those who originally opposed the customer).* | | | | | | |
| Protestants | 42 | 33 | 31 | 23 | 25 | 23 | 19 |
| Number | (164) | (176) | (153) | (92) | (106) | (87) | (58) |
| Catholics | 47 | 52 | 38 | 37 | 22 | 18 | 0 |
| Number | (26) | (33) | (53) | (38) | (23) | (11) | (3)[b] |
| | *Per cent who do not know ONE Jew well.* | | | | | | |
| Protestants | 17 | 21 | 26 | 29 | 31 | 41 | 46 |
| Number | (227) | (243) | (220) | (158) | (183) | (138) | (110) |
| Catholics | 9 | 19 | 17 | 23 | 24 | 5 | 33 |
| Number | (32) | (56) | (79) | (60) | (33) | (21) | (6)[b] |
| | *Per cent who have NEVER entertained a Jew in their home.* | | | | | | |
| Protestants | 8 | 17 | 24 | 29 | 30 | 41 | 56 |
| Number | (225) | (247) | (222) | (159) | (179) | (143) | (113) |
| Catholics | 9 | 11 | 20 | 24 | 47 | 38 | 43 |
| Number | (33) | (56) | (81) | (62) | (34) | (21) | (7)[b] |

[a] Respondents who did not answer a particular item are omitted from the percentages.
[b] Too few cases for stable percentage, presented for descriptive interest only.

the proportions within each category of the Religious Bigotry Index who said they would *not* be inclined to understand the customer's anti-Semitism in such circumstances. Among Protestants there is a moderate decline in those who would not understand the customer as one moves from the lowest categories of the Bigotry Index to the highest—74 per cent of those with zero scores would not understand, while 58 per cent of these with maximum scores of 6 would not understand. Among Roman Catholics the relationship is somewhat stronger and more systematic, ranging from 78 per cent among those with a score of zero down to 46 per cent of those with a score of 5. The 42 per cent for Catholics with a score of 6 is based on too few cases to be offered in evidence and is presented for its descriptive interest.

The second item in the table is more clearly a measure of anti-Semitism, and asks whether or not respondents would feel sympathetic toward the Jewish store owner during such an incident. Consequently, responses to this item are much more powerfully related to the Index of Religious Bigotry. Among Protestants, the proportions who would sympathize with the owner fall from 64 per cent of those with zero scores on the index to 35 per cent of those with scores of 6. A similar pattern can be seen among Roman Catholics. It should be recognized that the relatively small number of cases on which Catholic statistics are based in this table makes findings subject to a certain amount of random fluctuation—for purely statistical reasons, patterns among Catholics can be expected to be somewhat less consistently systematic than patterns among Protestants.

Perhaps the most important, if somewhat ambiguous, question asked about this incident in the store concerned changing one's mind if it happened that the store owner had actually cheated the customer. It has been remarked earlier in this chapter that many respondents likely did not recognize the moral implications of such a change of mind: that a general anti-Semitic indictment of Jews is hardly justified by the duplicity of a single shopkeeper. Still, looking at the data in the third item, it is apparent that willingness to change one's mind in these circumstances is in fact strongly related to religious bigotry, even though only a small minority of Christians said they would *not* change their minds. Among Protestants, 36 per cent of those with zero scores on the Bigotry Index refused to change their minds, and this proportion declines across the index until only 14 per cent of those with scores of 6 showed this resistance. A relatively similar pattern characterizes the Roman Catholics.

In summary, then, the model of the religious roots of anti-Semitism does predict the way people anticipate acting in situations charged with anti-Semitic behavior.

The last two items in the table reveal that social contact with Jews is also markedly affected by religious bigotry. Only 17 per cent of those with scores of zero on the Bigotry Index indicated they do not know at least one Jew well, while nearly half (46 per cent) of those who scored 6 do not. Among Catholics a similar, but slightly weaker, relationship obtains.

Religious bigotry even more powerfully predicts whether or not Christian church members have entertained Jews in their homes. Only 8 per cent of those Protestants with zero scores on the index report they have *never* entertained a Jew in their home, while 56 per cent of those with scores of 6 have never done so. Similarly, 9 per cent of the Roman Catholics with zero scores have not entertained Jews, while approximately 40 per cent of those with scores of 4, 5, and 6 on the index have not done so.

We have already acknowledged that social contact with Jews not only reveals patterns of discrimination, but that lack of such contact may stem from other sources while acting to facilitate the maintenance of anti-Semitic beliefs and feelings. Nevertheless, the extensive discrimination against Jews that does take place in contemporary social life is contained within these data—some portion of this lack of contact obviously represents avoidance. The powerful correlation between our model and knowing and entertaining Jews amply illustrates the degree to which such avoidance is connected with religious influences.

### Conclusion

We have now assembled all the elements of our major thesis and have examined the way in which they fit together. Beginning with an examination of orthodox Christian beliefs, we have traced out the process through which they lead to a particularistic outlook which ultimately comes to impose a hostile religious definition upon modern Jews. Subsequently, it has been demonstrated that this contemptuous religious image of Jews predisposes Christians to embrace a purely secular variety of anti-Semitism as well.

Approximately 80 per cent of these church members held some explicitly negative beliefs about Jews as a group, and nearly half acknowledged they bore unfriendly feelings toward Jews because of these beliefs. We have just seen that fewer than half these Christians believe that Jews ought to have the right to be admitted to any vacation resort, that fewer than half would sympathize with a Jewish store owner who had just been called "a crook like all the Jews," that the overwhelming majority would countenance such a remark if the owner had actually cheated, and that 86 per cent would at least condone such anti-Semitic behavior through remaining silent in the face of it. Not only is anti-Semitism very characteristic of Christian church members, but all of these aspects of anti-Semitism were found to be strongly correlated with our model of the religious sources of anti-Semitism.

But even though the empirical world does seem greatly to correspond to our model, much remains to be done before we can be reasonably certain that the causal relations we have posited actually exist. While our model may be descriptively true, it has still not been determined that our explanation for the high interrelation of these phenomena is accurate. Are religious factors really producing anti-Semitism, or are these phenomena found together because some yet unexplored factor is the cause of all of them? Consequences of the same cause will always be highly correlated even if there is absolutely no independent connection among them. So it still remains to be seen whether or not there is a reasonable basis for confidence that religion is actually at the root of much current anti-Semitism. The three chapters making up Part IV of this volume will be devoted to testing the explanations we have developed: that there is a peculiarly religious element in anti-Semitism that is absent from other kinds of racial and ethnic prejudice; that these relationships are probably not artifacts of some outside cause; and that they apply nationwide and not just to northern California.

# PART IV.  A MATTER OF CERTAINTY

*Religious factors seem to be a potent source of contemporary anti-Semitism. In the following chapters we shall attempt to rule out a number of alternatives for "explaining away" these findings in order to provide a reasonable basis for having confidence that these connections between religion and prejudice are not just apparent, but real.*

# CHAPTER 10

# Christianity and Race

> Now therefore ye are cursed, and there shall none of you be freed
> from being bondmen, and hewers of wood and drawers of water for
> the house of my God.
>
> —Josh. 9:23 (A.V.)

Our concern in the present study is anti-Semitism, not intergroup prejudice
in general. Still, two rather important contributions can be made to understanding anti-Semitism by pausing briefly to consider prejudice against
Negroes. For one thing, examining the attitudes of Christians toward
Negroes gives a comparison for evaluating the depth and meaning of the
anti-Semitism we have already uncovered. Because of the explosion of
the civil rights movement, we have some reasonably accurate estimates
of the widespread hostility toward the Negro. The more covert nature
of feelings toward Jews has suggested to many that they enjoy much
friendlier relations with Christians than Negroes do with whites. While
this is likely true, it seems relevant to ask: How much better off are the
Jews actually?

The second important reason to turn our attention to anti-Negro
prejudice concerns our thesis that a considerable portion of anti-Semitism
stems from religious sources. We have seen that our model of religious
factors powerfully predicts anti-Semitism. But it would greatly strengthen
our case if it could be shown that this model *does not* similarly predict
prejudice against Negroes. The logic of this position may not be immediately apparent, for clearly prejudiced attitudes toward Jews and Negroes,
as well as against other racial and ethnic groups, are very highly correlated

—bigots tend to be well rounded in this respect. However, we have not been attempting to account for anti-Semitism in general, but to uncover and isolate specifically religious sources for hatred of the Jews. Since Negroes are largely Christians, these same religious factors should *not* operate to generate hostility toward them. To the degree that we have successfully uncovered *purely* religious sources of prejudice, then, our model ought to fail to account for racial prejudice. If the analysis in this chapter shows this to be the case, it will be, in our view, an extremely persuasive confirmation of our thesis.

To achieve these dual purposes, we shall first examine a number of questions designed to reveal racial prejudice in order to get some picture of the interracial attitudes of American Christians. These items will also be used to see if our model does or does not predict attitudes toward Negroes.

Peter L. Berger has called 11 to 12 A.M. on Sunday the most segregated hour in American life.[1] The truth of this judgment can be seen in the fact that fewer than 1 per cent of both our Protestant and Roman Catholic respondents were Negroes. It is true, of course, that many Negroes are active in Christian churches, but they are almost entirely to be found in segregated Negro congregations, even in metropolitan northern California. A failure in our data collection among specifically Negro congregations (see Appendix A) resulted in their omission from the data. In our sample of congregations which are *not* specifically Negro, there are, for all practical purposes, no Negroes. For this reason, race does not appear as a control variable in this chapter, or in Chapter 11, although this would be essential were there any appreciable number of Negroes in the sample. Thus, the data we shall now examine are based on white Christians, who, whatever their attitudes and practices on race relations, do not attend church with Negroes.

At first glance, the attitudes of Christian church members on civil rights and the Negroes seem incomprehensible. On the one hand, the data show that virtually all Christians thought the moral imperative to "love thy neighbor," applied to Negroes and that Negroes ought to have equal rights. On the other hand, when it came to applying these righteous sentiments to specific matters like allowing Negroes to live in their neighborhood, there was a massive loss of fervor. It almost seemed as if Christians were very concerned to keep Negroes out of their neighborhoods for fear that then they would have to love them.

Upon careful examination, it is apparent that vast numbers of Christians are able safely to compartmentalize their religious morality so that it will not intrude into their practical affairs. Consequently, within the

[1] *The Noise of Solemn Assemblies* (Garden City, N.Y.: Doubleday, 1961).

context of a half page of the questionnaire they were able to espouse both high moral sentiment and unambiguous prejudice. These generalizations are clearly demonstrated by the data in Table 61.

The first two items in the table have been classified as moral clichés to indicate both the overwhelming support given them and their contradiction of sentiments expressed on more specific matters of consequence in race relations. Ninety-one per cent of both Protestants and Roman Catholics agreed that " 'love thy neighbor' means that we should treat all races alike." There are no meaningful variations among Protestant denominations on this item. Virtually identical proportions in all denominations also agreed that "Negroes ought to have the same rights and opportunities as others." This all seems very promising for the future of race relations.

But having proclaimed their Christian love and advocated equal rights and opportunities for Negroes by a nearly unanimous majority, the picture of Christian racial sentiments changed radically when it came to putting these beliefs into practice. As can be seen on item three in the table, almost *half* of the sample admitted they would probably move if several Negro families moved into their block. There are no meaningful differences among the various Christian bodies in their determination to flee black neighbors—42 per cent of the Congregationalists would move and 43 per cent of the Southern Baptists said they would too.[2] Slightly higher proportions of Christian church members indicated they would sympathize with friends who decided to move under such racial circumstances.

The rationalization for moving is apparent in item five. Here half of the Protestants and 53 per cent of the Roman Catholics agreed that "Most Negro neighborhoods are run down because Negroes simply don't take care of property." Again there are no especially interesting denominational contrasts.

Item six displays the willingness of about half of the sample to dismiss the civil rights movement as the unjustified artifact of radical agitators— "The races would probably get along fine in this country if Communists and other radicals didn't stir up trouble." Forty-five per cent of the Protestants and 54 per cent of the Roman Catholics agreed with this statement. It must be pointed out that these data were collected in the spring of 1963, and that the white "backlash" in the North against the civil rights movement was just setting in. It is likely that agreement on this and other items would have been considerably higher a year or two later.

This item is of further interest because it is one on which an appreciable difference exists among the various denominations. Here, and

[2] The relatively small number of cases on which the Disciples of Christ findings are based requires that here as elsewhere in this volume they be interpreted cautiously.

Table 61.   ATTITUDES TOWARD NEGROES

| | Cong. | Meth. | Epis. | D.of Christ | Pres. | A.Luth. | A.Bap. | M.Luth. | S.Bap. | Sects | Total Prot. | Cath. |
|---|---|---|---|---|---|---|---|---|---|---|---|---|
| Number | (151) | (415) | (416) | (50) | (495) | (208) | (141) | (116) | (79) | (255) | (2,326) | (545) |
| MORAL CLICHÉS: | | | | | | | | | | | | |
| 1. " 'Love Thy Neighbor' means that we should treat all races the same." | | | | | | | | | | | | |
| Agree[a] | 93% | 93% | 88% | 90% | 89% | 92% | 93% | 89% | 93% | 92% | 91% | 91% |
| 2. "Negroes ought to have the same rights and opportunities as others." | | | | | | | | | | | | |
| Agree | 92 | 93 | 89 | 94 | 89 | 89 | 93 | 89 | 96 | 89 | 91 | 88 |
| MATTERS OF CONSEQUENCE: | | | | | | | | | | | | |
| 3. "Suppose you owned your own home and several Negro families moved into your block. Would you be apt to move elsewhere provided you could get a fair price for your house?" | | | | | | | | | | | | |
| Would probably move | 42 | 37 | 50 | 26 | 43 | 42 | 41 | 48 | 43 | 40 | 42 | 40 |
| 4. "Whether or not you think you would move under these circumstances, would you sympathize with friends of yours who decided to move?" | | | | | | | | | | | | |
| Would sympathize | 53 | 44 | 58 | 40 | 54 | 42 | 44 | 51 | 52 | 49 | 49 | 44 |
| 5. "Most Negro neighborhoods are run down because Negroes simply don't take care of property." | | | | | | | | | | | | |
| Agree | 46 | 40 | 55 | 34 | 52 | 54 | 51 | 66 | 58 | 55 | 50 | 53 |
| 6. "The races would probably get along fine in this country if Communists and other radicals didn't stir up trouble." | | | | | | | | | | | | |
| Agree | 33 | 36 | 45 | 36 | 46 | 56 | 45 | 50 | 70 | 61 | 45 | 54 |
| 7. "It's too bad, but in general, Negroes have inferior intelligence compared to whites." | | | | | | | | | | | | |
| Agree | 33 | 24 | 35 | 24 | 31 | 28 | 25 | 38 | 38 | 28 | 30 | 29 |
| 8. "It would probably be better for Negroes and whites to attend separate churches." | | | | | | | | | | | | |
| Agree | 22 | 21 | 23 | 26 | 28 | 34 | 30 | 34 | 67 | 55 | 29 | 15 |
| 9. "It would probably be better all around if Negroes went to separate schools." | | | | | | | | | | | | |
| Agree | 19 | 13 | 22 | 14 | 20 | 23 | 20 | 29 | 46 | 32 | 22 | 18 |
| 10. "It's a shame that Negroes are so immoral." | | | | | | | | | | | | |
| Agree | 28 | 26 | 24 | 12 | 28 | 22 | 25 | 36 | 33 | 32 | 26 | 28 |

[a] A combination of "definitely agree" and "agree somewhat."

on two subsequent items concerning church and school segregation, the Southern Baptists are considerably higher than any other church body, although they respond like all other Christian denominations on other items. As it turned out, Southern Baptists in our sample, although presently living in northern California, were overwhelmingly of Southern origin. Apparently these three items are more characteristic of Southern racial beliefs, and consequently these Southerners display much more extensive agreement with them. But they are no more (and no less) inclined to move away from Negroes, or, as we shall see, to discredit Negro intelligence and morality than were Northern Christians.

Reading further in the table, it may be seen that approximately 30 per cent of all respondents agreed that "It's too bad, but in general Negroes have inferior intelligence compared with whites."

Item eight is in many ways the ultimate test of Christian sentiments; even if Negroes have to live somewhere else, should not they at least be allowed in white churches? Approximately 30 per cent of the Protestants and 15 per cent of the Catholics would rather they were not—"It would probably be better for Negroes and whites to attend separate churches." As remarked above, the Southern Baptists stand in sharp relief from other denominations on this item, the difference being attributable to their Southern upbringing. But this fact does not explain these sentiments in other denominations.

Similarly, the Southern Baptists are appreciably more inclined to favor school segregation (46 per cent did), but 22 per cent of all Protestants and 18 per cent of the Roman Catholics also felt that "It would probably be better all around if Negroes went to separate schools." Finally, 26 per cent of the Protestants and 28 per cent of the Roman Catholics agreed "It's a shame that Negroes are so immoral."

With the exception of segregated schools and churches, and the responsibility of radicals for racial unrest, there are simply no systematic differences among Christian bodies on attitudes toward Negroes. In summary, it must be concluded that racial prejudice is very common among Christian church members. But how much more common is it than anti-Semitism? This is a difficult judgment because the content of negative beliefs about Jews and Negroes is different. Thus, it is hard to conclude much one way or the other from knowing, for example, that while 30 per cent of these Christians thought Negroes had an inferior intelligence, approximately the same proportion thought Jews cheat in business.

It is of course patent that Jews are not denied the right to vote while great numbers of Negroes are, and Jews have not suffered the same degree of exclusion, discrimination, or brutality in America that Negroes have so endlessly borne. But it is possible that Jews have escaped this misery primarily because they arrived in America with the cultural equipment to attain economic parity with white Christians and thus are incomparably less vulnerable to the overt cruelties worked upon the Negro. One wonders what kind of an anti-Semitic "backlash" might develop if Jews began staging sit-ins at country clubs. But lacking the burden of poverty which provides the mainspring of the Negro struggle, Jews do not raise much of a public out-cry against the injustices worked upon them.

Considering the nature of both the anti-Semitic and anti-Negro sentiments uncovered in these data, however, it seems probable that Jews have more in common with Negroes in the disdain in which they are held by white Christians than with Christians vis-à-vis Negroes in being white. Undoubtedly many fine private clubs would rather have Jewish than Negro members, but since they admit *neither,* this preference is of little value to the Jew, who must stand outside while Negroes enter only to work as servants.

### Religious Bigotry and Racial Prejudice

Our second reason for examining Christian attitudes toward Negroes is to lend confidence to our claim to have isolated peculiarly and specifically *religious* roots for anti-Semitism. Since religion is not at issue between whites and Negroes, for both are overwhelmingly Christians, our model of religious contempt ought not predict anti-Negro prejudice. Thus, we mean to show that our model is not related to ethnocentrism and prejudice in general, but responds to religious differences exclusively.

Table 62 makes it apparent that our expectations are generally confirmed. The Index of Religious Bigotry, which so powerfully predicted anti-Semitism, is essentially unrelated to prejudice toward Negroes. For purposes of comparison, the relationship between religious bigotry and anti-Semitic beliefs is shown in boldface at the top of the table. Directly beneath this relationship, in which anti-Semitism is seen to increase 68 percentage points across the index, the proportions responding in a prejudiced way on a series of Negro items increase only slightly from left to right across the index. Among Protestants these mild relationships were caused by an overrepresentation at the high end of the Bigotry Index of persons raised in the South. With Southerners removed there were no systematic differences across the index, and even with them present, as they are in this table, no relationship of any particular importance emerges.

These findings greatly increase our confidence that we have isolated specifically religious factors to account for much contemporary anti-Semitism, because they fail to have any important effect on racial atti-

Table 62. RELIGIOUS CONTEMPT AND RACIAL PREJUDICE

| | Religious Bigotry Index | | | | | | |
|---|---|---|---|---|---|---|---|
| | Low 0 | 1 | 2 | 3 | 4 | 5 | High 6 |
| Per cent High or Medium High on Index of Anti-Semitic Beliefs. | | | | | | | |
| Protestants | 10 | 15 | 28 | 37 | 46 | 57 | 78 |
| Catholics | 6 | 17 | 19 | 39 | 40 | 58 | 83 |
| Per cent who would probably move to avoid Negroes[a] | | | | | | | |
| Protestants | 36 | 40 | 41 | 41 | 41 | 44 | 52 |
| Number | (226) | (251) | (223) | (162) | (184) | (142) | (122) |
| Catholics | 36 | 35 | 34 | 34 | 47 | 50 | 43[b] |
| Number | (33) | (55) | (80) | (64) | (36) | (24) | (7) |
| Per cent who would sympathize with friends who moved to avoid Negroes.[a] | | | | | | | |
| Protestants | 46 | 46 | 48 | 49 | 50 | 54 | 59 |
| Number | (227) | (249) | (222) | (162) | (185) | (142) | (122) |
| Catholics | 43 | 36 | 41 | 58 | 41 | 50 | 43[b] |
| Number | (33) | (56) | (80) | (64) | (36) | (24) | (7) |
| Per cent who agreed, "It's a shame Negroes are so immoral."[a] | | | | | | | |
| Protestants | 21 | 23 | 23 | 29 | 32 | 35 | 50 |
| Number | (223) | (245) | (217) | (157) | (184) | (139) | (117) |
| Catholics | 30 | 24 | 23 | 31 | 50 | 41 | 29[b] |
| Number | (33) | (56) | (81) | (64) | (35) | (24) | (7) |
| Per cent who favored school segregation.[a] | | | | | | | |
| Protestants | 13 | 14 | 15 | 17 | 28 | 26 | 42 |
| Number | (226) | (249) | (221) | (161) | (186) | (141) | (120) |
| Catholics | 6 | 18 | 17 | 18 | 26 | 9 | 14[b] |
| Number | (33) | (56) | (81) | (63) | (36) | (22) | (7) |
| Per cent who agreed that Negroes have lower IQ's than whites do.[a] | | | | | | | |
| Protestants | 24 | 28 | 27 | 28 | 32 | 32 | 49 |
| Number | (226) | (251) | (221) | (161) | (187) | (143) | (119) |
| Catholics | 21 | 30 | 23 | 32 | 27 | 41 | 42[b] |
| Number | (33) | (56) | (80) | (64) | (36) | (24) | (7) |

[a] Persons who failed to answer the question were omitted from these percentages.
[b] Too few cases for a stable percentage; included here for descriptive interest.

tudes.[3] But there are still questions left to be answered before we can say we have dealt with the more reasonable alternative explanations of our findings. In the next chapter a number of these alternatives will be tested.

[3] This is not to say that religion has no effect on racial attitudes, but that the particular religious factors that we have isolated as influencing anti-Semitism do not do so. Other aspects of religion might be found strongly to influence interracial sentiments one way or the other, but this is another issue.

# CHAPTER 11

# Alternative Explanations and the Problem of Spuriousness

Doubt is not a pleasant condition, but certainty is an absurd one.
—VOLTAIRE

A typical and most useful response to any proposed scientific explanation is to ask: What other possible explanations could account for these same data? As such alternatives come to mind, we then want to know whether or not they have been eliminated empirically as possible explanations. If so, then the case in support of the proposed explanation is greatly strengthened. But if likely alternatives have not been ruled out, they remain as challenges to the explanation being proposed. In a manner of speaking, the scientific enterprise consists of exploding theories. It is entirely possible definitely to disprove any theory, but the converse is not true: No theory is ever definitely proved. Yet some theories have a much greater probability than others of being true. This probability increases as repeated tests fail to disprove a given theory and as competing explanations of the same events are disproved. Consequently, the theories we come to treat *as if* they were proved are those that have emerged from this process of elimination and have repeatedly survived attempts to disprove them.

We have clearly demonstrated in previous chapters that our theory concerning the religious roots of much contemporary anti-Semitism is *descriptively* true, that the world does indeed hang together in the way we have hypothesized. Now we must confront the possibility that our explanation of *why* these relationships occur is false, that some other explanation of these correlations will show our theory to be incorrect. Consequently, this chapter will be devoted to determining whether or not certain plausible alternative explanations can be empirically invalidated, or whether our own theory fails to survive these confrontations and can be explained away.

In approaching these matters we shall act as Devil's advocates on behalf of several important counterexplanations of our data in order to make this process of elimination as effective as possible. These are no mere straw men that we are erecting simply to knock down. A priori they offer serious objections to our theoretical position, and any competent investigator would be required to take account of them. Indeed, many readers will likely have already been wondering whether or not one of them is not the "real" explanation for the data we have used to support our theory.

## Social Class as an Alternative Explanation

There is virtual unanimity that anti-Semitism is most widespread and virulent among the uneducated, unenlightened, and poorer members of American society. It is also generally believed that religiousness, especially commitment to "Old Time" traditional Christianity, is primarily found among these same backward, downtrodden, classes. The empirical evidence that the lower classes are more anti-Semitic than the middle and upper classes has been relatively persuasive. However, recent research has shown that religious involvement, whether it be fundamentalist or liberal in theology, is largely a middle- and upper-class phenomenon, and that by comparison, the lower classes are relatively less religious.[1] However, while the notion that the lower classes are more prone to religious beliefs is not generally true, research indicates it *is* true among church members.[2] That is, while the lower classes on the whole are the least likely to hold traditional religious beliefs, those lower-class persons who do in fact participate in religion are more inclined than middle- and upper-class persons to possess fundamentalist religious outlooks. Since our sample is entirely made up of church members, these class differences do apply to our findings.

On the basis of these two correlations, it may be argued, and indeed

[1] Charles Y. Glock and Rodney Stark, *Religion and Society in Tension* (Chicago: Rand McNally, 1965), Chapters 10 and 11.
[2] Yoshio Fukuyama, "Styles of Church Membership" (New York: United Church Board of Homeland Ministries, 1961, mimeo), esp. p. 16; N. J. Demerath III, *Social Class in American Protestantism* (Chicago: Rand McNally, 1965).

has been by many with whom we discussed our findings during the course of this study, that social class lies at the bottom of our apparent relationships. The case for this alternative explanation can be put in the following way. The lower classes are *both* more likely than other classes to score high on our model of religious bigotry and *also* to be anti-Semitic. But their anti-Semitism does not stem from their religious outlook; rather both are a product of their insular and deprived circumstances. Statistically, the implication of this alternative explanation is that if social class were controlled, the relationship between religious bigotry and anti-Semitism would vanish—that social class is the cause of both religious bigotry and anti-Semitism.

Fortunately, this explanation may be rather easily put to the test. Either status measures such as education, occupational prestige, and income wash out the relationship between religious bigotry and anti-Semitism or they do not. If they do, then our theory is obviously incorrect. If they do not, our theory still may not be correct, but the social class explanation is clearly false.

Perhaps the most plausible aspect of a status explanation of our findings is education. Education is probably negatively related to anti-Semitism—educated persons are presumably less likely to be anti-Semitic than are the uneducated. Similarly, it seems likely enough that the educated will have less primitive religious outlooks. Perhaps, then, the uneducated are greatly overrepresented at the high end of the Religious Bigotry Index, and the educated overrepresented at the low end, and this accounts for the apparent relationship between the index and anti-Semitism. This explanation is both possible and sensible, but it is wrong nonetheless. Looking at the data in Table 63, it is apparent that if highly educated persons meet the conditions of the model they are as anti-Semitic as those poorly educated persons who also meet it. Whether persons failed to complete high school or did postgraduate work following graduation from college, their beliefs about Jews are equally influenced by their religious outlook. Reading from left to right across the table within each category of education, it is seen that the proportion of Protestants who score High or Medium High on the Index of Anti-Semitic Beliefs increases greatly as their religious bigotry increases. Among Catholics a similar pattern obtains, although for lack of cases the Bigotry Index had to be collapsed into only three categories, thus reducing the possible size of the relationship.

In these data the degree to which church members are overselected from the middle class is also apparent. Indeed, 63 per cent of the total sample had at least some college training, and 14 per cent had attended graduate school. It is true that the most educated were less likely than the least

Table 63.    EDUCATION, RELIGIOUS BIGOTRY, AND ANTI-SEMITIC BELIEFS

(Per cent of respondents who scored High or Medium High on
Anti-Semitic Belief Index)

Religious Bigotry Index

| Education of Protestants | 0 | 1 | 2 | 3 | 4 | 5 | 6 | Total |
|---|---|---|---|---|---|---|---|---|
| Did not complete high school | 33[a] | 16 | 33 | 30[a] | 56 | 67 | 77 | 50 |
| | (9) | (19) | (15) | (7) | (25) | (15) | (31) | (121) |
| High school graduate | 11 | 27 | 17 | 47 | 29 | 50 | 76 | 37 |
| | (18) | (34) | (42) | (38) | (42) | (32) | (21) | (217) |
| Some college | 7 | 18 | 34 | 37 | 59 | 66 | 79 | 37 |
| | (73) | (69) | (62) | (44) | (53) | (47) | (28) | (376) |
| College graduate | 12 | 12 | 26 | 32 | 53 | 36 | 70 | 24 |
| | (60) | (58) | (51) | (28) | (17) | (14) | (10) | (238) |
| Postgraduate | 9 | 6 | 30 | 31 | 30 | 50 | 86[a] | 22 |
| | (54) | (51) | (34) | (29) | (22) | (14) | (7) | (211) |

Rank on Religious Bigotry Index

| Education of Catholics | Low (0, 1) | Medium (2, 3) | High (4, 5, 6) | Total |
|---|---|---|---|---|
| Did not complete high school | 25[a] | 25 | 67 | 42 |
| | (8) | (16) | (12) | (36) |
| High school graduate | 29 | 21 | 50 | 31 |
| | (14) | (42) | (24) | (80) |
| Some college | 10 | 43 | 48 | 33 |
| | (31) | (42) | (19) | (91) |
| College graduate | 11 | 27 | [b] | 19 |
| | (18) | (22) | (3) | (43) |
| Postgraduate | 0 | 31 | [b] | 17 |
| | (14) | (13) | (2) | (29) |

NOTE: Total number of respondents is shown in parentheses.
[a] The stability of these percentages, being based on so few cases, is questionable.
[b] Too few cases to compute stable percentages.

educated to score high on the Religious Bigotry Index. But those who
did acted like anyone else who scored high on the index. The attitudes
toward Jews of a fundamentalist with a Ph.D. were like those of other
fundamentalists, not like those held by the majority of Ph.D.'s.

Looking at the totals column, an important finding comes to light.
Education does greatly affect anti-Semitism. While 50 per cent of those
Protestants who did not complete high school scored High or Medium
High on the Index of Anti-Semitic Beliefs, only 22 per cent of those who
attended graduate school were similarly anti-Semitic. However, when the

religious factors summarized in our model were controlled, these educational differences vanished. This suggests that the way in which education affects anti-Semitism is through a changing of religious views of the world. Education is accompanied by religious changes, the more educated taking up a less traditional religious outlook[3] and, consequently, tending to lose a religious basis for anti-Semitism. Thus, education may be seen as a major factor in reducing anti-Semitism in American life, but it in no way explains away our findings. Reading down the table within categories of religious bigotry, it is seen that anti-Semitism does not systematically decrease with education and that the relationship between religion and anti-Semitism remains powerful. Thus, education fails to explain away the effects of religion on anti-Semitism.

A second status variable available in our data is the occupational prestige of the head of the family. Although correlated with education, this is a commonly used measure of social class. Perhaps this will explain away our findings.

From Table 64, it is apparent that occupational status[4] has no appreciable effect on the powerful relationship between religious bigotry and anti-Semitism. Among Protestants in the upper white-collar group, made up entirely by those holding professional or high-status managerial or business positions, 8 per cent of those with a zero score on religious bigotry were High or Medium High on anti-Semitic beliefs, while 78 per cent of those with a score of 6 on religious bigotry held similar anti-Semitic beliefs. This same powerful correlation can be observed, reading from left to right, within the other levels of occupational prestige. Among Catholics virtually identical patterns can be seen where sufficient cases were available to provide stable percentages.

Furthermore, while high occupational status and education clearly predispose persons toward an unorthodox and permissive religious viewpoint, with a consequent or concurrent decline in anti-Semitism, *social class does not seem to have any direct or independent impact on attitudes toward Jews*. No matter how high their education or occupational status, persons remain very likely to be anti-Semites so long as they retain a religious perspective which facilitates an image of the Jew as a religious outsider.

Another common operationalization of the notion of social class is income. To do justice to a social class explanation of our findings we

[3] Glock and Stark, *op. cit.*, Chapter 14.
[4] The four status categories are made up of the following occupational groups: Upper white collar: professionals, proprietors, managers, officials; lower white collar: clerical, sales workers; upper blue collar: craftsmen, foremen, service workers; lower blue collar: laborers, operatives, domestics.

Table 64.   OCCUPATIONAL STATUS, RELIGIOUS BIGOTRY, AND ANTI-SEMITIC BELIEFS

(Per cent of respondents who scored High or Medium High on
Index of Anti-Semitic Beliefs)

| Occupational Status of Breadwinner | Religious Bigotry Index | | | | | | | |
|---|---|---|---|---|---|---|---|---|
| | 0 | 1 | 2 | 3 | 4 | 5 | 6 | Total |
| *Protestants:* | | | | | | | | |
| Upper white collar | 8 | 12 | 27 | 33 | 43 | 58 | 78 | 27 |
| Number | (142) | (129) | (121) | (76) | (75) | (47) | (31) | (621) |
| Lower white collar | 9 | 19 | 32 | 42 | 48 | 75 | 81 | 37 |
| Number | (44) | (52) | (41) | (24) | (25) | (20) | (21) | (227) |
| Upper blue collar | 26 | 20 | 27 | 42 | 41 | 48 | 71 | 40 |
| Number | (23) | (31) | (30) | (36) | (37) | (42) | (31) | (230) |
| Lower blue collar | ª | 10 | 29 | 51 | 75 | 50 | 78 | 48 |
| Number | (2) | (10) | (7) | (8) | (12) | (10) | (9) | (58) |
| *Catholics:* | | | | | | | | |
| Upper white collar | 0 | 15 | 18 | 53 | ª | ª | ª | 22 |
| Number | (21) | (27) | (34) | (21) | (4) | (2) | (2) | (111) |
| Lower white collar | ª | 23 | 26 | 45 | 54 | 50 | ª | 36 |
| Number | (2) | (13) | (19) | (11) | (13) | (8) | (1) | (67) |
| Upper blue collar | ª | 17 | 0 | 24 | 30 | 72 | ª | 26 |
| Number | (4) | (12) | (10) | (21) | (10) | (7) | (1) | (65) |
| Lower blue collar | ª | ª | 33 | ª | ª | ª | ª | 44 |
| Number | (1) | (2) | (12) | (5) | (4) | (3) | (2) | (29) |

ª Too few cases to compute stable percentages.

shall briefly examine yearly income as a control variable. As can be seen
in Table 65, income too has no particular effect on the relationship between religious contempt and anti-Semitic beliefs. The findings remain as
powerful among persons earning $11,000 a year or more as among those
earning $6,000 or less. A glance at the number of cases on which these
percentages are based reveals, as did the tables on education and occupational prestige, that church members are heavily middle class. Church
membership is not characteristic of the lower and working classes; rather,
it is primarily a middle- and upper-middle-class affair. Indeed, 50 per cent
of the church members in this sample are in upper white-collar occupations (or the head of their family is), and an overwhelming 70 per cent
are in the white-collar class. Only 8 per cent were in lower blue-collar
jobs. Similarly, 37 per cent earn $11,000 a year or more, and only 14 per
cent earn $6,000 or less.

The Roman Silus Italicus was probably wrong in 75 A.D. when he
said, "It is when we are in misery that we revere the gods; the prosperous

Table 65.    INCOME, RELIGIOUS BIGOTRY, AND ANTI-SEMITIC BELIEFS

(Per cent of respondents who scored High or Medium High on
Index of Anti-Semitic Beliefs)

| Yearly Family Income of Protestants | Religious Bigotry Index | | | | | | | |
|---|---|---|---|---|---|---|---|---|
| | 0 | 1 | 2 | 3 | 4 | 5 | 6 | Total |
| $6,000 or less | 16 | 13 | 16 | 50 | 45 | 67 | 85 | 42 |
| Number | (19) | (24) | (25) | (14) | (20) | (21) | (26) | (149) |
| $7,000 to $10,000 | 6 | 17 | 31 | 34 | 41 | 56 | 66 | 33 |
| Number | (77) | (106) | (89) | (68) | (85) | (63) | (44) | (532) |
| $11,000 and over | 11 | 12 | 32 | 35 | 56 | 56 | 87 | 29 |
| Number | (115) | (95) | (74) | (63) | (47) | (29) | (22) | (445) |

| Yearly Family Income of Catholics | Religious Bigotry Index | | | |
|---|---|---|---|---|
| | Low (0, 1) | Medium (2, 3) | High (4, 5, 6) | Total |
| $6,000 or less | 0 | 11 | 72 | 31 |
| Number | (12) | (18) | (18) | (48) |
| $7,000 to $10,000 | 14 | 30 | 40 | 27 |
| Number | (49) | (77) | (30) | (156) |
| $11,000 and over | 14 | 31 | 38 | 25 |
| Number | (22) | (39) | (8) | (69) |

seldom approach the altar" (*Punica,* VII). Such a viewpoint has been commonly accepted down through the centuries and is widely believed currently by well-informed persons. But it is simply not true today, and probably never was. It is primarily the prosperous who most commonly do approach the altar. So much, too, for the possibility that our findings were an artifact of social class. The data conclusively disprove it.

### Rural–Urban Differences as an Alternative Explanation

A second basis on which our findings might be challenged as spurious is closely akin to social class explanations. However, instead of the correlation being attributed to differences among social classes, they are attributed to contrasts between the more cosmopolitan and enlightened religious and ethnic attitudes of urbanites, and the more fundamentalist religion and xenophobia of rural and small-town America. Thus it may be argued that it is an overrepresentation of rural Christians, newly moved to the city, that produces this apparent relationship between religion and anti-Semitism. Clearly there is some truth in this argument—rural America is vastly more superstitious in both its religion and its beliefs about unfamiliar ethnic groups and nationalities. Furthermore, a general antipathy for "city folk" probably reinforces negative evaluations of the overwhelmingly urbanite Jews. But, regardless of how much more readily anti-Semitism may flourish in rural areas, the question remains whether rural origins account for the relationships on which our model rests.

Looking at Table 66, it is apparent that whether church members were

Table 66.   SIZE OF COMMUNITY OF ORIGIN, RELIGIOUS BIGOTRY,
AND ANTI-SEMITIC BELIEFS

(Per cent of respondents who scored High or Medium High on
Index of Anti-Semitic Beliefs)

| Size of Community[a] in Which Respondent Was Raised | Index of Religious Contempt | | | | | | |
|---|---|---|---|---|---|---|---|
| | 0 | 1 | 2 | 3 | 4 | 5 | 6 |
| *Protestants:* | | | | | | | |
| Farms and small towns under 15,000 total population | 11 | 14 | 30 | 32 | 44 | 63 | 84 |
| Number | (80) | (90) | (92) | (69) | (84) | (62) | (61) |
| Cities of 100,000 or less | 8 | 7 | 21 | 50 | 52 | 44 | 69 |
| Number | (39) | (48) | (33) | (34) | (25) | (23) | (19) |
| Cities over 100,000 | 11 | 18 | 29 | 40 | 33 | 52 | 72 |
| Number | (62) | (68) | (52) | (38) | (39) | (33) | (14) |
| *Catholics:* | | | | | | | |
| Farms and small towns under 15,000 total population | 0 | 0 | 28 | 30 | 27 | 80[b] | [c] |
| Number | (9) | (13) | (25) | (20) | (15) | (10) | (2) |
| Cities of 100,000 or less | | | | Insufficient cases | | | |
| Cities over 100,000 | 14 | 10 | 15 | 48 | 50 | 60[b] | [c] |
| Number | (14) | (29) | (41) | (27) | (14) | (9) | (3) |

[a] Suburbs of cities over 100,000 excluded from the data for lack of cases.
[b] The stability of these percentages, being based on so few cases, is questionable.
[c] Too few cases to compute stable percentages.

raised in large cities, on farms, or in small towns, their anti-Semitic beliefs are equally predictable on the basis of their religious perspective. Among Protestants who grew up in cities of more than 100,000 persons, 11 per cent of those with zero scores on the Bigotry Index were High or Medium High on anti-Semitic beliefs, while 72 per cent of these urbanites with scores of 6 were similarly anti-Semitic. The same findings also hold among Catholics.

It is true, looking at the bases of the table, that persons raised in small towns and on farms are more likely to score at the high end of the Religious Bigotry Index than are urbanites. But when these religious factors are controlled, they seem not to be particularly more prone to anti-

Semitism than are urbanites. This suggests that anti-Semitism may be more widespread in rural areas primarily because the religious factors which we have postulated to be a major source of anti-Semitism are more generally operative.

It should also be noted that a very high proportion of the Protestant church members, although currently residing in a major metropolitan area, were raised in small towns or on farms. The widely discussed difficulties Protestantism has had in establishing or maintaining a firm foothold in the city are reflected here. Not only are Protestants very much a minority in the city, but a great many of their members are recent migrants from the hinterlands.

Rural-urban differences can also be examined in terms of the part of the country in which respondents grew up. In Table 67 it is clear, how-

Table 67.   REGION OF ORIGIN, RELIGIOUS BIGOTRY, AND ANTI-SEMITIC BELIEFS

(Per cent of respondents who scored High or Medium High on
Index of Anti-Semitic Beliefs)

| Area of Country in Which Respondents Were Raised[a] | Religious Bigotry Index | | | | | | |
|---|---|---|---|---|---|---|---|
| | 0 | 1 | 2 | 3 | 4 | 5 | 6 |
| *Protestants:* | | | | | | | |
| Outside the U.S. | 15 | 33[b] | 60 | 64 | 71[b] | c | c |
| Number | (13) | (9) | (10) | (11) | (7) | (4) | (2) |
| Midwest | 14 | 17 | 25 | 47 | 53 | 59 | 90 |
| Number | (63) | (59) | (61) | (36) | (53) | (29) | (40) |
| Mountain states | 0 | 16 | 38 | 37 | 50[b] | c | c |
| Number | (10) | (13) | (13) | (11) | (8) | (4) | (4) |
| South | 0 | 8 | c | 20 | 41 | 82 | 70 |
| Number | (19) | (33) | (16) | (14) | (11) | (10) | (10) |
| Far West | 11 | 9 | 25 | 34 | 39 | 51 | 67 |
| Number | (89) | (96) | (78) | (61) | (57) | (55) | (24) |

[a] Data for persons raised in the Southwest are not presented for lack of cases. Data are shown for Protestants only because so few Catholics had been raised anywhere other than the Far West that regional comparisons were not possible.
[b] The stability of these percentages, being based on so few cases, is questionable.
[c] Too few cases to compute stable percentages.

ever, that no matter where in the nation Protestant church members were raised, their anti-Semitism is equally related to religious bigotry. Catholics are not shown because so few grew up elsewhere than in the Far West that comparisons were not possible—which also rules out the possibility that regional differences could have produced the relationship observed among them.

While region of origin in no way explains away our findings, it does seem to have some independent effect on anti-Semitism. While the estimates may be somewhat questionable because they are based on few cases, it appears that persons raised outside of the United States are more likely to be anti-Semitic than persons raised here. Inside the country, the Middle West—that bastion of rural life—seems to produce the highest propensity for anti-Semitic beliefs. The finding that persons raised in the South are apparently less likely to be anti-Semitic than Midwesterners or persons from the Mountain states seems unusual. The likely explanation is that Southerners who move to California are less typical of the South than migrants from the Midwest are of their region. Thus, although the Southerners in our sample retain much of their native prejudice against Negroes, they are not as anti-Semitic as persons still living in the South. Persons raised on the West Coast seem least likely of all to be anti-Semitic. It must be emphasized that *all* of these respondents lived in California at the time of the study. A more comprehensive examination of regional variations will be made in the next chapter when we re-examine our thesis using data from a nationwide sample.

## Cultural Change as an Alternative Explanation

In recent years there has been a degree of optimism expressed in most evaluations of the future of anti-Semitism in American life: Times are changing; people are becoming more enlightened and tolerant. In particular, the impact of the Nazi atrocities on the attitudes of the younger generations of Americans is expected to have made them less given to prejudice than their forebears. In this view, anti-Semitism is old-fashioned, a lingering relic of times past that can be expected to pass away with the older generations.

To the degree that such intergenerational trends of decreasing anti-Semitism are in fact occurring, they pose the possibility of a counter-explanation to our theory. For it is also widely presumed that religion too has been changing, becoming less orthodox and more secularized in past decades. Thus it is possible that our empirical relationship between religious bigotry and anti-Semitism is a mere artifact of uncontrolled age differences; that the elderly will be overrepresented at the high end of the index, and, for reasons having nothing to do with their religious outlooks, will also be considerably more prone to be anti-Semitic.

Table 68 suggests that there is a good deal of truth in these notions that the younger generations are both less anti-Semitic and less likely to resemble our model of religious bigotry than are the older generations. Among those who scored a high of 6 on the Religious Bigotry Index (reading down the table), 60 per cent of the Protestants 39 or under

Table 68.   AGE, RELIGIOUS BIGOTRY, AND ANTI-SEMITIC BELIEFS

(Per cent of respondents who scored High or Medium High on
Index of Anti-Semitic Beliefs)

Religious Bigotry Index

| Age | 0 | 1 | 2 | 3 | 4 | 5 | 6 |
|---|---|---|---|---|---|---|---|
| *Protestants:* | | | | | | | |
| 39 or under | 10 | 15 | 18 | 35 | 34 | 43 | 60 |
| Number | (106) | (107) | (100) | (65) | (69) | (58) | (32) |
| 40–59 | 12 | 14 | 38 | 38 | 53 | 60 | 84 |
| Number | (103) | (107) | (87) | (64) | (70) | (48) | (52) |
| 60 and over | 0[a] | 16 | 32 | 41 | 60 | 89 | 100 |
| Number | (7) | (19) | (19) | (17) | (20) | (18) | (13) |
| *Catholics:* | | | | | | | |
| 39 or under | 10 | 13 | 22 | 30 | 39 | 56[a] | [b] |
| Number | (20) | (31) | (41) | (27) | (13) | (9) | (3) |
| 40–59 | 0[a] | 20 | 15 | 45 | 40 | 56[a] | [b] |
| Number | (8) | (20) | (34) | (28) | (20) | (9) | (0) |
| 60 and over | | | | Insufficient cases | | | |

[a] The stability of these percentages, being based on so few cases, is questionable.
[b] Too few cases to compute stable percentages.

scored high or medium high on the Index of Anti-Semitic Beliefs, while 84 per cent of the 40-to-59 group did so, and 100 per cent of those 60 and over. Similar increases with age occur in most categories of the Religious Bigotry Index. Among Catholics the findings are not quite so consistent, but the same age trend appears to exist. Thus, the older generations do seem to be more anti-Semitic than the younger even when they share similar religious outlooks. Nevertheless, these age trends do not explain away our findings; whether they are young or old religious bigotry greatly predicts church members' attitudes toward Jews—within each group the relationship remains extremely powerful.

We have never suggested, of course, that religion is the *only* source of anti-Semitism in American life, or that only religious factors affect its maintenance. Clearly something has been going on to make younger Americans less anti-Semitic than their elders. But despite such changes, religion apparently remains a potent force in shaping their attitudes toward Jews.

### Politics as an Alternative Explanation

It is widely known that, at least among Protestants, religious involvement is strongly associated with a penchant for conservative politics.

Indeed, had the nation voted the way our sample of Protestant church members did, Richard M. Nixon would have been elected President in 1960 by the largest landslide in political history, beside which Lyndon Johnson's 1964 victory would have seemed won by a modest margin. Seventy-one per cent of these church-member Protestants said two and a half years after the election that they preferred Nixon. Conversely, 75 per cent of the Roman Catholics preferred John F. Kennedy.

Republicans and political conservatives are known to be more inclined to be prejudiced against all varieties of "aliens," and against Jews in particular, than are Democrats and liberals. Thus it is possible, at least among Protestants, that it is not religion but the political conservatism of the more religious that has produced these correlations with anti-Semitism. Table 69 shows that there is indeed a tendency for Nixon supporters,

Table 69. PRESIDENTIAL CHOICE IN 1960, RELIGIOUS BIGOTRY, AND ANTI-SEMITIC BELIEFS

(Per cent of respondents who scored High or Medium High on Index of Anti-Semitic Beliefs)

| Preference | Religious Bigotry Index | | | | | | |
|---|---|---|---|---|---|---|---|
| | 0 | 1 | 2 | 3 | 4 | 5 | 6 |
| *Protestants:* | | | | | | | |
| Nixon | 13 | 15 | 29 | 38 | 46 | 61 | 79 |
| Number | (139) | (166) | (141) | (104) | (113) | (84) | (76) |
| Kennedy | 6 | 15 | 24 | 34 | 44 | 47 | 71 |
| Number | (69) | (60) | (59) | (41) | (43) | (36) | (17) |
| *Catholics:* | | | | | | | |
| Nixon | [a] | 15 | 30 | 44 | [b] | [b] | [b] |
| Number | (7) | (20) | (27) | (16) | (3) | (4) | (0) |
| Kennedy | 8 | 16 | 14 | 37 | 42 | 53 | 80[a] |
| Number | (24) | (32) | (50) | (41) | (29) | (17) | (6) |

[a] The stability of these percentages, being based on so few cases, is questionable.
[b] Too few cases to compute stable percentages.

among both Protestants and Catholics, to be more anti-Semitic than persons who preferred Kennedy. However, regardless of the Presidential choice, religious bigotry remains powerfully related to anti-Semitism. The proportions High or Medium High on anti-Semitic beliefs increase from 6 per cent to 71 per cent across the Bigotry Index among Protestants who preferred Kennedy, and from 13 to 79 per cent among those who preferred Nixon. Turning from Presidential preference to political party affiliation, shown in Table 70, a similar pattern can be seen. Republicans seem to be moderately more predisposed toward anti-Semitism than are

Table 70.   PARTY AFFILIATION, RELIGIOUS BIGOTRY, AND ANTI-SEMITIC BELIEFS

(Per cent of respondents who scored High or Medium High on
Index of Anti-Semitic Beliefs)

| | Religious Bigotry Index | | | | | | |
|---|---|---|---|---|---|---|---|
| | 0 | 1 | 2 | 3 | 4 | 5 | 6 |
| *Protestants:* | | | | | | | |
| Republicans | 12 | 15 | 29 | 35 | 47 | 58 | 87 |
| Number | (130) | (156) | (125) | (93) | (96) | (56) | (60) |
| Democrats | 7 | 14 | 23 | 38 | 41 | 58 | 68 |
| Number | (58) | (50) | (56) | (45) | (46) | (50) | (28) |
| Independents | 9 | 10 | 29 | 53[a] | 53 | 60 | [b] |
| Number | (23) | (22) | (21) | (8) | (15) | (15) | (4) |
| *Catholics:* | | | | | | | |
| Republicans | 0 | 10 | 22 | 53 | 60[a] | 72[a] | [b] |
| Number | (12) | (21) | (23) | (19) | (5) | (7) | (1) |
| Democrats | 12 | 16 | 16 | 33 | 36 | 46 | 80[a] |
| Number | (16) | (25) | (43) | (33) | (25) | (13) | (6) |
| Independents | [b] | 28[a] | 10 | 33[a] | [b] | [b] | [b] |
| Number | (3) | (7) | (12) | (6) | (1) | (1) | (0) |

[a] The stability of these percentages, being based on so few cases, is questionable.
[b] Too few cases to compute stable percentages.

Democrats, but within both groups the correlation between religious bigotry and anti-Semitism remains massive.

Political preferences do affect anti-Semitism, but they are ruled out as a counterexplanation of our findings.

## Sex as an Alternative Explanation

Sex must also be considered as a possible counterexplanation. It is recognized that women are more apt to be involved in religion than are men. Indeed, 63 per cent of our Protestant respondents and 66 per cent of the Catholics are females.[5] It is conceivable that women are more likely to be anti-Semitic than are men and that our correlations were produced by uncontrolled sex differences. Table 71 shows that this is not the case. If anything, women appear somewhat less likely to be anti-Semitic than men, and among both Protestants and Roman Catholics the relationship between religious bigotry and anti-Semitic beliefs remains extremely powerful among both men and women. Sex is clearly ruled out as a possible alternative explanation.

[5] This is accurate of the church population sampled (See page 237, Appendix A).

Table 71. SEX, RELIGIOUS BIGOTRY, AND ANTI-SEMITIC BELIEFS

(Per cent of respondents who scored High or Medium High on
Index of Anti-Semitic Beliefs)

| | Religious Bigotry Index | | | | | | |
|---|---|---|---|---|---|---|---|
| | 0 | 1 | 2 | 3 | 4 | 5 | 6 |
| *Protestants:* | | | | | | | |
| Men | 9 | 17 | 32 | 31 | 55 | 60 | 79 |
| Number | (112) | (110) | (90) | (72) | (70) | (54) | (28) |
| Women | 12 | 13 | 25 | 34 | 39 | 54 | 77 |
| Number | (104) | (123) | (116) | (74) | (89) | (70) | (69) |
| *Catholics:* | | | | | | | |
| Men | 8 | 14 | 32 | 50 | 42 | 80[a] | [b] |
| Number | (12) | (29) | (32) | (22) | (12) | (5) | (1) |
| Women | 5 | 20 | 11 | 33 | 39 | 50 | 80[a] |
| Number | (19) | (25) | (46) | (37) | (21) | (16) | (5) |

[a] The stability of these percentages, being based on so few cases, is questionable.
[b] Too few cases to compute stable percentages.

## Time Order as an Alternative Explanation

The logic of our model rests on certain assumptions about the sequence in which elements occur. We have postulated that religious hostility is a consequence of, and thus must develop subsequent to, those factors summarized as religious dogmatism. Furthermore, we have hypothesized that religious definitions of the Jew provide a basis for purely secular unfavorable ideas about Jews. For this to be the case, then religious hostility must precede, not follow, secular anti-Semitic beliefs.

It might be argued that we have postulated this developmental sequence backwards, that while our correlations cannot be denied, they can be interpreted in a way that removes all casual burden from religion. Thus, it might be claimed that secular anti-Semitism comes first and that persons then embrace religion to provide an additional justification for their anti-Semitism.

A definitive solution to this question of time order cannot be provided by a survey of persons taken only at one point in time. Conclusive proof could only be obtained through a longitudinal or panel study in which changes in individuals' religious outlooks and in their anti-Semitism could be examined to see which occur first. But the absence of conclusive proof does not mean the question must be left entirely open; some evidence can be adduced. First of all, there seems no persuasive theoretical reason to expect anti-Semitism to produce religious commitment. It seems reasonable to expect an anti-Semite to be attracted to hate groups, but why should we expect him to turn to abiding faith in God because of his bigotry? Furthermore, there seems to be strong inferential evidence that religious beliefs and traditions are typically learned earlier than are attitudes toward Jews. While there are obvious exceptions—persons who hear evil of the Jews at the same age as they are learning Christian doctrine—we would commonly expect little children to know a great deal about religion *before* they even know the word Jew or what it means. While no study has shown this to be the case, it strikes us as extremely plausible. Most people are more concerned about their religion than about their prejudices; there are thousands of books, pamphlets, movies, records, and classes devoted to teaching children Bible lessons, but there is no similar effort devoted to teaching children to hate Jews.

Another test of time order could be made by examining persons who have been exposed to Christian teachings, but not to a culture abounding in secular anti-Semitism. For such people, reared in non-Western cultures, it is impossible to argue that their anti-Semitism led to their hostile religious image of the Jew. Again no such study has been done, but we do have the personal observations of Horace M. Kallen:

> . . . I have discussed anti-Semitism with Christianized Chinese and Japanese who have never been exposed to the secondary, non-religious anti-Jewish prepossessions. The reaction seemed in all cases the unconscious response of a habit whose base was the religious preconception—the definition of the central role and status of the Jew in the Christian system.
>
> Wherever this system is taught the preconception is transmitted. . . . Attitudes that Sunday-schools the world over impart automatically to children at five may be deep buried and forgotten, but they are not extirpated, nor translated. They make a subsoil of preconceptions upon which other interests are nourished and from which they gather strength.[6]

Thus, although the question of time order cannot be entirely solved with available data, there are strong inferential grounds to justify the order we have postulated.

## Conclusions

At the beginning of this chapter we proposed to confront our findings empirically with a series of possible counterexplanations in order either to eliminate them or to explode our own theoretical case. During the course

[6] Horace M. Kallen, "The Roots of Anti-Semitism," *Nation*, February 28, 1923, pp. 240–242.

of the chapter, education, occupational prestige, income, rural-urban origins, age, politics, and sex have all been definitely disproved as possible alternative explanations of our findings. As was pointed out, disproving these counterexplanations in no way proves that our own explanation is true. But, since these particular counterexplanations cannot be true, there are that many fewer chances that our explanation is false, and the probability that it is true is thereby greatly increased. In acknowledging that our theory logically cannot ever be definitely proved, we do not mean to provide a source of comfort to those whose personal commitments are threatened by it. For it is neither persuasive nor legitimate to dismiss our explanation as "only a theory" without admitting that it is the *only* theory at present that adequately accounts for the powerful relationship between religion and anti-Semitism. For that matter, all statements of any importance, whether they assert the existence of God or the law of gravity, are "only theories" in precisely this same sense. And while we recognize that the law of gravity may be disconfirmed tomorrow, such a possibility provides a slim basis for ignoring it. The explanation we have postulated concerning the religious roots of anti-Semitism is hardly comparable to the law of gravity. However, the rules of evidence for dismissing either are the same.

Clearly the task of confronting our theory with chances for disconfirmation has only been begun in this chapter. Other scholars will undoubtedly conceive of a great many alternative explanations that we have neither considered nor tested. It is hoped that they will undertake such tests. It is hoped, too, that our more general notions concerning the origins and consequences of religious particularism will be applied and tested on other instances of religious conflict among men. Does religious particularism *always* arise in religions that claim universal applicability for a highly specified set of tenets and that develop in the midst of others who do not share this religious outlook? And does the hostility arising from such invidious definitions of religious legitimacy *always* infect men's perceptions of other nonreligious aspects of those who are outside the True Faith? It would be especially interesting to test these hypotheses in non-Western cultures.

CHAPTER 12

# A Nationwide Replication

> There's no law West of Dodge City, and no God West of Laramie.
> Frisco's West of both of them.
>
> —A Forty-niner heading West

No matter how scrupulous we might have been so far in attempting to establish the validity of our findings, it would still be possible to dismiss them as a local phenomenon. All of the analysis in preceding chapters is based on a sample made up entirely of Christian church members in four counties along the Western coast of San Francisco Bay. What reason is there to accept this picture of the religious roots of anti-Semitism as bearing any resemblance to conditions elsewhere in the nation? Indeed, it is commonly believed that religion in California is characterized by weird cults and sects that are alien to religion as it exists in the rest of the country.

Clearly, we did not think that our choice to carry out the study in northern California would distort our findings, or we would have gone elsewhere. We anticipated that, if anything, the fact that religious fervor is somewhat lower,[1] and libertarian traditions perhaps greater, here than

[1] Gallup's surveys consistently find church attendance is rather lower on the West Coast than in any other region of the country. His most recent findings, released December 27, 1964, were as follows:

| Region | Per Cent Attending Church in Typical Week |
|---|---|
| New England | 59 |
| Mid-Atlantic | 47 |
| East Central | 41 |
| West Central | 46 |
| South | 48 |
| West | 35 |

188

elsewhere in the nation might work against our central hypotheses. Hence, we were confident that any relationships between religion and prejudice uncovered in a study based on northern California would hold elsewhere in the nation, and would perhaps be borne out even more strongly. But there is no reason to dismiss this problem of generalizing to the nation-at-large with plausible arguments. Fortunately, our budget permitted us to obtain comparable data on a representative sample of the entire adult population of the United States.

In collecting data from the northern California sample an attempt was made to concentrate on information in depth. That is, a large number of questions were devoted to each aspect of our major thesis—many more questions than our resources would permit us to ask of a national sample. Such detail we deemed necessary for an adequate investigation of the variety of ways in which religion might generate hostility toward Jews. But having completed such a detailed examination, a retest of our major findings required much less detail. Consequently, the descriptive breadth of a national sample could be usefully added to our investigation. A few of the most central questions bearing on each major concept in our theoretical scheme were included in a national study of the American adult population conducted in October 1964.[2]

These national data will enable us to confirm empirically that the findings presented in previous chapters apply to the nation as a whole, and to the general public as well as to church members. They also provide an occasion briefly to recapitulate our central thesis and interpretations. To facilitate such a summing up, the national findings will be presented in an order corresponding to that of preceding chapters.

## Orthodoxy

We reported in Chapter 1 that Christian denominations differ greatly in the degree to which they have retained their commitment to traditional beliefs. Furthermore, these differences are not restricted to secondary matters, but are to be found even on a primary premise of all Christian doctrine: the existence of a sentient God. It is immediately apparent in Table 72 that these findings are not to be dismissed as California Christianity. Differences in the proportions who "know God really

[2] The primary purpose of the survey was a broad assessment of the extent and sources of contemporary anti-Semitism. This study, being prepared by Dr. Gertrude Jaeger Selznick and Stephen Steinberg, is another of those making up the series of anti-Semitism studies being conducted by the Survey Research Center, University of California, Berkeley. The results of all of these studies will soon be published by Harper & Row as companions to the present volume.

Table 72.   BELIEF IN GOD (NATIONAL SAMPLE)

|  | "I know God really exists and I have no doubts about it." |
|---|---|
| Unitarian (9) | 22% |
| Congregational (44)ᵃ | 63 |
| United Presbyterian (75) | 67 |
| Protestant Episcopal (56) | 72 |
| Methodist (217) | 78 |
| Presbyterian Church USA (40) | 70 |
| Disciples of Christ (42)ᵇ | 73 |
| American Lutheran bodies (146)ᶜ | 70 |
| **Total moderate Protestants (628)** | **72** |
| Lutheran, Missouri Synod (45) | 70 |
| Evangelical and Reformed (28)ᵃ | 71 |
| American Baptist (91) | 82 |
| Southern Baptist (187) | 93 |
| Other Baptist bodies (90) | 86 |
| Sects (128)ᵈ | 90 |
| **Total conservative Protestants (569)** | **86** |
| Total Protestants (1,197) | 79 |
| Catholics (507) | 85 |

NOTE: Figures in parentheses show total number of respondents.

ᵃ The Congregational and the Evangelical and Reformed denominations merged several years ago to form a single body under the name of the United Church of Christ. However, because of the extreme contrasts in religious outlook between members of the two original bodies we have presented them here separately under their old names.

ᵇ Officially the Christian Church.

ᶜ Included here are the Lutheran Church in America and the American Lutheran Church. There were no important differences between members of these two bodies.

ᵈ Included in the category of sects were: Assemblies of God, Church of Christ, Church of God, Four Square Gospel, Free Methodist, Mennonite, Nazarene, Pentecostal, Salvation Army, Seventh Day Adventist, Campbellite, Jehovah's Witnesses, Christian Missionary Alliance, Mission Covenant, and various tiny holiness bodies. Excluded were such groups as Christian Science, Unity, Divine Science, Theosophy, Spiritualists, and other such bodies which most properly should be classified as cults for our analysis, but since only 11 persons in the sample claimed affiliation with bodies of this type, such a general category seemed futile. Also excluded were persons who claimed affiliation with the various Eastern Orthodox churches, and one member of each of the major Asian faiths.

exists and have no doubt about it" range from 22 per cent of the Unitarians, 63 per cent of the Congregationalists, and up to 93 per cent of the Southern Baptists. Over-all, roughly three-fourths of the Protestants and 85 per cent of the Roman Catholics indicated undoubted faith in God.[3]

Recalling responses to this same question as reported in Chapter 1 (Table 1) it will be noted that the proportions giving this response are

[3] The 272 respondents who gave their religious affiliation as Jews, Mormons, none, one of the Eastern or Asian faiths, or various small cults were omitted from the denominational tables.

somewhat higher in the national data, especially in the most liberal bodies. There are several reasons for this contrast. The California data were collected by an anonymous questionnaire, while the national data are the product of personal interviews. It seems reasonable to expect that on a matter so heavily sanctioned by social norms as belief in God, having to state one's belief to a stranger (most often a middle-aged, middle-class housewife) would introduce a bias in favor of the most "proper" answer. A second factor is also not a California-America difference but rather a rural-urban effect. All of the respondents in the California data were then residents of a major metropolitan area. However, persons living on farms and in the small towns and middle-sized cities in America are considerably more traditional in their religious beliefs than are urbanites. The presence of such persons in the national data produced an increase in the proportions claiming certain belief in God. This rural-urban factor is also largely responsible for other differences between the national and the California data. For example, the Methodists appeared to be somewhat less traditional in their religious ideology than the Episcopalians in the California data, although the differences were quite small. However, in the national data they appear to be slightly more traditional than the Episcopalians. The reason for this shift is that the rural-urban effect is of greater significance among Methodists than among Episcopalians. That is, Episcopalians are more predominately urbanites than are Methodists and therefore when rurals are included in the sample the Episcopalian profile is less affected.

Data showing these regional variations in religious beliefs will be presented shortly, and eventually in this chapter we shall see if such variations necessitate any revisions in our central thesis concerning the effect of religion upon anti-Semitism.

An additional difference between the national and California data must also be noted: More denominations are represented in the national data. This *is* a function of regional differences, and broadens the scope of the study. Furthermore, many persons in the national sample were not members of any church congregation, although nearly all claimed some denominational tie. Thus, in the national data, findings apply to the churched and the unchurched alike.

The effect of having the unchurched in the national sample clearly shows up in Table 73. Belief is *lower* in all denominations (on the existence of the Devil) than was reported in Chapter 1 (Table 5) with the exception of the Congregationalists, where it is about equally absent.[4]

---

[4] The same effect was not present, as noted above, in response to the question on belief in God; the national sample was more likely than the church member

This clearly suggests that persons who actually belong to a congregation are much more likely to have retained their faith in the Devil than are persons who claim the same denomination without belonging to a congregation. Unfortunately, through an accident in preparing the final interview schedule this likely explanation could not be tested. The question that would have asked respondents in the national sample if they belonged to a specific congregation was inadvertently, and to our great embarrassment, left out.

Table 73.   BELIEF IN THE DEVIL AND LIFE BEYOND DEATH (NATIONAL SAMPLE)

|  | Absolutely Sure There Is a Devil | Absolutely Sure There Is a Life Beyond Death |
| --- | --- | --- |
| Unitarian (9) | 0% | 0% |
| Congregational (44) | 7 | 26 |
| United Presbyterian (75) | 20 | 36 |
| Protestant Episcopal (56) | 21 | 35 |
| Methodist (217) | 33 | 42 |
| Presbyterian Church USA (40) | 35 | 43 |
| Disciples of Christ (42) | 29 | 42 |
| American Lutheran bodies (146) | 31 | 52 |
| **Total moderate Protestants (628)** | **27** | **41** |
| Lutheran, Missouri Synod (45) | 44 | 50 |
| Evangelical and Reformed (28) | 39 | 50 |
| American Baptist (91) | 47 | 41 |
| Southern Baptist (187) | 55 | 65 |
| Other Baptist bodies (90) | 55 | 59 |
| Sects (128) | 61 | 67 |
| **Total conservative Protestants (569)** | **53** | **59** |
| Total Protestants (1,197) | 40 | 50 |
| Catholics (507) | 36 | 48 |

NOTE: See Table 72 for denominational definitions. Figures in parentheses show total number of respondents.

The same order of differences between our samples of church members and the general public can be seen on belief in life after death. In all denominations the national data indicate a smaller proportion believe in life after death than was found in the California data.

Perhaps a more important feature of Table 73 is the confirmation of our earlier findings that the religious bodies in America differ greatly in their commitment to traditional theological tenets. Vast differences can

---

sample to give the orthodox response. It is not entirely clear why this should be so. We suspect, however, that a face-to-face interview might operate to constrain a non-orthodox response on such a central article of faith as belief in God. This same reticence apparently did not operate where the questions pertained to more peripheral Christian beliefs.

be seen by reading down the table in the proportions of these denominations who believe in the Devil and in a life beyond death.

National figures, for all their descriptive interest, are something of a fiction. Culturally there are many Americas, and especially in religion Americans differ from place to place. National data, being a sum of these differences, conceal the regional diversity of American religion. In order to examine these regional variations, however, the question of racial differences must first be considered. Among moderate Protestants[5] as well as among Roman Catholics the data show that Negroes were more likely than whites to hold traditional and firm positions on the three belief items we have just examined. However, among conservative Protestants, Negroes were somewhat less likely than whites to hold these beliefs. Because the proportion of Negroes in the population differs greatly from one region of the country to another it is necessary to control for race in examining regional variations in religious belief. The shortage of sufficient numbers made such regional comparisons impossible for Negroes, so we shall only be able to examine variations among whites.

Turning to Table 74 it can be readily seen that among whites there are very substantial differences in religious outlook from region to region. Among moderate Protestants, for example, the proportions taking a firmly orthodox position on God range from 63 per cent in the Mountain

Table 74.   REGIONAL VARIATIONS IN RELIGIOUS BELIEFS
(NATIONAL SAMPLE, WHITES ONLY)

|  | East | Midwest | South | South-west | Mountain and Pacific |
|---|---|---|---|---|---|
| *"I know God really exists and I have no doubts about it."* | | | | | |
| Moderate Protestants | 70% | 67% | 85% | 74% | 63% |
| Conservative Protestants | 74 | 84 | 91 | 99 | 65 |
| Catholics | 83 | 86 | 90 | 90 | 81 |
| *Absolutely Sure There Is a Devil* | | | | | |
| Moderate Protestants | 22% | 24% | 38% | 37% | 20% |
| Conservative Protestants | 38 | 54 | 63 | 60 | 39 |
| Catholics | 32 | 39 | 57 | 38 | 29 |
| *Absolutely Sure There Is a Life Beyond Death* | | | | | |
| Moderate Protestants | 31% | 42% | 51% | 52% | 35% |
| Conservative Protestants | 56 | 64 | 76 | 67 | 45 |
| Catholics | 45 | 53 | 57 | 48 | 40 |
| *Number of Respondents* | | | | | |
| Moderate Protestants | (125) | (214) | (111) | (46) | (87) |
| Conservative Protestants | (34) | (97) | (147) | (81) | (51) |
| Catholics | (217) | (160) | (31) | (21) | (58) |

[5] The reader will have noticed the subtotals in boldface in tables 72 and 73. These subtotals classify the Protestant bodies into two general groups: the moderates and the conservatives.

and Pacific West region to 85 per cent in the South. Among conservative Protestants the range is from 65 per cent to 91 per cent, and among the Roman Catholics, from 81 to 90 per cent.

Similar regional contrasts can be seen on belief in the Devil and belief in life beyond death. Protestantism, especially its more conservative forms, differs greatly according to where it is located. Over-all, Roman Catholicism seems least subject to regional differences, but the Bible Belt atmosphere of the American South, and to a lesser extent the Southwest, influences Catholics too. In all religious bodies orthodoxy is weakest in the Far West and nearly as weak in the East. However, traditional Christian theological positions remain sufficiently widespread to serve as a source for a particularistic view of religious legitimacy.

## Particularism

If, as we have demonstrated quite clearly in Chapter 2, religious particularism is largely a result of commitment to a traditional Christian ideology, then we would expect to find less particularism nationally than in our regional sample, for religious orthodoxy is less widespread in the general public than among church members. That this is the case can be seen in Table 75. Here considerably lower proportions in each denomination asserted that a person who did not accept Jesus could be saved than did so in the California sample (Table 10, Chapter 2). For example 38 per cent of the California Congregationalists took this position, but only 23 per cent of the Congregationalists nationwide did so. A similar comparison for Missouri Synod Lutherans is 97 per cent versus 63 per cent, and for Catholics 51 per cent versus 29 per cent. Thus, the presence of a larger proportion of persons who are not committed to traditional Christian orthodoxy is reflected in a smaller proportion who would restrict salvation to Christians.

A second measure of particularism is provided by the notion of being God's Chosen People. As can also be seen in Table 75, the proportions of the denominations who think Christians are today's elect are smaller nationwide than among California church members.

On both measures of particularism the now familiar increase from the more liberal denominations to the more conservative is powerfully replicated for the nation. While none of the Unitarians thought Christians were God's Chosen People today, and only 14 per cent of the Congregationalists thought so, almost half of the Baptists thought Christians had this divinely sanctioned monopoly on virtue. Over-all, 35 per cent of the Protestants took this position and 21 per cent of the Roman Catholics did so. Thus, while particularism is considerably less common among

Table 75.  PARTICULARISM (NATIONAL SAMPLE)

| | Belief in Jesus Necessary to Salvation[a] | God's Chosen People Today | |
|---|---|---|---|
| | | "Christians" | "No One" |
| Unitarian (9) | 11% | 0% | 100% |
| Congregational (44) | 23 | 14 | 61 |
| United Presbyterian (75) | 41 | 36 | 47 |
| Protestant Episcopal (56) | 26 | 22 | 65 |
| Methodist (217) | 56 | 33 | 39 |
| Presbyterian Church USA (40) | 53 | 35 | 55 |
| Disciples of Christ (42) | 59 | 36 | 27 |
| American Lutheran bodies (146) | 55 | 33 | 42 |
| **Total moderate Protestants (628)** | **48** | **30** | **45** |
| Lutheran, Missouri Synod (45) | 63 | 37 | 46 |
| Evangelical and Reformed (28) | 54 | 47 | 29 |
| American Baptist (91) | 80 | 59 | 26 |
| Southern Baptist (187) | 85 | 45 | 21 |
| Other Baptist bodies (90) | 82 | 46 | 26 |
| Sects (128) | 87 | 42 | 23 |
| **Total conservative Protestants (569)** | **81** | **41** | **25** |
| Total Protestants (1,197) | 64 | 35 | 35 |
| Catholics (507) | 29 | 21 | 54 |

NOTE: Figures in parentheses show total number of respondents.
[a] Percentage of respondents who answered "no" to the question "Do you think a person who doesn't accept Jesus can be saved?"

the general public than among church members exclusively, it is far from an insignificant force. For these percentages represent millions of Americans who fully believe they are among God's Chosen People and that many of their fellow countrymen, particularly those who are Jewish, are denied this special status. The incidence of religious particularism differs from region to region in a pattern similar to that seen on religious beliefs: Particularism is highest in the South and lowest on the West Coast.

For the sake of brevity we shall not pause here to show, as is in fact the case, that the powerful relationship between orthodoxy and particularism found among California church members holds for the nation at large. These and other such relationships will be reported simultaneously after the national denominational data on all of the central concepts in our theoretical model have been presented.

### Religious Images of the Historic Jew

As was true of church members, the majority of Americans recognize the Jewishness of the Old Testament and report that the Chosen People meant in the Old Testament were the Jews. Recalling Table 16 in Chapter

3, the data in Table 76 clearly show that a smaller proportion in each denomination nationwide acknowledged the Jews as the Old Testament Chosen People. These differences seem largely to represent ignorance on the part of those who do not have membership in a church rather than anti-Jewishness, because the tendency to Christianize the Old Testament

Table 76.  THE HISTORIC JEW (NATIONAL SAMPLE)

| | "Who were Chosen People of the Old Testament?" | | Group most responsible for the Crucifixion: |
|---|---|---|---|
| | "Jews" | "Christians" | "Jews" |
| Unitarian (9) | 89% | 0% | 1% |
| Congregational (44) | 77 | 7 | 30 |
| United Presbyterian (75) | 68 | 12 | 41 |
| Protestant Episcopal (56) | 79 | 7 | 42 |
| Methodist (217) | 61 | 17 | 40 |
| Presbyterian Church USA (40) | 78 | 13 | 40 |
| Disciples of Christ (42) | 56 | 20 | 42 |
| American Lutheran bodies (146) | 61 | 11 | 39 |
| **Total moderate Protestants (628)** | **66** | **13** | **39** |
| Lutheran, Missouri Synod (45) | 65 | 15 | 41 |
| Evangelical and Reformed (28) | 68 | 18 | 68 |
| American Baptist (91) | 59 | 22 | 46 |
| Southern Baptist (187) | 63 | 15 | 38 |
| Other Baptist bodies (90) | 53 | 24 | 47 |
| Sects (128) | 71 | 15 | 58 |
| **Total conservative Protestants (569)** | **63** | **18** | **47** |
| Total Protestants (1,197) | 63 | 15 | 43 |
| Catholics (507) | 64 | 10 | 50 |

NOTE: Figures in parentheses show total number of respondents.

is no greater in the public at large than among church members. That is, proportionately fewer in the national samples responded that the Jews were God's Chosen People than in the California sample because a greater proportion in the nationwide sample said they "didn't know."

As was the case among church members, the tendency to Christianize the Old Testament is considerably more common in the conservative bodies than in the liberal Protestant denominations. Differences between Protestants and Roman Catholics are relatively minor.

If the majority of Americans acknowledge the mutual roots of Judaism and Christianity, nearly a majority also blame the Crucifixion on the ancient Jews. Forty-three per cent of the Protestants and 50 per cent of the Roman Catholics identified the Jews as the "group most responsible for the Crucifixion." Among Protestants the proportions blaming the Jews rise sharply from 11 per cent of the Unitarians and 30 per cent of the Congregationalists up to 68 per cent of the members of the Evangelical and Reformed and 58 per cent of those who belong to the myriad Protestant sects. Again these proportions are considerably lower than were found among church members, which is what we would expect. Still a vast number of Americans view the ancient Jews as "Christ-killers." Indeed, less than two months before the Vatican Council acted provisionally to pronounce the Jews innocent of the Crucifixion, half of America's Catholics held a contrary opinion. This fact emphasizes the potential importance of the council's action if its schema, now passed, is vigorously promulgated and taught by the American clergy. On the other hand, a number of America's Protestant bodies have made similar pronouncements in recent years, yet nearly half of their members remain unmoved, and those who actually participate in the church—the "best" members—are those most likely to retain this traditional belief about Jewish deicide.

This propensity of Christians to blame the Jews for the death of Jesus varies greatly in different parts of the country. It is a minority view in the East and West while a majority one in the Midwest, South, and Southwest.

Thus, the implication of the Jews in the Crucifixion of Jesus remains a common belief among American Christians. While such a belief need not, and often does not, imply any resentment toward modern Jews, we have seen in earlier chapters that it provides an important basis for generating hostile religious images of the modern Jew.

### Religious Images of the Modern Jew

The main theme in religious hostility toward Jews has been that they are under a curse. Matthew reported in the New Testament that the Jews forced Pontius Pilate to permit the Crucifixion, and when he refused to accept responsibility for such an act, the Jewish multitude took "His blood upon us, and on our children." This version of Jewish guilt has long served as a rationale for anti-Semitism; the Jews have brought their troubles on themselves. God is punishing the Jews and hence there is divine approval for Christians doing likewise.

We reported in Chapter 4 that approximately 40 per cent of both Protestant and Catholic church members at least considered it possible that the suffering of modern Jews actually stemmed from divine will. We had hardly anticipated that such a view would be so common. Yet Table 77 shows that this was not a California oddity—a great many Americans

Table 77. RELIGIOUS IMAGES OF THE CONTEMPORARY JEW (NATIONAL SAMPLE)

Reply to: "The reason the Jews have so much trouble is because God is punishing them for rejecting Jesus."

|  | Yes | Don't Know | No |
|---|---|---|---|
| Unitarian (9) | 0% | 11% | 89% |
| Congregational (44) | 7 | 5 | 88 |
| United Presbyterian (75) | 13 | 5 | 82 |
| Protestant Episcopal (56) | 14 | 4 | 82 |
| Methodist (217) | 19 | 16 | 65 |
| Presbyterian Church USA (40) | 8 | 12 | 80 |
| Disciples of Christ (42) | 17 | 12 | 71 |
| American Lutheran bodies (146) | 21 | 14 | 65 |
| **Total moderate Protestants (628)** | **16** | **12** | **72** |
| Lutheran, Missouri Synod (45) | 26 | 11 | 63 |
| Evangelical and Reformed (28) | 21 | 11 | 68 |
| American Baptist (91) | 32 | 15 | 53 |
| Southern Baptist (187) | 35 | 11 | 54 |
| Other Baptist bodies (90) | 28 | 21 | 51 |
| Sects (128) | 30 | 16 | 54 |
| **Total conservative Protestants (569)** | **31** | **14** | **55** |
| Total Protestants (1,197) | 23 | 13 | 64 |
| Catholics (507) | 15 | 8 | 77 |

NOTE: Figures in parentheses show total number of respondents.

support the statement "The reason the Jews have so much trouble is because God is punishing them for rejecting Jesus." Twenty-three per cent of the Protestants think this statement is true and an additional 13 per cent say they "didn't know." Similarly, 15 per cent of the Roman Catholics supported the view that Jewish troubles stem from God's wrath, while 8 per cent "didn't know."

These same proportions sharply differ between the more liberal and more conservative Protestant bodies. No Unitarian and only 7 per cent of the Congregationalists agreed with the statement, while 35 per cent of the Southern Baptists did so.

In contrast to the data on church members (Table 25, Chapter 4) Americans nationally are more likely to reject the belief that Jewish suffering is made in heaven.[6] Yet millions of Americans do believe it.

[6] Since the "uncertain" response was offered respondents in the California questionnaire, and the national respondents had to volunteer "don't know" there was a tendency for the Californians to pile up in "uncertain" making them appear less likely to agree in some denominations than persons in the national sample. However, by considering the percentage who disagreed in each sample, the extent to which this belief is more widespread among church members than in the nation at large is shown.

Little wonder that the facts of the German atrocities and the trial of Adolph Eichmann had so little impact on the American public.[7] Obviously, of course, the overwhelming majority of those Americans who think Jews are being punished by God do not therefore approve of the Nazi "final solution," although 7 per cent of the American adults interviewed in this sample did in fact feel Hitler was justified in destroying the Jews. But even if they feel the Nazis went too far, thinking that God is behind much Jewish suffering would seem a dubious basis for expecting such people to take much interest in the tribulations of Jewry, let alone feel any great sympathy for the Jewish victims of persecution.

## Religious Libertarianism

Two of the items on civil liberties for atheists which were included in the Religious Libertarianism Index used in Chapter 5 were asked of the national sample. It is on these items, which are shown in Table 78, that the greatest discrepancies between the California and national samples

Table 78.   RELIGIOUS LIBERTARIANISM (NATIONAL SAMPLE)

|  | Would Not Allow an Atheist to Hold Public Office | Would Not Allow an Atheist to Teach in a Public High School |
|---|---|---|
| Unitarian (9) | 0% | 0% |
| Congregational (44) | 44 | 50 |
| United Presbyterian (75) | 46 | 47 |
| Protestant Episcopal (56) | 42 | 47 |
| Methodist (217) | 62 | 67 |
| Presbyterian Church USA (40) | 50 | 65 |
| Disciples of Christ (42) | 65 | 76 |
| American Lutheran bodies (146) | 50 | 51 |
| **Total moderate Protestants (628)** | **53** | **57** |
| Lutheran, Missouri Synod (45) | 44 | 50 |
| Evangelical and Reformed (28) | 68 | 64 |
| American Baptist (91) | 68 | 70 |
| Southern Baptist (187) | 67 | 78 |
| Other Baptist bodies (90) | 69 | 84 |
| Sects (128) | 65 | 74 |
| **Total conservative Protestants (569)** | **65** | **74** |
| Total Protestants (1,197) | 59 | 65 |
| Catholics (507) | 47 | 51 |

NOTE: Figures in parentheses show total number of respondents.

[7] The lack of impact of the Eichmann trial on public awareness is studied in detail in a forthcoming companion volume in this series, by Charles Y. Glock, Gertrude Jaeger Selznick, and Joe L. Spaeth.

were found. Americans at large are considerably less tolerant of atheists than are northern California church members. While 28 per cent of the Protestants and 23 per cent of the Roman Catholics in the church-member sample would not allow an admitted atheist to hold public office, 59 per cent of the Protestants and 47 per cent of the Roman Catholics nationwide would politically disqualify a man who did not believe in God. Similarly, 65 per cent of the Protestants and 51 per cent of the Catholics nationally would not allow an atheist to teach in a public high school, while only 39 per cent of the Protestants and 36 per cent of the Catholics in the church-member sample would take similar action.

These striking contrasts turn out to be primarily differences in the libertarian climate prevailing in various parts of the nation. In northern California in particular, and the Pacific West in general, there is considerably greater tolerance of religious deviation, and indeed of dissent on a wide range of social, political, and ethical matters, than elsewhere in America. In contrast, the widespread reputation of the rural and Southern regions for intolerance and repression of dissent seems fully deserved.

## Anti-Semitism

Having introduced items bearing on each of the concepts from which our model of the religious sources of anti-Semitism was constructed we have only to operationalize anti-Semitism in order completely to retest our findings.

Because all of the anti-Semitism data collected in this national study will be reported in detail in another volume of this series, we shall not report the distributions on individual items here. To construct an index of anti-Semitic beliefs six items were chosen from those included in the interview schedule to parallel as closely as possible the index used in analysis of the California data. All of the items, on the face of them, seemed clearly to impute unfair and invidious traits to Jews.[8] The index was scored in the same way as all previous indexes in this study. Respondents were given a score of 2 for every item with which they agreed, 1 for each to which they replied "don't know," and zero for each item to which they responded "false." Thus, the original index ranged from a high of 12 down to zero. This original scoring was collapsed to form

[8] (1) Jews are more willing than others to use shady practices to get what they want. (2) Jews are more loyal to Israel than to America. (3) Jews have a lot of irritating faults. (4) Jews are always stirring up trouble with their ideas. (5) Jews should stop complaining about what happened to them in Nazi Germany. (6) You can usually tell whether or not a person is Jewish just by the way he looks.

a four-point index: High includes all who scored 7 or more on the index; Medium High includes all who scored 4, 5, or 6; Medium indicates a score of 1, 2, or 3; while None refers to persons who rejected the truth of all six negative beliefs about Jews. Because the items are particularly strong, it could be said that only persons who rejected all six can be exonerated of at least ambivalence toward Jews (at least on these beliefs), and surely those who scored 7 or higher can be said to hold a rather hostile image of Jews.

To validate the index it was used to predict agreement on a number of other clearly hostile attitudes toward Jews. The data appear in Table 79.

Table 79.  VALIDATION OF INDEX OF ANTI-SEMITIC BELIEFS (NATIONAL SAMPLE)

|  | High | Medium High | Medium | None |
|---|---|---|---|---|
| Number | (622) | (752) | (340) | (183) |
| *Per cent who believe that:* | | | | |
| "Jews don't care what happens to anyone but their own kind." | 56 | 17 | 6 | 3 |
| "Jews always like to be the head of things." | 77 | 53 | 34 | 20 |
| "Jews have stirred up a lot of the trouble between whites and Negroes." | 29 | 7 | 4 | 0 |
| "The trouble with Jewish businessmen is that they are so shrewd and tricky that other people don't have a fair chance in competition." | 69 | 28 | 9 | 3 |
| "Jews stick together too much." | 76 | 49 | 30 | 25 |

On each item the findings are clear and consistent, and provide good reason to suppose that the Index of Anti-Semitic Beliefs measures a wide range of negative beliefs about Jews.

Turning to Table 80 we see that the perhaps shockingly wide prevalence of anti-Semitism revealed among northern California church members is a nationwide phenomenon. In the total sample (Jews omitted) a third scored in the highest category on the Anti-Semitic Belief Index, while another 40 per cent were scored as Medium High. Thus 73 per cent of the American public showed a considerable propensity for anti-Semitic beliefs, while a mere 9 per cent resisted all six negative statements.

Among the Christian denominations the differences in anti-Semitism are marked, and consistent with the findings in the California sample. While 11 per cent of the Unitarians, 14 per cent of the Episcopalians, and about one-quarter of the Congregationalists and United Presbyterians

Table 80.   DENOMINATION AND ANTI-SEMITIC BELIEFS (NATIONAL SAMPLE)

| | Rank on Index of Anti-Semitic Beliefs | | | |
| | High | Medium High | Medium | None |
|---|---|---|---|---|
| Unitarian (9) | 11% | 0% | 22% | 67% |
| Congregational (44) | 27 | 32 | 36 | 5 |
| United Presbyterian (75) | 25 | 36 | 27 | 12 |
| Protestant Episcopal (56) | 14 | 39 | 38 | 9 |
| Methodist (217) | 35 | 40 | 16 | 9 |
| Presbyterian Church USA (40) | 30 | 38 | 20 | 12 |
| Disciples of Christ (42) | 50 | 33 | 7 | 10 |
| American Lutheran bodies (146) | 35 | 42 | 15 | 8 |
| **Total moderate Protestants (628)** | **32** | **38** | **20** | **10** |
| Lutheran, Missouri Synod (45) | 36 | 33 | 18 | 13 |
| Evangelical and Reformed (28) | 43 | 39 | 18 | 0 |
| American Baptist (91) | 43 | 39 | 13 | 5 |
| Southern Baptist (187) | 43 | 37 | 12 | 8 |
| Other Baptist bodies (90) | 47 | 41 | 8 | 4 |
| Sects (128) | 46 | 34 | 16 | 4 |
| **Total conservative Protestants (569)** | **44** | **37** | **13** | **6** |
| Total Protestants (1,197) | 37 | 37 | 17 | 9 |
| Catholics (507) | 22 | 43 | 21 | 14 |
| Total sample (Jews omitted) (1,604) | 33 | 40 | 18 | 9 |

NOTE: Rows add to 100 per cent. Figures in parentheses show total number of respondents.

scored High on anti-Semitic beliefs, more than 40 per cent of those in the various Baptists bodies did so. Over-all, 37 per cent of the Protestants and 22 per cent of the Roman Catholics scored High. Anti-Semitic beliefs are clearly still an ubiquitous feature of American life, found in greater incidence among religious conservatives, but common in all religious bodies.

As would also be expected, anti-Semitism among Christians varied a good deal from one region of the country to another, especially for Protestants, among whom 23 per cent of the Westerners and 48 per cent of the Southerners scored High. Over-all, anti-Semitism is least common on the West Coast (23 per cent High), followed by the East (24 per cent High), and much higher in the Midwest and South: 33 per cent and 44 per cent High, respectively.

## Religious Bigotry and Anti-Semitism

It is now possible to ask to what extent our model of the religious roots of anti-Semitism accounts for the anti-Semitism of the general

American public. In order to carry out such an examination an index of religious bigotry comparable to that developed in the California data had to be constructed. Items we have previously examined on each component of this index, are now combined into a single measure.[9] These are virtually identical with those used for the same purposes in previous chapters. Thus, we are able to confront our theoretical position with a legitimate replication—an attempt to obtain similar results from new data, in this case data sampled from a much broader population.

As is apparent in Table 81 the Religious Bigotry Index powerfully

Table 81.  RELIGIOUS BIGOTRY AND ANTI-SEMITIC BELIEFS

| Index of Anti-Semitic Beliefs | Religious Bigotry Index | | | | | |
|---|---|---|---|---|---|---|
| | Low 0 | 1 | 2 | 3 | 4 | High 5 |
| High | 9% | 20% | 31% | 39% | 50% | 55% |
| Medium High | 34 | 37 | 43 | 43 | 41 | 29 |
| Medium Low | 33 | 26 | 20 | 11 | 6 | 14 |
| None | 24 | 17 | 6 | 7 | 3 | 2 |
| Total | 100% | 100% | 100% | 100% | 100% | 100% |
| Number | (144) | (366) | (600) | (341) | (229) | (157) |

predicts anti-Semitic beliefs in the general population too. Of those who lack all those religious characteristics summarized in our model (scored zero on the Bigotry Index) only 9 per cent are High on the Index of Anti-Semitic Beliefs, while of those who have all of these religious characteristics (scored 5 on the Bigotry Index) 55 per cent scored High on anti-Semitic beliefs. Conversely, only 2 per cent of those High on the Bigotry Index rejected all six anti-Semitic statements, while 24 per cent of those Low on the index did so. These data provide a persuasive replication of our earlier findings: Clearly the model we have developed of the religious sources of anti-Semitism is a potent empirical predictor of prejudice against Jews. However, the question of spuriousness, to which the preceding chapter was devoted, must be briefly dealt with in order to

[9] The scoring was as follows: As in earlier chapters, the Bigotry Index is a summary of other indexes. An Orthodoxy Index was constructed of the three available belief items, belief in God, the Devil, and life beyond death, each item receiving the same weight. The resulting index was trichotomized into High, Medium, and Low categories. A Particularism Index was constructed from two items: belief that Christians are God's Chosen People today and belief that persons cannot be saved without belief in Jesus. A Religious Libertarianism Index was made up of the two items on civil liberties for an atheist. These three indexes were combined into a single index along with belief that the historic Jews crucified Jesus. All items received the same weight in the index. This index was in turn combined with belief that the modern Jews are being punished by God to make the Religious Bigotry Index. The final index ranged from scores of zero through 5, and was not collapsed.

complete the replication of our northern California findings on national data.

Table 82 shows the original relationship between religious bigotry and anti-Semitism with a series of controls to test possible counter-explanations. It is immediately apparent that none of these control

Table 82.   TESTING THE RELATIONSHIP

(Per cent of respondents who scored High on Index of Anti-Semitic Beliefs)

| | Religious Bigotry Index | | | | | |
|---|---|---|---|---|---|---|
| | 0 | 1 | 2 | 3 | 4 | 5 |
| *Race:* | | | | | | |
| Whites | 9 | 20 | 30 | 39 | 51 | 53 |
| | (135) | (336) | (526) | (282) | (183) | (129) |
| Negroes | 14 | 25 | 34 | 39 | 44 | 67 |
| | (7) | (24) | (73) | (56) | (46) | (27) |
| *Denomination:* | | | | | | |
| Protestants | 10 | 22 | 35 | 42 | 51 | 61 |
| | (78) | (193) | (358) | (243) | (174) | (115) |
| Catholics | 6 | 14 | 21 | 31 | 41 | 44 |
| | (34) | (133) | (194) | (72) | (39) | (23) |
| *Sex:* | | | | | | |
| Men | 11 | 21 | 33 | 45 | 57 | 59 |
| | (96) | (200) | (261) | (137) | (107) | (69) |
| Women | 4 | 19 | 29 | 35 | 43 | 41 |
| | (48) | (166) | (339) | (204) | (122) | (88) |
| *Education:* | | | | | | |
| Not high school graduate | 14 | 48 | 42 | 54 | 57 | 66 |
| | (14) | (62) | (142) | (136) | (103) | (62) |
| High school graduate | 14 | 16 | 32 | 36 | 45 | 53 |
| | (73) | (198) | (321) | (157) | (100) | (73) |
| At least some college | 2 | 11 | 15 | 11 | 38 | 40 |
| | (57) | (104) | (137) | (48) | (26) | (22) |
| *Region:* | | | | | | |
| East | 9 | 16 | 22 | 24 | 47 | 46 |
| | (45) | (111) | (136) | (47) | (42) | (26) |
| Midwest | 11 | 19 | 31 | 46 | 61 | 50 |
| | (46) | (108) | (201) | (101) | (54) | (40) |
| South | 22 | 30 | 37 | 46 | 50 | 71 |
| | (9) | (50) | (120) | (118) | (62) | (55) |
| Southwest | 0 | 38 | 42 | 40 | 47 | 55 |
| | (8) | (31) | (61) | (35) | (34) | (22) |
| Mountain and Pacific West | 6 | 18 | 23 | 28 | 38 | 43 |
| | (36) | (66) | (82) | (40) | (37) | (14) |

NOTE: Figures in parentheses show total number of respondents.

variables has any important consequences for our findings. In the national data the relationship between religion and prejudice is approximately the same among whites and Negroes, among Catholics and Protestants, among men and women, among the educated and the uneducated, and in all regions of the country. Furthermore, considerably more complex statistical tables, not presented here, showed that no combination of these control variables had any appreciable effect upon the original relationship. Clearly then, none of these possible counterexplanations is true, while the likelihood that our explanation of these correlations is accurate is thereby increased.

The power of this relationship, and its resistance to counterexplanation, lends confidence to our thesis that religion operates, under certain conditions, as a potent source of anti-Semitism. But an important question remains: How serious a source is religion? It is conceivable that our theory could be true, that religion does produce anti-Jewish sentiments in the way we have suggested, but that this process is trivial in the over-all pattern of anti-Semitism. For example, our thesis could be perfectly true but only characterize 0.05 per cent of the population and consequently be of little relevance to the general quest to learn the causes of anti-Semitism. *Thus, we now need to estimate how much of the total incidence of current American anti-Semitism can reasonably be attributed to religious sources.*

This question can be answered through some simple recomputations of the data in Table 81. Of those persons who are classified as High or Medium High on the Index of Anti-Semitic Beliefs, 23 per cent also have scores of 4 or 5 on the Index of Religious Bigotry, and another 21 per cent have scores of 3 on this index. Conservatively, these findings would suggest that at least one-fourth of America's anti-Semites have a religious basis for their prejudice, while nearly another fifth have this religious basis in considerable part. Indeed, only 5 per cent of Americans with anti-Semitic views lack all rudiments of a religious basis for their prejudice. On these grounds it seems reasonable to say, if our explanation of our empirical findings is correct, that an impressive proportion, no less than a fourth, of American anti-Semitism is attached to religious sources. In terms of absolute numbers rather than percentages, these data indicate that approximately 17.5 million Americans who hold fairly strong anti-Semitic beliefs would also be classified in the top two categories of the Religious Bigotry Index.[10] Far from being trivial, religious outlooks and religious images of the modern Jew seem to lie at the root of the anti-Semitism of millions of American adults.

[10] These projections are based on the 1960 U.S. census figures for the number of Americans over the age of 21.

Although religion seemingly accounts for the anti-Semitism of millions of people, it must be recognized that millions more are anti-Semitic who do not seem to be responding from religious motives or training. Clearly this leaves a good deal of room for other causes or sources of anti-Semitism to be operating in contemporary American life. While in this study we have concentrated primarily on seeing how much of a role religion continues to play in fostering anti-Semitism it never occurred to us that religion is the *only* cause. Indeed, other studies being carried out in this same series are concerned with examining other aspects of our society which may be contributing to anti-Semitism. Very little in human behavior can be attributed to a single cause; rather, multiple causation is very nearly the rule. Still, in any summation of causes certain factors will play a very minor role while others will be of major importance. Our data suggest not only that religion very probably influences anti-Semitism through the process that we have postulated, but that this process is an extremely important force in maintaining the endemic level of American prejudice against Jews.

# CHAPTER 13

# The Challenge to the Churches

All the interest of my reason (speculative as well as practical) comes in the following three questions:
1. What can I know?
2. What ought I to do?
3. What may I hope?

—IMMANUEL KANT

Since we began this study by postulating a theoretical model of the religious roots of contemporary anti-Semitism, obviously we anticipated that the empirical findings of the survey would support our explanation. However, the *descriptive* findings were completely unanticipated. Perhaps naïvely, we expected that this religious process had become more or less vestigial. We were entirely unprepared to find these old religious traditions so potent and so widespread in modern society. As it happens, one of us considers himself a Christian; the other does not. But as the findings were revealed, both of us shared equally a sense of shock and dismay that a faith which proclaims the brotherhood of man can be so perverted into a *raison d'être* for bigotry.

What must concern us now is that our findings be faced honestly and acted upon constructively. If we produce only an outrage—perhaps because in pursuing the sources of anti-Semitism we are perceived as having carelessly trod on sacred ground and been insensitive to matters which are, for many, the keystone of their lives—then we shall have failed in our ethical mission. On the other hand, unless we provoke significant and sympathetic concern among Christians we shall also have accomplished nothing.

207

We recognize that the issues raised by the study are both sensitive and difficult. All humane men would agree that an end to anti-Semitism ought to be passionately sought. Yet few Christians could agree to sacrifice their faith for such a cause. Herein lies a possible dilemma with which we must deal in this final chapter. Is traditional Christian orthodoxy incompatible with Christ's teachings of brotherhood? The modern Christian answer, it would seem to us, ought to be that no faith incompatible with love and brotherhood can possibly be called Christian. Yet, not only our findings, but centuries of history, reveal the difficulty in Christianity of making love triumph over self-righteousness, and of reconciling what people espouse with what they do.

We are not theologians, and it would be presumptuous of us to say how the doctrinal issues raised by our study might or ought to be resolved. There are likely a number of theological solutions, and these will probably be discussed and debated for some time to come. But, if it is not our place to draft new doctrines, it seems appropriate to suggest where the process by which religion fosters anti-Semitism is most vulnerable to intervention. To this end, a brief recapitulation of our findings is necessary.

The causal chain that links Christian belief and faith to secular anti-Semitism begins with orthodoxy—commitment to a literal interpretation of traditional Christian dogma. Orthodoxy, in turn, leads to particularism—a disposition to see Christian truth as the *only* religious truth. Particularism produces a two-fold response toward religious outsiders. On the one hand Christian particularism prompts missionary zeal: The faith is open to all mankind if only they will accept it. But when others reject the call to conversion the hostility latent in particularism is activated.

This hostility is directed against all religious outsiders whether they are of another faith or of none. Because of their historic link with Christianity, the Jews are singled out for special attention. The specifically religious hostility toward the Jews generated by particularism is not merely a result of blaming the historic Jews for the death of Jesus. Particularistic Christians are not alone in holding such a view; less orthodox and unparticularistic Christians are also likely to implicate the ancient Jews in the Crucifixion. The difference lies in the interpretation given this view of history. In the eyes of most particularists, the Jews *remain* guilty; the Jews provoked God's wrath by crucifying Jesus, and have suffered under divine judgment ever since. Their tribulations will not cease until they extirpate their guilt by accepting salvation through Christ. Less orthodox and less particularistic Christians are unlikely to draw this link between the ancient and the modern Jews.

This process—orthodoxy to particularism to religious hostility—culminates in secular anti-Semitism. Almost inexorably, those caught up in this syndrome of religious ideology are led to a general hostility toward the Jews. At what points can this process be interrupted and its harmful consequences eliminated?

A possible, but unpalatable and unnecessary, point of attack is to shatter this syndrome at its source, through a theological rejection of traditional Christian orthodoxy. Clearly, without its orthodox base, the whole structure would collapse. For many men of the modern Church a rejection of orthodoxy would seem not only an appropriate way to assault the religious roots of anti-Semitism, but a worthy end in itself. Surely, the theology of Paul Tillich or Bishop John Robinson constitutes such a rejection of orthodoxy. Widespread acceptance of similar views would undoubtedly help to reduce anti-Semitism. Indeed, as the data in previous chapters show, in those denominations where orthodoxy has been replaced with a more liberal doctrine, anti-Semitism is much less common.

But a solution of this kind, which would attempt to derail the process by which religion fosters anti-Semitism by combating orthodoxy, is unacceptable and unrealistic. Those committed to traditional orthodoxy simply would not yield to any such appeals, nor would it be moral to ask them to do so. Who can ask a man to surrender what he considers to be the ground of his being?

For those who subscribe to it, particularism is undoubtedly as sacrosanct an element of Christian faith as orthodoxy. The possibility, therefore, of halting the process by asking Christians to give up their particularism seems as untenable as asking them to abandon orthodoxy. Two considerations, however, mute such a conclusion.

Orthodoxy, as we have seen, is powerfully related to particularism, but the relationship is not perfect. Orthodox Christians are not necessarily particularistic, for although most are, some are not. How orthodox persons restrain themselves from taking up a particularistic view of their own religious superiority is not wholly explained by our data. But for many, the answer seems to be their commitment to ideals of religious liberty. Perhaps, if effectively taught, religious libertarianism can be made an even more effective instrument to forestall orthodoxy from becoming particularistic.

It seems also possible that the hostile consequences of particularism might be reduced and conceivably eliminated by simply confronting Christians with what these consequences are. A particularism of the sort which recognizes that what is a deeply felt religious truth for oneself need not apply to all others characterizes some, albeit a small minority, of Christian church members. Yet, such a particularism seems consistent both with this tradition in Christianity and with the Christian commitment to the brotherhood of man.

These are only partial answers, however. The issue of particularism must also be confronted theologically. Here, we suspect, conservative theologians could find common cause with their liberal colleagues to hammer out a solution. For the theological grounds for a militant particularism seem much less solid than those for orthodoxy even if one's theological perspective is essentially conservative.

Despite the optimistic tenor of these remarks, we are not so sanguine as to expect universal agreement that particularism is not an essential element of Christian belief. It must be admitted that militant particularism is a two-sided phenomenon, and if it has harsh effects on those beyond the pale, it also provides a powerful internal force welding the faithful into a moral community. The particularism of religion, when viewed against the background of a larger society, is clearly potentially harmful. But viewed from within any such religion it is a positive mobilizing and energizing force. It is this internal force of particularism that is largely responsible for all the great successes of religious movements. It was the impassioned conviction of its own virtue that made possible the victory of early Christianity over the Western world, and later inspired the incredible eruption of Islam. A similar particularism today moves Communism.

Clearly particularism causes serious social conflict. But as clearly it provides those who embrace it with a certain competitive advantage. It is difficult to proselytize for a religious perspective that is not the "absolute and only truth." And perhaps that is partly the reason that the most particularistic denominations and sects in America are growing at a faster rate than those who have surrendered their convictions of religious supremacy. These competitive fruits of particularism may promote its continued existence.

Despite the faster growth of these more zealous denominations, the main trend in American religion is a slow departure away from its particularistic past. But while even greater inroads on militant particularism will undoubtedly be made, there are many Christians for whom the particularistic elements of their faith will remain as intransigent as their orthodoxy. This raises the question of whether or not the causal link between faith and anti-Semitism can be severed as long as particularism remains a dominant theme in Christianity.

Our data strongly indicate that particularism is a mighty source of religious hostility toward the contemporary Jew. However, an important link between the two is provided by an invidious interpretation of the nature and meaning of the role of the Jews in the Crucifixion. Without the reinforcement provided by the deicide tradition, the link between particularism and religious hostility would probably still remain. The simple fact that Jews remain outside the "true" faith would be enough to sustain a degree of hostility. But it seems certain that this hostility could be significantly muted if the deicide issue could be laid to rest once and for all.

Horace Kallen wrote in 1923, "If you can end this teaching that the Jews are the enemies of God and of mankind you will strike anti-Semitism at its foundations."[1]

Since then there has been some shaking of the foundations, but the full moral power of the churches has not yet been exerted. Thus, the recent adoption of a new schema on the Jews by the Ecumenical Council carries a promise of truly major consequences. This statement goes to the heart of Christian anti-Semitism. Its effect will be to arm the lower clergy with appropriate theological means to denounce anti-Semitism in its religious trappings. If Christians everywhere take the spirit and the content of this historic pronouncement as an occasion for ridding their conscience of the stigma of bigotry, there is hope that a study like ours done in the next generation will report an outbreak of Christian love and brotherhood.

The final point at which the process by which faith is translated into anti-Semitism can be attacked is in the stereotypes and feelings making up secular anti-Semitism itself. While our data have shown that the church often provides the ground in which secular anti-Semitism grows, nothing we have learned suggests that the church is directly promulgating secular anti-Semitism. To be sure, there is an extremist fringe in the church given to vicious anti-Semitism. But, by and large, churchmen exhibit a sincere sympathy for the plight of the Jews and a willingness to take action to combat anti-Semitism.

In the midst of this increasing spirit of good will there has been a growing complacency too. Particularly in the last decade, the idea has become widespread that anti-Semitism is no longer really a problem in America. Churchmen, like most others, have accepted this comfortable and complacent view, which is reflected in the little attention given to the problem of anti-Semitism in present-day church educational programs.

In the words of Jeremiah, "They have healed the wound of my people lightly, saying, 'Peace, peace,' when there is no peace." The wounds of his people have not yet healed. Anti-Semitism is very much alive in our culture. There are no grounds for complacency, and especially none for the churches. For quite aside from the fact that religion actually operates to produce anti-Semitism, there is the evidence that, on whatever grounds,

---

[1] "The Roots of Anti-Semitism," *Nation*, February 28, 1923, p. 241.

the majority of American church members are rather prejudiced against Jews. Thus, even if the churches dispose of the deicide charge and reduce the tendency to particularism among their followers, the task will still be far from finished. A host of bigots will still remain in the bosom of the faith, their presence disfiguring the Christian conscience. A massive frontal attack on anti-Semitism per se is clearly required.

There can be no question that Christian ethics provide the basis for such a frontal attack. If the faithful would heed the message "Love thy neighbor as thyself," an account such as ours could not have been written. But a mere theological clarification of what Christian ethics imply for anti-Semitism will not be enough; the task is to make these pious words relevant in the concrete moral questions of daily life.

What is called for, then, is a systematic reappraisal of Christian education, *both* as it teaches its history and doctrines *and* in the way it deals with the question of anti-Semitism as such. In this book we have not tried to examine concretely the ways in which the church teaches the syndrome of beliefs that foster anti-Semitism. We have not analyzed the content of sermons, conducted our own review of Sunday school materials, nor observed Sunday schools in action. Neither have we looked systematically at precisely how the Crucifixion story is currently being told in the average American congregation. Yet, it is self-evident in the effects we have observed that, however inadvertently, the lessons which prejudice Christians against Jews are being effectively transmitted. The challenge to American Christianity is to root out all the concrete ways in which these lessons continue to pervade their religious training, and to eradicate them.

Until the process by which religion fosters anti-Semitism has been abolished, the Christian conscience must bear the guilt of bigotry. Even then, the moral duty of Christians, and of us all, remains clear: To oppose intolerance and prejudice wherever they are found until finally we learn to love one another.

# APPENDIXES

# APPENDIX **A**

---

# Methodological Observations on the Career of a Study*

Typically, methodological appendixes only present sufficient information concerning the design and procedures of a study to satisfy specialists that certain technical standards, particularly those concerning sampling, have been adequately met. Only rarely do such reports provide any clear picture of how the study was "really" done.[1] The problems that arose, and choices made among alternative strategies at various points in the research enterprise, pass unremarked, as do the reasons these particular choices were made and their consequences. As a result, future researchers profit little from the techniques others develop and the lessons they learn.

Methodological discussions that do take up such questions, and are written for the student as well as the specialist, belong to a tradition in social research which ought to be continued and expanded. A few major works are as celebrated for their contributions on how to do research as for their substantive findings.[2]

But beyond contributing innovations and extensions in the technology of social research, such discussions also can serve a second extremely useful pedagogical function. By providing an account of how the research was

---

* This is an account of the northern California study only. A later volume by Gertrude Jaeger Selznick and Stephen Steinberg will discuss the methodology of the national sample.

[1] This seems to be true of the physical sciences as well. For despite the detailed sections on methods and materials included in papers reporting experiments, researchers who actually attempt to replicate experiments or incorporate elements of a method find they must contact the author to learn critical details which were omitted [see Herbert Menzel, "Planned and Unplanned Scientific Communication," in Bernard Barber and Walter Hirsch (eds.), *The Sociology of Science* (New York: The Free Press of Glencoe, 1962), pp. 417–441].

[2] Among these are William F. Whyte, *Street Corner Society* (Chicago: University of Chicago Press, 1943), and David Riesman's field report in Paul F. Lazarsfeld and Wagner Thielens, Jr., *The Academic Mind* (Glencoe, Ill.: The Free Press, 1958), pp. 266–370; see also Philip Hammond, *Sociologists at Work* (New York: Basic Books, 1964).

accomplished, and evaluating procedures and decisions in the light of subsequent events, students are provided an opportunity to gain a concrete and, it is hoped, useful glimpse of the contingencies of actual research.

It is primarily this pedagogical function which prompted the addition of this rather detailed discussion of our research procedures. But because the problems which arose are common to surveys, and the design developed seems widely applicable to other research undertakings, it is possible that making our experience generally accessible will be of use to the specialist as well as the student.

## Defining the Universe

Given that the research decision has been made about what to study and how,[3] the questions remain: Who and where? Since available resources are rarely unlimited, each decision made in resolving these questions closes certain possibilities and restricts the scope of the study; all research designs represent a series of compromises. In this section we shall review the compromises made in defining the universe, or population, to be studied.

The problem of choosing the universe was made up, basically, of two interrelated sets of options: (1) to study a cross-section of the general population or to concentrate on some less inclusive special "religious" population; (2) to restrict the study to some particular locale or to include the entire country.

### Cross-section vs. Special Population

Ideally, we would have preferred reasonably large samples of all the generic religious orientations in American society: each of the Christian denominations, the Jews, members of other non-Christian world religions, the various cults, the unaffiliated, the agnostics, and the atheists. Since typically atheists and agnostics cannot be found in organized groups, they could only have been obtained by a cross-sectional sample of the general population. Since these types are uncommon, however, a cross-sectional sample would have to be extremely large to include them in appreciable numbers.[4] A sample of such size was beyond our means; hence, whether we chose some special population or a cross-section, these uncommon irreligious orientations were beyond our sampling techniques, and were perforce excluded from the scope of the study.

An additional problem concerning whom to study was raised by the questionnaire. As will be discussed later, operationalizing our theoretical concepts for a Christian group was a long and expensive undertaking. This questionnaire was not appropriate for studying non-Christians, and to produce parallel versions for each different non-Christian group would have multiplied expenses far beyond the proportion of increase in the study's scope; for, aside

[3] A discussion of the decision to use a mail questionnaire appears on pages 247–248.

[4] National surveys typically find 2 to 3 per cent who report no religious affiliation. Hence, a cross-sectional sample of 3,000 respondents would only include from 60 to 90 persons who were "irreligious," hardly a sufficient number to be of much use in analysis.

from the Jews, these groups play virtually no part in the religious culture of America. Thus, we were led to exclude members of non-Christian faiths, other than Jews. Those omitted included a variety of American cults as well as followers of major world religions such as Buddhism, and also several sects on the borderline of Christianity: Mormons, Christian Scientists, and Jehovah's Witnesses.[5]

Having made these restrictions, our plans were to study the three major American religious traditions: Protestantism, Roman Catholicism, and Judaism. Within these three groups there still remained the option of using a cross-sectional sample or placing further restrictions on the population to be sampled. The choice made was the result of further problems also related to the area to be studied.

### A National vs. a Regional Sample

A dual concern structured our decision of where to do the study: a desire that our data be reasonably representative of the nation in general, and our intention to investigate the social contexts of our respondents as well as their individual attitudes and behavior. With national samples respondents are widely scattered, and one can only guess about the character and behavior of the persons with whom they interact, although this network of social relations plays a primary role in shaping the behavior and attitudes of the respondents. When respondents are selected from social contexts which are also investigated, then their behavior can, it is hoped, be more completely understood, and the effects of different combinations of context and individual can be examined. For example, in the present study, it would be possible to contrast the behavior of the fundamentalist in the liberal religious congregation with that of the fundamentalist in a fundamentalist setting, etc.

The advantage of national samples, of course, is that they allow specification of how any particular trait is differentially distributed among various regions. In a sense, it can be said that the findings represent the entire nation. In a way, however, this "national representativeness" may be something of a fiction. The national data may be the sum of rather different distributions from each of the various cultural groups and regions, *none* of which is similar to the national distribution. In such a case it would be possible to say both that "America is like this" and "nowhere in America are people really like this." For example, no known instance of the statistically average American family has ever been found—if for no other reason than that it always contains fractional children. In any event, while a sample restricted to some region of the United States may yield *descriptions* slightly discrepant from conditions in other parts of the country, there is good reason to expect that *relationships* among variables in one area will hold for others. For example, the proportion of Democrats and of Catholics varies from place to place, but the correlation between being a Catholic and voting Democratic is relatively stable. Since

---

[5] In addition, Christian Scientists and Jehovah's Witnesses were not accessible to survey research through formal church auspices, the former due to restrictions against "numbering" members and the latter because of a general withdrawal from secular affairs.

the main interest in social research is with correlations rather than with distributions, the importance of a nationwide sample is correspondingly reduced. This, of course, does not mean there is anything wrong with national samples; indeed, given other features of adequate research they are desirable. However, since compromises are necessary, national samples often opt for breadth at the cost of depth. In some instances this is preferable. In this one it seemed undesirable.

A further concern in choosing the population and locale was raised by the decision to investigate persons in relation to their social contexts, which we plan to do in further volumes based on these data. To do this we needed to sample social networks. The theoretically relevant groups which suited this purpose were church congregations. By taking sizable samples from individual congregations we would be able to aggregate data on individual members to characterize the group. To this we could add other information gathered about the group, such as the neighborhood around the church, the physical condition of the building, the background of the pastor, the organization of the congregation and its round of activities, the group's history, etc. And, further, if these congregations were located close together, it would be possible for the researchers to visit them and gain direct experience of the social setting and systems of relationships in which respondents were embedded. This possibility strongly influenced the decision to concentrate the study in one area.

The decision to focus on church congregations, however, led to the exclusion of an important segment of the population from the study—persons not formally affiliated with a church. This was our most painful compromise. But the option of studying church members in depth rather than both members and nonmembers more superficially seemed to justify it. Furthermore, since samples of church members would include not only those who were active in religion, but also those with only nominal membership, it seemed possible to use these apathetic members as a basis for inferences about nonmembers.

A second compelling reason for restricting the locale of the study followed from the decision to sample members of church congregations, for this raised the need to obtain approval for the study from church officials. Had we selected respondents from the population at large through the usual survey procedures, we should only have had to seek the cooperation of the individuals sampled. But if samples were to be drawn from church rolls, then access to these rolls had to be managed. Among Protestants and Jews we felt we need only seek the approval of the particular congregations selected for the study. Since there was no reason to expect this to be any more difficult in one part of the country than in another, there was no reason why a nationwide sample of congregations could not be selected (although the logistical problems and expense of such a sample would have been much greater than for a sample confined to one region). But the organizational arrangements of the Roman Catholic Church necessitated obtaining such permission from the bishop of the diocese in which any sample parish was located. In the past there has been a certain reluctance among Catholic bishops to authorize social research. The possibility of obtaining permission from a number of bishops across the country was too remote for serious consideration. But we were encouraged to attempt to find a bishop of some major metropolitan diocese who would agree.

Thus, we resolved the various questions of where to do the study by deciding to concentrate our resources on a single community, as typical of urban

America as possible, with the ultimate selection depending on where Roman Catholic participation could be arranged. This proved difficult. We began with a list of a half-dozen communities that had a religious composition reasonably similar to that of the nation as a whole. Both formal and informal appeals to the bishops of these communities were rejected, and the list was quickly exhausted. Our difficulties grew greater in the fall of 1962, when the Ecumenical Council drew all the bishops to Rome, making it difficult for us to contact them. The prospects of Catholic cooperation grew dim. On impulse we sought permission to conduct the study in the Archdiocese of San Francisco. Quite frankly we would not initially have chosen to do the study in the San Francisco area, but at that point we would have settled for doing it almost anywhere. Actually it turned out for the best. His Excellency Thomas J. McGucken, Archbishop of San Francisco, graciously extended us his permission, and members of his staff greatly aided us in conducting the survey. Since we were subsequently able to obtain national data, the fact that northern California is not very similar to the country as a whole on religious matters was of little importance. Furthermore, it was much less expensive to conduct the study in home country where the facilities and staff of the Survey Research Center could be used easily. It was also very convenient, since the authors were familiar with the area to be studied and could easily visit any congregation in the sample at any time during the study when further observation would prove useful.

However, conducting the research in the Archdiocese of San Francisco, which comprises four Westbay counties of the metropolitan Bay Area, raised one serious reduction in the scope of the research. Although we had planned to include Jews in the study (indeed, a questionnaire had been specifically developed for them and preliminary contacts made with area rabbis), it became apparent that although Christians in the area were relatively similar to Christians in other metropolitan areas, Jews in the area were not very typical. For one thing, there were fewer Jews than in most similarly populous areas. Furthermore, it is reasonably accurate to state that any American Jew not living in an Eastern city is an atypical American Jew. Upon reconsideration it did not seem prudent to dissipate our resources on a Jewish sample of dubious significance. In addition, there arose prospects of obtaining a national sample of Jews at a later time. For these reasons we dropped our plans to sample local synagogues.

In the end, the population we picked to sample was defined as comprising members of Christian churches in the four counties constituting the Roman Catholic Archdiocese of San Francisco: Marin, San Francisco, San Mateo, and Santa Clara counties.

After we had made these sampling decisions and begun the data collection process, it developed that we could also afford to include some of our items in a nationwide sample study. Thus we could gain the advantages of both an in-depth regional study and national data. Because the national interviewing was not scheduled until October 1964, we had nearly a year to analyze our northern California data to determine what few items were most central to our research. These were subsequently included in the national study. Had we known in the beginning that both kinds of samples were within our means, this is the way we would have planned to do it. That we did it this way, however, was partly good fortune.

## The Sample: Design

### The Sampling Frame

Since the universe had clear-cut legal boundaries, there was no problem in deciding whether or not a particular congregation belonged in the sampling frame; rather, the difficulty was to locate all those which should be included and to determine the total membership of each. The paucity of church statistics, and the fragmentation of American denominations and sects, made this a vexing and time-consuming process. Neither local nor area councils of churches were of any use; their mailing lists were poorly kept, contained clergymen rather than congregations, and then only those who were members. The records of religion editors of area newspapers were, however, of considerable help, as were telephone books, and, for the major denominations, church yearbooks and information provided by regional denominational headquarters.[6] Cross-checking these sources readily produced reliable lists of all congregations of the major denominations which existed in the four-county universe. And relatively accurate information on the membership of each congregation was also obtained. But the "third-force" churches—the various small pentecostal, holiness, and evangelical sects—presented a good deal of difficulty. While several of these groups published yearbooks, most did not. Furthermore, these groups are less likely than the larger bodies to be listed in the telephone books,[7] and, even more important, they have a high rate of institutional turnover. Small storefront churches are constantly appearing and disappearing, almost unnoticed amid the swirl of metropolitan life.

While these third-force bodies, as it turned out, had only about 9 per cent of all Protestant church members in the four-county area, they constituted 26 per cent of all the congregations that could be located. The bulk of the time and expense in constructing the sampling frame went into this relatively small portion of the church-member population. After compiling a list from telephone books and newspaper files, we contacted clergymen of various third-force groups in different parts of the sampling area and got them to check the list, both for their particular denomination and for churches of other denominations located in their vicinity. Through these informants (twenty in all were contacted), we expanded our original list of third-force congregations by about 10 per cent. As we shall show shortly, the list thus constructed was probably entirely accurate for the larger and more stable third-force groups, such as the Nazarenes, Seventh Day Adventists, Church of God in Christ, etc., but failed to keep abreast of the rapid birth and death cycle of the more marginal, tiny sects. Of the three Pentecostal bodies drawn in the original sample, all were defunct by the time our field workers called to see the pastor. In one case even the building no longer existed, having been razed the previous week.

But beyond merely locating these third-force congregations was the problem of determining their adult membership. Since such information was not included

[6] However, one large denomination had no organized list of congregations or membership even in its office. A field worker was flown to the scene and compiled a list from the disorganized material in its files.

[7] Surprisingly, most did turn up in the church section of the Yellow Pages.

in our source materials (church yearbooks, etc.), we had either to carry out a census of these bodies, some 157 congregations, or, since they were all relatively small, rely on an average membership figure based on the enrollment of the third-force congregations whose pastors we contacted to help construct the list. The latter seemed feasible, and was considerably less expensive. Thus, we assumed all third-force congregations had 80 adult members. When completed, the Protestant sampling frame contained 556 congregations with a total membership of 161,288.

The Catholic sampling frame presented less difficulty. The chancery office provided a complete list of parishes. Membership of parishes, however, was not clearly known. Parish membership is determined on a geographical basis rather than on the basis of voluntary affiliation: A Catholic is a member of the parish in which he resides.[8] Thus, while technically all Catholics residing in the parish are members, the parish rolls tend to pick up only the names of those new arrivals who take the trouble to notify the pastor, and old names tend never to be removed.[9] Since membership interested us only as a basis for giving relative sampling weights to parishes, average Mass attendance figures were used, and served as well. These statistics, gathered four months prior to our research, showed 216,039 persons had attended Mass each Sunday in 137 parishes. The modal parish has an average Mass attendance of 1,500 adults; the largest reported 5,544, and the smallest, 50.[10]

## Sampling Procedure

Several factors entered into the strategy of sampling. We were interested in a sample which would be representative of the church-member population of these counties, and furthermore, we wanted sufficient cases to allow separate analyses at both the denominational and congregational levels. We also wanted sufficient numbers and varieties of congregations to allow us on occasion to treat congregations, rather than individuals, as the unit of analysis. Thus, a stratified procedure was required in which first a sample of congregations would be selected, and then a sample of members from each. The procedure also needed to be self-weighting so that, taken together (with restrictions we shall discuss), the individuals sampled would be representative of church members.

If sufficient numbers of persons for these purposes were to be obtained from small denominations, then we would be forced to take very large numbers of persons from the big denominations. In particular this would have required an enormous Catholic sample had we followed a simple random procedure. For this reason we decided to sample Protestants and Catholics separately. There seemed no reason to suppose we would ever desire to lump these two groups together in order to describe a collective population.

This same problem of proportions was repeated in microcosm within the Protestant universe. If we were to draw sufficient numbers of congregations and members from each third-force denomination, such as the Nazarenes, to

[8] Except for members of ethnic national parishes.

[9] To a lesser extent this is also true of Protestant congregations. This is discussed in detail below.

[10] Convict and cloistered populations were omitted.

enable us to analyze them separately, then we should have needed enormous samples from the mainline bodies in order to maintain proper proportions. For this reason we decided to treat the third-force collectively, as if it were a single denomination, aiming only for enough cases from these churches to allow separate analysis of this merged unit, rather than of specific denominations within it. The mainline denominations were all large enough so there was no problem getting sufficient cases from each.[11]

The selection of the Protestant and Roman Catholic samples was carried on then independently. For the Protestants, it was decided to select 100 congregations, or about 18 per cent of the total number of congregations in the sample area. This number would allow all Protestant groups to be adequately represented. It was also felt that 100 cases would be enough for whatever analysis was to be pursued at the congregational level. Within each congregation, we sought to obtain questionnaires from 45 respondents, a number considered sufficient to allow a margin for shrinkage through nonresponse, etc., and also to provide enough cases for analysis within congregations. For Protestants, then, our target was roughly 4,500 church members.

By giving each congregation in the sampling frame the number of chances of being drawn in the sample equal to its membership, and then taking the same number of members from each, a self-weighting sample was obtained which is representative of members. That is, all members of churches in the sampling frame had an equal chance in the beginning of being drawn in the sample. With certain modifications, this technique was used.

However, before this procedure could be applied several additional problems had to be dealt with. For one thing, given that congregations among third-force churches were so small, and given our desire to avoid placing two questionnaires in a single household, it would clearly not be possible to draw 45 respondents from these churches even if we took everyone. Thus, direct application of the sampling procedure would have left the third-force badly underrepresented. From previous experience with church rolls during the pretest, we estimated that we would be able to draw an average of 23 respondents from third-force churches. Thus, we decided to double the number of third-force churches included in the sample in order to obtain the proper proportion of third-force members. Since the third-force represented 9 per cent of church members, we chose 18 congregations from this group in making up our original 100 Protestant churches. Since we were forced to treat all of them as being of the same size, this was done by simple random techniques. From each we took all adult members, not to exceed a total of 50 and to include no more than one per household. We rarely expected to find 50 members, but did expect to find some groups where the mean of 23 could not be reached. Thus by allowing as many as 50 when available, we hoped to reach the expected number of cases. When several members occupied the same household, the respondent was chosen randomly. In the several instances where slightly more than 50 persons remained after these household restrictions had been completed, members were discarded randomly until only 50 remained.

The mainline Protestants also presented a further complication. Although about half of the mainline congregations had fewer than 300 members, more

[11] Actually this resulted in a smaller number of members of the Disciples of Christ than we would have liked. Because we did not anticipate losing quite so many cases, we thought our number of Disciples would be greater.

than three-fourths of all mainline Protestants were in churches having more than 300 members. By directly applying our sampling procedure we would have drawn very few of these smaller congregations. However, since we anticipated that congregation size would be an especially interesting variable, we wished to increase the number of such congregations in the sample without distorting the picture of membership in general. This was accomplished by sampling congregations with 300 or fewer members separately from those which were larger, *and* by taking 20 per cent fewer members from each small congregation than from the larger ones, thus allowing a 20 per cent increase in the number of small congregations while not increasing the number of members they contributed to the total Protestant sample. To do this we chose 50 members from the large churches sampled, and 40 from the small ones. Applying our sampling formula in each of the two size strata, 82 congregations were selected, 22 of which had fewer than 300 members.[12]

For the Catholic parishes the sampling formula was directly applied, and 20 parishes were selected. This seemed to yield a sufficient number of cases for analysis at the parish level. However, only two parishes that had an average Mass attendance of 500 or less were drawn by this procedure. Therefore it was decided to double this number by randomly selecting two more of these smaller parishes and taking 50 rather than 100 members from each. Thus, in all, 22 Catholic parishes were selected.

Having drawn our sample of congregations, there still remained the task of getting these bodies to agree to participate in the study and to give us access to their membership rolls for sampling. Each pastor whose church had been drawn in the sample was sent a letter which briefly outlined the study and requested an appointment for a field worker who would furnish him a copy of the questionnaire and further details of the study. After obtaining the pastor's permission,[13] the field worker interviewed him about the history and status of his congregation as well as about his own background and training.

Each church was asked to provide us with a list of its members, as it defined a member. Where a distinction was made between types of members—e.g., baptized and confirmed, we elected to use the broader rather than the narrower definition, since we were interested in encompassing in our study the complete range of membership from the nominal to the most active. The membership lists were then sampled in the following manner:

1. The total number of members of the church was divided by the number of respondents desired, to yield the sampling interval.

2. Then a random number was drawn between 1 and the number equal to the interval.

3. The church roll was counted, beginning with the first name, until the

[12] The sampling frame was ordered thus: Denominations were ordered randomly. Within each denomination counties were ordered randomly, and within each county congregations were ordered alphabetically by name of city, and within cities, alphabetically by name of congregation. This was done separately for smaller and larger congregations for the mainline Protestants.

[13] Often final approval was contingent upon the consent of governing boards of laymen. However, as soon as the pastor lent us his support we completed the field work for his congregation so that we did not have to call back. Several boards refused, but the waste in these cases was far offset by the time saved in the frequent instances where the board supported the pastor's decision.

random number was reached. The person indicated by this number became the first case in the sample.

4.   The count was begun again at 1, starting with the next name on the roll until the number equal to the sampling interval was reached. This person became the second case, and the counting procedure was begun at 1 again until the interval was reached, indicating the third case, and so on until the end of the list was reached.

Whenever the sampling interval came out as an even number or a fraction, it was rounded *down* to the next uneven number. This was done to avoid a systematic bias which might occur if the interval were an even number, such as getting only males from a long list of married couples. In some instances rounding resulted in too many cases being drawn from a congregation. In this event, cases were randomly discarded from the sample until it was reduced to the desired size.

## The Sample: Results

### Rate of Congregational Participation

As can be seen in Table A-1, of the original 100 Protestant congregations drawn in the sample, 83 agreed to participate in the study. Of the remaining 17, ten refused to take part and seven were lost because they had ceased to exist. The losses through refusal were all from mainline denominations, while six of the seven defunct congregations came from third-force groups.[14] Over-all, however, the data indicate that losses were fairly evenly spread among denominations. The poorer showing of the third-force is almost completely accounted for by the most marginal of these bodies, the Pentecostals, unaffiliated fundamentalist churches, and the Pillar of Fire.[15] Only one congregation was lost from the other third-force groups. Omitting these three peripheral groups, the third-force participation rate was 92 per cent, which compares extremely well with the mainline denominations. The only other slightly low participation rate was that of the Episcopalians. This arose through an unfortunate coincidence of our research and a census the Episcopalians were making of the diocese. Since our questionnaire would have followed the census questionnaire by only a few weeks, pastors and vestrymen were reluctant to expose members to both in such a short period. However, in most instances this objection was not raised.

To minimize the effects of lost congregations on the descriptive accuracy of the sample, and on the number of cases, lost congregations were replaced. We searched for a church of the same denomination, of the same size, in the same city if possible, and if not, then in a similar city in the same county. By this process, 14 of the 17 lost congregations were replaced by others which were

[14] Actually, the one mainline congregation so classified was not permanently defunct. The group had no pastor at the time of the study and was not meeting, but has subsequently reopened.

[15] The loss to the sample of congregations produced by these groups was greatly reduced when we were subsequently forced to omit all-Negro congregations from the analysis. All three Pentecostal bodies lost, and their replacements, were all-Negro groups.

Table A–1.  THE SAMPLE OF CONGREGATIONS

| Denomination | Original Number | Refused | Defunct | Total Lost | Number Replaced | Number Not Replaced | Total Sampled | Per Cent of Original Number Participating |
|---|---|---|---|---|---|---|---|---|
| Baptist (American) | 7 | 1 | 0 | 1 | 1 | 0 | 7 | 86 |
| Baptist (Southern) | 6 | 1 | 0 | 1 | 0 | 1 | 5 | 83 |
| Congregational | 6 | 1 | 0 | 1 | 1 | 0 | 6 | 83 |
| Disciples of Christ | 2 | 0 | 0 | 0 | 0 | 0 | 2 | 100 |
| Episcopal | 16 | 4 | 0 | 4 | 4 | 0 | 16 | 75 |
| Lutheran[a] | 12 | 0 | 0 | 0 | 0 | 0 | 12 | 100 |
| Methodist | 16 | 1 | 0 | 1 | 1 | 0 | 16 | 94 |
| Presbyterian | 17 | 2 | 1[b] | 3 | 3 | 0 | 17 | 82 |
| Mainline total | 82 | 10 | 1 | 11 | 10 | 1 | 81 | 87 |
| Assemblies of God | 3 | 0 | 1 | 1 | 1 | 0 | 3 | 67 |
| Church of God | 2 | 0 | 0 | 0 | 0 | 0 | 2 | 100 |
| Church of God in Christ | 2 | 0 | 0 | 0 | 0 | 0 | 2 | 100 |
| Nazarene | 3 | 0 | 0 | 0 | 0 | 0 | 3 | 100 |
| Seventh Day Adventist | 1 | 0 | 0 | 0 | 0 | 0 | 1 | 100 |
| Four-Square Gospel | 1 | 0 | 0 | 0 | 0 | 0 | 1 | 100 |
| Pillar of Fire | 1 | 0 | 1 | 1 | 0 | 1 | 0 | 0 |
| Pentecostal | 3 | 0 | 3 | 3 | 3 | 0 | 3 | 0 |
| Unaffiliated | 2 | 0 | 1 | 1 | 0 | 1 | 1 | 50 |
| Third-force total | 18 | 0 | 6 | 6 | 4 | 2 | 16 | 67 |
| Grand total | 100 | 10 | 7 | 17 | 14 | 3 | 97 | 83 |

[a] American Lutheran, 6; Lutheran Church in America, 2; Missouri Synod, 4.
[b] Not meeting; between pastors.

still operating and were willing to participate. The remaining three were not replaced for methodological reasons. The one mainline church not replaced was an all-Negro congregation which contained 70 per cent of the Negro members of this denomination in the four-county area. Clearly, no suitable replacement was to be found. (For this reason, and others we shall discuss later, our sample of all-Negro congregations fared badly.) The two third-force congregations were not replaced for a happier reason. As we began to receive membership lists from third-force groups, it became apparent that our estimates of the number of cases to be gained from each had been somewhat low. Since this would have resulted in overrepresentation of the third-force in the total sample, two lost congregations were left unreplaced to compensate for this trend.

In the end, our sample was made up of 97 Protestant congregations from which 4,488 members were selected as respondents.

With the splendid assistance of the Archbishop and the Chancery, cooperation of the sample Roman Catholic parishes was readily forthcoming. However, one of the sample parishes turned out to be a Portuguese-language national parish.[16] It was felt by the pastor that few, if any, of his members would be able to read English well enough to take part in the study, so the parish was dropped from the sample. Thus, our Catholic sample is limited to parishes other than national foreign-language congregations. Since such groups are rapidly receding from the American scene, it was felt that little of descriptive value was sacrificed. This left 21 parishes from which 1,900 respondents were drawn.

### Rectifying the membership rolls

From the beginning of the research we were aware of the problem of faulty membership lists. To keep a membership roll accurate and current would require a good deal more time and effort than it would be worth to most congregations. Little is lost by sending church bulletins, etc., to persons who have moved away, converted to another faith, are deceased, or have become incompetent. It is much more important, however, to see that the names of new members are quickly added to the list, since failure here could lead to disaffection. The pastors we talked to were well aware of these contingencies and all had well-developed procedures for adding to their membership lists, while admitting that revision of the lists to delete inactive names was only done infrequently; in some cases many years had passed since the last careful revision. This was strikingly illustrated when we learned that one man drawn in our sample of Roman Catholics had been dead since 1929.

[16] While parish membership is geographic, persons recently immigrated may choose to belong to a national parish, specially maintained for certain ethnic groups, where their native language is used. Even had we retained this parish it could not really have been argued that it was "representative" of foreign-speaking parishes, for surely a Portuguese parish would be markedly different from Spanish, Italian, German, or French national parishes. Hence, the option was actually either to omit all or include all. And since attempting to use a mail questionnaire written in English among persons with limited ability to read or even speak that language is a rather foolish venture, there really was no option at all. Even though avoiding these concentrations of non-English speakers, the study ran into large numbers of Catholics in polyglot San Francisco who could not read English.

Given that additions are made promptly, but that deletions are occasional, it is apparent that a reasonably accurate list of current members is included in the church rolls—virtually everyone who should be there, is, but many who should not be are there too. The problem is to sort them out and exclude the deadwood. Clearly our sample congregations and parishes could not be expected to take on such an elaborate task simply to satisfy our research needs. Nor could we possibly afford to revise the rolls for them. But we could afford to do so for those members chosen in the sample.

If a random sample is drawn from a list of names which contains a certain proportion of "accurate" names as well as a proportion which are "inaccurate," the sample should contain the correct proportions of both if it comprises a sufficient number of cases to be reliably representative. Given this, it follows that if the inaccurate names are removed from the sample, the result is the same as would have been attained by sampling an accurate list in the first place, except for a reduction in the number of cases.

Thus, we were faced with the considerably more manageable task of rectifying the sample rather than the lists. Initially, of course, there was no way of knowing which names ought to be deleted; so the first mailing of the questionnaire went to everyone drawn in the sample. Subsequently, we began to get back questionnaires as undeliverable mail. Each was carefully checked out. When we were able to determine that the addressee should have been deleted from the membership list of the sampled congregation because he had left the area or died, he was declared a legitimate loss from the original sample. In addition, persons who were permanently hospitalized or institutionalized were dropped, as well as some incompetents who were under home nursing care. Through these means 537 Protestants and 297 Roman Catholics were removed from the sample. The proportion of losses was about the same for all Protestant denominations.

Aside from these inaccuracies of the church rolls brought to our attention either because the questionnaire was undeliverable, or because a friend or relative contacted us, there were many additional inaccuracies that were not revealed through these means. Some guardians and relatives discarded the questionnaire without informing us, and many persons living at the old address of some former church member did not return the questionnaire to the postman as misdirected mail. These failures came to light during attempts to conduct telephone interviews with a random sample of nonrespondents.

At the end of the data collection campaign, random samples of nonrespondents were drawn, 300 from among the Protestants, and 200 from the Roman Catholics. Those who had telephones were interviewed, and the minority without phones were sent a brief mail questionnaire containing the same items as the interview schedule.

The purpose of these interviews was three-fold: to gather data which would allow a comparison of respondents and nonrespondents to see what, if any, sorts of bias in return might distort our findings; to find out the reasons people gave for not participating; and to see what portion of them should not have been in the sample in the first place. We shall take up the first two points shortly, but the last bears on rectifying the sample.

A summary of response to these interviews is shown in Table A-2. Eighty-six per cent of the Protestant sample of nonrespondents were either inter-

Table A–2.  INTERVIEWING A SAMPLE OF NONRESPONDENTS

|  | Protestants | Catholics |
|---|---|---|
| Interviews completed | 56% | 42% |
| Interviews refused | 7 | 5 |
| Discovered and discarded as legitimate losses | 30 | 40 |
| No response[a] | 7 | 13 |
| Total | 100% | 100% |
| Total number | (300) | (200) |

[a] Forty-eight Protestant and 44 Catholic nonrespondents for whom no telephone listing could be found were sent mail questionnaires containing the same items as the telephone interviews. Those who did not reply to the mail questionnaire are presented here separately from those who refused to be interviewed by telephone.

viewed or dropped from the sample. This included 30 per cent of the nonrespondents who could be conclusively established as deadwood. These additional losses were also spread evenly among the denominations. Since these findings were based on a sample of substantial size, they provided a rather firm estimate for further correction of the sample rolls, and, as we shall recount shortly, 30 per cent of the *remaining* Protestant nonrespondents were subtracted from the original sample prior to computation of the final return rate.

We were similarly successful in interviewing Catholic nonrespondents, and 83 per cent were either interviewed or declared as legitimate losses. In analysis of our interviews with Catholics, we not only uncovered 40 per cent who should have been deleted from the rolls, but found further inhibitions to a successful study: language and literacy.

Even though we had excluded specifically foreign-language national parishes from our Catholic sample, still we found a surprisingly large number of Catholics who were unable to fill out the questionnaire because they could not read and write English; indeed, many could not even speak it. Of the Catholics interviewed in the sample of nonrespondents, 24 per cent volunteered this information about themselves. The futility of sending a mail questionnaire to an illiterate is obvious. Had we been able to distinguish illiterate members of ethnic groups from the literate in advance, we would unquestionably have rectified the sample to be representative of only the literate. There is undoubtedly a certain loss to the study in excluding the illiterate foreign-born, but since they are beyond the reach of mail questionnaire techniques, this loss must be borne. Furthermore, such groups do not make up any very significant segment of the general population, and their omission does not seriously detract from a description of our general culture.

Although we were unable to delete these foreign-speaking persons from our sample a priori, and in fact did not expect to find them in so great a number, there was no reason why they could not be removed after the fact by the same logic as applies to the legitimate losses. Hence, for the Catholic sample, the correction factor subtracted from the original base combines the proportion of nonrespondents discovered to be legitimate losses with the proportion who were clearly established as foreign-speaking illiterates.

*Response Rate*

Having described the procedures for rectifying the sample, we may now turn to an examination of the proportion of eligible persons in the sample who eventually filled out and returned their questionnaire. For ease in explication we shall discuss generic blocks of denominations separately.

### Mainline Protestants

After removing two all-Negro and two all-Chinese congregations for separate treatment, our sample contained 78 Protestant congregations from mainline denominations. Questionnaires were sent to 3,745 persons listed on the membership rolls of the congregations. A complete statistical breakdown of response rate by denomination appears in Table A-3. As can be seen in column 2 of the table, during the course of the data collection process 466 persons were uncovered who should have been deleted from the original membership lists. Column 3 shows the sample base for each denomination after these legitimate losses had been subtracted, and column 5 shows the percentage of persons in column 3 who filled out and returned their questionnaire. Over-all, 64 per cent did so. An examination of major denominational groupings shows the rate fluctuated very little among them: from 68 per cent of the Congregationalists and Disciples of Christ to 60 per cent of the Episcopalians.[17] *Within* the Baptist group, however, the variation was slightly greater, with only 52 per cent of the Southern Baptists responding as compared with 71 per cent of the American Baptists. This slightly lower showing of Southern Baptists is only partly attributable to differences between conservatives and moderates. As we shall shortly show, although the sects did return in slightly smaller proportion than the mainline bodies, most of them surpassed the Southern Baptists. While it cannot be demonstrated, some portion of this lower response may have been produced by suspicion and resentment toward the University of California at Berkeley among Southern Baptists who had been exposed to recent right-wing attacks on the university by several Southern Baptist pastors in the area. Whether or not this was the case, the influence was minor, since the response rate was still reasonably good.

Because we had discovered through telephone interviews that an additional 30 per cent of the nonrespondents were also legitimate losses, these were also removed from the sample bases. This correction factor, shown in column 6, is 30 per cent of the nonrespondents shown in column 4. Column 7 shows the rectified sample bases, after the correction factor had been subtracted from the totals shown in column 3.

The number of persons in each denomination who actually took part in the study is shown in column 8. In all, 2,083 mainline Protestants responded out of a rectified sample base of 2,920. Column 9 shows these ratios in the form of the percentages who returned questionnaires. Over-all, 72 per cent responded. Again we see that fluctuations among denominations were very slight, indicating that no important denominational biases were operating in the data collection.

[17] This was probably the effect of having followed on the heels of the diocesan census; see page 224.

Table A–3.   QUESTIONNAIRE RETURN RATE OF MAINLINE PROTESTANTS[a]

| | Original Number (1) | Legitimate Losses (2) | Corrected Number (3) | Number of Nonrespondents (4) | Per Cent Returned (5) | Correction Factor (6) | Corrected Number (7) | Number Returned (8) | Final Per Cent Returned (9) |
|---|---|---|---|---|---|---|---|---|---|
| Baptist[b] | 446 | 97 | 349 | 119 | 66 | 36 | 313 | 230 | 74 |
| American | 230 | 32 | 198 | 57 | 71 | 16 | 182 | 141 | 78 |
| Southern | 216 | 65 | 151 | 72 | 52 | 22 | 129 | 79 | 61 |
| Congregationalist | 239 | 17 | 222 | 71 | 68 | 21 | 201 | 151 | 75 |
| Disciples of Christ | 100 | 26 | 74 | 24 | 68 | 7 | 67 | 50 | 75 |
| Episcopal | 780 | 84 | 696 | 281 | 60 | 84 | 612 | 416 | 68 |
| Lutheran[c] | 550 | 43 | 507 | 180 | 65 | 55 | 452 | 327 | 72 |
| Missouri | 180 | 13 | 167 | 51 | 69 | 15 | 152 | 116 | 76 |
| American[d] | 370 | 30 | 340 | 134 | 61 | 40 | 300 | 208 | 69 |
| Methodist | 760 | 101 | 659 | 244 | 63 | 73 | 586 | 415 | 71 |
| Presbyterian | 870 | 98 | 772 | 277 | 64 | 83 | 689 | 495 | 72 |
| Total | 3,745 | 466 | 3,279 | 1,196 | 64 | 359 | 2,920 | 2,086 | 72 |

[a] All-Negro and all-Chinese congregations have been excluded.
[b] For lack of information, 10 Baptist respondents could not be assigned to either American or Southern groups, but are included in the Baptist total.
[c] Five Lutheran respondents could not be assigned a synod for lack of information, but appear in the Lutheran total.
[d] Two bodies, the American Lutheran Church and the Lutheran Church of America have been treated as one.

Table A–4. QUESTIONNAIRE RETURN RATE OF THIRD-FORCE PROTESTANTS[a]

| | Original Number | Legitimate Losses | Corrected Number | Number of Non-respondents | Per Cent Returned | Correction Factor | Corrected Number | Number Returned | Final Per Cent Returned |
|---|---|---|---|---|---|---|---|---|---|
| Assemblies of God | 104 | 21 | 83 | 39 | 53 | 12 | 71 | 44 | 62 |
| Church of God | 90 | 26 | 64 | 20 | 69 | 6 | 58 | 44 | 76 |
| Church of God in Christ | 71 | 4 | 67 | 30 | 55 | 9 | 58 | 37 | 64 |
| Nazarene | 140 | 12 | 128 | 53 | 59 | 16 | 112 | 75 | 67 |
| Seventh Day Adventist | 50 | 3 | 47 | 12 | 74 | 4 | 43 | 35 | 81 |
| Four-Square Gospel | 12 | 0 | 12 | 0 | 100 | 0 | 12 | 12 | 100 |
| Unaffiliated Congregation | 28 | 5 | 23 | 15 | 35 | 5 | 18 | 8 | 44 |
| Total | 495 | 71 | 424 | 169 | 60 | 52 | 372 | 255 | 68 |
| Combined total | 4,420 | 537 | 3,703 | 1,365 | 63 | 411 | 3,292 | 2,341 | 71 |

[a] All-Negro and all-Chinese congregations have been excluded.

### Protestant Sects

After removing three all-Negro Pentecostal groups for separate treatment, the sample of sect groups consisted of 13 congregations from which 495 members were originally sampled. As in the mainline denominations, a number of ineligible persons subsequently came to light, and 71 legitimate losses were removed from the original sample base. As shown in Table A-4, over-all 60 per cent of the sect members completed and returned their questionnaires, ranging from an exemplary 100 per cent from the Four-Square Gospel[18] to 35 per cent of those in the unaffiliated tabernacle. When the sample base was further corrected for the legitimate losses disclosed by the telephone interviews, the final return rate was 68 per cent, which is only slightly below that of the mainline denominations. Altogether, 255 persons from the sects responded. Combined with those from the larger Protestant bodies, this gave us 2,338 completed questionnaires from Protestants.

### All-Negro and All-Chinese Congregations

As mentioned in the previous discussion of the sample of congregations, the loss of a huge Negro church immediately damaged our attempt to study Negro Protestants, most of whom, unfortunately, even in the very northern and liberal Bay Area, belong to segregated congregations.

To this was added our error of not drastically oversampling all-Negro congregations. As the sample turned out, even if we had obtained excellent returns from Negroes we would have been plagued by insufficient cases for any extensive multivariate analysis. In point of fact, our response rate among Negro Protestants was much poorer than among whites, as can be seen in Table A-5. Even after all the rectifications had been made of the sample base, the final return rate was only 40 per cent. Strangely enough, the tiny Pentecostal storefront churches responded much better than the mainline congregations. Since it seems certain that the Pentecostals, as a group, were much less educated and more ghettoized than the Methodists and American Baptists, these findings run counter to expectations based on social class. One possible explanation may be that the involvement of Pentecostals in their church was sufficiently greater to overcome the difficulties the questionnaire posed for the uneducated. In any event, the all-Negro groups were too under-represented to be of any use, and were subsequently discarded from the analysis.

When we discovered upon drawing the sample of congregations that we had included two all-Chinese Protestant groups, our first impulse was simply to discard them and exclude members of all-Chinese congregations from the population to which we could generalize. Since there are very few Chinese in America, and all-Chinese Protestant congregations are especially rare, it did not seem that such an omission would particularly reduce our description of American religion.

On the other hand, there are sufficient numbers of Chinese in the Bay

[18] The total of 12 represented one questionnaire from every household in the congregation, which was founded by Aimee Semple McPherson.

Table A–5.  QUESTIONNAIRE RETURN RATE OF ALL-NEGRO, ALL-CHINESE, AND CATHOLIC CONGREGATIONS

| | Original Number | Legitimate Losses | Corrected Number | Number of Non-respondents | Per Cent Returned | Correction Factor | Corrected Number | Number Returned | Final Per Cent Returned |
|---|---|---|---|---|---|---|---|---|---|
| *All-Negro Protestant congregations:* | | | | | | | | | |
| American Baptist | 40 | 6 | 34 | 29 | 15 | 9 | 25 | 5 | 20 |
| Methodist | 50 | 5 | 45 | 32 | 29 | 10 | 35 | 13 | 37 |
| Pentecostal | 78 | 17 | 61 | 35 | 43 | 11 | 50 | 26 | 52 |
| Total | 168 | 28 | 140 | 96 | 31 | 30 | 110 | 44 | 40 |
| *All-Chinese Protestant congregations:* | | | | | | | | | |
| American Baptist | 40 | 3 | 37 | 15 | 59 | 5 | 32 | 22 | 69 |
| Congregational | 40 | 11 | 29 | 24 | 17 | 7 | 22 | 5 | 23 |
| Total | 80 | 14 | 66 | 39 | 41 | 12 | 54 | 27 | 50 |
| Catholic | 1,900 | 297 | 1,603 | 1,058 | 34 | 575 | 1,028 | 545 | 53 |

NOTE: Other unassignable returns were: Unsampled Protestant denominations, 16; irreligious, 16; denomination unknown, 11. The total of all documents returned was 3,000.

Area so that this contingency arises in all local surveys. Since it cost very little to include these two churches we decided to do so in order to gain some experience of what research might be possible among the Chinese. The results indicate that language is the only real barrier to survey research among the Chinese. In one congregation 69 per cent responded, about the same as among white Protestants, while the other showed a 23 per cent return rate. These differences closely approximate estimates by the pastors of these churches of the proportions of members who could read English. Since there were only 27 persons in all from these congregations who replied, they could not be included in the analysis. However, we now know that if Chinese are sufficiently oversampled so that those who do not speak English can be dropped, they are accessible to survey research.

### Roman Catholics

Our initial sample of Roman Catholics contained 1,900 persons randomly drawn from the membership rolls of 21 parishes. Of these 297 were dropped as legitimate losses, a somewhat higher proportion than among Protestants. In all, 545 Catholics responded to the survey. When the sample base had been further rectified for additional legitimate losses and illiterates, as discussed earlier, the final response rate was 53 per cent. This was considerably poorer than responses from Protestants.

The most important reason for this difference was probably a resistance by many Catholics to the basic assumption of the questionnaire, namely, that people have *personal* religious opinions and beliefs as distinguished from the formal creed of their church. A number of Catholics took the position that a study of Catholicism ought to confine itself to official preachments, and that a study of individual Catholics was irrelevant since any deviations from normative Catholicism are either inadvertent or pernicious. This type of response took both a sophisticated and folk form. The sophisticate sent back his questionnaire with the suggestion that we obtain answers to all questions by consulting the hierarchy for official statements of Catholic doctrine and position. "While I must admit I do not know the Catholic position on many of these questions," one such Catholic respondent wrote, while refusing to take part in the study, "it is also true that I have never had occasion to seek it out. Should any of these issues confront me, the Catholic position would either be widely known or I would ask my Pastor to guide me."

With less eloquence, the folk responses made the same point. "I ain't the one to tell these things. If you call Father ——— at St. ——— and tell him I ask you he will teach you all these things. He is not strick. His number is ———."

As we shall discuss later, in our first follow-up letter to respondents we attempted to overcome this feeling that we were asking people to act as official spokesmen. Protestants, with a tradition of "everyman his own theologian," of course, took to the idea readily enough. But even though the Archbishop and their own pastor supported the study, which made it clear that the official hierarchy shared our perspective that people have personal beliefs, resistance continued among the Catholics. In all, 12 per cent of the nonrespondents interviewed voluntarily raised this objection to the study.

A second factor limiting response was anticipated by the chancery office before the data collection even began. We were advised that Catholics are continually approached by various church-connected groups seeking to enlist their aid or their support, and that consequently Catholics have a lot of "sales resistance" to appeals in the name of the church. This was borne out by interviews with nonrespondents, many of whom complained, as did one woman, that, "it's always something, the Cathedral fund, the nuns, the school, the Holy Names Society, it's too much. I go to Mass and confession and I just want to be let alone." This sales resistance was perhaps especially high at the time of the study since St. Mary's Cathedral had recently been destroyed by fire, and an extensive fund-raising campaign to replace it was in progress throughout the archdiocese.

*Representativeness*

So far we have been concerned with the proportion of the respondents who returned the questionnaire. But even more important is the degree to which those who responded accurately represent the population from which they were selected. On this depends, of course, the degree to which the data can be used to cipher out an accurate account of the religious life of church members in the Bay Area, and, by implication, the role of religion in the lives of Americans generally.

One criterion for establishing representativeness is the proportion of persons sampled who respond—the fewer persons who fail to participate the less possibility that important types and subgroups will be underrepresented in the data. As we have seen, nearly three-quarters of the sampled Protestants and more than half of the Roman Catholics took part in the study. The high Protestant rate gives some confidence in the descriptive reliability of the data, although there is some room for doubt about the Catholics. However, we need not rely too heavily on this kind of estimate of representativeness, since through telephone interviews we managed to find out a good deal about the Protestants and Catholics who did not respond. By comparing nonrespondents with respondents we could readily determine whether and to what extent a number of probable sources of bias did in fact influence response to the questionnaire.

The first potential distortion we shall examine which could have marred our data is religious involvement, that is, persons with a greater religious commitment could have been more likely to respond than those whose church membership was rather nominal. Since frequency of church attendance was asked of both respondents and the sample of nonrespondents, this possibility can be adequately examined.

As can be seen in Table A-6, respondents were slightly more likely to be frequent church attenders than were nonrespondents. Among Protestants these differences were too small to suggest any important bias in the response pattern; indeed, the variations were not statistically significant at the .05 level.[19] Among Catholics the differences in church-going between respondents and nonrespondents were slightly greater (and significant at the .02 level), but the variation was almost entirely restricted to the first two categories of attendance. Nonrespondents were less likely than respondents to be every-week attenders and more likely to fall into the at least once-a-month category.

[19] Chi-square was used.

Table A–6.    COMPARISON OF CHURCH ATTENDANCE OF
RESPONDENTS AND NONRESPONDENTS

| Frequency of Attendance | Protestants | | Catholics | |
|---|---|---|---|---|
| | Respond-ents | Non-respondents | Respond-ents | Non-respondents |
| Every week | 36% | 31% | 69% | 54% |
| At least once a month | 48 | 43 | 17 | 30 |
| At least once a year | 12 | 18 | 10 | 13 |
| Less than once a year or never | 3 | 6 | 4 | 2 |
| No answer | 1 | 2 | ᵃ | 1 |
| Total | 100% | 100% | 100% | 100% |
| Number | (2,413) | (169) | (545) | (85) |
| | | $p > .05$ | | $p < .02$ |

ᵃ Less than 0.5 per cent.

If these two categories were merged, the comparison would be: respondents, 86 per cent; nonrespondents, 84 per cent. Thus, while our data slightly overrepresent weekly attenders and correspondingly underrepresent the moderately frequent attenders, the proper proportion of infrequent and non-attenders was reached by the questionnaire. Thus, although the differences are statistically significant at the .02 level, the bias did not enter at the expected and most critical point—the disaffected and indifferent are adequately represented. Given their poorer return rate, the probability of bias in the Catholic sample was greater than for the Protestants. Finding so small a bias greatly increases confidence in the general descriptive quality of the data.

Even if our data escaped any important tendency of persons little involved in church to leave the questionnaire unanswered, we must still establish the representativeness of the sample on additional characteristics which have been found in the past to influence participation in survey studies.

Since women typically have considerably more free time than men, they have been found to be more likely to complete mail questionnaires. However, the comparisons in Table A-7 show that sex played no meaningful role in the response rate. Any tendency for men to underrespond was extremely slight. Again differences between respondents and nonrespondents were slightly greater in the Catholic sample, but in neither group were the differences statistically significant at the .05 level.

There was no age bias in response rate among Protestants. Among Catholics there appears to have been a slightly greater likelihood for the young to participate than the elderly, but again the differences fell below statistical significance at the .05 level.

Table A-7 does reveal, however, that our data slightly overrepresent the educated and, among Protestants, those with prestige occupations. Among both Protestants and Catholics the college-educated were more likely to respond than those with grade school or only some high school training. While this tendency does not introduce a major distortion into our description of church members, it must be taken into account in interpreting our findings. In particular, estimates of religious knowledge and sophistication must be qualified

Table A–7.    COMPARISONS BETWEEN RESPONDENTS AND NONRESPONDENTS
ON FOUR BACKGROUND CHARACTERISTICS

| | Protestants | | Catholics | |
|---|---|---|---|---|
| | Respond-ents | Non-respondents | Respond-ents | Non-respondents |
| *Sex:* | | | | |
| Men | 37% | 40% | 34% | 41% |
| Women | 63 | 60 | 66 | 59 |
| | | $p > .05$ | | $p > .05$ |
| *Age:* | | | | |
| Under 40 | 39% | 36% | 46% | 40% |
| 40–59 | 45 | 48 | 41 | 34 |
| 60 and above | 16 | 16 | 13 | 26 |
| | | $p > .05$ | | $p > .05$ |
| *Education:* | | | | |
| Grade school only | 6% | 8% | 8% | 18% |
| Some high school | 8 | 14 | 12 | 10 |
| Completed high school | 21 | 26 | 30 | 39 |
| Attended college | 63 | 51 | 48 | 32 |
| No information | 2 | 1 | 2 | 1 |
| | | $p < .01$ | | $p < .02$ |
| *Occupation:*[a] | | | | |
| Upper white collar | 52% | 43% | 38% | 26% |
| Lower white collar | 19 | 16 | 23 | 14 |
| Upper blue collar | 21 | 27 | 27 | 30 |
| Lower blue collar | 7 | 10 | 12 | 19 |
| Not in labor force | 1 | 4 | 1 | 0 |
| | | $p < .01$ | | $p > .05$ |
| Number | (2,386) | (169) | (545) | (85) |

[a] Head of household.

as slightly inflated by the presence of an oversupply of college-educated respondents. Similarly, the presence of a slightly higher proportion of upper
white-collar workers among Protestants must be taken into account. These
biases are probably inescapable for a mail questionnaire since the educated
find it much easier to respond than do the uneducated who in the extreme
cases simply cannot read the questions. Hence, the best that can be hoped
for with a mail questionnaire is that such biases can be minimized. In general,
our samples seem to be reasonably representative of the populations sampled,
the Protestant data being somewhat more accurate than the Catholic; but in
both samples the number of the better-educated and of persons with prestige
occupations is slightly inflated.

## The Strategy of Data Collection

As can be seen from the questionnaire, which contains more than 450
items,[20] we were asking respondents to give a good deal of time and effort to

[20] The numbering used obscures the actual number of independent items. In
some instances a dozen or more separate questions are grouped under a single item
number.

participation in the study. We estimated that the average person would be able to complete it in just over three hours, although one respondent reported taking 16 hours on the document. Given that mail questionnaires have often obtained poor response rates, one might well expect that using such a long questionnaire would insure failure. Yet, as we have just discussed, a very high return rate was forthcoming, and the data obtained seem reasonably representative of the sampled population. In this section we shall recount the data collection campaign which yielded these high returns, and offer some speculations about how and why it was effective.

Having obtained the name and address of all persons in the sample, an initial mailing was prepared. This consisted of a personal letter (Exhibit A-1),[21] the questionnaire, a prepaid return envelope, and a postcard to be used to inform us when the questionnaire had been mailed back. This last device was to insure anonymity to all respondents. The questionnaires were without any identification. When we received the postcard we removed the respondent's name from the list of those scheduled to receive further follow-up. Although it was possible to be credited with participating in the study by merely sending back the postcard, while discarding the questionnaire, this must have been a rare occurrence. The number of postcards always lagged slightly behind the number of questionnaires received. These provisions to insure anonymity were taken largely to satisfy the apprehensions of pastors. How important they were to respondents is unknown. However, despite instructions to the contrary, at least 20 per cent of the respondents signed their name to the questionnaire or the return envelope, and many commented that they were perfectly willing to be identified with their views. But, obviously, this added anonymity did not offend or discourage those who felt no need for it, and likely it did influence the decision of those who were less bold to participate.

Prior to mailing the questionnaires, the pastors of the sampled congregations and parishes were notified, and, in the majority of cases, responded by announcing the forthcoming study from the pulpit and in the church bulletin.

In the letter which accompanied the questionnaire, every effort was made to let the respondent know precisely what we were asking of him. In the opening sentence we admitted that the questionnaire would take several hours to complete, and indicated that we were willing to allow a reasonably long period of time for its return.

The consequences of this are clear in the pattern of returns (Table A-8). While responses to most mail questionnaires follow a sharply accelerated curve during the first several weeks which then rapidly falls to zero, the curve followed in this instance was elongated. There was an initial acceleration, but the rate of return did not become exceptionally high before it slumped. Following the drop-off, returns settled at a steady and sizable pace for eight more weeks and then declined very slowly. Indeed, a few questionnaires continued to come in each week even seven months after the initial mailing, and one came back two years later. While the table also indicated the impact of various follow-up devices in maintaining this return rate (which we shall

---

[21] Exhibit A–1 shows the letter sent to Protestants. The letter to Catholics was substantially the same but included the information that the study had the approval of the Archbishop.

# UNIVERSITY OF CALIFORNIA

DY OF RELIGION IN AMERICAN LIFE
VEY RESEARCH CENTER
KELEY 4, CALIFORNIA

I am writing to ask for two or three hours of your time over the next several
ks in helping on a study of religion in American life which is being conducted
the Survey Research Center of the University of California. I do this with the
roval of your Pastor, who has been consulted about the study, and who feels, as
ope you will, that it will produce a useful picture of American religion and be
remely valuable for church planning.

What I would like to ask you to do is to fill out the enclosed questionnaire.
you will see, it is a long one because a topic as important and complex as religion
not be discussed briefly. Because of its length, you may not be able to answer all
the questions at one time. I hope, however, that you will take a few spare moments
m time to time over the next week or so to answer them. When you have finished,
ld you kindly return the questionnaire to me in the enclosed envelope.

You are not asked to sign your name to the questionnaire so you can be sure that
ything you say will be entirely confidential. It would, however, be very useful to
to know when you have completed and mailed back your questionnaire. So when you
, would you kindly take the trouble to tell me that you have done so by also mailing
ck the enclosed postcard.

I know this is a lot to ask of busy people. However, as you look at the question-
ire, I think that you will agree that it deals with an important topic and that it
ll be useful to the churches in America to know how their members feel on these
tters. I also hope, by the way, that you will find it an interesting questionnaire
d of some personal help to you in your own life.

Your generosity in giving your time and effort to assist in this study is very
eply appreciated. I wish there were an opportunity to express my gratitude in
rson. My phone number is THornwall 5-6000, extension 4044, in case you have any
estions that you may wish to raise. If I happen not to be in, please ask for my
sociate, Mr. Rodney Stark. Again, many thanks for your help.

Cordially,

Charles Y. Glock
Director

S.  It occurs to me that you may be curious to know how you were chosen as a
spondent. Your Pastor supplied us with a list of the members of your Church.
then put all of the names in a hat, in effect, and picked out 50 names at random
be sent the questionnaire. You happened to be one of them. This procedure, which
are repeating in many congregations, assures us of scientifically accurate results,
everyone returns his questionnaire. We are anxious, as you can understand, to be
scientifically accurate as possible, which is another reason why we are hoping
hat you will find it possible to help.

Table A–8.    RETURNS BY WEEK

| | Week | Number Returned |
|---|---|---|
| April | 1<sup>a</sup> | 121 |
| | 2 | 360 |
| | 3 | 347 |
| May | 4 | 258 |
| | | *First follow-up letter* |
| | 5 | 454 |
| | 6 | 284 |
| | 7 | 106 |
| June | 8 | 106 |
| | | *Second follow-up letter* |
| | 9 | 150 |
| | 10 | 149 |
| | 11 | 116 |
| July | 12 | 102 |
| | | *Third follow-up letter with questionnaire* |
| | 13 | 136 |
| | 14 | 78 |
| | | *Parish follow-up began* |
| | 15 | 26 |
| | 16 | 56 |
| August | 17 | 37 |
| | 18 | 46 |
| | 19 | 16 |
| | 20 | 18 |
| September | 21–24 | 34 |
| Total | | 3,000 |

<sup>a</sup> Only a partial week since questionnaire took a day or two in the mail.

shortly discuss in detail), several additional factors probably played the most important roles in generating this long-term response rate.

It seems plausible that if the initial approach stresses immediate compliance, persons are forced to make what may be a *premature* decision on whether or not to participate. Many may refuse because the request came at an especially inconvenient time. But if persons in such circumstances are assured that they may defer responding until a more opportune occasion, many potential nonrespondents will make an initially favorable decision. Thus, rather than having them throw away the questionnaire, send it back unanswered, make up their minds not to cooperate, and otherwise become unamenable or inaccessible to further appeals, it is possible to create a nearly universal pool of persons disposed eventually to respond.[21] This favorable disposition is then available to be summoned up and reinforced by subsequent appeals. On the other hand, such "soft sell" probably encourages many who would respond quickly to take their time, and perhaps temporize until they end

[21] Of the nonrespondents interviewed, 42 per cent were still favorable to the study and hoped to "get around to it shortly."

up as nonrespondents. The gamble taken, then, was to reduce the urgency of the first approach, risking a lethargic reaction, in hopes of a higher, though slower and less certain, rate of response in the long run.

A second factor which seems to have led so many to respond was the extreme length of the questionnaire. Rather than being a handicap, it would seem from a number of comments made by respondents that the long document and the intensive exploration of single topics lent plausibility and substance to our claim to be attempting significant research. At least several hundred persons specifically mentioned the length of the questionnaire favorably. Only a handful complained about it, and an equal number took us to task for not writing an even longer questionnaire.

A third feature of the study also played a vital role in securing a high response rate. By sampling, typically, 50 persons from a single congregation and 100 from each parish, sufficient numbers of persons were contacted within acquaintance networks for the study to become a topic of conversation for many, and for most to be at least aware that others they knew were taking part in the study. Since the study was sanctioned by pastors, and often the lay leaders of the church as well, it was likely that majority opinion in these communications networks was favorable to the study, thus further predisposing members to take part. Some evidence of this favorable interaction was provided by a number of persons, not included in the sample, who wrote and asked to participate after having found out their friends were doing so. A few even complained of having been overlooked. Of course, we could not include these volunteers, but we sent personal answers to all such letters and enclosed sample questionnaires. This probably helped to continue the study as a topic of conversation. Moreover, the content of the questionnaire led to many discussions among church members, and we received numerous requests for sample copies to be used by adult Sunday school and discussion groups, and requests for questionnaires came from relatives and friends of respondents from as far away as India. Thus, an essential feature was a mediated rather than direct appeal. For a respondent, the study was not simply an impersonal correspondence with some unknown sociologists, but was instead an experience shared and supported by others to whom he was linked by acquaintance and common membership in a church. As we continued the data collection campaign, we made every effort to underline and retain this mediated character of the appeal.

After respondents had been given three and a half weeks to complete their questionnaire, the first follow-up letter was sent (Exhibit A-2). Again it was emphasized that respondents should take their time; the mere fact of a reminder letter adequately suggested they should speed up. In the letter we attempted to resolve a problem which had become apparent from letters and calls: many felt unworthy or unrepresentative to speak for their congregations. We tried to explain that these matters would take care of themselves through sampling and that we were particularly and specifically interested in each respondent.

After another month, a second follow-up letter was sent (Exhibit A-3). During the preceding weeks we had learned that if we could get any return communication from respondents, a telephone call or a letter, they were almost certain to complete their questionnaires. Activity in connection with the study

# UNIVERSITY OF CALIFORNIA

STUDY OF RELIGION IN AMERICAN LIFE
SURVEY RESEARCH CENTER
BERKELEY 4, CALIFORNIA

May 3, 1963

Dear Friend:

Several weeks ago, I took the liberty, with your Pastor's permission, of asking you to fill out a questionnaire -- a lengthy one, I'm afraid -- in connection with a study of religion in American life.

In my earlier letter, I suggested that you take your time in filling out the questionnaire and I hope that you will not interpret this letter as unduly pressure to hurry.

So far the response to our project has been very encouraging and those who have returned their questionnaires indicate they found it interesting and thought provoking. Some people, who felt they were not very "typical" church members, wondered whether we wanted them to fill out the questionnaire anyway. We are very interested in each person chosen in the sample and in the variety of religious outlooks people have, not just in "typical" members.

We tried very hard to follow scientific principles in picking the sample of people to whom to send the questionnaire. Whether or not we end up with scientifically accurate study will depend upon the cooperation we receive from people like yourself. I recognize that we are asking a lot of you. However, in light of the help that the study will be to the churches generally, to your denomination in particular, and to our overall understanding of religion in American life, I hope that you will find it possible to help us.

If you have already sent in your questionnaire, please disregard this letter and accept my apologies for having written you again. If you have misplaced your copy of the questionnaire, or have not received one, please write or call me or my associate Mr. Rodney Stark, at TH 5-6000, extension 4044.

I would like to take this opportunity to thank you for your help and patience.

Cordially,

Charles Y. Glock
Director

CYG:su

# UNIVERSITY OF CALIFORNIA

SURVEY RESEARCH CENTER
BERKELEY 4, CALIFORNIA

June, 1963

Dear Friend:

By this time you may feel that I am beginning to wear out my welcome by writing you once again about the study of religion in American life which the Survey Research Center is conducting. I do so only because your opinions are important to the study and without them the study cannot be complete.

Most people who have sent back their questionnaires--and a majority have done so by now--have found filling them out a worthwhile experience and I have been pleased at the large number of favorable comments that people have made. I guess the nicest comment came from a gentleman who said, "I would like to congratulate your staff on a very stimulating, educational, and inspiring questionnaire." More typically, people have said that they found the questionnaire "very interesting," or "well worth the time it takes to fill it out," or "it helped me in my own life."

According to my records, I have not yet heard from you. It may be that you haven't had time yet to fill out the questionnaire. Or, perhaps you have sent it back without sending the post card telling us you had done so. (You will recall that we didn't ask you to put your name on the questionnaire itself.) It may also be that you have mislaid the question- naire or even that you did not receive it.

It would be helpful at this stage to know where you do stand. If you could take a moment to fill out the enclosed post card and mail it back to me I would appreciate it very much. If you need another copy of the questionnaire, please indicate this on the post card and I shall be happy to send you one.

Many people have asked how they can find out about the results of the study. A summary of results for your congregation will be given to your Pastor sometime this fall, and I'm sure he will make these available to you. These summaries will not, of course, give the answers of any single individual, but will show the number of persons who chose each answer--very much like election returns. A more complete report will be published in book form, hopefully in a paperback edition that can be purchased inexpensively. While I can't be sure at the present time, there is a good possibility that the publisher will agree to make the book available at a reduced price to those who cooperated in the study.

If you have any questions about the study, my associate--Mr. Rodney Stark--or I will be very pleased to answer them. (TH 5-6000, extension 4044) Meantime, I hope that you will have the same favorable reaction to filling out the questionnaire that other people have had. Thank you very much.

Cordially,

Charles Y. Glock
Director

seemed to beget more activity. For this reason a prepaid postcard was enclosed in the second follow-up letter. On it respondents were asked to indicate their progress. They could check that they were working on the questionnaire and would send it back soon; that they had misplaced or not received the questionnaire and needed another; or that they had already sent it back. No provision was made for indicating refusal, since there seemed no point in suggesting that as an acceptable alternative. These cards came back quickly (617 were returned), and a large proportion of those who returned cards promised to complete the questionnaire and eventually did. It was our impression that, having made it very easy to pledge a forthcoming response, persons committed themselves and then felt obligated to follow through. In any event, the postcards provided a rationale for the next step in the follow-up campaign.

By this time, it seemed necessary to demonstrate our own concern about the study, and an easy way was to make further investment in the respondent. Thus, all persons who had not yet returned their questionnaire were sent a second complete packet—questionnaire, return envelope, postcard, and a new letter (Exhibit A-4). This was explained on the basis of indications from the earlier postcards that many might have misplaced their original questionnaire. This mailing prompted an increase in the return rate.

Coupled with this second mailing was an attempt to bring informal pressures from the congregation to bear on respondents. When the pastors of the sample congregations were interviewed by field workers at the start of the study, they were asked to suggest some lay members of their church who might volunteer to contact persons who had not yet replied late in the study. Such volunteers were obtained in nearly every congregation. During the week following the second questionnaire mailing, these volunteers were brought into action, and many nonrespondents were personally contacted. At this same time, most pastors made an announcement about the study in church or in the bulletin.

With this we let the data collection campaign rest, and conducted the telephone interviews with a sample of nonrespondents described in the preceding section. From the time of the first mailing, six months had been spent in pursuit of completed questionnaires.

### The Questionnaire

In this concluding section we shall take up three general points: the development and pretesting of the questionnaire; certain essential features of the finished questionnaire; and some advantages and disadvantages of using a self-administered questionnaire rather than interviews.

### Development

In the beginning, no particular attention was given to developing items or structuring the questionnaire. Instead, the concern was to specify some basic inquiries about religion and its relation to other aspects of life, and on the basis of these to block out an analytic scheme of elements to be examined, bound together by sets of hypotheses to be tested. During the early stage, our

# UNIVERSITY OF CALIFORNIA

JRVEY RESEARCH CENTER
ERKELEY 4, CALIFORNIA

July, 1963

Dear Friend

My last letter about our study of religion in American life produced a flood of post cards from people saying that they had misplaced their questionnaire and asking for another one. It occurred to me that people like yourself, from whom I didn't hear, may also have mislaid their questionnaires. Rather than ask you again, I thought that it might be easier to simply send you another copy.

In doing so, I know I run the risk of making you feel that you are being bothered too often. And, I guess I might feel the same way if I were receiving rather than sending out the questionnaire. The fact is that there is no one else who believes and thinks and feels exactly the way you do. If there were, I should ask him or her to take your place. Since there isn't, however, I continue to hope that I might hear from you.

Remember that you are not asked to sign your name to the questionnaire so that you can be sure that anything you say will be entirely confidential. So that I can know who has returned the questionnaire and who hasn't, however, would you send along (separately) the enclosed post card when you send back your questionnaire.

If you have already begun to fill out the first copy of the questionnaire which I sent you, please go on and complete it. You can keep this second copy as a souvenir, use it for a study group in your church as some people are doing, or simply discard it.

Thank you for your continuing patience and for your help.

Cordially,

Charles Y. Glock
Director

CYG:mch

conceptualization was aided by depth interviews with a variety of church members, including some children. These interviews were highly open-ended and ranged widely over the subject matter of our prospective research. Only after the conceptualization was completed and the depth interviews carefully studied was work begun on questions.

For some of our requirements, items already existed which were well tried and well understood. This was especially true of items included in the sections on politics, the Srole anomia scale, and many of the standard background items. But, for the most part, previous questions were not available. This was particularly true of items on religion, which has been little and briefly studied. For the greatest part of the questionnaire, we had to begin from scratch to build the pool of items ultimately used. Items were rewritten dozens of times before the first discussion draft of the questionnaire was completed. Fewer than 10 per cent of the items written for this draft survived to reach the final version in recognizable form.

The first discussion draft was distributed to colleagues and clergymen for criticism. Out of ensuing discussions came guidelines for extensive revisions which were made in the pre-pretest version which followed several months later. This questionnaire was administered in a group session to 20 volunteers from Protestant churches in the vicinity of the university. These volunteers gave us important insights into how a lay audience, similar to our intended respondents, might receive and interpret the questionnaire. The volunteers wrote extensive marginal notes about problems they had in fitting their personal points of view and patterns of activity into the structured categories offered them, and also discussed the document with us.

Again, extensive revisions were made to produce a pretest version. The pretest was primarily intended to help further refine the questionnaire, but the opportunity was also taken to test the planned data collection techniques. Five congregations were arbitrarily selected to represent the spectrum of Protestantism from liberal to fundamentalist,[23] pastors' permission was obtained, membership lists sampled, and the questionnaires were mailed out in August 1962. At that time it was thought that the questionnaire was far too long to achieve a satisfactory return rate, even though the entire political and leisure time sections were omitted.[24] Our intention was to use pretest findings as an empirical basis for selecting items to be retained in the final questionnaire. To our surprise, the return rate steadily climbed until 65 per cent finally came back. Such a return, with only moderate follow-up efforts,[25] and launched during the height of the summer vacation season, caused us to reconsider our notions about how long a questionnaire was feasible.

More importantly, the pretest did reveal a great deal about items in the questionnaire. In all, 109 questionnaires were returned and analyzed. On this basis, sufficient redundant items were eliminated to make room for the items not included in the pretest without increasing the length of the document. Through the winter revisions were carried out, further advice was sought from

[23] These were Episcopalian, Congregational, American Baptist, Missouri Synod Lutheran, and Nazarene, all located in Berkeley, California.

[24] The items planned for these sections were mostly well tested in previous studies. In the end, however, some original items were added to these sections without the benefit of pretesting.

[25] One letter and one postcard were sent.

colleagues and clergymen, and, finally, seventeen months after the project was formally begun, the questionnaire was completed.

## Content

Aside from the problems which beset all questionnaires, such as clarity, exhaustive answer categories, etc., we faced the need to probe sensitive and private areas of the lives of our respondents and obtain truthful answers on topics for which there are highly standardized and heavily sanctioned answers. In addition, through the centuries theologians have split up the possible positions which can be taken on many religious questions until the positions have become exceedingly numerous and the distinctions often rather obscure. We tried to overcome these difficulties by explaining what we were asking and why as we went along. By carefully defining alternative positions, and by using more personal language which avoided theological clichés, we sought to encourage respondents to say what they meant, rather than what they thought they ought to say.

The questionnaire's structure followed an outline, the bones of which were intentionally left showing. Questions with a common focus appeared together, and an introduction to each grouping explained the topic, and its relevance, to the reader. Thus, respondents were not left in the dark to conjure up suspicions or anxiety about what secrets the questions might be intended to reveal. Obviously this does not mean that many items did not make covert measurements, but the manifest purpose of questions was made clear.

We suspected, and subsequently established in the pretest, that theological clichés—excerpts from confessions and other ritualized statements of beliefs —elicit unconsidered, nearly muscle-twitch responses. While these are rather interesting in themselves, clearly such responses tell little about the actual beliefs and outlooks of people. For example, it is much more interesting to know that 50 per cent of the persons in some denomination *do not* agree that "a child is born into the world already guilty of sin," than to know that 98 per cent of these same people agree with the doctrine of "original sin." Thus, every effort was made to communicate the substance of theological positions and discover whether they were accepted, and avoid the automatic agreement produced by liturgical language or concepts. Our success in this can best be demonstrated by comparing the distribution of responses obtained by our relatively broad question on belief in God (item 31) with the responses given to the question commonly used by the Gallup organization. As discussed in Chapter 1, our sample made up entirely of church members revealed much less acceptance of "God" in a traditional sense than has been attributed to the population in general on the basis of the Gallup item. It seems clear that to ask, "Do you, personally, believe in God?" elicits an automatic "yes" from virtually every American, but obscures important differences in the kind of God believed in and the strength of belief.

## Questionnaire vs. interviews

The advantages of questionnaires over interviews are four-fold: they are much less expensive; more items can be asked in less time; they provide privacy, hence likely greater honesty on sensitive questions; and the respondent replies directly to the investigator, in his own words and hand, without his views being filtered through the perceptions and biases of an interviewer. On the other hand, personal interviews are somewhat surer to get a response; can probe for further details when answers are unclear; can avoid skipping and excessive "don't know" responses; and can provide observations which respondents would not or could not give, for example, the appearance, grammar, personal style, etc., of the respondent.

Any survey study must weigh these alternatives in terms of the goals of the particular research. In this case the questionnaire seemed clearly preferable. The most important task was to obtain candid answers on matters highly subject to normative responses. It is much less difficult to say one doubts whether his prayers are unanswered on an anonymous questionnaire, than to tell this to a middle-class, middle-aged, female interviewer. The fact that many respondents made use of the questionnaire to write unsolicited accounts of personal problems of all kinds strongly suggests that they found this privacy conducive to probing deeply into their own lives.

Furthermore, we wanted to collect a great deal of data. Questionnaires, being self-administered, can ask many more questions during comparable sessions than can interviewers. An interview schedule the length of our questionnaire would probably have taken five to six hours to complete. To conduct interviews of that length with 3,000 persons would have cost as much as ten times our total budget. To use interviews we would have had to settle for many fewer questions asked of many fewer persons.

By taking care in constructing items and asking a number on the same topic, we reduced the need for probing to avoid unclarity or excessive "don't knows." Finally, considering the return rate obtained, it seems that most of the advantages of the questionnaire were gained without seriously encountering their common disadvantages.

# APPENDIX B

---

## A Note on Index Construction

The indexes used in this book met (and typically greatly surpassed) the minimum requirements of conventional scaling procedures and could have been reported in that form. We chose, however, not to transform the data into scales, but to employ the simplest additive scoring procedures. In part this decision stemmed from our aversion to the false impression of precision that such scales encourage. Once the rather gross measurements provided by questions on attitudes and opinions have been transformed into a scale, there is a tendency to think that the scaling procedure has somehow created data as exact and reliable as feet or pounds. We have tried to avoid this sort of impression management.

A practice commonly used in scaling techniques is to supply missing data on respondents. For example, if a respondent gave a prejudiced answer on five items in a prejudice scale, but failed to answer the sixth item included in the scale, he would commonly be assigned a prejudiced answer on the sixth, the assumption being that this is what he *would* have done had he answered. While such procedures are sometimes necessary, and not without some justification, we have entirely avoided making assumptions about how respondents might have answered. Rather, all indexes include *only* those persons who answered all of the items on which a given index was based. By omitting persons who failed to answer, we faced the possibility of biasing our indexes. Failure to answer is itself often a meaningful response. For example, on prejudice items failure to answer might most commonly occur among persons who are prejudiced, but who would rather not answer than admit it. If this is the case, then eliminating persons who failed to answer one or more items from a prejudice index would seriously bias the results because a disproportionate number of the prejudiced would be omitted.

Our method for checking indexes to see that they were not biased in this way was similar to that used to validate the indexes. First we showed that a given index powerfully predicted responses to items not included in the index but judged to be measures of the same thing as the index. Then we inspected the answers of persons *not* scored on the index to these same validating items. If nonresponse was unrelated to the index, then both persons scored and those not scored should give similar answers to the validating items. Thus, if 30 per cent of those scored on an index answered "yes" to a validating question, then 30 per cent of those not scored should also have answered "yes."

This procedure was followed in analyzing the unscored on all indexes. In every case it was found that the index was not biased by the omission of persons who failed to answer all of the questions. If there had been biases, then we would have had to try to score persons on the basis of the items they did answer. The absence of bias made this unnecessary, and we therefore restricted our analysis to persons whose beliefs and feelings had been clearly indicated, not inferred by the investigators.

# Index

252    INDEX

Jews, 111 (*tab.*), 114 (*tab.*), 119 (*tab.*), 122 (*tab.*), 129 (*tab.*), 157 (*tab.*), 202 (*tab.*); survey participation, 225 (*tab.*) 230 (*tab.*)
"American Religion and American Political Attitudes" (Miller), 83 *n.* 8
American Revolution, 82
"Amblatt für die Erzdiözese Freiburg" (Gröber), 60 *n.* 1
Anti-Catholicism, 67, 86, 90
Anti-Communism, 87, 118–120
Anti-Defamation League of B'nai B'rith, *xii, xiii*
Anti-intellectualism, 85, 120–121
Anti-Semitism, *see* Prejudice; *and see specific aspects,* e.g., Images, of Jews
Apostles, 47 (*tab.*), 48
Arendt, Hannah, 115 *n.* 4, 116 *n.* 5
Armed services, Jews and, 119 (*tab.*), 120, 124 (*tab.*), 142 (*tab.*), 144
Assemblies of God, 5 (*tab.*), 47 *n.* 3, 190 (*tab.*); survey participation, 225 (*tab.*), 231 (*tab.*)
Atheism, 5 (*tab.*), 6, 65 *n.* 6; civil liberties and, 81, 85, 86–87, 88 (*tab*), 89 (*tab.*), 90, 199 (*tab.*), 200, 203 *n.* 9; survey methods and, 216
Austria, Reichsrat of 1848, 116
*Authoritarian Personality, The* (Adorno, et al.), *xvii*
Authority, *see* Orthodoxy; Power
"Avaricious Jew" image, 109–113, 117, 118, 123, 124 (*tab.*) 126, 131, 169, 200 *n.* 8, 201 (*tab.*); action and, 151–155, 158–159; feelings and, 141, 142 (tab.), 143–144

Bahai, 29
Ballard, Edna and Donald, 84 *n.* 9
Banking (international), 109, 110, 111 (*tab.*), 126 (*tab.*), 127
Baptism, 24, 25 (*tab.*), 223
Baptists: anti-Semitic beliefs index, 202 (*tab.*); on atheists, 199 (*tab.*); belief in God, 5 (*tab.*), 190 (*tab.*); historic Jew image, 196 (*tab.*); on life beyond death, and the Devil, 192 (*tab.*); particularism of, 194, 195 (*tab.*); on racial guilt, 198 (*tab.*); survey participation, 229, 230 (*tab.*). *See also* American Baptist Church; Southern Baptist Church
Barabbas, 43, 50
Barber, Bernard, cited, 215 *n.* 1

Becker, Frank, quoted, 83
Behavior, *see* Action
Belief, religious, *see* Doctrine; Images; Orthodoxy
Belief, secular anti-Semitic, 103–106, 107–138, 186; action and, 154, 155 (*tab.*), 157–161; Church efforts to combat, 211–212; feelings and, 109, 125–128, 139–146, 157; indexing, 121, 123–129, 200–202, 203, 205, 249; religious dogmatism and, 130–138, 157–161, 174, 185–187, 202–206, 208–209. *See also* Images; Prejudice
Bell, Arthur L. "The Voice," 84 *n.* 9
Bell, Daniel, cited, 117
Berger, Peter L., 166
Berlin, Germany, *xi*
Bible, The, 15, 17, 35, 91; on miracles, 8, 9, 10, 11; New Testament, 44, 45, 48, 74, 197; oaths on, 83; Old Testament, 44–49, 57 (*tab.*), 58, 59, 110, 195–196. *See also specific Books*
Bigotry (religious), *xv, xvi, xxi*; alternatives to, in explaining anti-Semitism, 172–187; anti-Semitic action and, 157, 158 (*tab.*), 159–161; Index of, 135–138, 146 (*tab.*), 174, 175, 183, 202–205; race prejudice and, 170, 171 (*tab.*). *See also* Hostility; Violence
Birchites, 20 *n.* 3
Birth control, salvation and, 25 (*tab.*), 26
Bishop of Rome, 33
Blum, Léon, 116
B'nai B'rith, Anti-Defamation League of, *xii, xiii*
Bolshevism, 34, 117
Brotherhood of man concept, *xv,* 208, 210, 211, 212
Brown, James, cited, *xviii nn.* 5–8
Buddhism, 65, 217
Bullock, Alan, 139 *n.* 1, 140 *n.* 3
*Bunds,* 118

California, *xx,* 84 *n.* 9, 161, 181; methodology of the survey in, 215–251; Negro churches in, 166; religious climate of, 188–206 *passim,* 219, 226 *n.* 13, 232, 234, 235; selection for survey, 188–189, 216–219; Southern whites in, 169
California, University of, *xii–xiii,* 101, 106, 229

Calvin, John, 33
Calvinists, 33–34
Cambellite Church, 190 (tab.)
Canaanites, Judaism and, 32
Canada, 84 n. 9
Canon law, 148–149
Caplovitz, David, cited, xi n. 1
Carthage, Illinois, 84 n. 5
Castration complex, xvi
Catholicism, see Roman Catholicism
Censorship, 87, 88 (tab.); of social research, 218
Cheating, see "Avaricious Jew" image
Chein, Isador, 103 n. 2
Chinese, 186, 229; Protestantism and, 232, 233 (tab.), 234
Chosen People concept: Christian, 20 n. 4, 27 (tab.), 37 (tab.), 40, 90–91, 194, 195 (tab.), 203 n. 9; Jewish, 44–45, 46 (tab.), 47 n. 3, 50, 58, 195, 196 (tab.)
Christianity, xv, xvii–xviii, 205–206, 207; anti-Semitic action and, 147–149, 160–161; anti-Semitic feelings index, 145 (tab.); class and, 173–174; doctrines, 3–15, 35, 189–194, 208 (See also Doctrine); dogmatism and, 96–98, 130–138, 173, 175, 178; Hinduism and, 76–78; "ignorance" of, 71, 73 (tab.)
images of contemporary Jews and, 60–80, 98, 100, 109, 130, 186, 197–199, 208–209; anti-Semitic belief index, 128, 129 (tab.), 130–138, 205
Judaism and, 44–59, 65, 74–80, 84, 110, 195–197
libertarianism and, 81–98, 130, 199–200, 209; bigotry index, 146 (tab.), 205; law and, 85; religious hostility index, 133, 134 (tab.), 135
Negroes and, 165–171; particularism and, 20–26, 27 (tab.), 28, 31–32, 33–34, 35–40, 130, 194–195, 208–212; ritual participation, 15–18 (See also Ritual). See also specific denominations, e.g., Roman Catholicism; and see specific aspects of faith, e.g., Jesus Christ
Christian Missionary Alliance, 190 (tab.)
Christian Science, 190 (tab.), 217 n. 5
"Christian Teaching and Anti-Semitism: Scrutinizing Religious Texts" (Brown), xviii nn. 5–8
Churches: attendance, 15, 16 (tab.), 17, 18, 137, 138, 188 n. 1, 221, 223, 235,

236 (tab.); interfaith cooperation, 65; measures against anti-Semitism, xix, 50, 197, 207–212; membership, 4, 6, 16 n. 5, 17, 22, 23 (tab.), 166, 168 (tab.), 169, 173, 191–192, 196, 216–217, 218, 220–221, 222–223, 226–228; Negro, 166, 168 (tab.), 169, 226, 229, 232, 233 (tab.), 234; survey sampling of congregations, 218–219, 220–224; synagogue desecration, xi, 103. See also specific denominations
Church of Christ, 5 (tab.), 190 (tab.)
Church of England, 82. See also Episcopalians
Church of God, 5 (tab.), 190 (tab.), 225 (tab.), 231 (tab.)
Church of God in Christ, 220, 225 (tab.), 231 (tab.)
Church of the Nazarene, 5 (tab.), 190 (tab.), 220, 221; survey participation, 225 (tab.), 231 (tab.), 246 n. 23
Circumcision, xvi
Citizenship, 115–120, 123
Civil liberties, 86–92, 199–200, 203 n. 9; of cultists, 84–85
Civil Rights Movement, xiii, 165, 166, 170; Jewish attribution, 201 (tab.); radical attribution, 167, 168 (tab.), 169
Class, xvi, 39 n. 13, 40, 82, 87 n. 12; anti-Semitism and, 173–178, 187; survey participation and, 232
Clergy, 85–86, 108; conversionism and, 79, 148; measures against anti-Semitism, xix, 50, 135, 209, 211–212; on punishment of Jews, 60, 63, 65; survey cooperation, 218–219, 220, 221, 223, 226, 234, 238, 241, 244, 246
Clermont, Synod of, 148
Clothing, 111 (tab.), 113, 126 (tab.), 127
Cohn, Werner, cited, 115 n. 4, 117; quoted, 116
Cold War, 118
Coleridge, Samuel Taylor, quoted, 20–21
Cologne, Germany, xi
Commentary (periodical), xvii n. 4, xviii nn. 5–8
Commitment, see Orthodoxy
Communion, 16, 91
Communism: civil liberties and, 87; Civil Rights Movement association with, 167, 168 (tab.), 169; Jewish associ-

254    INDEX

ation with, 117–120, 126 (*tab.*), 127; particularism of, 20 *n.* 3, 34, 210

*Communism, Conformity, and Civil Liberties* (Stouffer), 87 *n.* 12

Communist party, 117

Confirmation, 223

*Conflict of the Church and the Synagogue, The* (Parkes), 31 *n.* 9

Congregationalists: anti-Semitic action, attitudes toward, 150 (*tab.*), 152, 153 (*tab.*), 157 (*tab.*); anti-Semitic feelings index, 145 (*tab.*); atheists and, 88 (*tab.*), 199 (*tab.*); conversionism, 78 (*tab.*), 79; on Jewish view of Christians, 73 (*tab.*); on Negroes, 167, 168 (*tab.*); orthodoxy, 5 (*tab.*), 6, 7 (*tab.*), 8, 9 (*tab.*), 10 (*tab.*), 12 (*tab.*), 13 (*tab.*), 14, 16 (*tab.*), 22, 23 (*tab.*), 75 (*tab.*), 190 (*tab.*), 191, 192 (*tab.*), 194, 195 (*tab.*); religious image of Jews, 46 (*tab.*), 47 (*tab.*), 48, 49 (*tab.*), 51 (*tab.*), 52, 53 (*tab.*), 54 (*tab.*), 55, 56 (*tab.*), 57 (*tab.*), 58, 62 (*tab.*), 63, 64 (*tab.*), 80, 196 (*tab.*), 197, 198 (*tab.*); secular image of modern Jews, 111 (*tab.*), 112, 114 (*tab.*), 119 (*tab.*), 122 (*tab.*), 128, 129 (*tab.*), 156, 157 (*tab.*), 201, 202 (*tab.*); survey participation, 225 (*tab.*), 229, 230 (*tab.*), 233 (*tab.*), 246 *n.* 23

Constantine I, emperor, 31

Conversion, 31 *n.* 11, 32, 210; of Jews, 45, 48, 61, 62 (*tab.*), 66, 78 (*tab.*), 79 (*tab.*), 80, 148, 208; non-Christian missionaries, 89 (*tab.*), 90

Cook, Stuart, 103 *n.* 2

II *Corinthians,* 19

Coser, Louis, 118 *n.* 8

Coughlin, Charles E., 60, 117 *n.* 7

Cracow, Poland, 116

Cremieux, Benjamin, 116

Cross-sectional samples, 216–217

Crucifixion, The, *see* Racial guilt, for the Crucifixion

Cults, 84–85, 188, 190 (*tab.*), 216, 217

Danforth Foundation, 63 *n.* 6

Data collection, 219; mailing lists, 226–228, 237–244; procedure, 221–224; sampling frame, 220–221, 241. *See also* Index construction; Questionnaires; Respondents

David, 45, 47 (*tab.*), 48, 59

Death camps, 103, 139 *n.* 2

Deicide, *see* Racial guilt, for the Crucifixion

Demerath, N. J., III, 173 *n.* 2

Democracy, *xii,* 55, 116, 118

Democratic party, 183, 184 (*tab.*), 217

Denominations, *see* Sectarianism; Sects; *and see specific denominations*

Depression, 117, 118

*Destruction of the European Jews, The* (Hilberg), *xvii n.* 3, 149 *n.* 3

Deutsch, Morton, 103 *n.* 2

*Deuteronomy,* 19, 27 *n.* 8

Devil, The 54; belief in, 11, 12 (*tab.*), 191, 192 (*tab.*), 193 (*tab.*), 194, 203 *n.* 9

*Devil and the Jews, The* (Trachtenberg), 54 *n.* 4

"Dimensions of Prejudice" (Kramer), 103 *n.* 2

Disciples of Christ: anti-Semitic action, attitudes toward, 150 (*tab.*), 151, 153 (*tab.*), 157 (*tab.*); anti-Semitic feelings index, 145 (*tab.*); atheists and, 88 (*tab.*), 199 (*tab.*); conversionism, 78 (*tab.*); on Jewish view of Christians, 73 (*tab.*); on Negroes, 167 *n.* 2, 168 (*tab.*); orthodoxy, 5 (*tab.*), 7 (*tab.*), 9 (*tab.*), 10 (*tab.*), 12 (*tab.*), 13 (*tab*), 16 (*tab.*), 23 (*tab.*), 75 (*tab.*), 190 (*tab.*), 192 (*tab.*), 195 (*tab.*); religious images of the Jews, 46 (*tab.*), 47 (*tab.*), 49 (*tab.*), 51 (*tab.*), 53 (*tab.*), 54 (*tab.*), 56 (*tab.*), 57 (*tab.*), 62 (*tab.*), 64 (*tab.*), 195 (*tab.*), 196 (*tab.*), 198 (*tab.*); secular images of modern Jews, 111 (*tab.*), 114 (*tab.*), 118, 119 (*tab.*), 122 (*tab.*), 129 (*tab.*), 157 (*tab.*), 202 (*tab.*); survey sampling of, 222 *n.* 11, 225 (*tab.*), 229, 230 (*tab.*)

*Discours et Conferences* (Renan), 91 *n.* 14

Dissent: Christian, within Judaism, 44–45; majority power and, 30–32, 34, 35–36; the Papacy and, 33; religious liberty and, 81–82

Divine Science, 190 (*tab.*)

Doctrine: anti-Semitic, *xii, xviii–xix,* 148–149, 186, 208; belief and, 3–18, 29, 189–195, 247; dogmatism and, 3, 96–98, 130, 131 (*tab.*), 132–38, 172–187; interpretation of, 35, 110,

208, 210–211, 234, 247; Judaic, 44–45, 110; particularism and, 28–29, 34, 36, 37, 38–39, 65, 208–212; Protestant-Catholic confrontation, 90–91, 92; religious libertarianism and, 83, 93; specificity of, 29–30, 34, 35–36, 93, 94–95, 187. *See also specific doctrines*
Dogmatism, *see* Doctrine, dogmatism and
"Draft-dodgers," 119 (*tab.*), 120, 124 (*tab.*), 142 (*tab.*), 144
Dreyfus, Alfred, 116

East, The, 188 *n.* 1, 202, 204 (*tab.*)
Eastern Orthodox Church, 190 (*tab.*)
Eating, 147, 148
Ecumenical Council, *xix,* 197, 211, 219
Education, 45, 67, 211, 212; anti-Semitism and, *xi, xiii, xvi, xviii, xix,* 173, 174, 175 (*tab.*), 176, 177, 186, 187, 204 (*tab.*), 205; survey response and, 228, 232, 234, 236, 237 (*tab.*)
*Education and Attitude Change* (Stember), 107 *n.* 1
"Egocentric Jew" image, 113–115, 118, 123, 124 (*tab.*), 201 (*tab.*); feelings toward, 143 (*tab.*), 144
Eichmann, Adolph, *xiii,* 199
Eisenhower, Dwight D., quoted, 20
Emotions, *see* Feelings; Hostility
Employment: of atheists, 87, 88 (*tab.*), 199 (*tab.*); of gentiles, by Jews, 147, 148; occupational prestige and anti-Semitism, 174, 176, 177 (*tab.*), 187; survey response and, 237 (*tab.*)
*Encyclical Mirari Vos* (Pope Gregory VI), 81
Entertainment, extended to Jews, 155–157, 160
Episcopalians: anti-Semitic action, attitudes toward, 150 (*tab.*), 152, 153 (*tab.*), 157 (*tab.*); anti-Semitic feelings index, 145 (*tab.*); atheists and, 88 (*tab.*), 199 (*tab.*); conversionism, 78 (*tab.*); on Jewish view of Christianity, 73 (*tab.*); on Negroes, 168 (*tab.*); orthodoxy, 5 (*tab.*), 6, 7 (*tab.*), 8, 9 (*tab.*), 10 (*tab.*), 12 (*tab.*), 13 (*tab.*), 16 (*tab.*), 23 (*tab.*), 75 (*tab.*), 190 (*tab.*), 191, 195 (*tab.*); religious images of the Jew, 46 (*tab.*), 47 (*tab.*), 48, 49 (*tab.*), 51 (*tab.*), 53 (*tab.*), 54 (*tab.*), 56 (*tab.*), 57 (*tab.*), 62 (*tab.*), 64 (*tab.*), 65, 195 (*tab.*),

196 (*tab.*), 198 (*tab.*); secular image of modern Jews, 111 (*tab.*), 114 (*tab.*), 119 (*tab.*), 122 (*tab.*), 128, 129 (*tab.*), 156, 157 (*tab.*), 201, 202 (*tab.*); survey participation, 224, 225 (*tab.*), 229, 230 (*tab.*), 246 *n.* 23
*Epistles,* 45
Ethics, 209, 211; anti-Negro prejudice and, 166–167, 168 (*tab.*), 169, 171 (*tab.*)
*beliefs about Jewish ethics,* 111 (tab.), 112, 113, 124 (tab.), 169; feelings aroused by, 141, 142 (*tab.*), 143–144
perception of issues, 154, 159, 160–161, 212; of renegades, 108; scientific, 102
"Ethnic Groups," (Weber) 20 *n.* 4
Ethnicity, *see* Race
Eugenius IV, pope, quoted, 147
Europe, 4, 82, 110; Catholic Church in, 67; democratic movement in, 116, 117; Islam in, 32; Nazism in, *xvi–xvii,* 101; post-Nazi anti-Semitism, *xi. See also specific countries*
Evangelical Church, 5 (*tab.*), 190 (*tab.*), 192 (*tab.*), 195 (*tab.*); anti-Semitic beliefs index, 202 (*tab.*); on atheists, 199 (*tab.*); images of Jews, 196 (*tab.*), 197; on "punishment" of Jews, 198 (*tab.*)
Evolution, theory of, 84
"Exclusive Jew" image, 113–115, 118, 123, 124 (*tab.*), 131, 201 (*tab.*); feelings aroused by, 143 (*tab.*), 144

*Faith and Prejudice* (Olson), *xviii n.* 5
Fascism, *xi, xvii,* 118. *See also* Nazis
Father Divine, 30
Feelings, anti-Semitic, 102, 103–106, 107, 125–126, 127, 139–146, 179; action and, 149–161; index of, 145–146; perception of identity distinguished from, 107–109. *See also* Hostility; Prejudice
Feuer, Lewis, cited, 81–82
Flying Saucer cult, 84 *n.* 9
Foreign-language congregations, 226, 228, 232–234
*Fortune* (periodical), 110 *n.* 2
Forty-niner adage, quoted, 188
Four square Gospel Church, 5 (*tab.*), 190 (*tab.*), 225 (*tab.*), 231 (*tab.*), 232
Fourth century, 147

House of David, 84 *n.* 9
Howe, Irving, 118 *n.* 8
Hyman, Herbert, 132 *n.* 12

Identity, religious, 2, 3–40, 107–109, 209
Ideology, *see* Doctrine; Images
Illiteracy, 228, 234
Images: feelings and, 125–128, 139, 146, 158–159, 179; of God, 4–6, 15, 30, 31, 44; of Jesus Christ, 7 (*tab.*), 8, 44, 58; Jewish image (presumed) of Christians, 71, 73 (*tab.*)
  *of Jews, xiii, xviii,* 44–59, 60–80, 86, 90, 92, 94–95, 96–98, 100, 104, 105–106, 176, 186, 195–199, 203 *n.* 9; as avaricious, 109–113, 117, 118, 123, 151–155, 158–159, 169, 200 *n.* 8, 201 (*tab.*); Church efforts to change, 211–212; as deicide (*See* Racial guilt); as egocentric and exclusive, 113–115, 118, 123, 201 (*tab.*); as intellectuals, 120–121, 200 *n.* 8; measurement of anti-Semitism in, 107–109, 121, 123–138, 200–201, 202 (*tab.*); as unpatriotic and subversive, 115–120, 123, 200 *n.* 8
  of non-Christians, 40, 76–78, 89 (*tab.*), 90–91
  *of other Christians,* 27–28, 67, 90–91; Negro, 105, 106, 128, 167, 168 (*tab.*), 169, 171 (*tab.*)
  of self, 26–27 (*See also* Particularism); of social scientists, 102
Immigrants, 117, 180 (*tab.*), 181, 226 *n.* 16; literacy of, 228
*Immortale Dei* (Pope Leo XII), 81 *n.* 1
Immortality, *see* Life after death
Income, *see* Wealth
Independent political parties, 184 (*tab.*)
Index construction, 249–250; action measurement, 149–157; anti-Semitic belief, validation, 125–129; factor analysis in, 123, 221–222; index of feelings, 145–146; index of religious bigotry, 135–138, 146; "pure affect" measures, 140; scaling procedures, 249
India, 241
Industry, *xii,* 110 *n.* 2, 111 (*tab.*), 126
Innocent III, pope, 32 *n.* 12; quoted, 148
Inquisition, The, 19, 32
Intelligence, 85; Jewish image, 118, 120–121, 122 (*tab.*), 200 *n.* 8; Negro image, 168 (*tab.*), 169, 171 (*tab.*)

International banking, 109, 110, 111 (*tab.*), 126 (*tab.*), 127
Interviews, 247–248; of non-respondents, 227–228, 229, 234–235, 241 *n.* 21, 244; in questionnaire conceptualization, 246
Intolerance, *see* Bigotry (religious); Hostility; Prejudice; Violence
*Inventory and Appraisal of Research on American Anti-Semitism, An* (Tumin) *xvi n.* 1, 101 *n.* 1
Islam, 19, 33, 65, 78, 210; conversionism and, 31 *n.* 11, 32, 78
Isolation, particularism and, 30
Israel, 119 (*tab.*), 120, 124 (*tab.*), 143 (*tab.*), 144, 200 *n.* 8

Jahoda, Marie, 103 *n.* 2
Japanese, 186
Jehovah's Witnesses, 20 *n.* 3, 190 (*tab.*), 217 *n.* 5
*Jeremiah,* quoted, 211
Jesus Christ: crucifixion of, *xv, xvii, xviii, xix,* 43, 44, 48, 50–54, 59, 60, 61, 63, 66, 69, 70 (*tab.*), 71, 72 (*tab.*), 73, 80, 93, 94 (*tab.*), 95, 96–98, 130, 131, 135, 197–199, 203 *n.* 9, 208, 210–211, 212; divinity of, 7 (*tab.*), 8, 22 *n.* 5, 44, 45, 48, 58, 61; Jewish motives in rejecting, 54–59; Jewish (presumed) attitudes toward Christianity, 71, 73 (*tab.*); miracles of, 8–10, 14 (*tab.*); as Saviour, 8, 22, 23 (*tab.*), 44, 45, 94, 96, 194, 195 (*tab.*), 203 *n.* 9, 208
Jews: anti-Semitic wave of 1959, *xi;* Christian images of (*See* Images, of Jews); conversionism and, 45, 48, 61, 62 (*tab.*), 66, 78 (*tab.*), 79 (*tab.*), 80, 148, 208; emancipation of, 115, 116, 117; identification of, 107–109; Mediterranean, 31; Negroes and, 165–171; survey of, 216, 217. *See also* Judaism
*Jews: Social Patterns of an American Group, The,* (Sklare, ed.) 115 *n.* 4
John XXIII, pope, *xix*
John Birch Society, 20 *n.* 3
Johnson, Lyndon B., 183
*Joshua,* quoted, 165
*Journal of Psychology* (periodical), 103 *n.* 2
Judaism: American politics and, 85–86; Christian view of, 44–59, 65, 74–80, 84, 195–197; classical world and,

Steinberg, Stephen, *xxi n.* 10, 189 *n.* 2, 215 *n.*
Stember, Charles Herbert, quoted, 107
Stouffer, Samuel A., 87 *n.* 12
Strang, James J., 84 *n.* 9
*Street Corner Society* (Whyte), 215 *n.* 2
"Styles of Church Membership" (Yoshio Fukuyama), 173 *n.* 2
"Subversive Jew" image, 115–120, 123, 131, 200 *n.* 8, 201 (*tab.*)
Suci, George J., cited, 140 *n.* 4
Sunday Schools, 186, 212; survey participation, 241; textbooks, *xviii*, 45
*Survey Design and Analysis* (Hyman), 132 *n.* 12
Surveys, 215–251; controls in, 39–40, 132–133, 165–166, 193, 204, 205; correlations vs. distributions, 217–218; counterexplanations and, 172–173, 186–187, 204–205; language and, 226, 228, 234; letters to respondents, 239, 241, 242–243, 244, 245; location, 188–189, 216–219; mediated appeal and, 241; nationwide replication of sample, 189–206, 215 *n.*, 217–218, 219; participation rate, 224, 225 (*tab.*), 226, 238, 240 (*tab.*), 241, 244; pretesting, 244, 246–247; representativeness, 235–237, 238; response, 227–237, 238, 240 (*tab.*), 241, 244; sample design, 220–224, 241. *See also specific aspects, i.e.,* Data collection; Index construction; Questionnaires; Respondents
*Swastika 1960: The Epidemic of Anti-Semitic Vandalism in America* (Caplovitz and Rogers), *xi n.* 1
Synagogues, *xi*, 103
Synods, Roman Catholic, 148
*Systematic Theology* (Tillich), 3 *n.* 1

Table grace, 15, 17
*Table Talk* (Luther), 148 *n.* 2
Taborites, 19
Talmud, 148
Tannenbaum, Percy H., cited, 140 *n.* 4
Telephone books, 220
Television industry, 111 (*tab.*), 126
Ten Commandments, 74
Textbooks, *xviii*, 45
Theology, 44–45; cliché responses, 247; libertarianism and, 81, 83–84; particularism and, 28–29, 65, 209, 210. *See also Doctrine*

*Theories of Society* (Parsons, et al.), 20 *n.* 4
Theosophists, 190 (*tab.*)
Thielens, Wagner, Jr., cited, 215 *n.* 2
"Third force" churches, 220–221, 222, 224; survey participation, 225 (*tab.*), 226, 229, 231 (*tab.*), 232. *See also* Sects
Thirteenth century, 148
"Three Decades of the Radical Right: Coughlinites, McCarthyites, and Birchers" (Lipset), 117 *n.* 7
Tillich, Paul, 209; quoted, 3
Tithing, 85
Tory party, 82
Trachtenberg, Joshua, cited, 54 *n.* 4
Transubstantiation Doctrine, 91
Trinity Doctrine, 91
Trotskyism, 117
*True Believer, The* (Hoffer), 20 *n.* 2
Truman, Melvin M., cited, *xvi n.* 1, 101 *n.* 1
Tyranny, particularism and, 34

Unaffiliated congregation, *see* Sects
Unitarians, 29, 190 (*tab.*), 192 (*tab.*); on atheists, 199 (*tab.*); on Crucifixion guilt, 196 (*tab.*), 197; particularism of, 194, 195 (*tab.*); on "punishment," 198 (*tab.*)
United Church of Christ, 5 (*tab.*), 190 (*tab.*). *See also* Congregationalists
United States of America: anti-Semitism and, *xi–xii, xvi n.* 1, *xviii, xix–xx,* 60–61, 65, 73–74, 98, 117, 118, 149, 155, 176, 188–206, 211–212; Catholic role in, 67, 86; conversionism in, 78, 210; cultural changes, 181–182; fascism in, 118; foreign language groups in, 226, 228, 232–234; Jewish loyalty and, 117–120, 124 (*tab.*), 127, 142 (*tab.*), 143 (*tab.*), 144; Negro position in, 170; particularism in, 30–31, 36, 194–195, 210; piety in, 4, 6, 83, 98, 189–194; regional differences, 178–181, 188–189, 219; religious "pluralism" of, 82–86; survey location, 188–189, 216–219
United States Congress, 83
United States Constitution, 82 *n.* 5, 83
United Presbyterians, 190 (*tab.*), 192 (*tab.*), 195 (*tab.*), 196 (*tab.*); anti-Semitic beliefs index, 201, 202

SURVEY RESEARCH CENTER

UNIVERSITY OF CALIFORNIA

BERKELEY 4, CALIFORNIA

_____

A Study
of Religion
in American Life

# INSTRUCTIONS

The questionnaire, as you will see, is organized in a series of sections concerning various aspects of religion. At the beginning of each section, we have tried to explain our purpose in asking the questions which follow.

Almost all of the questions can be answered by making a simple check mark with pen or pencil in the box beside the answer you choose. Please ignore the extra numbers beside questions and answers. These are there to help in tabulating the answers by IBM machines.

We should like you to feel that you are expressing your true feelings as you answer the questionnaire. Please write your comments in the margin when you feel a question is unclear, or doesn't allow you to express exactly how you feel. We are not asking you to sign your name so you can be sure that your answers will be confidential.

When you have finished the questionnaire, please mail it back to us in the enclosed pre-paid envelope. At the same time, would you please also mail back the enclosed post card to notify us that you have sent back the questionnaire.

We hope you enjoy filling out the questionnaire and we thank you for your cooperation.

CHARLES Y. GLOCK
*Project Director*

RODNEY STARK
*Assistant Project Director*

**001**

To begin we would like to ask about your present church going habits and about your religious activities more generally.

1. What is the name and denomination of the church to which you presently belong?

   Name of church...................................................................

   Address........................................................................
   (city)

   Denomination ..............................................................

2. How long have you been a member of your present Congregation or Parish? Check the answer which is closest.

   13   ☐ I have always been a member
        ☐ Less than 1 year
        ☐ 1 to 2 years
        ☐ 3 to 5 years
        ☐ 6 to 10 years
        ☐ More than 10 years

3. Have you ever been a member of a denomination other than your present one?

   14   ☐ Yes    ☐ No

   IF YES: What denomination was that? (If more than one, list them in order from the most recent to the earliest)

   ...............................................................
   ...............................................................
   ...............................................................
   ...............................................................

4. How often do you attend Sunday worship services? (Check the answer which comes closest to describing what you do)

   19   ☐ Every week
        ☐ Nearly every week
        ☐ About three times a month
        ☐ About twice a month
        ☐ About once a month
        ☐ About every six weeks
        ☐ About every three months
        ☐ About once or twice a year
        ☐ Less than once a year
        ☐ Never

5. Have you received Holy Communion in the last year?

   20   ☐ Yes   ☐ No

6. Have you been Baptized?

   21   ☐ Yes, in my present denomination
        ☐ Yes, in another denomination
        ☐ No

7. Have you been Confirmed?

   22   ☐ Yes, in my present denomination
        ☐ Yes, in another denomination
        ☐ No

8. In an average week, how many evenings do you spend in church, including church meetings such as study groups which may not actually meet in the church building?

   23   ☐ 1   ☐ 2   ☐ 3   ☐ 4   ☐ 5   ☐ 6   ☐ 7

9. IF YOU HAVE CHILDREN WOULD YOU PLEASE ANSWER THE QUESTIONS IN THE BOX BELOW. IF YOU HAVE NO CHILDREN, SKIP TO QUESTION 10.

   ---

   What kind of a school do your children attend?

   24   ☐ a parochial or church affiliated school
        ☐ a public school
        ☐ a private school not affiliated with any church
        ☐ they do not attend school

   How frequently, if at all, do your children attend Sunday school or religious instruction classes which are not part of their regular school day?

   25   ☐ They do not attend
        ☐ They attend regularly
        ☐ They attend often
        ☐ They attend sometimes

   ---

10. All in all, how important would you say your church membership is to you?

    26   ☐ Extremely important
         ☐ Quite important
         ☐ Fairly important
         ☐ Not too important
         ☐ Fairly unimportant

11. *In Column A,* please list all of the church organizations, groups, or activities in which you participate, such as choir, church committees and boards, men's clubs, women's clubs, etc.

    *In Column B,* please indicate how many of the last five meetings of each of these organizations you have attended.

    *In Column C,* please indicate whether or not you have *ever* held an office in each organization you list.

| Column A (List each organization) | Column B (How many of the last five meetings did you attend?) | Column C (Have you ever held an office in this group?) |
|---|---|---|
| ....................................... | ....................................... | ☐ Yes   ☐ No |
| ....................................... | ....................................... | ☐ Yes   ☐ No |
| ....................................... | ....................................... | ☐ Yes   ☐ No |
| ....................................... | ....................................... | ☐ Yes   ☐ No |
| ....................................... | ....................................... | ☐ Yes   ☐ No |
| ....................................... | ....................................... | ☐ Yes   ☐ No |

12. IF YOU ARE NOW OR EVER HAVE BEEN MAR-
RIED, PLEASE ANSWER THE QUESTIONS IN
THE BOX BELOW. If you have been married more
than once, answer for your most recent spouse.

To what denomination does (or did) your spouse
belong? ....................................................................

In what denomination was your spouse raised?

....................................................................

Would you say you are (or were) more or less interested in religion than your spouse?

34 ☐ More ☐ Less ☐ About the same

About how often does (or did) your spouse attend
Sunday worship services?

35 ☐ Every week
☐ Nearly every week
☐ About three times a month
☐ About twice a month
☐ About once a month
☐ About every six weeks
☐ About every three months
☐ About once or twice a year
☐ Less than once a year
☐ Never

13. All in all, how well do you think you fit in with the
group of people who make up your church congregation (or parish)?

36 ☐ I really don't fit in too well with this group
of people
☐ I fit in, but not too well
☐ I fit in quite well
☐ I fit in very well

14. Generally speaking, would you say most of the people
you associate with in activities aside from church
affairs are or are not members of your congregation
(or parish)?

37 ☐ Most are members of my congregation (or
parish)
☐ About half are and half aren't
☐ Most are not members of my congregation

15. Of your five closest friends, how many are members
of your congregation (or parish)?

38 ☐ None
☐ One
☐ Two
☐ Three
☐ Four
☐ Five

16. Turning now to other religious activities besides attending church, how often, if at all, are table prayers
or grace said before or after meals in your home?

39 ☐ We say grace at all meals
☐ We say grace at least once a day
☐ We say grace at least once a week
☐ We say grace but only on special occasions
☐ We never, or hardly ever, say grace

17. How often do you read the Bible at home?

40 ☐ To be frank, I never read the Bible or I read
it so rarely that it probably shouldn't even
count
☐ I read it regularly once a day or more
☐ I read it regularly several times a week
☐ I read it regularly once a week
☐ I read it quite often, but not at regular
intervals
☐ I read it once in a while
☐ I read it only on very special occasions

18. Thinking now of your daily life and the decisions that
you have to constantly make about how to spend your
time, how to act with other people, how to bring up
your children, presuming you have them, and so on,
to what extent does what you have read in the Bible
help you in making everyday decisions in your life?

41 ☐ To be frank, I hardly ever think of the Bible
and what it has to say as I go about my daily
life.
☐ While I can't think of specific examples,
nevertheless I feel sure that the Bible is still
of help in my daily life.
☐ I can think of specific times when it has
helped me in a very direct way in making
decisions in life.
☐ Other (please specify)..................................
....................................................................

19. If you were asked, do you think you could recite the
Ten Commandments?

42 ☐ Yes, but not the exact words
☐ Yes, the exact words
☐ I'm not sure that I would remember all ten

20. Which of the following were Old Testament prophets?
(check as many answers as you think are correct)

43 ☐ Elijah
44 ☐ Deuteronomy
45 ☐ Jeremiah
46 ☐ Paul
47 ☐ Leviticus
48 ☐ Ezekiel
49 ☐ None of these

21. Which one of Christ's Disciples denied Him three
times?

50 ☐ James
☐ Paul
☐ Judas
☐ Mark
☐ Peter
☐ Jacob

22. Would you say that the Book of Acts was an eye-
witness account of Jesus' ministry?

51 ☐ Yes ☐ No ☐ Don't know

2

23. Now would you please read each of the following statements and do *two* things: *first*, decide whether the statement is from the Bible or not; and *second*, would you please indicate whether or not you agree with the statement. (Please do this even if you think the statement is not from the Bible.)

For it is easier for a camel to go through a needle's eye, than for a rich man to enter into the kingdom of God.
From the Bible?
52 ☐ Yes ☐ No
Do you agree?
53 ☐ Yes ☐ No

Blessed are the strong: for they shall be the sword of God.
From the Bible?
54 ☐ Yes ☐ No
Do you agree?
55 ☐ Yes ☐ No

Thou shalt not suffer a witch to live.
From the Bible?
56 ☐ Yes ☐ No
Do you agree?
57 ☐ Yes ☐ No

Blessed are the meek: for they shall inherit the earth.
From the Bible?
58 ☐ Yes ☐ No
Do you agree?
59 ☐ Yes ☐ No

Let your women keep silence in the churches: for it is not permitted unto them to speak.
From the Bible?
60 ☐ Yes ☐ No
Do you agree?
61 ☐ Yes ☐ No

For I the Lord thy God am a jealous God, visiting the iniquity of the fathers upon the children unto the third and fourth generation of them that hate me.
From the Bible?
62 ☐ Yes ☐ No
Do you agree?
63 ☐ Yes ☐ No

We'd like to shift now from asking about the Bible to asking about prayer. Prayer is a very private thing and we frankly are not sure whether we should ask people about their prayers. We hope that you will not find the questions too delicate to answer, but if you do, please tell us by writing in the margins.

24. How often do you pray privately? (Check the answer which comes closest to what you do.)
64 ☐ I never pray, or only do so at church services
☐ I pray only on very special occasions
☐ I pray once in a while, but not at regular intervals
☐ I pray quite often, but not at regular times
☐ I pray regularly once a day or more
☐ I pray regularly several times a week
☐ I pray regularly once a week

IF YOU EVER PRAY, OTHER THAN IN CHURCH, PLEASE ANSWER THE QUESTIONS IN THE BOX BELOW

When you pray, why do you pray? (Check as many as apply)
65 ☐ As a Christian duty
☐ To find comfort when I am feeling low
☐ To strengthen my faith
☐ To try to learn God's will
☐ To ask God's guidance in making decisions
☐ Because it gives me a feeling of being closer to God
☐ To ask forgiveness for something I have done
☐ To ask God to bring someone else to Christian faith and belief
☐ To give thanks to God
74 ☐ To be worshipful of God

**002**

Now look back at the list above, and please circle the answer which you feel is the *most* important reason that you pray.

Have you ever prayed during your adult years for the following purposes? (Check each you have done)
9 ☐ To ask for some material thing, for example, a new car or a new house
10 ☐ To ask God to keep some misfortune from happening to me
11 ☐ To ask God to restore my health
12 ☐ To ask God to restore someone else's health
13 ☐ None of these

Do you feel your prayers are answered?
14 ☐ Yes, I have no doubt that they are
☐ I feel that they are, but I'm not entirely sure
☐ I don't really know
☐ I feel that they aren't, but I'm not entirely sure
☐ I guess I don't feel that they really are
☐ Other (please specify).....................................
..........................................................................

How important is prayer in your life?
15 ☐ Extremely important
☐ Fairly important
☐ Not too important
☐ Not important

25. How important is the idea of sin in your life?
16 ☐ I am rather concerned with trying to live as sinless a life as possible
☐ I accept the idea of sin, but do not really think about it very often
☐ The idea of sin means very little to me
☐ None of the above represents my feelings; what I do feel is that.....................................
..........................................................................
..........................................................................

3

26. How often do you ask forgiveness for your sins?

17    ☐ Very often
       ☐ Quite often
       ☐ Occasionally
       ☐ Rarely
       ☐ Never

27. How certain are you that your sins are forgiven?

18    ☐ I am absolutely certain they are
       ☐ I am fairly certain
       ☐ I feel they are forgiven sometimes, but not always
       ☐ I am never quite sure whether my sins are forgiven or not
       ☐ I usually feel that my sins are not forgiven
       ☐ I don't think of sin in this way

28. Have you personally ever tried to convert someone to your religious faith?

19    ☐ Yes, often
       ☐ Yes, a few times
       ☐ Yes, once or twice
       ☐ No, never

29. There has always been a good deal of discussion among Christians about how people ought to act in their daily lives. It is not always clear what characteristics ought to be admired and which ones we should disapprove of. Below you will find a series of descriptions of ways in which people act. For each would you decide how much you would admire or disapprove of a person who acted in this way?

If a person were like this, I would:

| | Admire him for it | Think it was all right | Be mildly disapproving of him | Be highly disapproving of him |
|---|---|---|---|---|
| drinks moderately 20 | ☐ | ☐ | ☐ | ☐ |
| is very ambitious | ☐ | ☐ | ☐ | ☐ |
| thinks he is better than others | ☐ | ☐ | ☐ | ☐ |
| dresses in a flashy way | ☐ | ☐ | ☐ | ☐ |
| prefers to be with people like himself | ☐ | ☐ | ☐ | ☐ |
| is very patriotic | ☐ | ☐ | ☐ | ☐ |
| feels that Christian holidays should not be celebrated in the public schools | ☐ | ☐ | ☐ | ☐ |
| is very rich | ☐ | ☐ | ☐ | ☐ |
| is very anxious to be thought of as an intellectual | ☐ | ☐ | ☐ | ☐ |
| is satisfied with his lot in life 29 | ☐ | ☐ | ☐ | ☐ |

30. We would like you to imagine, for a moment, that for some reason you could no longer continue to attend a church of your present denomination. Below is a list of other denominations that it would be possible for you to attend. We would like you to consider each and decide for yourself how comfortable and "at home" you think you would feel in each.

| | Very comfortable | Comfortable | A little uncomfortable | Uncomfortable | Don't know enough about this denomination to say |
|---|---|---|---|---|---|
| Baptist 30 | ☐ | ☐ | ☐ | ☐ | ☐ |
| Jehovah's Witnesses | ☐ | ☐ | ☐ | ☐ | ☐ |
| Jewish | ☐ | ☐ | ☐ | ☐ | ☐ |
| Lutheran | ☐ | ☐ | ☐ | ☐ | ☐ |
| Presbyterian | ☐ | ☐ | ☐ | ☐ | ☐ |
| Roman Catholic | ☐ | ☐ | ☐ | ☐ | ☐ |
| Unitarian | ☐ | ☐ | ☐ | ☐ | ☐ |
| Mormon 37 | ☐ | ☐ | ☐ | ☐ | ☐ |

4

We now turn to another part of religious life—religious belief. We are concerned to learn not only what people believe, but also how important their beliefs are to them. We hope you will find that the questions allow you to express your own beliefs. If not, would you write a comment next to any question which you consider to be inappropriate.

31. Which of the following statements comes closest to expressing what you believe about God? (Please check only one answer)

38　☐ I know God really exists and I have no doubts about it

　　☐ While I have doubts, I feel that I do believe in God

　　☐ I find myself believing in God some of the time, but not at other times

　　☐ I don't believe in a personal God, but I do believe in a higher power of some kind

　　☐ I don't know whether there is a God and I don't believe there is any way to find out

　　☐ I don't believe in God

　　☐ None of the above represents what I believe. What I believe about God is................

　　............................................................

　　............................................................

　　(please specify)

32. Which of the following statements comes closest to expressing what you believe about Jesus?

39　☐ Jesus is the Divine Son of God and I have no doubts about it

　　☐ While I have some doubts, I feel basically that Jesus is Divine

　　☐ I feel that Jesus was a great man and very holy, but I don't feel Him to be the Son of God any more than all of us are children of God

　　☐ I think Jesus was only a man, although an extraordinary one

　　☐ Frankly, I'm not entirely sure there really was such a person as Jesus

　　☐ None of the above represents what I believe. What I believe about Jesus is...................

　　............................................................

　　............................................................

　　(please specify)

33. The Bible tells of many miracles, some credited to Christ and some to other prophets and apostles. Generally speaking, which of the following statements comes closest to what you believe about Biblical miracles. (Check only one answer)

40　☐ I am not sure whether these miracles really happened or not

　　☐ I believe miracles are stories and never really happened

　　☐ I believe the miracles happened, but can be explained by natural causes

　　☐ I believe the miracles actually happened just as the Bible says they did

34. Would you please think about each of the religious beliefs listed below and then indicate how certain you are that it is true by putting an X in the appropriate box.

| | Completely true | Probably true | Probably not true | Definitely not true |
|---|---|---|---|---|
| There is a life beyond death.............. 41 | ☐ | ☐ | ☐ | ☐ |
| Jesus was born of a virgin................. | ☐ | ☐ | ☐ | ☐ |
| The Devil actually exists .................. | ☐ | ☐ | ☐ | ☐ |
| Jesus was opposed to all drinking of alcohol... | ☐ | ☐ | ☐ | ☐ |
| What we do in this life will determine our fate in the hereafter.................... | ☐ | ☐ | ☐ | ☐ |
| Jesus walked on water..................... | ☐ | ☐ | ☐ | ☐ |
| Man cannot help doing evil............... | ☐ | ☐ | ☐ | ☐ |
| The Pope is infallible in matters of faith and morals .......................... | ☐ | ☐ | ☐ | ☐ |
| Jesus was born a Jew...................... | ☐ | ☐ | ☐ | ☐ |
| Only those who believe in Jesus Christ can go to heaven...................... | ☐ | ☐ | ☐ | ☐ |
| A child is born into the world already guilty of sin......................... 51 | ☐ | ☐ | ☐ | ☐ |

5

35. When you think of salvation, do you think primarily of being granted eternal life beyond the grave, or do you think primarily of being released from sin and protected from evil in this life?

52  ☐ I think primarily of being granted eternal life beyond death

☐ I think primarily of being released from sin and protected from evil in this life

☐ Other ...........................................................................................................
                                     (please specify)

36. Would you please read each of the items listed below and decide whether you think it is:
   (a) absolutely necessary for salvation
   (b) probably would help in gaining salvation
      or
   (c) probably has no influence on salvation

| | Absolutely necessary | Would probably help | Probably has no influence |
|---|---|---|---|
| Belief in Jesus Christ as Saviour................... 53 | ☐ | ☐ | ☐ |
| Holy Baptism ................................. | ☐ | ☐ | ☐ |
| Membership in a Christian church................ | ☐ | ☐ | ☐ |
| Regular participation in Christian sacraments, for example, Holy Communion .................... | ☐ | ☐ | ☐ |
| Holding the Bible to be God's truth.............. | ☐ | ☐ | ☐ |
| Prayer ....................................... | ☐ | ☐ | ☐ |
| Doing good for others.......................... | ☐ | ☐ | ☐ |
| Tithing ...................................... | ☐ | ☐ | ☐ |
| Being a member of your particular religious faith..... | ☐ | ☐ | ☐ |
| Loving thy neighbor .......................... 62 | ☐ | ☐ | ☐ |

37. Now looking at the following list of items, would you please indicate for each whether you think it will:
   (a) definitely prevent salvation
   (b) may possibly prevent salvation
      or
   (c) probably has no influence on salvation

| | Definitely prevent | Possibly prevent | No influence |
|---|---|---|---|
| Drinking liquor .................................. 63 | ☐ | ☐ | ☐ |
| Breaking the Sabbath ............................ | ☐ | ☐ | ☐ |
| Being completely ignorant of Jesus as might be the case for people living in other countries................. | ☐ | ☐ | ☐ |
| Taking the name of the Lord in vain................ | ☐ | ☐ | ☐ |
| Being of the Jewish religion....................... | ☐ | ☐ | ☐ |
| Practicing artificial birth control.................... | ☐ | ☐ | ☐ |
| Being of the Hindu religion....................... | ☐ | ☐ | ☐ |
| Marrying a non-Christian ......................... | ☐ | ☐ | ☐ |
| Discriminating against other races.................. | ☐ | ☐ | ☐ |
| Being anti-Semitic .............................. 72 | ☐ | ☐ | ☐ |

**003**

38. Do you believe Jesus will actually return to the earth some day?

8  ☐ Definitely  ☐ Probably  ☐ Possibly
   ☐ Probably not  ☐ Definitely not

IF YOU THINK JESUS WILL DEFINITELY OR PROBABLY RETURN: Please answer the question in the box:

━━━━━▶

How soon do you expect this is apt to happen?

9  ☐ In the next 10 years
   ☐ In the next 25 years
   ☐ In the next 50 years
   ☐ In the next 100 years
   ☐ 200 to 500 years from now
   ☐ 1,000 to 10,000 years from now
   ☐ 50,000 or more years from now
   ☐ Other...................................................
                     (please write in)

39. What do you feel will probably happen to you after death?
I feel that I will:
10   ☐ go to purgatory
      ☐ go to hell
      ☐ simply stop existing
      ☐ go to heaven

40. How certain do you feel about the answer you have just given?
11   ☐ Very certain
      ☐ Fairly certain
      ☐ Not very certain
      ☐ Fairly uncertain

41. How sure are you that you have found the answers to the meaning and purpose of life?
12   ☐ I am quite certain and I pretty much grew up knowing these things
      ☐ I am quite certain, although at one time I was pretty uncertain
      ☐ I am uncertain whether or not I have found them
      ☐ I am quite sure I have not found them
      ☐ I don't really believe there are answers to these questions

So far, we have asked about your religious activities, your religious knowledge, and your religious beliefs. The next series of questions has to do with your religious experiences, that is, with what feelings you may have had which you would think of as religious.

42. To begin, would you describe briefly any experience which you have had in your life which at the time you thought of as a distinctly religious experience.

.................................................................
.................................................................
.................................................................
.................................................................
.................................................................
.................................................................

43. Listed below are a number of experiences of a religious nature which people have reported having. Since you have been an adult have you ever had any of these experiences, and how sure are you that you had it?

|  | Have you had such an experience? (Mark answer with X) | | |
|  | Yes, I'm sure I have | Yes, I think that I have | No |
| --- | --- | --- | --- |
| A feeling that you were somehow in the presence of God............ 17 | ☐ | ☐ | ☐ |
| A sense of being saved in Christ................................ | ☐ | ☐ | ☐ |
| A feeling of being afraid of God................................ | ☐ | ☐ | ☐ |
| A feeling of being punished by God for something you had done....... | ☐ | ☐ | ☐ |
| A feeling of being tempted by the Devil.......................... 21 | ☐ | ☐ | ☐ |

IF YOU HAVE ANSWERED NO TO ALL OF THE ABOVE, do you feel that it is possible for people to have religious experiences?
22   ☐ Yes   ☐ No   ☐ I'm not sure

The following questions give attention to still another topic—the history of Christianity. Here we are interested to learn how church people view the events of early Christianity and of the Reformation period.

44. The Old Testament tells that God picked a certain group to be His "Chosen People." Can you tell us who God picked as His "Chosen People"?
23   ☐ the Romans
      ☐ the Greeks
      ☐ the Jews
      ☐ the Christians
      ☐ none of these

45. Who do you think are God's "Chosen People" today?
24   ☐ the Americans
      ☐ the Roman Catholics
      ☐ the Jews
      ☐ the Christians
      ☐ the Protestants
      ☐ none
      ☐ other..................................................
                   (please write in)

46. Do you think of Moses, David, and Solomon as:
25   ☐ Romans
      ☐ Greeks
      ☐ Jews
      ☐ Christians
      ☐ none of these

47. When you think of Peter and Paul and the other Apostles, do you think of them as:
26   ☐ Romans
      ☐ Greeks
      ☐ Jews
      ☐ Christians
      ☐ none of the above

48. When you think of Judas, who betrayed Christ, do you think of him as:
27   ☐ a Roman
      ☐ a Greek
      ☐ a Jew
      ☐ a Christian
      ☐ none of these

49. The Bible tells of Christ going to a Temple in Jerusalem to talk with the Scribes and the Pharisees. To what religious group did that Temple belong?

28   ☐ The Romans
     ☐ the Greeks
     ☐ the Jews
     ☐ the Christians
     ☐ none of these
     ☐ don't know

50. What group do you think was most responsible for crucifying Christ?

29   ☐ the Romans
     ☐ the Greeks
     ☐ the Jews
     ☐ the Christians
     ☐ none of these
     ☐ don't know

51. Do you think Pontius Pilate wanted to spare Jesus from the Cross?

30   ☐ Yes   ☐ No   ☐ Don't know

IF YES, please answer the question in the box below:

---

If you think Pilate really wanted to spare Jesus, why didn't he? Because:

31   ☐ a group of powerful Romans wanted Jesus dead
     ☐ a group of powerful Greeks wanted Jesus dead
     ☐ a group of powerful Jews wanted Jesus dead
     ☐ a group of powerful Christians wanted Jesus dead
     ☐ other.................................................
                         (please specify)

---

52. Why did the Jews reject Christ? (Check all answers with which you agree.)

32 ☐ The Jews were sinful and had turned against God.

33 ☐ They made an unfortunate but honest mistake.

34 ☐ They were deceived by wicked priests who feared Christ.

35 ☐ God did not reveal the truth to the Jews because He was angry with them.

36 ☐ They couldn't accept a Messiah who came from humble beginnings.

37 ☐ Jesus did not actually fulfill the Old Testament prophesies concerning the Messiah, so the Jews saw no reason to accept Him.

38 ☐ Because the Jews hated Gentiles they could not accept Christ's message of brotherhood.

53. How do you think Jews in America today feel about Jesus? (Check as many as you tend to agree with.)

39 ☐ They don't believe He every really existed and feel Christians are foolish to believe in Him.

40 ☐ They respect Him as a great teacher, but they are still sure He is not the Son of God.

41 ☐ They regard Jesus as a misguided fanatic.

42 ☐ They don't give much thought to Jesus and His message.

43 ☐ They secretly worry that they may be wrong for not accepting Jesus as the Saviour.

44 ☐ They are sorry about Christ's Crucifixion.

54. The Jews can never be forgiven for what they did to Jesus until they accept Him as the True Saviour.

45   ☐ agree   ☐ disagree   ☐ uncertain

55. The reason the Jews have so much trouble is because God is punishing them for rejecting Jesus.

46   ☐ agree   ☐ disagree   ☐ uncertain

**The split between Protestants and Catholics began when Martin Luther led the first group of German Protestants out of the Catholic Church. Below are a series of statements concerning this event. Will you please decide whether you agree or disagree with each.**

56. At the time when Luther broke with the Roman Catholic Church it was sinful and corrupt.

47   ☐ agree   ☐ disagree   ☐ uncertain

57. Luther was excommunicated for breaking his vows as a monk *before* he began his religious revolt.

48   ☐ agree   ☐ disagree   ☐ uncertain

58. It would have been much better for Christianity if the split between Protestants and Catholics had never occurred.

49   ☐ agree   ☐ disagree   ☐ uncertain

59. Both Luther and the Roman Catholic Church were partly right and partly wrong in the dispute which led to their split.

50   ☐ agree   ☐ disagree   ☐ uncertain

60. Luther was a monk who left the Catholic Church because he wanted to marry a nun.

51   ☐ agree   ☐ disagree   ☐ uncertain

8

The questions we have asked until now have been mainly concerned with the religious beliefs and practices of church members. Our study is also concerned with learning how church people feel about inter-group relations, that is relations between Protestants and Roman Catholics, between Christians and Jews, and between people of different races. We hope you will feel that the following questions on this topic are important and that they will allow you to express your true feelings. If not, we would ask once again that you let us know by writing a comment whenever you think we have worded a question poorly or perhaps have asked the wrong question.

For each of the religious beliefs and practices listed below, decide whether or not you think it is generally true of each of the three major American faiths—Catholicism, Judaism, and Protestantism—then mark your decision for *each* group.

|  | Protestants | | | Catholics | | | Jews | |
|---|---|---|---|---|---|---|---|---|
| Worship God ..................... 8 | ☐ Yes | ☐ No | 17 | ☐ Yes | ☐ No | 26 | ☐ Yes | ☐ No |
| Believe in life after death........... | ☐ Yes | ☐ No | | ☐ Yes | ☐ No | | ☐ Yes | ☐ No |
| Regard the Old Testament as God's word ................... | ☐ Yes | ☐ No | | ☐ Yes | ☐ No | | ☐ Yes | ☐ No |
| Believe in Christ ................. | ☐ Yes | ☐ No | | ☐ Yes | ☐ No | | ☐ Yes | ☐ No |
| Honor the Holy Saints............. | ☐ Yes | ☐ No | | ☐ Yes | ☐ No | | ☐ Yes | ☐ No |
| Circumcise their sons for religious reasons ....................... | ☐ Yes | ☐ No | | ☐ Yes | ☐ No | | ☐ Yes | ☐ No |
| Regard the New Testament as God's word ................... | ☐ Yes | ☐ No | | ☐ Yes | ☐ No | | ☐ Yes | ☐ No |
| Believe in the Ten Commandments... | ☐ Yes | ☐ No | | ☐ Yes | ☐ No | | ☐ Yes | ☐ No |
| Are truly religious ................ | ☐ Yes | ☐ No | | ☐ Yes | ☐ No | | ☐ Yes | ☐ No |

61. How do you feel about the future of the Protestant Church in America?

    35   ☐ It will probably gain more and more influence

    ☐ It will continue about the same as it is

    ☐ It will probably lose some influence

    ☐ It will probably grow rather weak

62. How do you feel about the future of the Catholic Church in America?

    36   ☐ It will probably gain more and more influence

    ☐ It will continue about the same as it is

    ☐ It will probably lose some influence

    ☐ It will probably grow rather weak

63. How do you feel about the future of the Jewish religion in America?

    37   ☐ It will probably gain more and more influence

    ☐ It will continue about the same as it is

    ☐ It will probably lose some influence

    ☐ It will probably grow rather weak

64. How do you feel about the future of atheistic beliefs in America?

    38   ☐ They will probably gain more and more influence

    ☐ They will continue about the same as they are

    ☐ They will probably lose some influence

    ☐ They will probably grow rather weak

65. It sometimes happens when we first meet a person that we know only *one* thing about him. We may know what he does for a living, or what his religion is, or where he comes from, and so on. We all tend to form a first impression of this person on the basis of this one thing we know about him. Now, would you put yourself in the situation of just having met a person and the *only* thing you know about him is that he is a Baptist. Knowing only this *one* thing about him, what would your immediate reaction tend to be?

39
- ☐ I think I would feel friendly and at ease
- ☐ I think I would feel friendly, but somewhat uneasy
- ☐ I think I would feel uneasy and somewhat unfriendly
- ☐ I think I would feel quite unfriendly
- ☐ I guess I would feel nothing either way

Now we would like you to read each of the following characteristics and assume for each that it is the ONLY thing you know about a person, and do the same thing you just did above.

I think I would feel:

| | Friendly and at ease | Friendly, but some-what uneasy | Uneasy and somewhat unfriendly | Quite unfriendly | Nothing either way |
|---|---|---|---|---|---|
| A Communist ..................... 40 | ☐ | ☐ | ☐ | ☐ | ☐ |
| A Methodist ......................... | ☐ | ☐ | ☐ | ☐ | ☐ |
| A German .......................... | ☐ | ☐ | ☐ | ☐ | ☐ |
| An African ......................... | ☐ | ☐ | ☐ | ☐ | ☐ |
| An Alcoholic ....................... | ☐ | ☐ | ☐ | ☐ | ☐ |
| A Roman Catholic .................. | ☐ | ☐ | ☐ | ☐ | ☐ |
| A Leftwinger ...................... | ☐ | ☐ | ☐ | ☐ | ☐ |
| An Episcopalian .................... | ☐ | ☐ | ☐ | ☐ | ☐ |
| A Puerto Rican ..................... | ☐ | ☐ | ☐ | ☐ | ☐ |
| A Jehovah's Witness ................ | ☐ | ☐ | ☐ | ☐ | ☐ |
| A Conservative .................... | ☐ | ☐ | ☐ | ☐ | ☐ |
| A Jew ............................. | ☐ | ☐ | ☐ | ☐ | ☐ |
| An Irishman ....................... | ☐ | ☐ | ☐ | ☐ | ☐ |
| A Fascist .......................... | ☐ | ☐ | ☐ | ☐ | ☐ |
| A Negro ........................... | ☐ | ☐ | ☐ | ☐ | ☐ |
| An Englishman ..................... | ☐ | ☐ | ☐ | ☐ | ☐ |
| A Rightwinger ..................... | ☐ | ☐ | ☐ | ☐ | ☐ |
| A Pole ............................ | ☐ | ☐ | ☐ | ☐ | ☐ |
| An Atheist ......................... | ☐ | ☐ | ☐ | ☐ | ☐ |
| A Liberal .......................... | ☐ | ☐ | ☐ | ☐ | ☐ |
| A Teetotaler ....................... | ☐ | ☐ | ☐ | ☐ | ☐ |
| A Zionist .......................... | ☐ | ☐ | ☐ | ☐ | ☐ |
| An Italian ......................... | ☐ | ☐ | ☐ | ☐ | ☐ |
| A Spiritualist ...................... | ☐ | ☐ | ☐ | ☐ | ☐ |
| A Russian ......................... | ☐ | ☐ | ☐ | ☐ | ☐ |
| An Oriental ........................ | ☐ | ☐ | ☐ | ☐ | ☐ |
| An Israeli ......................... 66 | ☐ | ☐ | ☐ | ☐ | ☐ |

## 005

66. Below are listed several kinds of people. We would like you to think back over your lifetime and recall whether you have ever known at least one person quite well who was a member of such a group. Mark each group from which you have known at least one person quite well.

- 8 ☐ Jew
- 9 ☐ Catholic
- 10 ☐ Protestant
- 11 ☐ Negro
- 12 ☐ Someone who did not believe in God
- 13 ☐ Communist

10

67. How many persons from each of the following groups would you say you are acquainted with at the present time?

| | None | 1 | 2–3 | 4–10 | 11 or more | don't know |
|---|---|---|---|---|---|---|
| Jews ................. 14 | ☐ | ☐ | ☐ | ☐ | ☐ | ☐ |
| Catholics .............. | ☐ | ☐ | ☐ | ☐ | ☐ | ☐ |
| Protestants ............ | ☐ | ☐ | ☐ | ☐ | ☐ | ☐ |
| Negroes .............. | ☐ | ☐ | ☐ | ☐ | ☐ | ☐ |
| People who don't believe in God........ | ☐ | ☐ | ☐ | ☐ | ☐ | ☐ |
| Communists ........... 19 | ☐ | ☐ | ☐ | ☐ | ☐ | ☐ |

68. How many persons from each of the following groups would you say you know well?

| | None | 1 | 2–3 | 4–10 | 11 or more | don't know |
|---|---|---|---|---|---|---|
| Jews ................. 20 | ☐ | ☐ | ☐ | ☐ | ☐ | ☐ |
| Catholics .............. | ☐ | ☐ | ☐ | ☐ | ☐ | ☐ |
| Protestants ............ | ☐ | ☐ | ☐ | ☐ | ☐ | ☐ |
| Negroes .............. | ☐ | ☐ | ☐ | ☐ | ☐ | ☐ |
| People who don't believe in God........ | ☐ | ☐ | ☐ | ☐ | ☐ | ☐ |
| Communists ........... 25 | ☐ | ☐ | ☐ | ☐ | ☐ | ☐ |

69. How many families of each of the following groups would you say live in your neighborhood?

| | Many | Some | Hardly Any | None |
|---|---|---|---|---|
| Jews ................................... 26 | ☐ | ☐ | ☐ | ☐ |
| Catholics ................................. | ☐ | ☐ | ☐ | ☐ |
| Protestants ............................... | ☐ | ☐ | ☐ | ☐ |
| Negroes ................................... | ☐ | ☐ | ☐ | ☐ |
| People who don't believe in God............... | ☐ | ☐ | ☐ | ☐ |
| Communists .............................. 31 | ☐ | ☐ | ☐ | ☐ |

70. Have you ever entertained members of the following groups in your home, and if so how often would you say you had done this?

| | Never | Once or twice | Occasionally | Fairly often | Quite often |
|---|---|---|---|---|---|
| Jews ............................. 32 | ☐ | ☐ | ☐ | ☐ | ☐ |
| Catholics ........................... | ☐ | ☐ | ☐ | ☐ | ☐ |
| Protestants ......................... | ☐ | ☐ | ☐ | ☐ | ☐ |
| Negroes ........................... | ☐ | ☐ | ☐ | ☐ | ☐ |
| People who don't believe in God........ | ☐ | ☐ | ☐ | ☐ | ☐ |
| Communists ........................ 37 | ☐ | ☐ | ☐ | ☐ | ☐ |

71. How interested would you say you were in knowing the religious affiliation of people you meet? Would you say you were:

38 ☐ Very interested
☐ Quite interested
☐ Somewhat interested
☐ Not very interested
☐ Not interested at all

72. If a person refuses to tell people his religious affiliation, what would you think of this? (Check as many as you agree with)

39 ☐ He must have something to hide or be ashamed of his religion
☐ A man should be proud of his religion or change it
☐ A man has a right to keep his religious affiliation to himself
☐ Even though a man has a right to keep his religious affiliation to himself, I would wonder about someone who refused to admit what it was
☐ Someone who refuses to tell his religious affiliation is probably covering up the fact that he has no religion.

11

73. One of the ways used in research to help understand people's opinions and attitudes is to ask them to complete sentences by saying the first thing that comes into their minds. We would ask you now to finish the following sentences, putting down whatever comes to your mind as you read the opening phrase.

1. I can't understand why Protestants.................................................................................................................................................

.................................................................................................................................................................................................

2. It's a shame that Jews........................................................................................................................................................

.................................................................................................................................................................................................

3. I can't understand why Catholics....................................................................................................................................

.................................................................................................................................................................................................

4. It's a shame that Negroes..................................................................................................................................................

.................................................................................................................................................................................................

**006**

5. It's a shame that Protestants............................................................................................................................................

.................................................................................................................................................................................................

6. I can't understand why Jews............................................................................................................................................

.................................................................................................................................................................................................

7. It's a shame that Catholics................................................................................................................................................

.................................................................................................................................................................................................

8. I can't understand why Negroes......................................................................................................................................

.................................................................................................................................................................................................

9. It's a shame that heavy drinkers......................................................................................................................................

.................................................................................................................................................................................................

**007**

74. As you probably know, there are a number of people in this country who claim they do not believe in God. Suppose a man publicly admitted he did not believe in God. Would you agree or disagree that the following actions should be taken against him?

| | AGREE | DISAGREE | |
|---|---|---|---|
| 8 | ☐ | ☐ | A book he wrote should be removed from the library |
| 9 | ☐ | ☐ | He should be fired from a job in a supermarket |
| 10 | ☐ | ☐ | He should not be allowed to teach in a private university |
| 11 | ☐ | ☐ | He should not be allowed to teach in a public high school |
| 12 | ☐ | ☐ | He should be fired from a defense plant |
| 13 | ☐ | ☐ | He should not be allowed to preach his beliefs to others |
| 14 | ☐ | ☐ | He should not be allowed to hold public office |

12

75. How serious a problem do you think exists in this country because of people who do not believe in God?

    15    ☐ Very serious

            ☐ Fairly serious

            ☐ Not very serious

            ☐ Not serious at all

IF YOU THINK THE PROBLEM IS VERY OR FAIRLY SERIOUS, ANSWER THE QUESTION IN THE BOX BELOW

> What would you say was the most important way in which these people create a problem? (please specify) ..................................................................
> ..................................................................
> ..................................................................
> ..................................................................
> ..................................................................

76. Would you agree that a person who says there is no God is likely to hold dangerous political ideas?

    26    ☐ Agree    ☐ Disagree    ☐ Uncertain

77. I tend to distrust a person who does not believe in Jesus.

    27    ☐ Agree    ☐ Disagree    ☐ Uncertain

78. Most of my friends could not like someone who didn't believe in Jesus.

    28    ☐ Agree    ☐ Disagree    ☐ Uncertain

79. We turn now to relations between Christians and Jews. There is a great deal of disagreement about what Jews are like. Here are some things people have said at one time or another about Jews. For each statement, we would ask you to do two things:

*First* read the statement and decide whether you tend to think Jews are like this or not, and put your answer in Column A.

*Then,* whether or not you think Jews are like this or not, we would ask you to suppose that the statement actually were true. If the statement were true, how would it tend to make you feel toward Jews? Would you tend to feel friendly or unfriendly toward them because of this? Put your answer in Column B.

| COLUMN A | | | | COLUMN B | | |
| --- | --- | --- | --- | --- | --- | --- |
| Do you feel Jews tend to be like this? | | | | If Jews were like this would it tend to make you feel: | | |
| Yes | Somewhat | No | | Friendly | Unfriendly | Neither Way |
| 29 ☐ | ☐ | ☐ | Jews are particularly generous and give a great deal of money to charity | 40 ☐ | ☐ | ☐ |
| ☐ | ☐ | ☐ | Jews like to be with other Jews and tend to avoid non-Jews | ☐ | ☐ | ☐ |
| ☐ | ☐ | ☐ | Jewish parents tend to be very concerned about making sure that their children marry Jews | ☐ | ☐ | ☐ |
| ☐ | ☐ | ☐ | On the average, Jews are wealthier than Christians | ☐ | ☐ | ☐ |
| ☐ | ☐ | ☐ | Jews are more likely than Christians to cheat in business | ☐ | ☐ | ☐ |
| ☐ | ☐ | ☐ | Jewish children tend to get better grades in school than Christian children do | ☐ | ☐ | ☐ |
| ☐ | ☐ | ☐ | Jews are less likely than Christians to oppose Communism | ☐ | ☐ | ☐ |
| ☐ | ☐ | ☐ | On the average, Jews tend to drink less than non-Jews | ☐ | ☐ | ☐ |
| ☐ | ☐ | ☐ | The movie and television industries are pretty much run by Jews | ☐ | ☐ | ☐ |
| ☐ | ☐ | ☐ | Jews are ambitious and work hard to succeed | ☐ | ☐ | ☐ |
| ☐ | ☐ | ☐ | Jews tend to wear flashy clothes and jewelry | ☐ | ☐ | ☐ |

13

|  | COLUMN A<br>Do you feel Jews<br>tend to be like<br>this? | | | | COLUMN B<br>If Jews were like<br>this would it tend<br>to make you feel: | | |
|---|---|---|---|---|---|---|---|
|  | Yes | Somewhat | No |  | Friendly | Unfriendly | Neither<br>Way |
| 51 | ☐ | ☐ | ☐ | Jewish organizations have been strong supporters of Negro 'sit-in' campaigns | 64 ☐ | ☐ | ☐ |
|  | ☐ | ☐ | ☐ | Jews, in general, are inclined to be more loyal to Israel than to America | ☐ | ☐ | ☐ |
|  | ☐ | ☐ | ☐ | An unusual number of the world's greatest men have been Jews | ☐ | ☐ | ☐ |
|  | ☐ | ☐ | ☐ | Because Jews are not bound by Christian ethics, they do things to get ahead that Christians generally will not do | ☐ | ☐ | ☐ |
|  | ☐ | ☐ | ☐ | While many Jews attend synagogues and worship God, most Jews are not very religious | ☐ | ☐ | ☐ |
|  | ☐ | ☐ | ☐ | International banking tends to be dominated by Jews | ☐ | ☐ | ☐ |
|  | ☐ | ☐ | ☐ | Many Jews oppose allowing Christian holidays, such as Christmas and Easter, to be celebrated in the public schools | ☐ | ☐ | ☐ |
|  | ☐ | ☐ | ☐ | Jewish boys were less likely than Christian boys to volunteer for service in the armed forces during the last war | ☐ | ☐ | ☐ |
|  | ☐ | ☐ | ☐ | Jews have tended to be ardent supporters of labor unions | ☐ | ☐ | ☐ |
|  | ☐ | ☐ | ☐ | Among themselves, Jews think Christians are ignorant for believing Christ was the Son of God | ☐ | ☐ | ☐ |
|  | ☐ | ☐ | ☐ | Jews provide most of the funds for planned parenthood centers and other birth control programs | ☐ | ☐ | ☐ |
|  | ☐ | ☐ | ☐ | Jews believe they are better than other people | ☐ | ☐ | ☐ |
| 63 | ☐ | ☐ | ☐ | Jews want to remain different from other people, and yet they are touchy if people notice these differences | 76 ☐ | ☐ | ☐ |

**008**

80. Some people are of the opinion that serious problems exist between Catholics and Protestants in America today, while others say these problems are not really serious. How do you tend to feel about this?

8   ☐ The problems are very serious

☐ The problems are fairly serious

☐ The problems are not very serious

☐ There really aren't any problems at all

81. One of the ways to help reduce tensions between groups is to get out into the open things about one group that bother people in the other group. Here is a list of things that Protestants have said about Catholics and that Catholics have said about Protestants. For each statement would you please indicate how you feel—do you feel that it is true, tends to be true, tends to be false, or is false.

| | | True | Tends to be true | Tends to be false | False |
|---|---|---|---|---|---|
| Protestants attack Catholic religious beliefs without knowing anything about them...................... | 9 | ☐ | ☐ | ☐ | ☐ |
| Catholics stick to themselves and have as little to do with Protestants as possible......................... | | ☐ | ☐ | ☐ | ☐ |
| Protestant employers often discriminate against Catholics, for example, by not hiring or promoting them........... | | ☐ | ☐ | ☐ | ☐ |
| Catholics try to impose their religious practices on others.. | | ☐ | ☐ | ☐ | ☐ |
| Protestants don't really take their religion seriously as compared to Catholics ............................. | | ☐ | ☐ | ☐ | ☐ |
| Catholics believe they belong to the only true church..... | | ☐ | ☐ | ☐ | ☐ |
| Protestants have tried to exclude Catholics from political offices ...................................... | | ☐ | ☐ | ☐ | ☐ |
| Catholics tend to vote as a bloc for Catholic political candidates ................................. | | ☐ | ☐ | ☐ | ☐ |
| The Catholic Church supports dictators in Catholic countries in South America and Europe................ | | ☐ | ☐ | ☐ | ☐ |
| Compared to Catholics, Protestants do not oppose divorce as strongly as they should.................... | | ☐ | ☐ | ☐ | ☐ |
| Protestants have often spread false rumors about Catholic priests and nuns........................... | | ☐ | ☐ | ☐ | ☐ |
| Catholics are very lax about drinking and gambling as compared to Protestants......................... | | ☐ | ☐ | ☐ | ☐ |
| Catholics interfere with the rights of others to practice birth control if they wish........................... | | ☐ | ☐ | ☐ | ☐ |
| By denying tax support to parochial schools, Protestants unfairly make Catholics support schools they do not use... | | ☐ | ☐ | ☐ | ☐ |
| Protestants are not given religious freedom in Catholic countries the way Catholics are given freedom here...... | | ☐ | ☐ | ☐ | ☐ |
| The Catholic church is unfair to demand that children of a Protestant-Catholic couple must be raised Catholics...... | 24 | ☐ | ☐ | ☐ | ☐ |

82. Some people tell us there are serious problems between Negroes and whites in America today, while others say the problems are not really serious. How do you tend to feel about this?

25    ☐ The problems are very serious
      ☐ The problems are fairly serious
      ☐ The problems are not very serious
      ☐ There really aren't any problems at all

15

83. Below are a number of statements people have made about Negro and white relations in America. Would you please read each and decide whether or not you tend to agree with it?

| | Definitely agree | Agree somewhat | Disagree somewhat | Definitely disagree | |
|---|---|---|---|---|---|
| 26 | ☐ | ☐ | ☐ | ☐ | Negroes are getting ahead as fast as we can hope for. |
| | ☐ | ☐ | ☐ | ☐ | The Bible makes it quite clear that God meant for the races to be separate. |
| | ☐ | ☐ | ☐ | ☐ | It's too bad, but in general Negroes have inferior intelligence compared to whites. |
| | ☐ | ☐ | ☐ | ☐ | Negroes ought to have the same opportunities and rights as others. |
| | ☐ | ☐ | ☐ | ☐ | We can be proud of what we have done for the Negro in recent years. |
| | ☐ | ☐ | ☐ | ☐ | It would probably be better for Negroes and whites to attend separate churches. |
| | ☐ | ☐ | ☐ | ☐ | Negroes would advance as far as white people if they had the same opportunities as whites. |
| | ☐ | ☐ | ☐ | ☐ | The races would probably get along fine in this county if Communists and other radicals didn't stir up trouble. |
| | ☐ | ☐ | ☐ | ☐ | The Christian church is not doing enough to help the Negro. |
| | ☐ | ☐ | ☐ | ☐ | It would probably be better all around if Negroes went to separate schools. |
| | ☐ | ☐ | ☐ | ☐ | "Love thy neighbor" means that we should treat all races the same. |
| | ☐ | ☐ | ☐ | ☐ | It's a shame that Negroes are so immoral. |
| 38 | ☐ | ☐ | ☐ | ☐ | Most Negro neighborhoods are run down because Negroes simply don't take care of property. |

This section of the questionnaire concerns many situations in which people often find themselves in real life. Try to imagine yourself in each situation and then try to tell us how you would most likely feel and act.

84. Suppose you heard an argument between three of your friends over the practice of many vacation resorts of not permitting Jews as guests. One friend said Jews have a right to be admitted to any vacation resort. The second said Christians have a right to their own private resorts if they want them. The third said regardless of what Christians or Jews might expect, any resort owner has the right to run his business and pick his customers any way he wants to. With whom would you tend to agree?

39 ☐ The Jews have a right to be admitted anywhere

☐ Christians have a right to their own resorts if they want them

☐ Resort owners have a right to pick their own customers

85. What if you were in a store operated by a Jew, and a customer came in to complain about a purchase, and during the argument with the storekeeper called him "a crook like all the Jews." How would you feel and act in this circumstance?

1) Would you be inclined to understand the customer's feelings?

40 ☐ Yes ☐ No ☐ Uncertain

2) With whom would you be inclined to feel sympathetic?

41 ☐ the customer ☐ the owner
☐ both ☐ neither

3) What would you most likely do?

42 ☐ Leave the store quietly
☐ Stay and say nothing
☐ Speak up on the side of the customer
☐ Speak up on the side of the owner

4) What if you knew the owner had actually cheated the customer? Would it change your feelings about the customer's remark or not?

43 ☐ It would likely change my feelings in that case

☐ It would not change my feelings

☐ I don't know what effect it would have

86. Suppose a friend told you he had been offered an attractive business deal by a Jewish businessman, but wondered if he should risk trusting a Jew in business. What would you most likely advise him?

44 ☐ To avoid deals with a Jew
☐ To be very careful of dealing with a Jew
☐ To go ahead, but be somewhat careful
☐ To go ahead because Jews are no more likely to be dishonest in business than Christians are
☐ To go ahead because Jews are especially honest in business

16

87. Suppose you own your own home and several Negro families moved into your block. Would you be apt to move elsewhere provided you could get a fair price for your house?

45  ☐ Would almost certainly move
     ☐ Would probably move
     ☐ Probably wouldn't move
     ☐ Almost certainly would not move

88. Whether or not you think you would move under these circumstances, would you sympathize with friends of yours who decided to move?

46  ☐ Sympathize very much
     ☐ Sympathize somewhat
     ☐ Disapprove somewhat
     ☐ Disapprove strongly
     ☐ Feel nothing either way

*If you have come this far in answering the questionnaire, you are probably wondering when it is going to end. Actually, we are coming very close and ask your kind cooperation for another few pages. We know we are asking a lot from you. We hope, however, that you will agree that the study will produce the most significant body of information that the churches in America have ever had about their memberships, and that you might feel a certain pride in having been part of it.*

**As you perhaps know, some denominations issue statements from time to time on current social issues. We are interested to learn how church people feel about this being done and also how they feel about some of the issues on which denominations have taken stands.**

**You will find below a series of statements on current affairs with which some people agree and some disagree. Would you kindly indicate how you feel about each of them by checking the appropriate box.**

*On the Church Speaking Out on Social, Economic, and Political Questions:*

89. Churches should stick to religion and not concern themselves with social, economic, and political questions.
47  ☐ agree  ☐ disagree  ☐ uncertain

90. Aside from preaching, there is little that churches can really do about social and economic problems.
48  ☐ agree  ☐ disagree  ☐ uncertain

91. It is proper for churches to state their positions on practical political questions to the local, state, or national government.
49  ☐ agree  ☐ disagree  ☐ uncertain

*War and Peace*

92. War is justified when other ways of settling international disputes fail.
50  ☐ agree  ☐ disagree  ☐ uncertain

93. The United States and Russia cannot live side-by-side without fighting.
51  ☐ agree  ☐ disagree  ☐ uncertain

94. Red China ought not be admitted to the United Nations at the present time.
52  ☐ agree  ☐ disagree  ☐ uncertain

95. War cannot be avoided in our time.
53  ☐ agree  ☐ disagree  ☐ uncertain

96. The United States ought to invade Cuba.
54  ☐ agree  ☐ disagree  ☐ uncertain

*World Problems*

97. The United Nations ought to have the continued strong support of the United States.
55  ☐ agree  ☐ disagree  ☐ uncertain

98. The United States should do everything it can to help "underdeveloped countries" raise their standard of living.
56  ☐ agree  ☐ disagree  ☐ uncertain

99. The United States should follow a policy of opening its doors to displaced persons (refugees) whoever they may be.
57  ☐ agree  ☐ disagree  ☐ uncertain

*National Problems*

100. Nowadays people are more afraid to speak their mind on controversial social issues than they used to be.
58  ☐ agree  ☐ disagree  ☐ uncertain

101. There is no room in church for people who believe in Communism.
59  ☐ agree  ☐ disagree  ☐ uncertain

102. Church people ought to recognize the right of conscientious objectors not to bear arms.
60  ☐ agree  ☐ disagree  ☐ uncertain

103. There's little use writing to public officials because often they aren't really interested in the problems of the average man.
61  ☐ agree  ☐ disagree  ☐ uncertain

104. The way they are run now, labor unions do this country more harm than good.
62  ☐ agree  ☐ disagree  ☐ uncertain

105. Church people ought to take a bold stand in protecting freedom of speech even for people whose views are unpopular.
63  ☐ agree  ☐ disagree  ☐ uncertain

106. Nowadays a person has to live pretty much for today and let tomorrow take care of itself.
64  ☐ agree  ☐ disagree  ☐ uncertain

107. Communism is as much a threat inside the United States as outside it.
65  ☐ agree  ☐ disagree  ☐ uncertain

108. Big companies control too much of American business.
66  ☐ agree  ☐ disagree  ☐ uncertain

109. In spite of what some people say, the lot of the average man is getting worse, not better.
67  ☐ agree  ☐ disagree  ☐ uncertain

17

## 009

110. The House Un-American Activities Committee ought to be encouraged in the work it is doing.

68 ☐ agree ☐ disagree ☐ uncertain

111. A high school teacher who "pleads the fifth amendment" while being questioned by a Congressional Committee ought to be fired at once.

69 ☐ agree ☐ disagree ☐ uncertain

112. It's hardly fair to bring children into the world the way things look for the future.

70 ☐ agree ☐ disagree ☐ uncertain

113. The Federal Government ought to provide medical care for the aged.

71 ☐ agree ☐ disagree ☐ uncertain

114. These days a person doesn't really know whom he can count on.

72 ☐ agree ☐ disagree ☐ uncertain

115. In the past 25 years this country has moved dangerously close to socialism.

73 ☐ agree ☐ disagree ☐ uncertain

116. We should not allow missionaries from non-Christian religions to spread their teachings in a Christian community.

74 ☐ agree ☐ disagree ☐ uncertain

117. Basically, I feel this is a Christian nation and persons who are not Christians and want religion kept out of public affairs ought to recognize this and stop complaining.

75 ☐ agree ☐ disagree ☐ uncertain

*Prayer in Public Schools*

118. Because not all Americans have the same religious beliefs, it would be better not to have prayers said in the public schools.

8 ☐ agree ☐ disagree ☐ uncertain

119. Because many children do not have religious parents it is our Christian duty to teach their children to pray in school.

9 ☐ agree ☐ disagree ☐ uncertain

120. Since a majority of Americans are religious they have a right to expect their children to learn prayers in public school.

10 ☐ agree ☐ disagree ☐ uncertain

121. Because of the separation of church and state, it is unconstitutional for any kind of prayers to be said in public schools.

11 ☐ agree ☐ disagree ☐ uncertain

122. If the Federal Government in Washington decides to give money to aid education, should the money go only to public schools, or should the money go to help Catholic and other private schools as well?

12 ☐ Public schools only
☐ Catholic and private schools as well
☐ I can't really decide

123. How do you feel about the state of morals in this country at the present time?

13 ☐ They are pretty bad and getting worse
☐ They are pretty bad, but getting better
☐ They are pretty good, but getting worse
☐ They are pretty good and getting better

124. Now we would like you to tell us how you think your pastor feels about a variety of things. We realize that this may be somewhat difficult for you to decide, but we ask you to do the best you can. For each of the following items we would like you to decide whether your pastor approves or disapproves of it, or really has no preference either way, and mark this answer in *Column A*. Then we would like you to tell us how you feel about each item and put your answer in *Column B*.

| | Column A | | | | Column B | | | |
| | How does your Pastor feel about this? | | | | How do you feel about this? | | | |
| | Approves | Dis-approves | Doesn't Care | I don't really know | Approve | Dis-approve | Don't Care | I don't really know |
|---|---|---|---|---|---|---|---|---|
| Dancing .......... | 14 ☐ | ☐ | ☐ | ☐ | 24 ☐ | ☐ | ☐ | ☐ |
| Racial integration .. | ☐ | ☐ | ☐ | ☐ | ☐ | ☐ | ☐ | ☐ |
| Bible reading in public schools ... | ☐ | ☐ | ☐ | ☐ | ☐ | ☐ | ☐ | ☐ |
| Converting Jews to Christianity ..... | ☐ | ☐ | ☐ | ☐ | ☐ | ☐ | ☐ | ☐ |
| Gambling ......... | ☐ | ☐ | ☐ | ☐ | ☐ | ☐ | ☐ | ☐ |
| Artificial birth control ....... | ☐ | ☐ | ☐ | ☐ | ☐ | ☐ | ☐ | ☐ |
| Mixed religious marriages ......... | ☐ | ☐ | ☐ | ☐ | ☐ | ☐ | ☐ | ☐ |
| Censorship of movies and books... | ☐ | ☐ | ☐ | ☐ | ☐ | ☐ | ☐ | ☐ |
| Capital punishment.. | ☐ | ☐ | ☐ | ☐ | ☐ | ☐ | ☐ | ☐ |
| Racial mixing ...... | ☐ | ☐ | ☐ | ☐ | ☐ | ☐ | ☐ | ☐ |

18

125. Many people say some groups have too much power in this country and some have not enough; but they often disagree on which groups have too much or too little. For each of the following groups of people in America, please decide whether you think they have too much power, too little power, or about the right amount of power in our nation's affairs.

|  | Too much power | Too little power | Just the right amount of power |
|---|---|---|---|
| Catholics .......................... 34 | ☐ | ☐ | ☐ |
| Rich people ........................... | ☐ | ☐ | ☐ |
| Labor unions .......................... | ☐ | ☐ | ☐ |
| Jews ................................. | ☐ | ☐ | ☐ |
| Protestants ........................... | ☐ | ☐ | ☐ |
| People who don't believe in God............ | ☐ | ☐ | ☐ |
| Big corporations ........................ | ☐ | ☐ | ☐ |
| Communists ........................... | ☐ | ☐ | ☐ |
| Negroes .............................. | ☐ | ☐ | ☐ |
| The liquor industry ...................... | ☐ | ☐ | ☐ |
| Liberals .............................. | ☐ | ☐ | ☐ |
| Rightwingers .......................... | ☐ | ☐ | ☐ |
| Voters ............................... | ☐ | ☐ | ☐ |
| College professors ...................... 47 | ☐ | ☐ | ☐ |

126. Do you tend to agree or disagree with Darwin's theory of evolution—which maintains that human beings evolved from lower forms of animal life over many millions of years?

48 ☐ The theory is almost certainly true
☐ The theory is probably true
☐ The theory is probably false
☐ The theory could not possibly be true
☐ I have never really thought about this before

This is the last section of the questionnaire. Here we would like to know about some of the things you do and enjoy aside from religious activities, and to learn something of your personal history. This information is particularly important if we are to understand the ways in which religion fits into the lives of Americans.

127. Now we would like to know something about the organizations and clubs you belong to. Below are listed various kinds of organizations. In the blank in front of each kind of organization, write in the number of organizations like this to which you belong. If none, mark 0.

49 ........ FRATERNAL GROUPS, such as Elks, Eagles, Masons, Knights of Columbus, Eastern Star, and women's auxiliaries to groups like this, etc.

50 ........ SERVICE CLUBS, such as Lions, Rotary, Zonta, Jr. Chamber of Commerce, etc.

51 ........ VETERANS GROUPS, such as the American Legion, VFW, Amvets, etc.

52 ........ POLITICAL GROUPS, such as Democratic or Republican clubs, and political action groups such as voter's leagues, NAACP, etc.

53 ........ LABOR UNIONS, such as International Typographical Union, Teamsters, etc.

54 ........ SPORTS GROUPS, such as bowling teams, bridge clubs, or sports sponsoring groups such as Downtown Quarterbacks, etc.

55 ........ YOUTH GROUPS, such as Boy Scouts, Girl Scouts, 4-H, etc.

56 ........ SCHOOL SERVICE GROUPS, such as PTA, or alumni associations, etc.

57 ........ HOBBY OR GARDEN CLUBS, such as stamp or coin clubs, flower clubs, pet clubs, etc.

58 ........ SCHOOL FRATERNITIES OR SORORITIES, such as Sigma Chi, Delta Gamma, etc.

59 ........ NATIONALITY GROUPS, such as Sons of Norway, Hibernian Society, etc.

60 ........ FARM ORGANIZATIONS, such as Farmer's Union, Farm Bureau, Grange, etc.

61 ........ LITERARY, ART, DISCUSSION, OR STUDY CLUBS, such as book review clubs, theater groups, painting groups, etc.

62 ........ PROFESSIONAL OR ACADEMIC SOCIETIES, such as the American Dental Association, Phi Beta Kappa, etc.

63 ........ OTHER ORGANIZATIONS NOT LISTED ABOVE (please write in)..........
............................................................
............................................................

19

128. Aside from church organizations and activities, about how many times a week do you attend a meeting or other activity connected with organizations to which you belong?

64 □ 0 □ 1 □ 2 □ 3 □ 4 □ 5
□ 5 □ 6 □ 7 □ 8 □ 9 □ 10
(x)

129. How often do you have friends visit you at home? Check the answer which is closest to what you do.

65 □ More than four times a week
□ Two to three times a week
□ Once a week
□ Once every several weeks
□ Once a month
□ Once every three months
□ At least once a year
□ Less than once a year

130. How often do you visit friends in their homes?

66 □ More than four times a week
□ Two to three times a week
□ Once a week
□ Once every several weeks
□ Once a month
□ Once every three months
□ At least once a year
□ Less than once a year

131. How did you meet most of the people who are now your friends?

67 □ in the neighborhood
□ at school
□ at work
□ at church
□ at parties
□ through my family
□ other ..................................................................
..........................................................................................

132. Do you usually take a vacation out of town each year?

68 □ Yes, always
□ Yes, often
□ No, not often
□ Never or hardly ever

133. How much time do you usually spend watching TV each week? Check the answer which is closest to what you usually do.

69 □ 1 to 5 hours
□ 6 to 10 hours
□ 11 to 15 hours
□ 20 to 30 hours
□ more than 30 hours
□ watch TV rarely or not at all

134. What is your favorite kind of television program? Place an X in the right hand column beside the kind of TV programs you like *best*. Then in the left hand column, put an X by the kind of program you like *least*.

| Like least (one only) | | Like best (one only) |
|---|---|---|
| 70 □ Westerns | | 72 □ |
| □ Comedies | | □ |
| □ Drama | | □ |
| □ Detective | | □ |
| □ Movies | | □ |
| □ Popular music | | □ |
| □ Variety shows | | □ |
| □ Symphony and concert music | | □ |
| □ Religious programs | | □ |
| □ Panel shows | | □ |
| □ News | | □ |
| □ Current events | | □ |
| 71 □ Sports | | 73 □ |
| □ Quiz | | □ |

135. Do you ever make a point of listening to of watching religious services on radio or television?

74 □ Yes, regularly
□ Yes, sometimes
□ Very seldom
□ No, never or practically never

136. How many books have you read in the past year?

75 □ None
□ One
□ Two
□ Three
□ Four to ten
□ Ten to twenty
□ More than twenty

137. What kind of books were these mostly?

76 □ Did not read
□ Fiction
□ Textbooks
□ Non-fiction
□ Religious
□ Other..............................................................
(please write in)

## 010

138. Which, if any, of the following magazines do you read regularly? Check each one which you regularly read.

    8 ☐ Reader's Digest
    9 ☐ Saturday Evening Post
  10 ☐ Ladies Home Journal
  11 ☐ Time
  12 ☐ Newsweek
  13 ☐ Saturday Review of Literature
  14 ☐ Christian Century
  15 ☐ Life
  16 ☐ American Legion Magazine
  17 ☐ New Republic
  18 ☐ Esquire
  19 ☐ Others...................................................

................................................................................
(please write in)

139. Are you presently employed?

  20  ☐ Yes
      ☐ No, but I usually am
      ☐ No

140. Is your family better off, worse off, or about the same as they were 10 years ago?

  21  ☐ Better now
      ☐ Worse now
      ☐ About the same

141. Do you think that your family will be better off, worse off, or about the same 10 years from now?

  22  ☐ Better off 10 years from now
      ☐ Worse off 10 years from now
      ☐ About the same

142. How much formal education have you had? Check nearest answer.

  24  ☐ Some grade school
      ☐ Finished grade school
      ☐ Some high school
      ☐ Finished high school
      ☐ Some college
      ☐ Finished college
      ☐ Attended graduate school or professional school after college

143. Was any of your education in parochial or church affiliated schools?

  25  ☐ Yes   ☐ No

IF YES: please indicate what portion of your education was in parochial schools.

Check One answer for *each* level of school you attended

| | Grade School | High School | College |
|---|---|---|---|
| All in parochial schools ......... | 26 ☐ | 27 ☐ | 28 ☐ |
| Part in parochial schools ......... | ☐ | ☐ | ☐ |
| None in parochial schools ......... | ☐ | ☐ | ☐ |

144. What is your sex?

  29  ☐ Male
      ☐ Female

145. What is the occupation of the head of your family?

...................................................................................

...................................................................................

146. Now, looking at the chart below, find the category that is closest to the occupation of the head of your family, and check the category which comes closest.

  30  ☐ *Clerical and related workers* such as: bookkeepers, stenographers, cashiers, mail carriers, shipping clerks, secretaries, ticket agents, telephone operators, office machine operators, etc.

      ☐ *Craftsmen, foremen, and related workers* such as: tinsmiths, bakers, carpenters, masons, shoemakers, electricians, inspectors, cement workers, jewelers, machinists, painters, etc.

      ☐ *Laborers* such as: garage laborers, car washers, stevedores, lumbermen, teamsters, gardeners, unskilled helpers in construction, manufacturing.

      ☐ *Operatives and related workers* such as: chauffeurs, delivery men, laundry workers, apprentices, meat cutters, semi-skilled and unskilled employees in manufacturing establishments (bakers, tobacco, textiles, etc.), wholesale and retail workers, mine laborers, bus drivers, motormen, etc.

      ☐ *Private household workers* such as: servants, laundresses, employed housekeepers.

      ☐ *Professional, technical, and similar workers* such as: teachers, editors, dentists, clergymen, professors, instructors, doctors, lawyers, nurses, architects, librarians, social workers, accountants, funeral directors, photographers, dancers, optometrists, aviators, surveyors, chiropractors, athletes, etc.

      ☐ *Proprietors, managers, and officials* such as: public officials, credit men, buyers, officers, floor managers, proprietors, railroad conductors, etc.

      ☐ *Sales workers* such as: salesmen, insurance and real estate agents and brokers, stock and bond salesmen, newsboys, demonstrators, etc.

      ☐ *Service workers, except domestic,* such as: fire, police, barbers, beauticians, janitors, porters, waiters, ushers, practical nurses, etc.

      ☐ *Other* (specify) ...........................

147. By and large, do you think of your family as being of the working class, the upper class, or the middle class? Of which of these groups do you consider your family a member?

  31  ☐ Working class
      ☐ Upper class
      ☐ Lower class
      ☐ Middle class

147. Will you please indicate your present marital status, and fill in the information requested following your answer?

    32   ☐ MARRIED—

        How long have you been married? ............

        ☐ WIDOWED—

        How long were you married? ....................

        How long have you been widowed? ............

        ☐ DIVORCED—

        How long were you married? ....................

        How long have you been divorced? ............

        ☐ SINGLE—

        Are you engaged?  Yes ☐  No ☐

        Are you dating anyone steadily?

        Yes ☐  No ☐

IF YOU ARE WIDOWED, DIVORCED OR SINGLE: please answer the questions in the box below.

---

How likely do you think you are to eventually marry (or remarry)?

45   ☐ Very likely

     ☐ Quite likely

     ☐ A possibility

     ☐ Not too likely

     ☐ Quite unlikely

Whether or not you think you might marry, would you consider doing so?

46   ☐ Yes    ☐ No    ☐ Uncertain

---

149. How many children do you have? ..........................'.. (If none write 0)

150. Using the spaces provided below, indicate the age of each of your children. Child 1 refers to your oldest child, and so on.

48–49  ........(Child 1)     56–57  ........(Child 5)

50–51  ........(Child 2)     58–59  ........(Child 6)

52–53  ........(Child 3)     60–61  ........(Child 7)

54–55  ........(Child 4)     62–63  ........(Child 8)

        write in additional ages if necessary

151. What was your age at your *last* birthday? ................

152. Were you born in this country?

    66   ☐ Yes    ☐ No

    IF NO: in what country were you born? ....................

..................................................................................

153. Check the figure that comes closest to your present yearly family income:

69–70   ☐$1,000  ☐$5,000  ☐$9,000  ☐$13,000

          ☐$2,000  ☐$6,000  ☐$10,000 ☐$14,000

          ☐$3,000  ☐$7,000  ☐$11,000 ☐$15,000

          ☐$4,000  ☐$8,000  ☐$12,000 ☐$16,000

                                   or more

## 011

154. In what part of the country were you raised?

    8   ☐ I was not raised in the United States

       ☐ The East

       ☐ The Northeast

       ☐ The South

       ☐ The Middle-West

       ☐ The South-West

       ☐ The Rocky Mountain West

       ☐ The Far West

155. What was the size of the community in which you were raised?

    9   ☐ Raised on a farm

       ☐ A town of less than 2,500 persons (not a suburb of a large city)

       ☐ A town of less than 15,000 persons (not a suburb of. a large city)

       ☐ A town of less than 50,000 persons (not a suburb of a large city)

       ☐ A city of less than 100,000 persons

       ☐ 100,000 to 250,000 persons

       ☐ 300,000 to 750,000 persons

       ☐ A million or more persons

       ☐ A suburb of a city of 100,000 or more persons

       ☐ A suburb of a city of 500,000 or more persons

156. Thinking of the community in which you were raised, how many of each of the following groups would you say lived there?

| | | Many | Some | Very few | None |
|---|---|---|---|---|---|
| Protestants | 10 | ☐ | ☐ | ☐ | ☐ |
| Catholics | 11 | ☐ | ☐ | ☐ | ☐ |
| Jews | 12 | ☐ | ☐ | ☐ | ☐ |
| Negroes | 13 | ☐ | ☐ | ☐ | ☐ |

157. Were *both* your father and mother born in this country?  14  ☐ Yes  ☐ No

IF NO, in what country were they born?

.............................Father .............................Mother

158. During the time you were growing up, what was the religious affiliation of your parents?

Father.................................................................
      (denomination)

Mother.................................................................
      (denomination)

159. When you were of high school age, what was your father's occupation?

...........................................................................

23 (If you were not being supported by your father at that time, please indicate the occupation of the person who was supporting you)

160. Please indicate how much formal education your father had. Check the nearest answer.

24
  ☐ Some grade school
  ☐ Finished grade school
  ☐ Some high school
  ☐ Finished high school
  ☐ Some college
  ☐ Finished college
  ☐ Attended graduate school or professional school after college

161. From what countries did your ancestors mostly come? ...........................................................

...........................................................................

162. In all, how much time would you say you have spent in the hospital in the past five years? (Check the closest answer)

29
  ☐ None
  ☐ One week or less
  ☐ About two weeks
  ☐ About one month
  ☐ About three months
  ☐ About six months
  ☐ About a year
  ☐ More than one year

163. Do you have any physical handicaps or disabilities?
30   ☐ Yes   ☐ No

IF YES, would you briefly explain...........................

...........................................................................

...........................................................................

164. What is your height? ...............................

165. What is your present weight?...........................

166. In the list below, please indicate each of the various financial activities of your church to which you make *regular* contributions. Check as many as apply.

41   ☐ Expenses of your local church
42   ☐ Benevolences, such as missionary work
43   ☐ Local church organizations
44   ☐ Church building fund
45   ☐ A church college or university
46   ☐ Theological seminary
47   ☐ Church elementary or secondary school
48   ☐ Social or community welfare

167. Do you give funds regularly to any of the following? Check *each* you contribute to.

49   ☐ Clubs and groups not affiliated with your church
50   ☐ Red Cross, or Community Fund
51   ☐ Medical or health funds, such as Christmas seals
52   ☐ Charities such as the Salvation Army
53   ☐ Political campaign funds
54   ☐ A private or public college or university

168. What is the range of your family's WEEKLY contribution to your church?

55
  ☐ Less than $1
  ☐ 1.00 to 2.99
  ☐ 2.00 to 2.99
  ☐ 3.00 to 3.99
  ☐ 4.00 to 4.99
  ☐ 5.00 to 7.49
  ☐ 7.50 to 9.99
  ☐ 10.00 to 12.49
  ☐ 12.50 to 14.99
  ☐ 15.00 or more

169. How far is your home from your church building? (Check the answer which is closest)

56
  ☐ 1 to 5 blocks
  ☐ 6 to 10 blocks
  ☐ 11 to 20 blocks
  ☐ 2 to 3 miles
  ☐ 4 to 6 miles
  ☐ 7 miles or farther

170. What is your race?

57
  ☐ White
  ☐ Negro
  ☐ Oriental
  ☐ Other........................
          (please specify)

171. Do you think of yourself as:

58
  ☐ A liberal Democrat
  ☐ A moderate Democrat
  ☐ A moderate Republican
  ☐ A conservative Republican
  ☐ An Independent
  ☐ Other........................
          (please specify)

172. For whom did you vote for President in 1960? (If you did not vote, indicate whom you tended to favor)

59
  ☐ Nixon
  ☐ Kennedy
  ☐ Other........................
          (please specify)

**We sincerely appreciate your help in this study. Thank you very much for completing the questionnaire. Please remember to mail the post card as well as the questionnaire.**

**This page has been left for any comments you would like to make**